Cracking the
Hard-Boiled Detective

Cracking the Hard-Boiled Detective

A Critical History from the 1920s to the Present

LEWIS D. MOORE

McFarland & Company, Inc., Publishers
Jefferson, North Carolina, and London

LIBRARY OF CONGRESS CATALOGUING-IN-PUBLICATION DATA

Moore, Lewis D.
    Cracking the hard-boiled detective : a critical history from
the 1920s to the present / Lewis D. Moore.
       p.   cm.
    Includes bibliographical references and index.

    ISBN 0-7864-2581-4 (softcover : 50# alkaline paper)

    1. Detective and mystery stories, American — History and
criticism.   2. Detective and mystery stories, English — History
and criticism.   3. Crime in literature.   I. Title.
PS374.D4M66 2006
813'.08720905 — dc22   2006001513

British Library cataloguing data are available

Cover image ©2006 Index Stock

Manufactured in the United States of America

*McFarland & Company, Inc., Publishers
  Box 611, Jefferson, North Carolina 28640
   www.mcfarlandpub.com*

For Colin and Ryan

Contents

Preface

When I was twelve, I read Mickey Spillane's *I, the Jury*. My brother had a copy and left it lying around the house. My mother told him not to let me read it, but I was engrossed from the first pages. I returned to the hard-boiled detective novel in the middle sixties when I read Dashiell Hammett's *The Maltese Falcon*, Raymond Chandler's *The Big Sleep*, and John D. MacDonald's *The Deep Blue Good-by*. I developed a serious interest in MacDonald's work in graduate school in the early 1970s at American University in Washington, D.C., and contemplated writing my dissertation on his fiction but changed to the nineteenth-century English novelist George Gissing. However, I published two of my earliest articles on Gissing and MacDonald. In 1994, I published *Meditations on America: John D. MacDonald's Travis McGee Series and Other Fiction*. In that year, I also began to work on books on Gissing and on the hard-boiled detective novel.

From 1994 on, I have given talks at academic conferences on Gissing and hard-boiled detective fiction. Gissing and MacDonald are social and psychological realists; hard-boiled detective novelists work in the same literary tradition. Applying a thematic critical approach to these writers clarifies the development of ideas both in their works and in the genre as a whole. This analytical focus also helps distinguish the periods of the genre.

With so many writers and their works, the difficulty often was to locate the novels, especially from the Early Period between 1927 and 1955, and the secondary sources. I discovered it best to buy the books if they were available, and for these writers, the Internet and mystery and detective bookstores were invaluable. The Library of Congress and the British Library contained many works that were difficult to find or whose costs were beyond my budget. For example, one Internet search revealed that some of Carroll John Daly's novels were selling for $600 to $1300. University libraries in the Washington, D.C., area such as American University, Georgetown University, George Washington University, and the University of the District of Columbia provided secondary sources as well.

I wish to thank the many people who suggested primary and secondary sources for this book. I met most of them initially at academic conferences in the United States and abroad. Specifically, I feel grateful for the help and encouragement of Professors Donna Harper, Sarah Fogle, William Klink, Priscilla Ramsey, and John Springhall. Also, I wish to thank the members of the Mystery Book Club with whom I have met to discuss mystery and detective fiction for over ten years. They are Charlotte Desilets, our organizer, Janice Rahimi, and Jacquie Whitley.

Finally, I owe a huge debt of gratitude to friends and family who have listened patiently as I talked about the book. Of the former, Terry Flood has performed this task more kindly and more often than I deserve. My wife Barbara and my sons Colin and Ryan have always supported me in this study, and I cannot thank them enough.

Introduction

This book analyzes the development of the hard-boiled detective novel from the 1920s to the present. During the 1920s, Prohibition and the rise of the gangster provide a backdrop against which the genre develops. Increasing urbanization and the many problems it entails also give a realistic air to the violence that fills the hard-boiled detective novels. The private detective seems an inevitable result of strained police forces, honest or corrupt, and a wealthy economy in which people with money can obtain private as well as public help. Whether a social or, partly, a literary reality, the hard-boiled detective story and novel flourish and establish a genre that continues to this day. The thesis of the book is that while the genre has undergone many changes it still employs a recognizable form and thematic focus throughout.

The first chapter examines the connection between Edgar Allan Poe's Dupin and Arthur Conan Doyle's Holmes and the hard-boiled private detective. Another important nineteenth century influence is Charles Dickens' Inspector Bucket in *Bleak House* (1853). These three progenitors, along with Wilkie Collins' Sergeant Cuff in *The Moonstone* (1863), are the most significant early detectives. While the list includes two private and two official detectives, the distinction, especially in the case of Inspector Bucket, is not always clear. Other sources for the hard-boiled detective's character are epic heroes from classical Greek and Roman literature; medieval knights; American frontiersmen, especially the fictional Natty Bumppo in James Fenimore Cooper's Leatherstocking Tales; and the Western gunfighter.

The remainder of the book is divided into three main periods: the Early (1927–1955), Transitional (1964–1977), and Modern (1979–present).

The genre begins with Carroll John Daly's *The Snarl of the Beast* (1927) and Dashiell Hammett's *Red Harvest* (1929). Raymond Chandler published *The Big Sleep* in 1939, initiating the Philip Marlowe series. These three writers, especially the latter two, with the addition of Mickey Spillane and Ross Macdonald set the early boundaries of the genre. Stylistically crude when compared to Hammett and Chandler, Daly nonetheless leaves his mark by being first. Daly situates his first novel in New York and pictures a dark, violent city where it takes a violent man to confront the pervasive evil. Race Williams calls himself hard-boiled on the first page of *The Snarl of the Beast*. *The Hidden Hand* (1928) uses Miami as a setting for much of the novel, foreshadowing the manner in which the idea of place will expand. The use of a criminal gang led by a mastermind, adapted from Conan Doyle's Dr. Moriarty, appears in *The Hidden Hand*, but aside from Spillane's *My Gun Is Quick* (1950), proves generally short-lived. Hammett's *Red Harvest* uses a variation of the gang, but examples of the latter's obvious violence, greed, and corruption forestall the need for the evil genius.

John D. MacDonald's Travis McGee series and Michael Collins' Dan Fortune series initiate the Transitional Period. Joseph Hansen's Dave Brandstetter, the first homosexual hard-boiled private detective, Bill Pronzini's Nameless, and Robert B. Parker's Spenser follow soon after. MacDonald rejuvenates the hard-boiled detective novel, connecting it to the Early Period in various ways and opening it up in directions that are yet to be fully dramatized. He abundantly explores the idea of sexuality in Travis McGee's life and revives the partnership tradition first used by Poe and Conan Doyle. McGee's psychological and emotional experiences expand the range of the detective's character. Hansen, Pronzini, and Parker continue to show the vitality of the ideas of love and loss in the genre.

Finally, Stephen Greenleaf's John Marshall Tanner, Loren D. Estleman's Amos Walker, Jonathan Valin's Harry Stoner, Liza Cody's Anna Lee, Sara Paretsky's V.I. Warshawski, Sue Grafton's Kinsey Millhone, Jeremiah Healy's John Francis Cuddy, and Gillian Slovo's Kate Baeier lead the Modern Period's expansion both into new American cities and into England, in the use of black detectives, and in the increased presence of female and homosexual private investigators. The above lists of new detectives and the additional settings only suggest what has occurred since 1979. With over forty new writers and each one with multiple titles to his or her credit, it is difficult to encompass the possibilities for the form or to prophesy the direction it will take. In contrast to the dismissive caricatures in Hammett, Chandler, and Spillane, Hansen's Brandstetter, Sandra Scoppetone's Lauren Laurano, and J.M. Redmann's Michelle "Micky" Knight introduce homosexual detectives serious about their work and their love lives. Certainly in the Early Period, sexuality is not unknown, but after MacDonald's Travis

McGee, writers increasingly integrate love and sexuality into their characters' lives. As this book will demonstrate, the hard-boiled detective novel can incorporate most literary themes into its form and deal with them in a substantial way.

Each of the three periods is organized into chapters that analyze selected themes. The analyses will focus particularly on the principal writers in each period and on early works in each detective series. Not all themes will be used for each period. Some will be limited to one period. Those that appear in each period include character, violence, space and place, work, love and sexuality, and friendship. This thematic flexibility allows an analysis of those ideas that underpin and shape the direction of the genre. In addition, references to earlier writers as the book progresses give it a sense of continuity and demonstrate those fundamental generic elements that make the connection between Hammett's and Chandler's detectives and John Baker's Sam Turner's series and Carolina Garcia-Aquilera's Lupe Solano series. When Laura Lippman introduces Tess Monaghan in *Baltimore Blues* (1997), one instantly recognizes the essential aspects of the hard-boiled detective's character. Initially unlicensed, Monaghan, a former newspaper reporter, proceeds to investigate cases while occasionally working for a lawyer. Arthur Lyons' Jacob Asch, in the Transitional Period, works in similar ways with a similar newspaper past.

Although this book is not an historical overview of the writers covered, it does give a sense of change and development through time in the genre. Only by means of a thematic analysis can the stability and change in the genre be demonstrated. With so many writers and novels, this approach clarifies both the ideas in the writers' works and the changes that occur over time.

1

Poe, Conan Doyle and the Hard-Boiled Detective Novel

Edgar Allan Poe is generally recognized as the father of the detective story. In the three tales featuring C. Auguste Dupin, Poe introduces many of the genre's identifying traits. In *The Perfect Murder: A Study in Detection* (1989, 2000), David Lehman observes, "Critics who may disagree on everything else concur in regarding Poe as the most significant figure in the detective story's history and development [...]" (xiv). However, less obvious is Poe's influence on the hard-boiled detective story and novel introduced in the United States in the 1920s. At first glance, Dupin and his friend, the unnamed narrator of the tales, differ greatly from Carroll John Daly's Race Williams and Dashiell Hammett's Continental Op and Sam Spade, the first major detectives in the new genre. Yet, in five areas, i.e., the use of an urban environment, the idea of a detective duo, the narrative stance, the locus of violence, and the role of reason and analysis, the hard-boiled detective writers use and alter Poe's approaches to the broader detective genre. John G. Cawelti notes in *Adventure, Mystery, and Romance: Formula Stories as Art and Popular Culture* (1976), "the special role of the modern city as background" to the hard-boiled formula, tracing it to Poe and Conan Doyle (140). In addition to Daly and Hammett, Raymond Chandler, Brett Halliday, Mickey Spillane, Thomas B. Dewey, Ross Macdonald, Richard S. Prather, and William Campbell Gault, all writers in the Early Period of the hard-boiled detective novel (1927–1955), consciously and, at times seemingly unconsciously, employ Poe's models as they struggle to benefit by, while distinguishing themselves from, their great progenitor. Like a palimpsest, they write over their original just as authors from at least two other distinct periods in the hard-boiled detective form write over them. Each period adds details and variety to their predecessors' examples while occasionally introducing new elements, but Poe's stories stand, with the particular aid of Sir Arthur Conan Doyle's Sherlock Holmes series, as an interpretive model for both development and divergence in the hard-boiled detective tradition.

Poe introduces the city as a place of darkness, a darkness that simultaneously liberates and conceals. And, the city is not just any city but rather, Paris. The first story, "The Murders in the Rue Morgue," appears in 1841, during the second decade of the reign of Louis-Phillipe (1830–1848), the Citizen King. The last true monarch, if one excepts Napoleon III (1852–1871), an elected president turned emperor, Louis-Phillipe gave promise of an enlightened rule but was forced out like his predecessor Charles X (1824–1830). However, in 1841, Paris was the center of a reviving nation that dominated European culture in literature and art. Jules Michelet, Honore Balzac, Alexandre Dumas, Victor Hugo, and Charles-Augustin Sainte-Beuve as well as Jean-Auguste-Dominique Ingres, Eugene Delacroix, Honore Daumier, Jean-Baptiste-Camille Corot, and Jean Francois Millet were prominent writers and artists. Like London, Paris had also reformed its police force. In the city with professional police, the fictional private detective emerges, in Dupin's case, as a pure amateur but forty-some years later as a consulting detective in the London of Sherlock Holmes. The public and private detective are thus bound together from the beginning of the detective story in an urban environment. The cities expand with people, trade, and crime, the latter making police reformation absolutely necessary. In Poe, Paris is a dimly lit city but not one in which Dupin and his narrator friend fear to walk at night. Poe does not equate the physical darkness with a moral one. The fact that an orangutan murders the woman and her daughter in his first story deflects the horrible deed from man to brute. Similarly, Conan Doyle fits Holmes comfortably into London starting with *A Study in Scarlet* (1887). Julian Symons remarks in *Bloody Murder: From the Detective Story to the Crime Novel: A History* (1992):

> We should remember, as most critics do not, that this was not "period" material for [Conan] Doyle when the first three collections of short stories and three of the four novels were written. He was writing of the world around him, a world transformed by his imagination [85].

Carroll John Daly begins *The Snarl of the Beast* (1927), the first hard-boiled detective novel, at night in New York City with gunfire and a chase through crowded buildings. A policeman dies, and Race Williams, the protagonist, plunges into the middle of the violence. The antagonist, Raphael Dezzeia, aka the Beast, also appears early and confronts Williams. A showdown is initially averted when Dezzeia retreats rather than being shot by Williams whom he apparently believes will carry out his threat to do so. A possible allusion to the orangutan in Poe's "Murders," Dezzeia is the chief source of danger in the city and novel. Dashiell Hammett's Continental Op, who works out of San Francisco, arrives in Personville, also known as Poisonville, in *Red Harvest* (1929) in the afternoon but encounters a social and moral darkness produced by the open vice and corruption. It might be argued that he brings no more light to Personville than Holmes does to London, but, like Holmes, he achieves a stasis in the social decline. Neither English criminals nor Montana ones succeed, but no particular hope exists in Conan Doyle or Hammett that they have been eradicated. San Francisco's dark streets and alleys in Hammett's *The Maltese Falcon* (1930) contain Sam Spade's efforts to discover who killed his partner Miles Archer, as well as several other men, but are not scenes of a recovered city. Spade successfully concludes the case when he turns over Brigid O'Shaughnessy, the killer, to the police but does not change the city's quality of life any more than the Continental Op does when Elihu Willsson, the man responsible for Personville's debacle, remains in control at the end. Philip Marlowe's arrival in Raymond Chandler's *The Big Sleep* (1939) at the Los Angeles mansion of Gen. Sternwood takes place, symbolically, in the moral darkness of the city. Some scenes occur at night, but neither day nor night affects the miasma of vice and corruption surrounding the Sternwoods and those with whom they interact. Thus, when Marlowe turns the homicidal Carmen over to her sister Vivian at the end of the novel, nothing has improved though many are dead. And, the city promises to reveal many Carmens but few Rusty Regans, Vivian's unfortunate husband whom Carmen killed for rejecting her sexual advances prior to the novel's commencement. Cawelti remarks that Poe's setting

> abstracts the story from the complexity and confusion of the larger social world and provides a rationale for avoiding the consideration of those more complex problems of social injustice and group conflict that form the basis of much contemporary realistic fiction [*Adventure* 97].

However, the hard-boiled detective novel becomes increasingly realistic in its expansion of the setting into "the threatening chaos of the outside world" (97). Frank MacShane in *The Life of Raymond Chandler* (1976) also sees a divergence from Poe's tale of ratiocination:

> Like Hammett and [Joseph T.] Shaw before him, he was dissatisfied with the deductive kind of story and associated himself with writers who tried to use

the detective story to say something about the nature of contemporary life and the injustices that infest it [47].

The city continues to be the focus in the transitional hard-boiled detective novel (1964–1977). This focus especially involves an expansion in the number and kinds of cities. Not only do significant new series in New York, San Francisco, and Los Angeles appear, but smaller cities become prominent, e.g., Indianapolis, Boston, St. Louis, Saratoga Springs, and Fort Lauderdale. Some writers follow the model of Hammett's Continental Op and work in a variety of places. John D. MacDonald's Travis McGee frequently leaves Fort Lauderdale and often the United States. Joseph Hansen's David Brandstetter necessarily investigates cases of insurance fraud wherever they take him and must sometimes depart Los Angeles in the process. For the most part, Robert B. Parker's Spenser works in and around Boston, though he is not originaly from there, but in *Judas Goat* (1978), Spenser and Hawk travel to London. The question arises as to whether or not the city remains a venue substantially defined by the ominous qualities reflected in Poe and Conan Doyle. While there may be an atmosphere of uncertainty in the transitional cities, the detectives partially domesticate them in their confrontations with power and corruption. Parker's Spenser confronts dangerous people and situations, but, like the settings for many of the transitional detectives, Boston is his city, his home. He takes possession, as it were, of some part of the city's life. If not all, many of the transitional detectives are less alienated than those in the Early Period. In this they resemble Dupin and Holmes for whom alienation is a distinctly odd concept. Even the frequently lonely Nameless in Bill Pronzini's San Francisco series finds Kerry Wade in *Hoodwink* (1981), the seventh novel in the series, after earlier abortive relationships. In Stephen Dobyns' *Saratoga Longshot* (1976), Charlie Bradshaw spends most of the novel in New York City but returns to Saratoga Springs as his natural, if occasionally uncomfortable, environment.

In the Modern Period (1979 to present), writers, through allusion and example, explore the role of the detective in the city. Hammett, Chandler, Spillane, and Ross Macdonald might be the writers most frequently alluded to, but many of the aspects used in Poe and Conan Doyle function as foundations for plot and idea and find their expression inevitably in an urban setting. Every new city added and former one used increase the sense of danger, conflict, and corruption expected in this generic environment. Detroit; Santa Teresa, California; Cincinnati; Washington, D.C.; Oakland; Sacramento; Seattle; Portland, Oregon; Denver; Philadelphia; Cleveland; Newark; and east-central and southern Florida are just some of the modern venues. Even James W. Hall's Thorn, first introduced in *Under Cover of Daylight* (1987), contends with aspects of the city minus the buildings and crowds. Following John D. MacDonald's example, Hall shows that the moral darkness of the city fits quite well in sub-tropical Florida. Karen Kijewski's Kat Colorado in *Katwalk* (1989) works in Sacramento but investigates her first case in Las Vegas, shifting from one locale to another and suggesting a move from a lesser to a greater degree of corruption in the process. The arrival of the hard-boiled detective novel in the United Kingdom in the Modern Period suggests a return to the setting of one of the nineteenth-century progenitors in that four of the first five writers set their series in London and the fifth works in Manchester. In London, Liza Cody's Anna Lee in *Dupe* (1980), Gillian Slovo's Kate Baeier in *Morbid Symptons* (1984), Mark Timlin's Nick Sharman in *A Good Year for the Roses* (1988), and Sarah Dunant's Hannah Wolfe in *Birth Marks* (1991) and in Manchester, Val McDermid's Kate Brannigan in *Dead Beat* (1992) reveal the city as dangerous for the young and the old but especially the former. Kathleen Gregory Klein suggests that Anna Lee's work as a detective "is boring, circumscribed, and controlled" yet "much more realistic" than "her American counterparts" and not lacking in danger (*Woman Detective* 158). Taking into account the reputed cultural similarities between the United States and the United Kingdom, the strength of the genre shows itself in its ability to adapt to new requirements while still using the city as setting and theme.

The early hard-boiled period has few detective duos resembling those found in Poe and Conan Doyle. Both of the latter use the narrator friend to introduce the detective, whom George Grella mockingly calls in Poe "his deferential narrator-stooge" ("Murder and Manners" 42). This narrative device highlights and distances the detective from the voice that reveals him. The companion also becomes the foil to the detective's brilliant analytical abilities. Poe's narrator and Conan Doyle's Dr. Watson, in "The Murders in the Rue Morgue" (1841) and *A Study in Scarlet*, respectively, explicitly state the methods used by their friends and draw the reader into an admiration of their genius. These narrators not only display the initial arrogance of the police in dismissing the detectives' special abilities, even after they bring cases to them, but also the subsequent confounding of the official detectives. Dupin's friend resides with him, and Dr. Watson, until he marries, shares an apartment with Holmes in Baker Street. Each narrator explains the manner in which he came to live with his detective friend, giving one a hint of past history that the authors, especially in the case of Holmes, carefully expand. Conan Doyle's emphasis on a personal historical background as starting point differs from Poe's more dramatic *in medias res* structure, e.g., Dupin and the narrator walk in the city fairly early in "Murders." Dupin, essentially, has no past apart from his life with the narrator while Holmes has a past only briefly alluded to in the novels and stories. The mysteriousness of their origins is also a principal ingredient in the lives of the hard-boiled detectives and aids the forward-moving direction of the narratives by limiting past motivations for their conduct.

Race Williams, the Continental Op, Sam Spade, Philip Marlowe, Mike Hammer, and Lew Archer, the chief early hard-boiled detectives, with few exceptions work alone. Sam Spade's partner Miles Archer dies in the first chapter of *The Maltese Falcon*, and while the Continental Op works for the Continental Detective Agency and occasionally calls on other operatives, he generally sets the stage for their help. Although Earl Stanley Gardner's Perry Mason works with Paul Drake and Rex Stout's Nero Wolfe employs Archie Goodwin, these duos function on the periphery of the hard-boiled detective novel. Neither Halliday's Michael Shayne, Prather's Shell Scott, Spillane's Mike Hammer, nor Macdonald's Lew Archer have partners. Spade, Shayne, and Hammer have secretaries, but except occasionally for Hammer's Velda, they stay largely in the background. Paradoxically, Spillane is a forerunner for many changes in the genre, in this area as well as others, notwithstanding dismissals of him by Grella as "the perversion" and "a kind of end" of the hard-boiled detective novel ("Hard-Boiled Detective" 116, 118) and by Cawelti as "everybody's supreme embodiment of the tasteless, vulgar, obsessive, sadistic, and unredeemable dregs of popular formula literature" (*Adventure* 162).

John D. MacDonald gives Travis McGee a partner who by the seventh novel engages in most aspects of his cases. Meyer first appears in *A Purple Place for Dying* (1964) but only as an acquaintance who lives on a nearby boat at Bahia Mar, Fort Lauderdale. *Darker than Amber* (1966) deeply involves Meyer in discovering who killed Vangie Bellmeer, the woman they "meet" one night when she seems to catapult over a bridge as they fish underneath it. However, someone conveniently wired a concrete block to her ankles and dropped her into the tidal stream near their boat. McGee rescues her, he and Meyer talk with her, and in the process their real partnership begins. While McGee narrates the stories, Meyer is the center of rationality in the series. Edgar W. Hirshberg observes:

> But his most important function is as an additional brain. Sometimes he is a sounding board, off which Travis can bounce his ideas or hypotheses. Often he is the voice of reason and sense in instances when McGee may be carried away by his passions or resentments [59].

Partnerships resembling Poe's, Conan Doyle's, and MacDonald's are rare in the transitional period, but writers create other ways to lessen their detectives' isolation. In *Act of Fear* (1967), Michael Collins places Dan Fortune in Chelsea, the New York neighborhood in which he grew up. Roger L. Simon's Moses Wine in *The Big Fix* (1973) set in Los Angeles must contend with his Aunt Sonya, an early and continuing political radical, and his ex-wife Suzanne who has custody of their two children, Jacob and Simon. Michael Z. Lewin's Albert Samson operates in his hometown Indianapolis in *Ask the Right Question* (1971), writes to his daughter, and regularly eats at his mother's diner. Robert B. Parker's Spenser meets his lover Susan Silverman in *God Save the Child* (1974), the second novel in the series; Hawk in *Promised Land* (1976), the fourth novel; and takes fifteen-year old Paul Giacomin to live with him in *Early Autumn* (1981), the seventh novel. Stephen Dobyns' Charlie Bradshaw acquires a *de facto* partner in Victor Plotz whom he meets in *Saratoga Longshot*. Bradshaw resigns from the Saratoga Springs police force in that novel. In addition to growing up there, Bradshaw must deal with three businessmen cousins, an ex-wife, and his mother, who works as a waitress in town before winning money and buying one of the old hotels. Bradshaw subsequently performs some security work for her. Finally, Marcia Muller's Sharon McCone investigates in *Edwin of the Iron Shoes* (1977) for All Souls Cooperative in San Francisco. Many of the personnel are friends, and some live on the second floor of the Cooperative's office building.

The partnership tradition makes a stronger comeback in the Modern Period than in the Transitional era. However, the details of the partners' associations are just as varied in the 1980s and 1990s as in Poe's and Conan Doyle's times. First, partners are often seen as mentors rather than as equals. Janet Dawson's Jeri Howard, first introduced in *Kindred Crimes* (1990), learned her craft under Errol Seville, now retired. She still sees him from time to time and runs cases by him. Three British female hard-boiled detectives have mentors as partners. Liza Cody's Anna Lee, Sarah Dunant's Hannah Wolfe, and Val McDermid's Kate Brannigan all, in slightly different ways, learn from their mentor partners. Bernie Schiller, a retired policeman, coaches the young Anna, an ex-policewoman, and helps her overcome the difficulties she encounters at Brierly Security. Wolfe's ex-partner, Frank Comfort, another retired policeman, teaches her more through indirection than overt statement and after she leaves him gives her work. Brannigan's partner Bill Mortensen is also more experienced, but they divide their work in such a way that both do what they know best. Michelle Spring's Laura Principal operates similarly in Cambridge in *Every Breath You Take* (1994) with Sonny Mendlowitz, but he is also her lover. Of course, neither Dupin's nor Holmes' partner is superior to them in investigative work, but the other voice and mind add significantly to the stories while the detectives remain the principal focus.

Other partnerships in the modern period are more balanced. Robert Crais's Elvis Cole and Joe Pike in *The Monkey's Raincoat* (1987) bring overlapping gifts and styles to their agency. A.E. Maxwell's Fiddler and Fiora, an ex-banker when they begin to work as partners, also have varied backgrounds and knowledge that complement each other. Another modern Los Angeles private detective has a partner who would be better described as an anti-partner. Let go from his well-paying job at Champion Aircraft, Easy Rawlins slides into the role of private investigator in Walter Mosley's *Devil in a Blue Dress* (1990). The murderous Mouse, from whom he fled Houston years ago, writes to Easy that he would like to visit him in Los Angeles. Mouse responds positively to Easy's subsequent invitation to join him. Although Easy states they were best friends (148), Mouse has no conscience, and Easy knows that Mouse would kill him over money without thinking and with no remorse (152). Mouse's type of inhumane bonhomie goes back at least to one of his most famous predecessors, John D. MacDonald's Howie Brindle in *The Turquoise Lament* (1973). The jovial Howie has left a trail of bodies as the novel opens, and a comparison of Mouse to Howie underscores the former's danger to others. Mouse is not a partner in the strict sense, but he involves himself in Easy's case in *Devil in a Blue Dress* in order to "protect" him. Unlike in Poe and Conan Doyle, the genre has stretched the idea of the partnership tradition so that the detective loses some of his or her autonomy. One final modern variation on the partnership tradition, examples of which also occur in the transitional period, involves the detective and a support group. This ranges from family in Carolina Garcia-Aguilera's Lupe Solana series set in Miami, to Linda Barnes' Carlotta Carlyle's friends in Boston, to Reginald Hill's Joe Sixsmith series set in Luton, England, which includes friends and a bossy aunt. In addition, John Baker's Sam Turner in York, England, gathers friends to help him in his detective business, often just from the need to be with people, to feel connected to others. Other examples suggest the endless possibilities for partnerships and emphasize the important role they play in hard-boiled detective fiction.

The first-person voice of the detective's friend and confidant in Poe and Conan Doyle set the standard for narrating the hard-boiled detective novel. Even though Dupin and Holmes do not tell their stories as later becomes the norm, the consciousness of a character immediately involved in the action is the general narrative pattern. Commenting on Poe, LeRoy Lad Panek in *An Introduction to the Detective Story* (1987) states the important role of these narrators: "In the Dupin stories, Poe covered up facts by employing an obtuse narrator [...]" (30). Even if told in the past tense, the immediateness of perception by someone who does not, at the time of the unfolding events, know their outcome provides a dramatic tension tempered by the shaping of the story after the events. An unedited diary or journal or a series of letters would be more immediate and less under the selective control of the narrator, but twentieth-century authors seldom choose this form. Poe's unnamed narrator and Conan Doyle's Dr. Watson thus act in special roles relative to the detectives' expressed thoughts, actions, moods, and emotional states. The detective's life and career are filtered through their companions. One only acquires a partial, limited view of the detective as the narrator observes, reflects, and analyzes his friend's many emotional and mental states. Panek credits Poe with "new ways of telling stories," and they include "telling the story backward" and the even more important "manipulation of point of view" (*Introduction* 32). However, as the hard-boiled detective tradition unfolds, the typical first-person narration by the detective admits the reader to greater intimacy even while one remains aware of the detectives' corresponding control. Dr. Watson publishes his accounts of Holmes' cases and unavoidably raises the question of audience interest: What will the reader want to know about the detective besides what becomes known in pursuing a case? With the first-person narration by the detective, one most immediately notices in this regard that the detective often suppresses his past life unless it is relevant to the story. Usually, these bits of personal history appear in the most casual manner, inserted in passing even if connected to the plot.

Asked by Otto Penzler to write a biography of Travis McGee, Mac-Donald refused ("Introduction and Comment" 68). As a result, McGee sparingly parcels out references to his youth, family, and past activities. Some of the latter involve cases referred to but not written in story form. This is a device that Dr. Watson uses in the Sherlock Holmes' tales. Both Daly and Hammett (for the Continental Op and Sam Spade) mention earlier experiences and cases, but the detectives have no real pasts in the solid sense a novel would establish if that past were to be thematically important. This presentness dominates the genre, giving it one of its most distinctive qualities. One most immediately hears the voice of Daly's Race Williams boasting, justifying, threatening, promising, and generally boosting his spirits with remarks that ring true because he has done much of what his rhetoric asserts. Spillane's Mike Hammer will continue this narrative tone. Chandler's Philip Marlowe is quiet compared to Williams and Hammer but nonetheless present to himself and the case. The past is grudgingly allowed to intrude. Much like Ross Macdonald's Lew Archer, what happened, happened. It of course affects the present, and the detective on occasion acknowledges this. The narrative thrust of the first-person novels of Daly and Spillane are thus connected to Chandler and some Hammett novels. The Continental Op narrates his stories and novels, but Hammett uses the third person limited point of view in *The Maltese Falcon*. However, Sam Spade is as laconic and apparently unwilling to reveal his past as are the first-person narrators.

The transitional and modern hard-boiled detectives nearly all narrate their novels, but with the possible exception of MacDonald's McGee,

Parker's Spenser, Bill Pronzini's Nameless, and a few others, they speak more about their pasts than the detectives in the Early hard-boiled Period. Dupin's unnamed narrator and Holmes' Dr. Watson, seemingly reluctant to reveal too much about their friends, no longer influence the mid-to-late-twentieth-century narrator detectives. With more of their past lives intruding into the stories, the detectives' present situations deepen in complexity and inevitably become part of the plot. In *Pepper Pike* (1988), Les Roberts' Milan Jacovich beats up Victor Gaimari, the heir apparent to the Cleveland crime syndicate, when the latter appears to threaten his ex-wife and children (155). Gaimari has Jacovich beaten up in turn as a lesson (163). Jacovich, unable to leave well enough alone, tells Gaimari that the next time his men better kill him because he will shoot them (167). All of this adds to the drama in this modern hard-boiled detective series but radically alters the narrative structures and conventions. If her past before Kip Adams is somewhat nebulous, Sandra Scoppetone's Lauren Laurano shares a life with her partner measuring some eleven years. And, this past is integral to the series Lauren narrates, for Kip not only is her lover but also a practicing psychiatrist. The moods and crises have become crucial to the detective's image at least since Holmes, but the modern hard-boiled detective, again with some few exceptions, expands the degree to which the detective's everyday life, not only his or her problem-solving skills, becomes crucial to the cases.

The father of G.M. Ford's Leo Waterman in *Who in Hell Is Wanda Fuca?* (1995) was a Seattle politician whose reputation confronts Leo wherever he goes. Bartenders, fellow city council members, and shady figures who suggest possible illegality committed by his father — all of these factor into how Leo works his cases. Waterman's ability to deal with the many influences from the past and still function somewhat independently defines him. However, his many narrative choices regarding his father mark him off from other first-person accounts that limit such details. A similar effect, from a different perspective, occurs in Jeremiah Healy's John Francis Cuddy Boston series. Cuddy must deal with the devastating effects of his wife Beth's death. In *Blunt Darts* (1984), Cuddy visits his wife's grave on a hill in South Boston overlooking the bay. During that and subsequent visits, Cuddy speaks with her and "hears" her responses. Healy treads a fine line between strong sentiment and bathos with this narrative device but manages, with some restrictions on its use, to keep the focus on Cuddy's need for her and his difficulty in going on without her. One aspect of the narrative structures in Ford and Healy is that the focus is often strongly on characters other than the detectives. For Poe and Conan Doyle, their detectives are center stage, and the authors partly achieve this through the companion narrators. Liza Cody's Anna Lee narrates her series set in London, but in *Dupe*, the first novel, Lee becomes so engrossed in searching out the life and death of Deirdre Jackson in order to satisfy the parents' desire to know what happened to her that she manages to conceal herself while still always present.

The Modern Period also contains detectives who parallel the narrative patterns of Williams, the Continental Op, Spade, Marlowe, Hammer, and Archer. This might be seen either as a distinct lack of progress or as the continued vitality of the early models. Stephen Greenleaf's John Marshall Tanner, Loren D. Estleman's Amos Walker, Jonathan Valin's Harry Stoner, Sara Paretsky's V.I. Warshawski, Sue Grafton's Kinsey Millhone, and John Lutz's Fred Carver narrate their novels. Some incidents from earlier periods of their lives surface, but, much like in Poe and Conan Doyle and the early hard-boiled detectives, the work is forward moving, involving little effort to pull revelatory material from the past. Some is essential to frame their novels and stories; however, the early information is seldom structured into the narrative with the story revolving around it. Mark Timlin's Nick Sharman is an exception to this pattern in the Modern Period. His being a private investigator derives from his forced resignation from the police in a corruption scandal. His ex-wife and daughter also figure largely in his life, and he often refers to them. People in the police and criminal worlds with whom he interacted in the past also impact the direction of the novels. Sharman does have new experiences, but the past is frequently a factor in how the experiences pan out. In contrast to Timlin, Paretsky, Grafton, and Lutz carefully insert past experiences, e.g., family and/or professional, that suggest an effect on the detectives' characters without over-emphasizing it.

In Poe and Conan Doyle, violence and its resolution is a principal focus in their tales. R. Gordon Kelly observes in *Mystery Fiction and Modern Life* (1998):

> The introduction of murder into ["The Murders in the Rue Morgue"] greatly increases the stakes associated with the exercise of analysis, and serves to define an essential feature of Dupin's world. In his world, as in the growing cities of the 1840s, violent crime is a predictable, recurrent feature, bringing demands for its control, questions about its etiology, and debate about how and with what techniques and at what costs violent crime might be reduced [33–34].

Even though theft is the occasion for Dupin's involvement in "The Purloined Letter" (1844), Minister D, as Dupin reflects, is capable of murder and is therefore someone of whom to be wary (138). Similarly, Holmes investigates a variety of crimes, but murder or attempted murder rank high on the list. As a divergence that underscores the fundamental representation of violence in human culture, Poe and Conan Doyle occasionally use animals and/or reptiles as agents of violence. The escaped orangutan in "The Murders in the Rue Morgue" begins Poe's accounts of criminal predators.

Conan Doyle uses a snake in "The Adventure of the Speckled Band" (1902) and a giant dog in *The Hound of the Baskervilles* (1902). Humans may encounter violence anywhere and anytime; it surrounds them. In "The Adventure of the Speckled Band," Dr. Grimesby Roylott has killed one daughter and plans to kill another while she sleeps in order to claim her inheritance. The mother and daughter in "The Murders in the Rue Morgue" are in their own room when attacked from a seemingly impossible route, impossible of course to humans but not the animal perpetrator. If the animal escapes from his handler by accident in Poe's story, Conan Doyle's criminals purposefully employ animals for violent ends, thus crossing a moral and legal line prohibiting such actions. While Dupin is under a perceived threat in "The Purloined Letter," he does not use violence or much physical action to solve his cases. Dupin employs his observation and intellect. Paradoxically, Howard Haycraft in *Murder for Pleasure: The Life and Times of the Detective Story* (1984) remarks, "'The Murders in the Rue Morgue' [...] is really dominated by sensational physical event — not by detection, excellently as Poe conceived it" (15). However, this refers to the readers' probable memory of the story rather than Dupin's thorough investigative role. As will be seen, the balance between thought and action is a major thread in the hard-boiled detective novel as well. In contrast to Dupin, the occasionally lethargic Holmes shows himself capable of forceful, even violent, action when necessary. The body as well as the mind becomes crucial in Holmes' cases. Dickens' Inspector Bucket of the Detective in *Bleak House* (1853) is the principal progenitor for this development. With Esther Summerson's aid, Bucket's restless activity takes him back and forth across London and its suburbs. However, Holmes is seldom physically assaulted, and thus his short-lived "death" along with Professor Moriarty's as they presumably plunge over the Reichenbach Falls is an aberration.

Violence moves to the fore with the advent of the hard-boiled detective story and novel. What distinguishes its use in this genre is the presentation of violence in progress, both by and against the detectives and others. The general lack of violence in progress in the formal detective novel is what underlies Grella's observation of "the peculiar nonviolence of the form" ("Murder and Manners" 40). Holmes admires Irene Adler's intelligence and daring, but in Dashiell Hammett's *The Maltese Falcon*, Brigid O'Shaughnessy murders several men to gain the statue. Murder frequently becomes the preferred solution to most problems. Other influences, both literary and historical, partly account for this shift, but a reaction against the almost exclusively rational focus in the detective genre, which predominates before the 1920s and continues long afterward, also plays a role. Daly's Race Williams and Hammett's Continental Op often carry two or more guns, thus vividly demonstrating the new atmosphere in the detective novel.

Possibly only Prather's Shell Scott and Spillane's Mike Hammer reveal a penchant equal to Daly's Williams for shooting first and asking questions later. A reaction to violent solutions especially sets in with Chandler's Philip Marlowe and Macdonald's Lew Archer, but there is no easy way to return to the Poe–Conan Doyle model in which violence plays a correspondingly lesser role. The stories involving Hammett's Continental Op expand from individual violence to those in which criminal gangs invade and loot towns. The Continental Op usually calls on other operatives from the Continental Detective Agency to suppress the spiraling violence as he does in *Red Harvest*. This type of large-scale action, however, similar to Cawelti's description of the hero's struggles against the Western outlaw gangs (*Six Gun* 93–94), reaches a dead end in the early hard-boiled detective novel, and later writers generally avoid it. Mike Hammer acts violently in order to resolve his cases, but whether it is the shooting of Charlotte Manning in *I, the Jury* (1947) or the communist agents in *One Lonely Night* (1951), Hammer does not see killing as a socially-shared act. Individuals and their actions motivate his reactions, and he responds accordingly, even personalizing his violent solutions to groups as in the latter novel. Referring to "the high level of violence (even from the perspective of the '80s, this 1951 novel seems shocking)" (73), Max Allan Collins and James L. Traylor in *One Lonely Knight: Mickey Spillane's Mike Hammer* (1984) describe the end of *One Lonely Night*, "[...] the Communist cell members, led by an agent imported from Russia, kidnap Hammer's beloved secretary Velda, and are torturing her to find the whereabouts of the documents, when Hammer bursts in with a machine gun and massacres them" (74), acting alone as he does in the opening scene of the novel.

In the Transitional Period, the idea that violence is largely personal continues to operate. True, people bring salvage work to John D. MacDonald's Travis McGee, and this galvanizes him into action. But, many times clients also become lovers, however briefly. The cases have an erotic charge that often carries over into sexual intimacy. McGee's moral radar, as in the case of Vangie Bellmeer in *Darker than Amber*, will not always allow him to act on his physical responses to an attractive woman. Even so, McGee's admiration for Vangie's stubborn unwillingness to give in to her former colleagues' desire to kill her pushes him into avenging her murder. MacDonald is careful to account for McGee's hard nature and his ability to put this hardness to use when he feels that the criminals have stepped into his world and have attempted to arrange it to their own satisfaction. In at least thirteen of the twenty-one novels, McGee sets out to shift the balance between good and evil to the former. This happens most dramatically in *The Deep Blue Good-by* (1964), *A Purple Place for Dying*, *Bright Orange for the Shroud* (1965), *Pale Gray for Guilt* (1968), *The Long Lavender Look* (1970),

The Turquoise Lament, The Green Ripper (1979), and *Cinnamon Skin* (1982). While McGee might not kill every antagonist, their options narrow when he confronts them. Robert B. Parker's Spenser comes closest to McGee in seeing his opponents as morally evil and thus deserving of a violent response on his part. Parker's use of Hawk as the representative of ultimate violence in many dangerous situations allows the reader to see Spenser's somewhat more restrained violence in greater perspective.

The novels in the Modern Period generally support the concept that violence is personal though many demonstrate a belief in a socially-based evil. In the Early Period, Daly, Hammett in the Continental Op stories, and Spillane, the best exemplars of a belief in a socially-based evil, are counterbalanced first by Hammett himself in *The Maltese Falcon*, Halliday, Chandler, Prather, Ross Macdonald, and William Campbell Gault who confront an evil whose source largely comes from individuals. Thus, from the beginning the character of the detective protagonists partially pulls against absorption into any group dynamic. Les Roberts' Milan Jacovich, like Parker's Spenser, must deal in the modern period with organized crime figures, but the criminals are drawn into the detectives' stories and not vice versa. From their individual pasts and needs, the detectives come to their professions and control both their stories and the violence that occurs in them. Many individual detectives are attacked, but their responses to specific acts of violence are multifarious. At the most violent extreme lies Mark Timlin's Nick Sharman and at the other Stephen Greenleaf's John Marshall Tanner. Like Tanner, Sue Grafton's Kinsey Millhone generally eschews violence but kills Charlie Scorsoni in *"A" Is for Alibi* in order to save her own life. Very few modern hard-boiled private detectives repeat Race Williams' boast that he only shoots those who deserve it (*Snarl* 60–61). Rather, violence raises moral dilemmas that must be faced. Williams does reflect, however, in *The Snarl of the Beast*, "That the end justifies the means was made for me all right — but no end would justify the taking of an innocent life" (136). John Baker's Sam Turner and Jeremiah Healy's John Francis Cuddy do not easily turn, as it were, to cleaning their guns while dismissing the image of ruined, even if guilty, lives.

Early in *The Snarl of the Beast*, Race Williams says, "I'm a man of action but I can think occasionally" (63). And he is right; he does act, but along with his many and violent actions, Williams must decide how to deal with Daniel Davidson's opponents before they can kill his client. Thus, the seeds of reason and analysis exist in Daly's hard-boiled detective fiction. In contrast, Poe's Dupin is primarily a thinker. Grella remarks, "[...] Dupin exhibits the striking characteristics of intellectual brilliance and personal eccentricity which indelibly mark all later detective heroes" ("Murder and Manners" 42). His reasoning powers extend out of the context of those intellectual activities of which his friend speaks at the beginning of "The Murders in the Rue Morgue." All that day he and Dupin work on various artistic and scientific problems. They walk out late into the dark city for relief from their intellectual labors. Poe places the mind in the forefront and thus gives the detective a *raison d'être*. When Dr. Watson first meets Sherlock Holmes through a man named Stamford in regard to sharing lodgings, Holmes is working on a scientific experiment in the chemistry laboratory at Bart's. This and playing the violin, often in a desultory manner, are Holmes' chief preoccupations when not plying his profession as a consulting detective. Although intellectually engaged from the first moment he meets a client, witness his comments to Helen Stoner in "The Adventure of the Speckled Band" (259), there frequently comes a moment of deep abstraction during which Holmes figures out the case. Rex Stout will use this image of the thinker, there but not there. Nero Wolfe unconsciously signals this moment to his assistant Archie Goodwin when he leans back in his chair, closes his eyes, and moves his lips in and out. Then, like Holmes' sudden bursts of activity when he comes out of his trances, Wolfe opens his eyes and begins to issue orders to Goodwin that lead to the cases' solutions.

Unlike Race Williams, Hammett's Continental Op places both thought and action in the forefront. Short, broad, and armed, the Op looks the part of the man of action. However, he is sent out on cases by the Old Man of the Continental Detective Agency because of his ability to question extensively, observe closely, and reason his way through the lies and deceits he encounters. Both in the short stories and novels, the Op must see the pattern and then close the case. He must deal with a variety of citizens and policemen in order to satisfy his agency's clients. Chandler's Philip Marlowe and Ross Macdonald's Lew Archer come closest among the early hard-boiled detectives to Dupin's and Holmes's dependence on reason rather than action to resolve their cases. As noted, Holmes relies more on action than Dupin, and Marlowe resembles him in this. Marlowe's world-weary cynicism is alien to both early figures, but it does not inhibit his reasoning abilities nor his loyalty to his clients. Archer's Los Angeles differs from Poe's image of nineteenth-century Paris, but Archer is also more reliant on thought than action. He varies from Dupin's and Holmes's patterns in that he extensively interviews, questions, observes, and then presents the solution. Dupin and Holmes include elements of these, but their stories do not show the detective's experiencing the developing steps as fully as the hard-boiled detective novels. Aside from a Nero Wolfe, most detectives in the hard-boiled genre do not function as geniuses delivering the solution from an Olympian height.

What becomes obvious as the genre develops as a blend of thought and

action is the lessening of gratuitous violence, and though violence, gratuitous or otherwise, does not disappear, it becomes enmeshed in greater
human complexity in the Transitional and Modern Periods. Exceptions, at
least for the detectives, like Timlin's Nick Sharman, do exist, but many novels approach the condition of being novels of manners and morals with a
murder rather than strictly a detective novel with murder. Both Chandler
and John D. MacDonald argue for the novelists' right to see their detective
or suspense novels as "good fiction" or "art" (Chandler, "Simple Art" 2) or
"move [them] as close as I can get to the 'legitimate' novels of manners and
morals, despair and failure, love and joy" (MacDonald, "Introduction" 73).
Also, more traditional novels begin to include elements of detective fiction,
if not only the hard-boiled variety. Umberto Eco's *The Name of the Rose*
(1981) is a famous example. One effect of this novelistic shift on the use of
reason and analysis in the hard-boiled detective novel is their application
by the detective to himself or herself. The ways detectives look at the world,
their personal dilemmas, and their past experiences direct their thought
processes. The Op does not analyze himself but rather the people and circumstances of the cases. Certainly Marlowe reflects on many aspects of his
life, but he differs from most other early hard-boiled detectives in this. In
the Transitional Period, in addition to McGee's thorough attention to his
mental and emotional states, Prozini's Nameless, Lawrence Block's Matthew
Scudder, Muller's Sharon McCone, Lewin's Albert Samson, Dobyns' Charlie Bradshaw, and Hansen's Dave Brandstetter examine themselves, both in
terms of emotions and motives, as well as their cases. Parker's stoical Spenser
proves the exception to the rule in contemplation of self in this period but
not in reasoning closely about his cases. Spenser's long relationship with
Susan Silverman, a psychiatrist, provides opportunities for her insights on
his character, insights with which he frequently agrees.

In the Modern Period, the detectives emphasize the importance of reason and analysis to the successful conclusion of their work. While most
modern hard-boiled detectives are well educated, few have any pretensions
to being intellectuals. In fact, they generally go out of their way to avoid
this attribute. Kinsey Millhone's mixture of intuition and reason in solving her cases emerges in her use of index cards on which to note information but also to rearrange the order of events so as to counteract any
stalemates in her thinking. Dupin appears to work his way through a problem once he becomes interested in a case, but Holmes is the moody con-
templator of his ideas and facts until he achieves a result. Hill's Joe Sixsmith
uses his mind as a way both to solve his cases and destroy the stereotypes
his fellow Luton citizens, police and civilians alike, have of him as a redundant lathe operator not up to the tasks of his newly chosen profession.
Michelle Spring's Laura Principal left academia to become a private detec-

tive. While neither she nor Sixsmith have Holmes' brooding genius, they both think through their cases relying on action when necessary or unavoidable. If only from the group with whom he works, Baker's Sam Turner gets his due as a thinker. He often makes leaps that connect parts of a case to one another in ways not easily followed. To think back to Daly's Race Williams and his action creed makes one, at first, realize how far the genre has come; then, one is aware that reason and analysis are staples in the genre's development and transcend place, age, and country.

Eighty-six years separate Poe's "Murders in the Rue Morgue" and Daly's *The Snarl of the Beast*. A little more than half way between these two writers, Conan Doyle publishes his first Sherlock Holmes novel, *A Study in Scarlet*. If Poe and Conan Doyle were removed from the detective literature, it is hard to imagine the hard-boiled detective novel coming in to existence. Their many examples, especially Poe, cast a long shadow that points the direction for hard-boiled detective fiction. At the beginning of the twenty-first century, the narrative possibilities for the form continue to evolve.

2

History as Recovery

Set in the 1920s, 1930s, 1940s, and 1950s, the early hard-boiled detective novels are elements of their decades' intense present but also have, paradoxically, reconstituted themselves through time into histories and cultural myths. Geoffrey O'Brien in *Hard-Boiled America: Lurid Paperbacks and the Masters of Noir* (1981, 1997) argues for the importance of "realism" to this reconstitution:

> Following Hammett's lead, the crime novel became a major vehicle for social analysis. Even allowing for generous doses of fantasy and melodrama, it is possible to get a coherent picture of the underside of American life from the works of Hammett, James M. Cain, Raymond Chandler, Horace McCoy, David Goodis, Ross Macdonald, John D. MacDonald, and such latter-day practitioners as George V. Higgins, Donald Westlake, and Elmore Leonard [62].

And, as John G. Cawelti states in *Adventure, Mystery, and Romance*, that picture is set in the city. Raymond Chandler's "mean streets" is an evocation of an urban world that experienced Prohibition, the rise of the gangster, and the Depression. Dashiell Hammett's Continental Op cleans up Personville in *Red Harvest*, a microcosm of the failed city, and ironically has to escape before he becomes any more like the killers whom he has set in motion. Analogously, the nineteenth century novel is a rich mine of historical and mythic impressions of which the early twenty-first century reader/critic struggles to gain a clear sense. From Jane Austen to William M. Thackeray to Charles Dickens to Anthony Trollope to George Eliot to Henry James, among others, that century's fiction offers a retrievable historical source. Reversing the usual process of a Lillian De La Torre, Ellis

Peters, Robert van Gulik, or Julian Symons, the modern reader/critic of the early hard-boiled detective novel creates a historical mystery from a text not written from that perspective. Historicizing the early hard-boiled novels and speculating on the cultural myths they contain, a vision of a social and literary past appears, more pungent, complex, and elusive than one can project onto the frame of time.

While Edgar Allan Poe writes of a Paris in his Dupin stories that he did not know first-hand, Dickens, Wilkie Collins, and Sir Arthur Conan Doyle write of a London that they knew well. However transformed in their fiction, the London employed is the city with which they engaged on a daily basis. It vividly appears in their novels and stories in all its complexity, and not even through painting can one recover a more powerful visual image of the dynamic processes that make up the city's life. Contemporary nineteenth-century writers present different images of the city. Through their imaginative responses to their environments, one gets a feeling of the present, lived world. Dickens, for instance, reflects a vivid sense of the London streets and houses. This is in addition to the stories in which they occur. The tone and mood of the works, Dickens' particular gifts, will affect his descriptions of houses and streets, but from an examination of many works, some general awareness begins to appear. Jaggers' office and home in *Great Expectations* (1861), Tulkinghorn's home in *Bleak House*, and Dombey's in *Dombey and Son* (1848) take one into the feeling of place and the way of seeing that Dickens experiences. And, those are nineteenth century visions of houses as is Pip's first experience of the London streets in *Great Expectations* and Oliver's in *Oliver Twist* (1838). Influenced partially by Dickens, George Gissing conveys a late-nineteenth century feel for the streets and houses of the London slums in *Workers in the Dawn* (1880), *Thyrza* (1887), and *The Nether World* (1889) as well as the spreading suburbs in *The Paying Guest* (1896). Wilkie Collins in *Basil* (1852, 1862) prefigures Gissing's use of the suburbs. The protagonist follows two women whom he sees on an omnibus. The beauty of the younger one strikes him: "They went on, until we reached a suburb of new houses, intermingled with wretched patches of wasteland, half built over. Unfinished streets, unfinished crescents, unfinished squares, unfinished shops, unfinished gardens, surrounded us" (31–32).

In his Sherlock Holmes stories, Conan Doyle's London, in particular, mixes his portraits of buildings and their interiors with that of the streets to create a sharp sense of the city and its life, an evocation later caught by the many films based on the fiction. Writing about the contemporary world, Conan Doyle portrays what is ineluctably of his time. He writes, to modern readers, historical novels.

But streets and houses are just some of what one recovers from the novels-turned-history of nineteenth-century writers. One also gets portraits of intellectual and emotional aspects of that time. Mrs. Humphry Ward's *Robert Elsmere* (1888) details the struggle of loss of faith and what replaces it. Margaret Oliphant's *Hester* (1883) presents the image of a strong woman triumphing through necessity in the man's world of provincial banking. Thomas Hardy's *Tess of the d'Urbervilles* (1891) narrates the story of a woman of deep feeling betrayed by herself and others set in Wessex in southern England. While the characters react to their natural surroundings, Hardy sensuously describes a now long-ago world but one still vividly present to him. His novels frequently are historical records of emotional responses to nature dramatized in their imaginative presentations. What one must realize is that imaginative works might in part transcend their times while still being of those times. Thus, Becky Sharp in Thackeray's *Vanity Fair* (1848) speaks to modern sensibilities regarding conflict and passion but remains in the mid-nineteenth century. This is not to diminish her character but remind one of the duality of fictional creations. Trollope's *Framley Parsonage* (1861) demonstrates the temptations that wealth and power present to a country vicar, a work especially relevant to early twenty-first century America but redolent of nineteenth-century English life. Social and political movements, moral struggles and evanescent moods of feeling live in works of fiction that reflect their present realities but have become, in part, historical records.

Love, passion, and desire, as ideas for historical research, reveal that while much changes much remains: human nature drives romantic and sexual experiences, lending a semblance of permanence to this most conflicted of human areas. That the expressions of these ideas from the 1920s to the 1950s will resemble earlier and later epochs is not an issue. What is important is to recover the varied rhythms the novelists create. Carroll John Daly's sentimentalism in the Race Williams' novels contrasts sharply with the Continental Op's blunt, business-like approach to the emotional life in Hammett's *Red Harvest* and Sam Spade's cynical hardness in *The Maltese Falcon*. In Daly's *The Snarl of the Beast*, Williams works to prevent Ralph Dezzeia's plot against Daniel Davidson. The waif-like Milly joins with Williams to help the sickly Davidson. Williams' complicated reaction to Milly is a compound of elevating her above the world's baseness, even though he recognizes her as "A girl of the night" (34), and a longing to merge in some way with her. The action-prone Williams cannot move beyond placing her on a pedestal though he implies that something more will happen. In their end results, Williams, except for his admiration of Florence Drummond, The Flame; the Continental Op; and Spade wind up without any long-standing romantic interests. This functions both as an element of the genre and a broader social attitude that strong men in dangerous professions have an inability to cross over to a more "normal" life where love and its fulfillment are possibilities. Cawelti notes, "The function of the woman in the hard-boiled formula then is not simply that of appropriate sexual consort to the dashing-hero; she also poses certain basic challenges to the detective's physical and psychological security" (154). Spade and his involvement with Brigid O'Shaughnessy support this latter interpretation. He is attracted to Brigid but tells her that he would never be able to trust her (*Maltese* 226–27). Given their work, none of the above detectives is likely to meet women who want a family and a home.

Chandler's Philip Marlowe and Mickey Spillane's Mike Hammer support this image. The Sternwood sisters that Marlowe encounters in *The Big Sleep* and Hammer's Charlotte Manning in *I, the Jury* are the reverse of any conventional idea of "normal" romantic and/or married life. Carmen kills Rusty Regan, her sister Vivian's husband, and Vivian tries to protect her. Through that act, Vivian unfortunately involves herself with Eddie Mars, the owner of a local nightclub, and Carmen throws herself at any man she sees, Marlowe included. This 1930s image of a corrupt Southern California upper class with only Gen. Sternwood showing any moral depth reflects Chandler's sense of a breakdown in the possibility of human intimacy. The unreachable Marlowe is not a model but rather the lack of any alternative. Without the chance to connect with someone, physically, emotionally, and intellectually, one may as well remain apart. Where Marlowe retreats, Mike Hammer cuts off the illusion of connectedness that the murderous Charlotte offers. He shoots her, reflecting Spillane's more direct way of dealing with insoluble problems. In *My Gun Is Quick* (1950), three women, two of them prostitutes, respond to Hammer, and in each case Spillane underscores the temporary nature of their connections to him. Nancy Sanford, one of the prostitutes, is killed shortly after meeting Hammer and so is Ann Minor, a nightclub hostess. Lola Bergan, the other prostitute, speaks passively of her tainted life. Hammer sleeps with her and receives her loving gratitude before someone kills her. Although at times Spillane describes more positive human emotions than Chandler, Hammer achieves no more stable relationships than does Marlowe. Only his secretary Velda, set aside in the early novels from his sensual life, remains.

Ross Macdonald's first two Lew Archer novels, *The Moving Target* (1949) and *The Drowning Pool* (1950), continue this sense of failure to achieve some permanence in emotional relationships. Elaine Sampson in the first novel claims that she is an invalid but in fact can walk. It is not so much that she wants to avoid her husband's sexual advances as a desire to separate herself from others for those things in her present context that please her, e.g., being waited on and being secure from any expectations that she can or should do anything more than simply be. Her husband follows his own desires that lead to an escape into some aspect of spiritualism and a denial of self. Miranda, his daughter and Elaine's stepdaughter, seems the only normal member of the family as she flirts with Alan Taggert, her father's pilot. Albert Graves, the family lawyer and an acquaintance of Lew Archer, arranges her father's abduction in order to manipulate her into marrying him. Archer, hired to find Sampson, cannot prevent Graves from murdering him. Archer responds physically to Miranda, but both back off from any involvement. Graves kills Taggert as well as the father, and Elaine and Miranda are left alone and incompatible. Miranda's youth is the only positive note. *The Drowning Pool* also uses different generations and the various conflicts that time exacerbates to emphasize the idea of damaged emotional relationships. In *Dreamers Who Live Their Dreams: The World of Ross Macdonald's Novels* (1976), Peter Wolfe writes of the importance of family in Macdonald: "Like the later novels, *Pool* shows family-centered, rather than professional, crime as Ross Macdonald's true subject. The family or the closed social circle is what Ross MacDonald knows best and writes about best" (117).

Olivia Slocum is the dominant female who controls the family finances. James Slocum, her son, is a homosexual and married Maude to deflect curiosity about his lifestyle. Cathy Slocum is not James's daughter but rather the daughter of Maude and Police Lt. Ralph Knudson. After Cathy kills her grandmother and Maude commits suicide, Cathy goes to Chicago with Knudson, leaving the "father" she loves and going away with someone she hardly knows. Macdonald rarely ever constructs a bleaker vision of damaged emotional lives and families. From Maude's and Knudson's frustrated desires to be together to James's need to keep his sexual nature secret from his mother to Cathy's ruined childhood and the burden of killing her grandmother to avenge her supposed father, Macdonald leaves nothing whole for anyone confidently to build on. Archer decides not to turn Cathy into the police and lets her go with Knudson. This, the action of an outsider, is the only positive move made to heal the family.

The early hard-boiled detective novel is a repository of largely unselfconscious attitudes toward gender. The women's movement in America traces its roots to the nineteenth century, but not until the 1970s is there a wide-ranging examination of gender relations that call into question most social patterns between male and female. In Daly's *The Snarl of the Beast* and *The Hidden Hand* (1928), women seldom do anything wrong unless they cannot avoid it. Both Milly (*Snarl*) and Tina (*Hidden*) work to protect or avenge others. Men, evil men, propel them into these actions. Men surround and engulf them, robbing them of a sense of independence in choosing their courses of actions. The male antagonists in each novel take away their choices by harming those near to them. At the moment of peril, they are diverted into protecting others, fleeing from danger, and living different lives than what they planned. In contrast, Daly presents men in a full range of human activity, from good to evil, from effectiveness to ineffectiveness. Though there is some complexity regarding individual motivations among the characters, men have a greater chance as a sex to act autonomously. Only other men or their own limitations can divert them from taking a particular action or thinking a particular way. Sexual desire can control them or affect their behavior, but among the early hard-boiled detectives, only a few like Sam Spade, Brett Halliday's Michael Shayne, and Mike Hammer seem vibrantly interested in sex. Daly's Race Williams falls back on sentimentality or the case at hand and expresses his separation from women through these distancing techniques. With no secretary to create an ongoing *de facto* relationship that suggests sexual and/or romantic overtones, Williams is free to go or stay. And, as the narrator, he sketches his imaginative world that by necessity reduces both men and women to occasional players in his central drama as a hard-boiled private detective. Daly, thus, marginalizes both other men and women but especially the latter. He does so without any counter-pressure from another viewpoint within the genre.

In any social continuum of gender roles, these four decades, of course, do not create the unequal power relationships between men and women. The hard-boiled detective genre, however, does accentuate what appears as a slowly growing expansion in what women can do, especially as villains. Raymond Chandler consistently portrays women as capable of any evil that men can imagine or perform. While not the most admirable of equalizations, Chandler's women murder and betray with tenacity. Hammett's Brigid O'Shaughnessy helps set the tone for the genre, but she kills primarily for gain. *The Big Sleep*'s Carmen Sternwood is twisted, free to do what she wants until Marlowe stops her. She is also, except for the element of mental illness, close to an uncaused evil. However, she represents a freedom of action, reprehensible though it may be. William Ruehlmann melodramatically states, "Nubile castle denizen Carmen Sternwood, initially a victim, turns out to resemble more dragon than damsel" (80). Velma in *Farewell, My Lovely* (1940) kills to maintain her position. Not so much a social position, it is more the space she inhabits; any move to invade or shake her hold on that space brings swift, merciless violence, culminating in her killing her former lover Moose Malloy and finally herself. Her actions are the very definition of self-referentiality. In *The High Window* (1942), Mrs. Elizabeth Bright Murdock has killed only one person by the end of the novel and that happened years before the action began, but she torments her rather unstable secretary Merle Davis by convincing her that she killed Horace Bright, Mrs. Murdock's first husband. She is a hard woman, but she controls her sphere of action including her son and exerts a sense of independence that asks nothing of anyone.

The language used by the early hard-boiled detective novelists reflects stylistic aspects of the period from the crude to the sophisticated. Howard Haycraft writes, "[...] Hammett's lean, dynamic, unsentimental narratives created a definitely *American style*, quite separate and distinct from the accepted English pattern" (*Murder* 169). Daly falls into the crude category, and his prose might be seen as a compendium of 1920s slang and cliches. His words and phrases, put into the mouths of Race Williams and others, reveal a violent vulgarian operating, roughly, on the side of the law with a contradictory attitude toward women both sentimental and harsh. Referring to his reputation for violence, Williams states, "I've killed in my time, and I daresay I'll kill again. There — let the critics of my methods paste that in their hats" (*Hidden* 2). Gregory Ford, "a well-known operator" (*Hidden* 2), says to Williams:

> "The feared name of McCleary is built on blood and murder — but mark my words: He'll turn out to be a pawn in the game. If we can make him holler, buy him, or knock a squeal out of him — we'll lay our hands on the biggest brain that ever backed a crime ring" [*Hidden* 2].

The melodramatic tone and use of slang continues throughout the book. Ford says, "'If we catch the big gun behind McCleary, I'll cut you in for ten per cent of the melon [...]'" (*Hidden* 2). Early hard-boiled writers often use a similar style that sets their works in time, but some manage to govern their quality of language while recognizably writing in the same literary genre. The first few pages of Hammett's *Red Harvest* demonstrate a writer in greater control of his language than Daly. After quoting from Hammett's "The Gatewood Caper," O'Brien states:

> What distinguishes it from the work of [his] predecessors is the lightness of the writing, the way he starts in midstream, the use of colloquial language as the fundamental idiom rather than as something added for "color" or humor. Above all, there is the command of syntax that enables him to hit the essential details without getting bogged down in the needless ones [65].

However, a few examples of painful metaphors and slang in *Red Harvest* connect his tone to Daly's. The Continental Op asks a man in a crowd near the police department about Donald Willsson's death. After a smart answer from the man, who turns out to be Bill Quint, a union leader, the Op replies, "'I'm a stranger in town. Hang the Punch and Judy on me. That's what strangers are for'" (7). The Op, as narrator, remarks about Quint, "As chief muckademuck of the I.W.W. in Personville, he considered it his duty to get the low-down on me [...]" (8). Quint, wearing "a red windsor tie that blossomed over his gray flannel shirt" (6), is a radical in the same ideological area as the Communist Party if not a member of it. The "Wobblies" represent a historic moment in the labor movement, and Hammett, sympathetic to the left-wing cause, works them realistically into the novel in the person of Quint and his activities in organizing and leading the local miners. Hammett, through the hired gunmen that Elihu Willsson brought in to destory the union, also incorporates organized crime. Quint says, "[...] old Elihu didn't know his Italian history. He won the strike, but he lost his hold on the city and the state" (9). Speaking of members of organized crime in Personville, Quint refers to Lew Yard who "'handles most of the burg's hot stuff'" (10). Quint says that Elihu Willsson would not "let anybody cop anything from him without hitting back. But he had to be cagey with these guys. He brought the boy and his French wife home from Paris and used him for his monkey — a damned nice fatherly trick" (10). Regardless of the serious historic references, slang is never far away in the hard-boiled detective genre and strongly appears in both Chandler and Spillane as well.

Raymond Chandler's use of language reflects the significance of the ideas of class, sexuality, and privacy. He achieves the dramatization of these and other themes with a controlled style. Philip Durham observes in *Down These Mean Streets a Man Must Go: Raymond Chandler's Knight* (1963): "How to use the American idiom to its fullest was constantly in Chandler's vision; to do but not overdo, to squeeze out all the good juice but not the pulp, to be realistic without sacrificing artistic prerogatives" (117).

In *The Big Sleep*, the Sternwoods represent a corrupt Southern California aristocracy. Philip Marlowe, a former investigator for the district attorney and now a Los Angeles private detective, meets General Sternwood on the same cultural level minus the money. Marlowe's education affects his view of the world and, along with his personality and profession, gives him a necessary status. Marlowe's observation of the knight in the stained glass window in the general's home is an instance of the mindset that produces his language. However, it is heavily ironic. The knight is part of the class that rules, that commands others. Marlowe wants no part of controlling others except as far as his profession requires. It may be going too far to say that he acts like a gentleman toward women, but he does have standards that he will not betray. After he takes Vivian away from Eddie Mars' casino and they stop and kiss, Marlowe says to her, "'[...] your father didn't hire me to sleep with you.'" Vivian responds, "'You son of a bitch'" (153). Marlowe's rejection of Vivian's favors is relatively gentle, but with better results than Rusty Regan's rejection of Carmen's; she shoots him and stuffs his body in an abandoned oil sump on their estate. Marlowe's choice in letting Vivian take care of Carmen at the end of the novel rather than turn her over to the police reflects an upper-class position, e.g., both he and

Vivian are capable of deciding what is best for society in the present circumstances and acting on the decision with no recourse to any outside confirmation of their rightness to do so. Marlowe says, "'You'll take her away,' I said. 'And do that awfully damn quickly'" (229). A few lines later, he says, "'Get her out of here and see that she's watched every minute. 'Promise?' 'I promise'" (230). Both Vivian and he do this for the sake of the General and that he not know that Carmen killed Rusty Regan (229–231). Marlowe's isolation from everyone involved is complete as he leaves the mansion:

> I went quickly away from her down the room and out and down the tiled staircase to the front hall. I didn't see anybody when I left. I found my hat alone this time. Outside the bright gardens had a haunted look, as though small wild eyes were watching me from behind the bushes, as though the sunshine itself had a mysterious something in its light. I got into my car and drove off down the hill [230].

From the perspective of the twenty-first century, the idea of the hero in the hard-boiled detective novel of the 1920s to the 1950s presents a note from the distant past. In the Transitional Period, John D. MacDonald's Travis McGee and Robert B. Parker's Spenser see themselves in heroic imagery but sometimes strike an anachronistic tone in the process. Earlier heroic figures in American fiction such as Leatherstocking and the Western gunfighter as savior of the isolated town often seem more certain in their roles. An important heroic ingredient is a clear sense of evil, the presence of which one has no difficulty in placing on the far side of any moral line that could be drawn. Thus, the strong contrast that the good gunfighter presents pulls the reader into his framework, his way of seeing the world. In *High Noon* (1952), Gary Cooper's portrayal of Sheriff Will Gentry leaves no doubt as to the good for which he fights. Similarly, Alan Ladd's eponymous character in *Shane* (1953) acts out of a certain moral rightness that the film does nothing to counter. Operating in the city, with its eerie sense of omnipresent darkness even when the sun is shining, the hard-boiled detectives, at times reminiscent of their progenitors, present a combination of good and evil. Grella writes:

> The hard-boiled detective novel thus employs a characteristically American hero and worldview, which it translates into the framework of a twentieth century mystery story. Its central problem is a version of the quest, both a search for truth and an attempt to eradicate evil ["Hard-Boiled Detective" 104].

David Geherin, writing of Carroll John Daly's Race Williams, states, "But despite all the talk about the financial angles of a case, it is the thrill of the hunt and the dangers of his profession that he finds equally rewarding" (*American Private Eye* 10–11).

By the 1920s, there is, of course, no more frontier for either the woodsman or the gunfighter to act out his role. The city represents an inversion of this American theme, and the city of darkness is both an echo of the dangerous forests into which Leatherstocking penetrates and fights his battles as friend and foe of Indians and a corruption of a world that has not yet turned completely in on itself. Daly's pursuit scene at the beginning of *The Snarl of the Beast*, reminiscent of Cooper's in *The Deerslayer* (1841) and *The Last of the Mohicans* (1826), is symptomatic of this dark danger and sense of evil that exists in the city, in this case New York, a city from which the idea of the frontier is necessarily viewed. Except for nineteenth century Boston and the surrounding New England towns, no place stands more for the East, a psychological and geographical starting point for cultural renewal, than New York. However, Daly's Ralph Dezzeia, drawn in melodramatic extreme, represents evil personified both internally and externally. Physically repulsive and of superhuman strength, he also lives by desires far removed from most other human beings. Five of the nine hard-boiled detective writers in the Early Period set their stories in California, four of these in Southern California. Brett Halliday's Michael Shayne operates in Miami, a southern frontier. These geographical end points do not bring cultural renewal but rather offer new city venues that echo New York both in Daly and Spillane and Chicago in Dewey in the degree of venality, violence, and corruption.

Metaphorically rebounding from California, the end of the dream of the West, Hammett's Personville in *Red Harvest* still has all the qualities of the frontier boomtown. Whatever law is present serves only to underscore its corruption. Decent citizens are left unprotected both from police and criminal. The Continental Op comes to Personville almost as an anti-hero in his appearance and manner. The Op produces no romantic overtones and, except for his sense of solidity in terms of personality and physique, is monochromatic. He wears plain brown suits and coats and depends on no grand gestures. However, he is the hero personified. The Op does not deviate from his goal other than to do more than he should in combating evil, but one notes both the taint that evil spreads and the relentlessness of his character. Echoes of Homer's Achilles, Hector, and Odysseus, Virgil's Aeneas, the Arthurian knights, and on to Natty Bumppo and the Virginian in Owen Wister's novel of that name (1902) sound strongly in this work. Like Sam Spade in *The Maltese Falcon*, who presents a more sinister figure that recalls Milton's Satan in *Paradise Lost* in the description of Spade as "a blond Satan" (3), the Op endures punishment and continues. What these heroes from Homer to Hammett have in common is a sense of duty and the destiny to fulfill it. For Achilles and Hector, it is their mutual deaths; for Odysseus, it is to wander for ten years only to kill many of his people on his return to Ithaca in order to recover his throne. Aeneas's duty is to start a process whereby Rome would come into being. King Arthur's knights hope to find the Holy Grail but know that if they believe they are worthy they will not. Bumppo feels compelled to disappear into the wilderness to escape from civilization. The Virginian, whose destiny appears the most conventional and one that he in reality achieves, has another hidden desire, and that is to remain whole and untouched. For each of these heroes, destiny is more abstract than concrete. This ironic quality appears time and again in the hard-boiled detective novel. Even Spillane's Mike Hammer, who produces violent results, demonstrates a duty not just to eradicate evil but also to protect the innocent, often but not always women, and to restore social order by killing the killers. It is possibly the ultimate irony to say it is all in his mind, but that nonetheless is often the case.

Both Chandler's Marlowe and Spillane's Hammer share this heroic trait along with the ability to punish and/or kill others. Both men might also be seen as a beginning fragmentation of the heroic image in the hard-boiled detective novel. Their villains are, with the possible exceptions of Spillane's, no more reprehensible than those of the two earlier writers. Marlowe's recognition of the knight motif at the beginning of The Big Sleep is a self-conscious gesture that indicates some awkwardness about heroes in sunny California. Chandler's use of homosexuality as a moral perversity and the twisted sexual actions of Carmen Sternwood—childish and deadly— do not give Marlowe a heroic purchase in the novel. Who is to be rescued? Who is the moral innocent that deserves his succor? The dead Rusty Regan and the aged Gen. Sternwood are the only candidates for these positions. Marlowe turns in on himself as a result, a far cry from the sense of mission and purpose that heroes traditionally have had even if they are going out alone as Bumppo does in Cooper's The Prairie (1827), chronologically the last novel of the series. Leslie A. Fiedler in Love and Death in the American Novel (1960, 1966) has described him as "a magnificent old patriarch who has come to die in ultimate loneliness in the ultimate West" (183). Similarly, Mike Hammer continues this inversion, reducing any possible image of public vengeance or retribution to a private one when in I, the Jury, Hammer swears to avenge his friend Jack Williams' murder. The very extremes of his anger and violence deduct from the image of a hero who puts his own goals aside for the good of some community. A veteran of World War II, as MacDonald's McGee is of the Korean War and as Robert Crais's Elvis Cole and Joe Pike in the Modern Period are of the Vietnam War, Hammer conveys the atmosphere of the battlefield in some of his killing rages, as in One Lonely Night. Achilles is the archetypal figure of the privatization of vengeance as he sits out most of the Trojan War while his comrades die but then confronts and kills Hector in their epic battle before the walls of Troy yet only after Hector kills his friend Patroclus. For the most part, not until the Transitional and Modern Periods does the hard-boiled detective recover some sense of his/her private action for public good.

History as an idea functions as a dynamic process in the early hard-boiled detective novel. Not only placed in a complex historical period, the novels call forth their own sense of the past through allusions to specific events and ideas as well as to literary, political, religious, and scientific works. Memory also brings to bear the personal lives of characters. Mrs. Bright Murdock's very suppression of memory, willfully controlled in *The High Window*, demonstrates the suggestive power of the many pasts swirling around the characters' present lives and awakening them to danger. The ability to recapture the immediacy of the past reveals its power in the fiction and contributes to one's ability to see some glimpse of its wholeness.

3

The Creation of Character

Raymond Chandler's statement in "The Simple Art of Murder" that "[...] down these mean streets a man must go who is not himself mean, who is neither tarnished nor afraid. The detective in this kind of story must be such a man. He is the hero; he is everything" (18) is a profound insight into the then-developing hard-boiled detective novel. In the twenty-first century, with the many changes in the genre, this observation remains remarkably accurate. Female, minority, and gay and lesbian hard-boiled detectives have appeared; family, love, and friendship are now central themes in the novels; and nearly every region in America and many in Britain serve as loci for the stories. Resisting the destructive post-modernist attacks on character and narrative and the attempts to de-center individual consciousness, the hard-boiled detective novel continually reinvents and rediscovers itself in the individual acting in the world. As discussed in Chapter 2, speculation about the origins of the hard-boiled detective type involves aspects from many centuries, e.g., medieval knighthood, the American frontiersman, the Western gunfighter, and more immediately fictional detectives such as Dupin and Holmes. As another influence, predating all of the above and disregarding the role of the gods and goddesses in their lives, the Greek and Roman epic heroes from Homer's Achilles and Odysseus to Virgil's Aeneas establish an image of the human will imposing itself on its environment. Both historical and thematic, the impact of these origins has influenced the general direction of the development of the detective. In addition to the character's origins, the many types of hard-boiled detectives in the Early Period reveal the wide possibilities in the genre and suggest the variety and narrative power contained in the form. Finally, with the aid of hindsight, one can see what patterns of development the origins and first-generation character types initiate and what areas of development they have left open and unexplored. The figure of the hard-boiled detective strongly coalesces in the initial stage of the genre's formation, paradoxically dominating future images of the type and leaving space for growth and development.

Critics seem generally agreed on the hard-boiled detective's avatars. Some associations are overt, such as Philip Marlowe's observation of the knight in the stained-glass window at the Sternwood mansion in Raymond Chandler's *The Big Sleep*, the Continental Op's imitation of a western gunfighter when he agrees to clean up Personville in Dashiell Hammett's *Red Harvest*, Race Williams' chivalric relationship to women in Carroll John Daly's *The Snarl of the Beast* and *The Hidden Hand*, and the general independent, fearless action of most of the early hard-boiled detectives resembling Cooper's Natty Bumppo. It is not that the authors copy these traits but rather that the above characteristics function as archetypes that permeate the genre. In addition, the ratiocinative practices of Edgar Allan Poe's Dupin and Arthur Conan Doyle's Sherlock Holmes also provide inspiration for the early hard-boiled detective novelists. The amalgamation of qualities in various combinations and emphases give the genre its distinctive flavor against, and influenced by, the specific historical background of the 1920s, 1930s, 1940s, and 1950s. George Grella notes:

> Postwar America provided the hard-boiled school with an abundance of subjects. Undergoing the disorder that accompanies explosive social change, the nation coped unsuccessfully with a variety of problems—the Boom of the twenties, Prohibition, the national spiritual hangover of the Depression, and gangsterism on a spectacular scale ["Hard-Boiled Detective" 105].

The remarkable sameness in diversity appears across the range of characters over time. For some such as Marlowe, an intensification of certain behavioral traits manifests itself. It would be difficult to claim any growth on the part of such detectives as Mickey Spillane's Mike Hammer or Ross Macdonald's Lew Archer. Rather one observes the waxing and waning of certain aspects of their characters. The literary and cultural archetypes together with the historical conditions produce this character type, not only not seen before in literature in this particular combination of qualities but impossible to be seen.

Among those writing about the origins of the hard-boiled detective novel, few focus on the classical Greek and Roman heroes. Given the gap in time and the varied cultural and literary movements in the West since those earlier centuries, it seems that attempting to connect Homer and Virgil to the post-Renaissance, post-industrial world of the present would be impossible. Yet, there are several promising similarities that give depth to the hard-boiled detective. First, the idea of will, mentioned above, connects appropriately to the modern hero. For instance, the Continental Op forces the direction of the plots. His will to uncover the truth or rectify situations unrelentingly acts until he achieves a satisfactory resolution. Hammett's description of him, while not an Achilles- or Hector-like model, does signify that nothing deters him. Achilles' declining to fight for the Greeks regardless of Hector's victories over them while he languishes in his tent indicates that personal will counts more for him than communal understanding and support. Odysseus's cunning shows in Sam Spade's actions, that and his ability to weave tales that even the experienced Gutman and the wily Cairo in *The Maltese Falcon* would at least act on if not believe. Aeneas projects an image of someone who steadfastly pursues an end forced on him by circumstances. It is not that he lacks heroic qualities but that he lacks an eagerness to strive eternally for some far off goal. Philip Marlowe best matches Aeneas's qualities of reluctance matched with readiness. Peter Wolfe in his analysis of *The Big Sleep* writes of Marlowe, "[...] he overcomes great odds to solve problems and to quiet suffering. Yet because he can't commit his heart to another, he finds life a burden rather than a privilege; his days are an ordeal to fight through" (*Something* 121). The violence that all the classical heroes display coupled with their abilities to get out of trouble functions across the hard-boiled detective novel. Race Williams and Mike Hammer probably answer best this comparison in the early period. Ajax, Pyrhhus, and Turnus, the latter two described most vividly in *The Aeneid*, also find their violent, willful counterparts in the hard-boiled detective.

The disparate origins of the hard-boiled detective character coalesce to form a code. The code finds its best expression in Chandler's "The Simple Art of Murder." Not the first instance of it, Chandler's is the most memorable. Of course, Daly, Hammett, and Spillane contribute in ways that sometimes conflict with Chandler's and with one another. John D. MacDonald and Robert B. Parker add elements in the Transitional Period, and in the Modern Period Sara Paretsky, Loren D. Estleman, Liza Cody, and John Baker both emphasize earlier versions or parts of versions and furnish new ideas. Thus, some account of the code is necessary to each hard-boiled detective. Being the first hard-boiled detective writer, both in short stories and novels, Carroll John Daly set the boundaries for the code either to be observed or transgressed. In *The Snarl of the Beast*, Daly lays out some of the ideas for the detective: Don't back down, confront anyone if necessary, be willing to die for your position, don't expect much of a future, stand alone if possible, don't let the police manipulate you, look out for yourself first, expect treachery. Hammett adds new points and confirms earlier ones. In *The Maltese Falcon*, Spade affirms the necessity of avenging one's partner's death. Also, he suggests some confrontation of the police in order to control a situation as much as possible. In addition, he advises one to keep one's counsel and reveal to the police only what is necessary. Like Williams, the detective must expect treachery. While ambivalent about how to handle women in a case, one must suspect them and deal with them as one would deal with a man. Finally, and Williams occasionally supports this, a detective thinks and then acts. The Continental Op in *Red Harvest* and *The Dain Curse* (1929) reflects many of these same points. All three detectives have a complex approach to the police, e.g., work with them if possible although some may be corrupt but respect the honest ones for the difficult job they perform.

Spillane's Mike Hammer resembles Daly's Williams more than he does Hammett's Continental Op or Sam Spade. He differs in the extent of his use of violence as a method of vengeance and in glorying in the violence. While Williams will shoot someone if he has to, he prefers working with the police. Spade turns Brigid O'Shaughnessy over to the police for the murder of Miles Archer; he does not shoot her as Hammer does Charlotte Manning. What does Chandler contribute to the code? First, he writes an essay about it. Philip Marlowe is the most prominent detective in the Early Period with intellectual leanings. Chandler's education at Dulwich College in south London, his extensive reading, and his wide experience in business and writing give him a cultural depth that he transfers effectively to Marlowe's character. Towards the end of his essay, Chandler says that the detective must be the best man in his world, a hero. This connects directly to the knight in the stained glass window in the entrance to the Sternwood mansion. His name echoes that of Sir Thomas Mallory, author of *Le Morte d'Arthur* (1485). Chandler does not extend his allusions to the classic epic hero, but his works reflect some of the traits of that archetypal figure. The most striking one is that the detective never allows someone to threaten or attack him without a commensurate response, a trait that Daly and Hammett also insist on for their heroes. Throughout his essay, Chandler shows his admiration for Hammett as a writer. Thus, as an example of the code, Hammett's work demonstrates how it all holds together in a world that pulls against a good man, a hero.

Once begun, the genre develops several character types that appear and reappear to the present. This reappearance of character types contributes to the genre's stability. Some of the types are seen in binary opposition — for example, the boastful versus the laconic or stoical private investigator. Race Williams and Mike Hammer are examples of the first half of this opposition and the Continental Op, Sam Spade, Philip Marlowe, and Lew Archer the second. The violent/emotional approach versus the professional/rational one is another opposition. Instances of the first pole of this second opposition are Race Williams, Mike Hammer, and, to a lesser extent, Brett Halliday's Michael Shayne. For the second pole, the Continental Op, Sam Spade, Philip Marlowe, Thomas B. Dewey's Mac, and Lew Archer generally act professionally, and for the most part, they also think through their cases in systematic fashion. An occasional if surprising addition to the group that employs reason is Mike Hammer. For all his violent feelings and behavior, Hammer constantly sifts through the available clues, interviews witnesses and suspects, and analyzes the available information. However, Hammer uses so much verbal and physical violence that one tends to overlook the rational aspect of his detective work. Richard S. Prather's Shell Scott is a rare instance of the comic type in the Early Period. While Prather's detective initiates a certain amount of violence, *de riguer* for the genre, he seems at times almost light-hearted. Most of these detectives have aspects of each type to a greater or lesser extent, but what they all seem to have in common in the Early Period is a singleness of purpose. A trait that will last to the present, each detective, after any temporary deviance, comes back to what his original purpose was and focuses all of his energies on completing the task. Even when the genre expands to include many new lifestyles and locales, this characteristic remains. A stubborn resistance to being pushed off, either with threats or violence, from their chosen investigative path marks the genre's protagonists from the beginning to the present decade.

Analysis of one aspect of the first oppositional pair shows the different ways that writers dramatize what might seem very similar manifestations of the same trait. For example, both Race Williams and Mike Hammer boast about their intended actions, what they will do to someone for their criminal or moral transgressions. One difference between them is that Race Williams uses boasting as a rhetorical device that, through repetition, contains more words than deeds. Mike Hammer, however, suits words to deeds and what he boasts about will most likely occur without the need for repetition. Both men are serious regarding what they will do, but Hammer's threats are more ominous by their very lack of repetition. In addition, Williams speaks of his past actions in order to buttress his present statements while Hammer says little concerning what he has done, occasionally stating that the criminals have little doubt that he will act. David Geherin observes that the creation of the private eye

> produced, among other things, a radically new kind of hero, one far better equipped than the brilliant logician to cope with violence and disorder. Even though he was often unable to deduce solutions from bits of evidence or rid the world of evil at the end of the story, he did his best to combat it wherever he could by relying on his fists rather than his wits, his brawn instead of only his brains [*American Private Eye* 5–6].

Williams' rhetorical device of referring to himself in the third person emphasizes this difference, mythologizing his image in order to convince his reader before the commission of an act. In *My Gun Is Quick*, echoing his statement in *I, the Jury* with regard to Jack Williams' killer, Hammer says that Red's killer will pay and pay hard. His reputation precedes him, as it were, for both reader and character.

Another oppositional pair that emerges from a close examination of the early detectives is the cheerful or upbeat personality versus the business-like type with, in some cases, an air of despondency or even alienation. Race Williams, Sam Spade, Michael Shayne, Shell Scott, and William Campbell Gault's Brock Callahan occupy the first pole of this opposition. Spade's manner reflects an ironic and satirical outlook steeped in his experience of criminal and even official duplicity. His taunting of Gutman and Cairo, his mocking of young Wilmer, and his brash effrontery toward the police show Spade in his most ebullient state of mind. Like Spade, Shayne delights in enraging the police, especially Chief of Miami Beach Detectives Peter Painter, pushing him to act in ways that reveal a frustrated inability to deal with Shayne. Shell Scott acts as a comic sensualist. With his over six-foot frame, his muscled body, and white blond hair complemented by a smile for most occasions, Scott focuses on the moment in a paradoxically fatalistic manner. The detectives who represent the other side of this opposition, e.g., Continental Op, Philip Marlowe, Mike Hammer, and Lew Archer, demonstrate the complex possibilities in the genre. The Continental Op is the business-like character *par excellence*. He is so business-like that his name is his job description. Just the suggestion of a private life or romantic feelings, as in his brief experience with Dinah Brand in *Red Harvest*, stands out strongly from his normal behavior. Marlowe exemplifies the alienated detective. And for him too, business largely becomes his life. Mike Hammer's dark personality sometimes overshadows his attentions to work but not for long. Work and all that it entails define him. Lew Archer, concentrating his life on work, not only resembles the Continental Op but also Philip Marlowe, whom he imitates in his despondent and alienated character. As will be seen, later detectives will duplicate these character types, creatively employing the suggestive ideas and enriching the genre.

Several other types occur in the Early Period and reappear later, sometimes with modifications to the originals. The brooding, self-reflective, self-focused character, reminiscent of Sherlock Holmes, appears fully formed in the person of Philip Marlowe. Possibly, only Macdonald's Archer comes close to portraying a detective with these traits. When added to descriptions of him from the other types noted above, Marlowe is a clear predecessor of MacDonald's Travis McGee, the first detective in the Transitional Period. Holmes, Marlowe, and Archer form McGee's lineage, especially

Marlowe. The many references to knights and knight-errantry and the scenes of alienated brooding that overcome McGee tie him into the early tradition and reveal a stable element in the genre. Finally, and most widely represented, is the active type. This type occurs in two forms. This may seem a redundant category, but the different manner in which the detectives act calls for an explanation. First, the overtly active detective overwhelms one with his moving, seemingly without pause, from one situation to another. He chases someone, he fights with another, he interrogates a third, sometimes with and sometimes without the police, and he never seems to relax; even his thinking is on the run. If he has an office, it is either little used or the scene of action when occupied. The nonstop pace is part of the *Black Mask* legacy and stays a constant in the legacy through the examples of Race Williams, the Continental Op and, to a lesser extent, Sam Spade, Shell Scott, Michael Shayne, and Mike Hammer. Daly's influence on Spillane especially occurs in the amount of activity that happens in a Mike Hammer novel. In contrast, Philip Marlowe, Lew Archer, and Thomas Dewey's Mac appear less active. These detectives are sometimes alone, in their home or offices, and these periods naturally interrupt the activity even though the detectives still ponder their cases. They drive to different locations and resist the urge to act. Even Sam Spade has moments that break the action but not many. Events overtake him and force him to act, especially in solving his partner's murder and preventing the police from making a case against him. When McGee appears in MacDonald's *The Deep Blue Good-by* in 1964, one especially finds the influence of Marlowe, Archer, and Spade in this area. The *Busted Flush*, his houseboat, is a haven from the world and an over-active life, one in which he has decided to take his retirement in segments while still young enough to enjoy it. The break-neck pace of Daly's Williams quickly wanes though there are spurts of activity by later detectives in the Early Period and examples of this in the Transitional and Modern Periods.

From the perspective of the first decade of the twenty-first century, the patterns of development, explored or unexplored, that one observes in the Early Period appear with varying degrees of clarity from one writer to another. For instance, Spillane's Mike Hammer begins several strands that significantly expand in the modern era. However, for various reasons, some of them quite sound, Hammer's violent actions make it difficult to see the direction of his contributions in the glare of his egregious beatings, shootings, etc., and his accompanying gloating that those who deserve to suffer have indeed done so. The violent-emotional type discussed above develops the possibility of feeling, of responding emotionally to life's conflicts without professional control concealing and limiting them. In short, Hammer cares and cares passionately. He can be as hard and cynical as Spade and

Marlowe, but he does not live there nor is he as self-concerned as Race Williams, who, however, does evince some of Hammer's qualities of feeling and passionate response. The difference lies in the rhetorical burden of Williams' statements compared with the belief one frequently has that what Hammer will do to someone who has harmed someone he cares for is prophetically stated: it is a personal condemnation and vow of vengeance that will be carried out. Detectives in the Transitional Period, and MacDonald's Travis McGee comes strongly to mind, project this almost biblical sense of doom facing their foes. MacDonald accomplishes this by having other characters describe McGee's look when he speaks of those whom he will make suffer for their sins. Parker's Spenser, as the series progresses through the first several novels, conveys this same feeling of absolute belief that wrongs should be punished and that he will unerringly perform the task. Modern detectives such as Les Roberts' Milan Jacovich exude this sense of passionate involvement, especially when someone like Victor Gaimari, the Cleveland mob boss heir apparent, threatens his family. Karen Kijewski's Kat Colorado responds emotionally to the injustices her clients suffer. But, like Sue Grafton's Kinsey Millhone or Jeremiah Healy's John Francis Cuddy, Colorado does not have Hammer's almost insane love of violence as the answer to those who harm others. Critics such as Cawelti and Grella correctly note the tendency to violence in Hammer's personality while ignoring the feeling component which, if not always absent in the Early Period, is at least rare.

After Race Williams, Sam Spade, and Philip Marlowe, the only direction in the idea of the detective's sexual involvement is toward a real-life portrayal. Discussing Race Williams in *The Snarl of the Beast*, Allen B. Crider refers to the "sexual isolation of the detective" (112). The Aristotelian concept of imitation, understood in this case as a sexual engagement in the world rather than a mere copying of sexual practices, best expresses the work of newer writers in this area. Even in the Early Period, with detectives such as Halliday's Michael Shayne, Prather's Shell Scott, and Hammer, sexual relations are not unknown. However, it is worth observing that Ross Macdonald's Lew Archer, introduced late in the Early Period in *The Moving Target*, is one of the most impressive additions to the genre, but he is, if not asexual, so focused on the conflicted lives of his clients that he finds little time to pursue his own desires. One probably should accept that if a theme remains unexplored by the most important writers of a period that it, at least, is unimportant to their conceptions of the hard-boiled detective. MacDonald's McGee, Parker's Spenser, Bill Pronzini's Nameless, and Stephen Dobyns' Charlie Bradshaw change this. From the Transitional Period forward, sexuality as a major theme features in the works of most hard-boiled detective novelists, American and British. The latter do not appear until the Modern Period with Liza Cody's Anna Lee, Sarah Dunant's Hannah Wolfe, Val McDermid's Kate Brannigan, Gillian Slovo's Kate Baeier, Mark Timlin's Nick Sharman, Reginald Hill's Joe Sixsmith, Michelle Spring's Laura Principal, and John Baker's Sam Turner. Stated or implied, sexuality is part of their lives, coupled with love in some cases, often lust in Sharman's, and steady relationships. Like their modern American counterparts, sexual relationships are ineluctably mixed with their cases and add to the complexity of their lives.

For many of the modern detectives, the desire for independence is almost a stronger motivation than sex, and so Sara Paretsky's V.I. Warshawski, Janet Dawson's Jeri Howard, and Loren D. Estleman's Amos Walker frequently go home alone or remain there in that state. Yet, they, for the most part, live in a web of personal relationships quite different than is the case with the detectives in the Early Period. How does this condition grow from such a different beginning? It is true that Jonathan Valin's Harry Stoner and Estleman's Walker live separately and, for the most part, alone, but Walker, especially, has past associations that reverberate through his series. Most detectives have a police opponent with whom they duel from case to case. However, Walker's police contact is an old acquaintance. They knew one another when young since their father's were in business together. Estleman provides the expected tension between public and private detective, but Walker and Lt. John Alderdyce's shared past intrudes into the present, influencing their responses. Aside from Stoner, Walker, and a few other transitional and modern detectives, the source for a web of relationships qualifying the independent image of the hard-boiled private detective derives from Marlowe and Hammer. Even Halliday's Michael Shayne, who marries Phyllis Brighton in *The Uncomplaining Corpses* (1940), the third novel of the series, does not for long change the way he lives. Wondering about his fidelity before she marries him, Phyllis afterwards helps him settle down prior to her death. Later, Shayne engages in different romantic relationships, but they often fail to make a significant difference to his life. Geherin states, "[...] he remains, if not celibate, at least measured in his relationships with women" (*American Private Eye* 85–86).

Chandler's Marlowe exudes a lonely independence, but it is the loneliness and isolation in his life that seem to mark him for change, either for good or ill. When Marlowe disentangles himself in *The Big Sleep* from the Sternwoods, and especially from Carmen and Vivian, and realizes that Mona Mars loves someone else, he seems to have swung free from the messy emotional lives of others. Even Moose Malloy in *Farewell, My Lovely* can be seen as an emblematic figure for what happens if one loves too much. Malloy's death at the hands of Velma, the woman he loves, and her subsequent suicide, all effectively outside his control, underscore the need for some degree of separateness. But Chandler, as John D. MacDonald later does with Travis McGee, gives Marlowe a life in time in which one lives from year to year, experiences new people and situations, and has a past against which to measure them. By *The Long Goodbye* (1953), Marlowe becomes emotionally involved with others, e.g., Terry Lennox who betrays him as a friend and reveals Marlowe's emotional vulnerability and Linda Loring whom he apparently loves but who leaves him only to return in *Playback* (1958) and ask him to marry her. With these changes, Marlowe's independence moves from one of isolation and alienation to one in which he can belong and maybe achieve happiness. Marlowe has not so much lost his independence as filled another need that must coexist with it.

Spillane's Hammer clearly foreshadows the direction in which the idea of independence will develop more than does Marlowe. Marlowe finds a single focus for his emotional needs while Hammer is eternally and passionately involved whether in a relationship that will lead, he hopes, to marriage in *I, the Jury* or brief sexual involvement with the twins in the same novel or friendship with Red in *My Gun Is Quick*, whom he does not really know but who becomes part of his emotional life through his determination to avenge her death, or the girl on the bridge in *One Lonely Night* whom he avenges more quickly than any other woman or Velda, his secretary, whom he rescues in the same novel, as she hangs naked from ropes in an abandoned warehouse, by shooting all her tormentors. Rather than finally merge his independent but alienated self with another as Marlowe does, Hammer's independence and passion are parallel and overlapping currents that aid and clash with one another. What remains after the furious battles, as it were, points the genre in the new direction that independence takes. For Hammer, independence not so much surrenders to the imperatives of a romantic relationship but rather fuses with it. In *The Snake* (1964), Hammer and Velda, also his fellow P.I., make love. It is only in the Modern Period with A.E. Maxwell's Fiddler and Fiora and Dennis Lehane's Patrick Kenzie and Angela Gennaro that one sees the mixing begin to work, but it does have staying power. Other instances, not involving professional partnerships, demonstrate that independence and romance can combine. If not blinded by his violent excesses, one can detect Spillane's influence in this area. Although Mark Timlin's Nick Sharman follows Hammer a little too closely, especially in his over-reliance on violence, one can see Sharman's independence and romantic and family relationships, if the latter only with his daughter, playing significant roles in his life. It might not be too much to argue that the turn to the emotional life rescues the idea of independence for the hard-boiled detective and prevents it from becoming a sterile concept. MacDonald's twenty-one Travis McGee novels vividly make this argument by showing the independent McGee going through the whole gamut of romantic relationships and finally discovering a daughter whom he plans to aid financially and support emotionally.

As with many first novels and their writers, the early hard-boiled detectives set the stage and standards for later characters. Spade, Marlowe, Hammer, and Archer will likely hover in the back of any writer who works in this genre. The many allusions to the Early Period both in the Transitional and Modern Periods testify to the influence of the first private eyes. If not exactly reflecting Harold Bloom's eponymous "anxiety of influence," certainly a recognition of the basic outlines of the hard-boiled detective exists for subsequent authors as model to imitate or change.

4

Violence:
Direction and Control

For the early hard-boiled detective novel, violence functions almost as a defining term. Examples of violence especially inundate the reader in the twenty-year span from Daly's *The Snarl of the Beast* to Spillane's *I, the Jury*. Daly's 1923 short story "Three Gun Terry," with Terry Mack as a prototype for Williams, uses the title as a literal description of his weaponry, three guns and all effectively and necessarily employed. Early critics on the genre attempt to put the genre in a historical context and thus explain the evolution of the quality and degree of violence it contains. William Ruehlmann states "The fact is that private eye novels are vigilante literature, and their peculiar appeal lies in reader identification with a hero whose brutality avenges not only fictional transgression but American urban frustration as well" (9). Certainly, murder and other forms of mayhem are not unknown in the detective story from Poe until the advent of the hard-boiled detective novel. Even Golden Age novels contain their allotted share of murders, that particular social evil adding a tension that other crimes do not. However, while admitting a certain level of gratuitous violence in hard-boiled detective novels, emphasized especially by the boasting of a Race Williams or Mike Hammer, the authors continue, surprisingly, the ratiocinative pattern, merging it with the newer element and giving the genre a distinct flavor that sets it off from other detective fiction. Thus, the hard-boiled detective novel employs the violent to serve the rational, the former directed and controlled by the latter while focusing and framing the more traditional narrative device.

Ross Macdonald's Lew Archer is one of the last hard-boiled detective novelists in the genre's early period. Macdonald published *The Moving Target* in 1949, two years after Mickey Spillane's *I, the Jury* began the Mike Hammer series. If nothing else, Archer, like Hammett's Sam Spade and Chandler's Philip Marlowe, is in sharp contrast to Hammer's use of and pleasure in violence. Dennis Porter writes:

> The Private eye is always a law unto himself, but with Hammett and Chandler there is an at least implicit commitment to a higher law when an assault on a criminal is represented. Mickey Spillane's private eye, on the other hand, often operates as a lynching party of one [Porter 168].

In part a throwback to the twenties image of the hard-boiled detective, nonetheless Hammer's respect for investigation in *I, the Jury*, the gathering and analysis of information regarding his case, is clearly apparent. Archer resembles Hammer in his own focus on investigation and analysis and in the urban settings they share, Hammer New York and Archer Los Angeles. For all that Southern California remains as an almost primordial setting for hard-boiled detective novels, Raymond Chandler did not publish *The Big Sleep* until 1939, twelve years after John Carroll Daly's *The Snarl of the Beast* (New York) and ten years after Dashiell Hammett's *Red Harvest* (San Francisco and Montana). Yet, Marlowe's and Archer's Los Angeles seems a place of simpler corruption and evil contrasted to the Los Angeles of A.E. Maxwell's Fiddler, Robert Campbell's Whistler, or Robert Crais's Elvis Cole. While the New York of Andrew Vaachs' Burke might not closely resemble that of Spillane's Hammer, the latter's greater level of personal violence closes the affective gap. The systemic centrifugal forces, however, of modern New York darken the urban picture so that not even a Mike Hammer can compete. For Lew Archer, violence is dealt with, controlled, and traced to its source; he only uses force as a last resort.

The Moving Target is a classic example of this paradigm shift from the early violence but one soon to be reversed in the novels of John D. MacDonald's Travis McGee and Robert B. Parker's Spenser. One is tempted to see these reversals almost completely in their cultural contexts, with Ross Macdonald's Post–World War II work a possible revulsion against that conflict's slaughter, unlike Spillane's indulgence in violence, and John D. MacDonald's and Robert B. Parker's works as immersed in the 1960s social crises and their consequent loosening of cultural bonds. However important the social contexts, one should not lose sight of the thread of violence which the genre never relinquishes as a theme for the exploration of modern American culture. It is of course present in Ross Macdonald and links John D. MacDonald and Parker to the early hard-boiled detective novelists. Placing the origin of violence as a theme either inside the genre or outside it over-simplifies the problem. First, the hard-boiled detective novel, as Grella, Ruehlmann, John G. Cawelti, and David Geherin, among others, observe, has both literary and historical antecedents. Thus, the post-World War I big city corruption-and Prohibition-influenced era is not unimportant for the shift in American detective fiction to the hard-boiled form. And the profound resonance in Western literature of violence as a theme traces its origins to the Homeric epics and recurs most importantly in Cooper's Leatherstocking tales and in the Western. The above is not to imply that the thematic origin of violence balances between historical/ social influences and literary ones. For the critic, the literary usually takes precedence.

Another way that violence acts as a defining characteristic of the hard-boiled detective novel lies in its ability to shape the direction and form of the genre. LeRoy Lad Panek states, "[...] portraying toughness on several levels became one of the aims of the hard-boiled writer" (*Introduction* 152). Violence deals with basic needs and desires; it opens up the possibility of primitive motivators. Although the latter are still undeniably human, when violence occurs, subtleties are often removed. Complex processes may have led up to the moment of brutal resolution, and the better artist brings this out, but the actual destructive release creates a quandary for the novelist if it occurs too often. A consistent criticism of the early hard-boiled detective novels is an over-reliance on violence as a solution to plot difficulties. The famous statement by Chandler, "'When in doubt, have a man come through a door with a gun in his hand'" (qtd. in Lehman 146), is a recognition of the simplifying role of physical confrontation. Of course, violence can effectively redirect the story or resolve a scene or group of scenes. This redirection or resolution can also be an inherent part of the story that fits in terms of theme and plot. Shakespeare's *Hamlet* suggests a relative balance between violence and other plot elements when he allows only a very brief time for the sword fight at the end of the play, the principal remaining figures dying almost simultaneously.

It is in the types of characters that violence plays its most complex role. Race Williams and Mike Hammer, paralleled above, so integrate violence into their world views that it functions not as an occasional response to threats but rather as an essential component to what is necessary for survival. As Geherin states, Daly's Race Williams pulls strongly against the ratiocinative pattern: "Williams' methods are also radically different from those of the intellectual sleuths. He is a man of action, not thought, a man schooled in the laws of survival rather than the laws of logic" (*American Private Eye* 11).

This extreme condition, pushing violent acts to the fore and describing them as part of the characters' personalities, does not dominate hard-boiled detective fiction so much as it gives it a distinctive signature. Thus, Lew Archer, at the other end of the spectrum in the early hard-boiled detective novel, connects with Williams and Hammer through the violence he investigates and the kind of world suggested by that violence. In contrast, murder is more individual and idiosyncratic in the Golden Age mystery novels rather than systemic and inevitable in the chronologically overlapping hard-boiled fiction.

Who gains? This is surely one of the main questions asked by detectives in fiction as in life. The hard-boiled detective, faced with a brutal murder, is helped by a cynicism that suspects nearly everyone. Regardless of appearances, witness the ethereal Eileen Wade in Chandler's *The Long Goodbye*, everyone is capable of violence. Two ideas are important in this context. One is the contrast between the violent act and the appearance of innocence or purity. The other is the toll on the detective because of his suspicions, e.g., his sense of alienation, and a weight of experience leading to the certainty of the often unthinkable. Linda Loring comments to Marlowe in the above novel about the false impression that Eileen gives as to her true nature. She calls her "'That anemic blond show piece'" (224) and "'that golden icicle'" (363). Possibly it takes a woman to know another woman, but for all that Eileen's looks affect Marlowe, he still distrusts her at the first wrong note. In *The Maltese Falcon*, Hammett's Sam Spade sets the pattern of attraction and distrust that Marlowe later demonstrates. Spade compartmentalizes his sexual attraction to Brigid O'Shaughnessy and her possible role in the death of his partner Miles Archer and the theft of the statue. Brigid's innocence is initially less compelling to Spade than Eileen's is to Marlowe even though Marlowe seems more affected by and cynical toward the world and people with whom he deals. Marlowe possibly has a residue of hope, frequently disappointed, concerning human nature that Spade does not share. Of course, Marlowe is not naive when he confronts evil and can distinguish between the sick Carmen Sternwood and the relative health of her sister Vivian in *The Big Sleep*.

In Richard S. Prather's *Case of the Vanishing Beauty* (1950), Shell Scott remarks, "After so long a time you get a little sick of violence" (95). Up to this point, Georgia Martin, Scott's client, has been murdered, and he has killed Paul Seipel, one of the twins threatening him and Tracy Martin, Georgia's sister. Shortly afterward, he shoots and kills Peter Seipel, and Miguel Mercado sticks a knife through Scott's hand. However, regardless of the effects on particular detectives from their confrontation with evil and treachery, and in this regard Scott is no different than the rest, they continue to conduct investigations to find out who gains from any particular crime. On a more general level, this is a necessary social response, a rational answer to the threat of violence. Growing out of the feelings of cynicism and distrust, the image of the detective as redeemer, the cleanser of a corrupt society, frequently occurs. This seems an inevitable, if paradoxical, role for the detective. However, one might legitimately question how effective the detectives see themselves in this position. Daly's Williams and Spillane's Hammer speak of victory and triumph, but the continual need to redeem society undercuts this idea. Discussing Race Williams as a "'hard boiled' detective," Allen B. Crider says, "[...] 'hard boiled' means a mental toughness developed as a defense against the kind of world in which the detective exists. His toughness alone keeps him from being too deeply affected by what he sees and experiences" (112). Although the Continental Op in *Red Harvest* is almost a reverse image in this regard, his methodical approach to the violence in Personville demonstrates its lure, and he tells Dinah Brand, "'This damned burg's getting me. If I don't get away soon I'll be going blood-simple like the natives'" (154). Is Personville ("Poisonville") cleansed? Many corrupt and violent figures are dead, but the Op does not speak of victory, only survival. He gets out of town. Ruehlmann remarks, "It is Hammer's role to be a sort of democratic scourge, a cleanser of community sinks" (91). A few pages later, he writes, "Instead of purging evil, Archer ministers to the little value he finds in a confined urban world where even the able are missing persons" (105). It is possible to interpret Archer's actions as more effectively redeeming, rectifying, or cleansing a corrupt world than Williams,' the Continental Op's, or Hammer's. Almost minimalist in his social vision, Archer brings some sanity and "empathy" (Ruehlmann 105) to the situation in which he finds himself.

Powerful forces confront the detectives as they determine who benefits from the death and disruption encountered. Rather than material greed as the prime motivation to kill someone or disrupt his or her existence, strong psychological and emotional currents such as a desire for power or revenge often motivate the actors. The ambiguities discovered in their investigations when these currents predominate initially blind the detectives on which avenue to take. Daly's *The Hidden Hand* and Spillane's *My Gun Is Quick* have antagonists who perpetuate the image of the master manipulator initiated by Poe's Minister D__ and Conan Doyle's Dr. Moriarty. And, Williams and Hammer find themselves hired by the men they pursue and eventually kill. Daly's Howard Quincy Travers and Spillane's Arthur Berin-Grotin, respectively in the above novels, seek power for power's sake. This is too abstract for either detective, and they spend the novels looking for the person in front of them. If this pattern is in stark contrast to Williams' conflict with Dezzeia in *The Snarl of the Beast*, Spillane repeats it from *I, the Jury* in which Hammer looks for Jack Williams' killer and finds her in the person he has engaged to marry. Travers, Dr. Charlotte Manning, and Berin operate from a twisted, if not closely examined, desire for power. The authors assert but do not explore the desire in great detail. The need for revenge and the feelings of satisfaction it brings are no more deeply analyzed in Chandler's *The High Window* or Macdonald's *The Drowning Pool*. In the former novel, Mrs. Murdock killed her first husband Horace Bright before the action begins and convinces her secretary Merle Davis that she did it. Her reason for killing him is that he occupied the space that she wanted for herself, i.e., controlling her family through her husband's wealth. In Macdonald's novel, Cathy Slocum, disturbed and confused by her parents' alienation from one another and desiring to liberate the man she believes is her father from her grandmother's monetary manipulation, drowns her. Lt. Ralph Knudson, her mother's lover and the Nopal Valley police chief, is her father. Macdonald thus removes any basis for revenge. Once Archer discovers the facts, he allows Cathy to leave with her father, for the most part a stranger to her, for Chicago. To Archer, no one gained from the death and violence, but the young girl might benefit with a new life away from California.

Violence is usually associated with some physical marker or attribute, e.g., size, strength, viciousness, beauty, etherealness, or duplicity, that sets the person off from others. Few have their immoral qualities so clearly delineated as Ralph Dezzeia in *The Snarl of the Beast* and Wilmer Cook in *The Maltese Falcon*, and those threatened do not always have a clear warning of danger. Chandler's Carmen Sternwood in *The Big Sleep* very quickly projects an anomalous atmosphere. However attractive, something is "off" about her. Deviant behavior on the part of other beautiful women does not in all cases reveal itself immediately. In *The Long Goodbye*, Marlowe has difficulty believing that Eileen is a killer. Even Sam Spade's suspicions of Brigid in *The Maltese Falcon* do not prevent him from having a relationship with her. While Spade protects himself, Carmen and Eileen put Marlowe in greater danger although he does not remain in ignorance as long as Mike Hammer does concerning Charlotte Manning in *I, the Jury*. What these and other characters have in common is that violence is frequently an expression of their personalities. For Charlotte, it would be as difficult to disentangle her violent actions from who she is as it would with Hammer. Though they exhibit these actions in different contexts and from different causes, their violent responses define them. Spillane's framing device, i.e., the description of Jack Williams' murder at the beginning of the novel and Hammer's revenge killing of Charlotte for this act at the end, mirror one another.

Spillane's portraits suggest an inevitability about what they do. Hammer's statement in *One Lonely Night* (6) concerning the war's effects on him weakens this argument, but there is a quality of fate in the way he turns to violence as a solution to many situations. Yet, the opening scene in *One Lonely Night*, in which Hammer both recoils from the judge's harsh comments about him and relishes the physical release in smashing the man on the bridge after the woman who runs to him for help commits suicide rather than accept his protection, demonstrates the difficulty in assigning causes for violence that limit possibilities. Hammer is not only the sole one left alive after the sudden confrontation; he is also the only one left on the bridge. Spillane's scene — rain and snow, Hammer isolated high up over the East River after the two deaths— is a convincing tableau of Hammer's moral predicament, particularly as he exults over the killing. While he clearly kills the man in self defense, his obliteration of the man's identity afterwards by mutilating his face, an example of what Grella calls Spillane's "sadistic scenes" ("Hard-Boiled Detective" 117), suggests an uncontrollable element in man that will surface at certain times and in certain conditions. Ultimately, the idea of fate does not answer questions raised about the processes of development and change that affect motives and actions.

Moose Malloy in Chandler's *Farewell, My Lovely* is an emblematic figure of the character marked for violence. Several ideas are important in understanding his role in this context. First, Malloy is a large man who is abnormally strong. In his "appropriation" of Marlowe at the beginning of the novel outside Florian's (5), he neither desires to use or not to use physical force in locating Velma. Malloy was recently released from prison, and he goes to Florian's as the last place with which he associated her. Thinking that Marlowe will aid him in his quest, he drags him upstairs. Malloy, in his single-minded pursuit, enters the bar completely out of place — it has become a black establishment, but neither he nor the bartender and bouncer appreciate his obsession. Consumed with his idea of finding Velma whom he believes wishes to be found, Malloy brings his considerable strength to bear on anyone who interferes in his quest. This interest focused onto the other, i.e., Velma, gives him an additional source of power. Those in the bar act out their roles not sensing the inevitability of fate inherent in Malloy's actions. He functions on the model of the ancient classical hero who performs rather than decides to perform. Calling Malloy a "brutal killer," Cawelti states:

> [H]e is a man of epic proportions whose motives derive from the simple code he lives by and from his love for Velma. He is an Ajax anachronistically thrust into the antiheroic twentieth-century city, a gargantuan Romeo whose innocent passion is betrayed and who is eventually murdered in cold blood by his Juliet [*Adventure* 179].

In both *The Iliad* and *The Odyssey*, Homer gives life to what in the modern world would be termed unconscious impulses. So, Athena's appearances to Odysseus and Thetis's visits to Achilles dramatize what to the modern era are those buried motivations for actions, motivations explained in more abstract terms when explained at all. Chandler leaves Malloy's motivations largely unexamined except for the idea of Velma. Without analysis or dramatization of his inner world, Malloy seems more an act of nature, one that cannot be understood or overcome but rather endured.

The early hard-boiled detective novel is not far removed in time from late-nineteenth century social Darwinist thought. However, Freud, Jung, and literary Modernism interpose ideas between either a strictly biological or a mythical determinism such as fate and open up avenues of understanding that employ environment, heredity, and that unique quality that individualizes each human. If one thus states that violence is an expression of some people's personalities, the potential for either social destabilization or social harmony arises in dramatic form. Any person could be violent or not at any time; living with outside influences, one nonetheless remains a creative force for good or evil. It is here that the early hard-boiled detective novel, admittedly with varying degrees of sophistication, feels its way to the depiction of violence. An acceptance of the classical idea of fate or a nearly complete biological determinism espoused by behaviorists such as B.F. Skinner in *Beyond Freedom and Dignity* (1971) leaves humans trapped in a world saturated by controls that deprive them of free will and individual choice. In *A Stroll with William James* (1983), Jacques Barzun calls their system a "twist[ing]" of William James's "naturalist psychology" "into a mindless Behaviorism" (216). Without some innate characteristics that both help define their humanity and individuality, humans become almost indistinguishable parts in a vast system. In *The Blank Slate* (2002), Steven Pinker best describes this balance of forces that illustrate human nature:

> I think we have reason to believe that the mind is equipped with a battery of emotions, drives, and faculties for reasoning and communicating, and that they have a common logic across cultures, are difficult to erase or redesign from scratch, were shaped by natural selection acting over the course of human evolution, and owe some of their basic design (and some of their variation) to information in the genome [73].

Several examples explore the manner in which individuals choose to act based largely on who they are and what they stand for.

The Continental Op in Hammett's *Red Harvest* and *The Dain Curse* and Mike Hammer in *One Lonely Night*, paradoxically, show the detectives' acting from individual motives that exemplify their personalities. Two violent episodes in Spillane's novel, the killing of the man on the bridge at the beginning and the shooting of the communist agents torturing Velda in the warehouse at the end, rather than acts of mindless violence in reality proceed from motivations, as suggested earlier, to help those who cannot help themselves or from self defense. In addition to what is stated about the early scene above, Spillane's dramatization of the action needs further analysis in order to understand his motivations. First, Hammer has walked out on the bridge to be alone when the young woman, filled with fear, hurries towards him out of the rainy, snowy night. This triggers a protective response from Hammer, who generally acts to support the weak and vulnerable. Second, a man walks "out of the 'wall of white'" (10) and threatens to kill both of them, not thinking Hammer would be armed. Third, Hammer shoots the man in the face with his .45. Fourth, frightened by that and believing he is "'one of them'" (11), the woman throws herself off the bridge. Even though he knows that he acted to protect the woman and himself, Hammer hears the judge's accusations once again that he is nothing but a murderer. What obscures his motivation to act here and at the end of the novel is his strong emotional reactions to the events. Hammer, after scraping the dead man's face on the bridge road, throws him into the water. As he shoots the communist agents, possibly the only way to save Velda, he exults over his actions. These emotional responses to save someone or protect himself are defensive; he does not precipitate either situation. The young woman's statement that he is "'one of them,'" however mistaken, might suggest Hammer's dilemma, i.e., forever misjudged in his violent reactions to violent confrontations.

Hard-boiled private detectives, while acting from personal motives, also demonstrate common traits that appear across the genre. The Continental Op in *Red Harvest* and *The Dain Curse* restores some sense of social order to the respective social environments. Nothing about his personality suggests that he would not use violence to protect himself or someone else. But, he does not violently begin his investigations. Rather, his assignments to the cases are to serve his clients, and in this, he apparently acts as an agent, both personally and professionally, of order. The result in *Red Harvest*, as described above, is imperfect. Yet, Elihu Willsson, as the Op's second client, becomes by default the only person capable of starting some recovery in Personville. In *The Dain Curse*, the Op's scope is more limited, and however complicated the violence, he must help the innocent, making choices in seemingly baffling circumstances. Peter Wolfe writes, "In place of [*Red Harvest*'s] Marxist melodrama, it offers a Gothic extravagance, a sealed room puzzle of sorts, and the related jobs of curing a young widow of morphine addiction while demythologizing a family curse" (*Beams Falling* 94).

The Op kills Joseph Haldorn to save his wife Aaronia and joins in shooting Harvey Whidden when he threatens to kill Owen Fitzstephan. Aside from those deaths, Alice Dain Leggett and Owen Fitzstephan kill most of the others accounted for, primarily acting in the case of Fitzstephan to gain someone or, for Alice, to prevent someone from exposing her past. While there are fewer deaths in *Dain* than in *Red*, violence and death still saturate the former novel, and the Continental Op's determination to solve the case is paramount in ending the chaos.

Morality and violence uneasily conjoin in the hard-boiled detective novel. Given the often fast-paced action, detectives have little time to think before they respond to danger. In Richard S. Prather's *Bodies in Bedlam* (1951), Shell Scott is knocked unconscious as he tries to escape Hallie Wilson's house. As he recovers his senses, he realizes that Dutch and Flem, two of Mace Garvey's thugs, have bound him hand and foot and tossed him on the floor in the back of their car. They drive him into the hills above Los Angeles and, as Dutch tells him with pleasure, they intend to kill him by forcing him to commit suicide. Scott manages to escape and runs them down with their own car. He eventually learns that only one of them dies. In such a clear-cut case of self-defense, who would say that Scott acted immorally? However, one fact makes his case less innocent. When Scott operates their car, tied up as he is, he does not attempt to drive away; instead, he intentionally backs into them. Surprisingly, few detectives take the law into their own hands. Mike Hammer's actions in shooting Charlotte Manning in *I, the Jury* and in making sure Arthur Berin in *My Gun Is Quick* is going to die before he manages to escape from the burning building himself are rare. More often than not, detectives step into violent situations, sometimes unarmed even when they own a gun. Before Scott shoots Paul Clark in *Bodies in Bedlam*, Roger Brane's murderer and the man who has already tried to shoot him, he reasons that he must give Clark a chance to surrender. By warning him, Scott gets shot before he can kill Clark. Scott makes a moral choice that almost costs him his life.

One question regarding the roles of morality and violence in hard-boiled detective fiction has to do with morality's source. Raymond Chandler rather preemptively decides this issue for some detectives by stating in "The Simple Art of Murder" that the detective is the best man in his world. His hero Philip Marlowe is not known for gratuitously shooting people. However, his profession puts him among the violent. He shoots Lance Canino in *The Big Sleep* to protect himself and Mona Mars and tries, but fails, to prevent Moose Malloy from being killed by Velma. The detective is tainted by association and is often suspected by the honest policemen he encounters because his cases involve him in violent circumstances. Chief Peter Painter of the Miami Beach detective bureau suspects Michael Shayne in Brett Halliday's *The Private Practice of Michael Shayne* (1940) of having shot Harry Grange when in fact the real killer has set up Shayne. Only through the help of his friend Chief Will Gentry of the Miami Detective Bureau; Timothy Rourke, another friend and a reporter for the *Miami News*; and his own efforts to solve the murder does he avoid being tried for the killing. Painter, as a conventional foil, assumes Shayne is guilty of something whenever he uncovers his involvement in a case. To him, Shayne is capable of almost anything, a thoroughly immoral man. Notwithstanding the upright nature of detectives like Thomas B. Dewey's Mac, they must adapt to this image of guilt by association. For the most part, the police might escape this charge, but the private investigator cannot. This is a strange twist in the detective fiction genre given its origins in such above-reproach men as Poe's Dupin and Conan Doyle's Holmes.

One detective agency frequently uses the services of another one. Les Roberts has Milan Jacovich in *Full Cleveland* call Saxon in California to check something for him and send him a bill. This obviously is an economic way to operate. It just so happens that Roberts is the author of both series. Mike Plasti of International asks Thomas B. Dewey's Mac in *Every Bet's a Sure Thing* (1953) to follow Harriet Mitchell and her two children on a train trip from Chicago to Los Angeles. The surveillance started in New York, but Plasti tells him that Mrs. Mitchell spotted their operative. Mac assumes that if he is careful he will have a relaxing trip to the west coast and the possibility of a paid vacation. However, before the novel ends, Mr. Doyle, Harriet Mitchell's husband, forces Mac to jump from the Los Angeles Limited in Utah; a man shoots at Mac with a shotgun; and only the intervention of Mac's Chicago police friend Lt. Donovan prevents his being charged with transporting dope. The Treasury department agents suspect Mac primarily because he is there. For the private detective, one is guilty until proven innocent. Only Dashiell Hammett's Continental Op seems immune to this attitude. However, this possibly unavoidable state preempts moral consideration. The police make no moral judgment about Mac; they judge him and his profession as guilty before they can act. From this dubious position, Mac and other detectives must assume the responsibility of clarifying their involvement in every case; Mac does this naturally by solving the problem. Race Williams' belligerent assertions of the rightness of his conduct, Sam Spade's confrontation of the police when they suspect him, and Philip Marlowe's cold irony and stubborn refusal to back down represent one counter-threat in the genre, but Michael Shayne's worry in *The Private Practice of Michael Shayne* that he will not be able to clear himself of the charge that he killed Harry Grange weaves another threat and adds complexity to the detective's general character portrait. Only by removing the moral cloud that circumstances and other characters place over him does Shayne have a temporary relief from the likes of a Peter Painter who naturally is always wrong about Shayne.

Just as violence solves little in the hard-boiled detective novel, it also brings few satisfactions to the characters involved. It rearranges lives as it rushes over a portion of the social fabric, dragging a literary and cultural reminder of the darker world without which mankind seems unable to live.

Raymond Chandler's paean to the detective in "The Simple Art of Murder" is slightly embarrassing but also conveys a warning of what societies need to confront this fundamental way of altering destiny — or at least trying to. And, in the detective's isolation one sees either danger or an assurance of success.

5

Decaying Worlds

The early hard-boiled detective exists in a world, whether New York, San Francisco, Los Angeles, Chicago, or Miami, that is at the end of a process rather than the beginning. This applies to the 1920s, 1930s, 1940s, and 1950s for different social and cultural reasons but resonates throughout the works of the Period's writers. Certainly the major events associated with these decades, e.g., Prohibition and the rise of the gangster, the Depression, World War II, and the Korean War provide stimuli for good or evil, but the images which dominate the novels of the above writers frequently project more failure than success. While the detectives' personalities contribute to this result, each writer portrays a society flooded with corruption, social and personal, that isolates the detectives as they often struggle against both police and criminals and react harshly to the world in which they must live. Specificity is important in order to place the detectives visually and intellectually. However, the call for specificity is challenged immediately by the detectives' sketchy backgrounds. As mentioned earlier, they generally are men with little or no known pasts, fully grown and cynical, hardened, and coping with their environments with varying degrees of emotional and professional success. They are seen running before training to run. Although an image more intellectual than figurative, in *media res* captures the mood in which the reader experiences them. The darkness and decay of the cities and their surrounding areas also underscore the atmosphere of failure in these writers' works. Carrol John Daly's *The Snarl of the Beast* and *The Hidden Hand* use these images as, among others, do Hammett's, Chandler's, and Spillane's novels. Choice and the desire for choice, either absent, or morally or psychologically impaired, dominate the moods of the early hard-boiled detective novels. Thus, from the beginning of the genre, the paradox of decline and development in the social environment begins its operations in the characters and lives of the hard-boiled detectives.

What one most immediately notices about Race Williams is his voice — aggressive, boasting, self-flattering. Little about the man appeals except his consistency. From stating what violence he will commit in a given situation to asserting that all, especially the criminals, know this to describing himself as "hard-boiled" (*Snarl* 38), Williams exists as a man with an extreme if sketchy past: "I stand on my own legs and I'll shoot it out with any gun in the city — any time, any place. Thirty-fourth street and Broadway, in the five o'clock rush hour, isn't barred either. Race Williams — Private Investigator — tells the whole story" (*Snarl* 2).

Daly describes this at the beginning of the novel in the context of a chase, a gun battle involving the police, and Williams' secretive meeting with his client, Daniel Davidson. The genre begins in action violence at night in an urban slum area of New York. Race Williams follows an almost unseen enemy who shoots a policeman, thus raising the stakes of the outcome. Williams' ambivalent position between criminal and policeman adds to the moral dilemmas that unfold (*Snarl* 1). He does not invest the setting with any positive or neutral overtones. Menace rules. In *The Hidden Hand*, set in post-boom Florida, the buildings' physical decay and frequent abandonment coupled with the bursting, sub-tropical plant growth create an ominous environment that almost requires an unheeding hero such as Williams. The detective character's antecedents discussed in Chapter 3 clearly lie behind the image of detectives like Williams, the Continental Op, Sam Spade, and Philip Marlowe. Each detective differs in the type and degree to which he reflects these forerunners, but the latter offer strong examples of literary influences. With the literary and historical antecedents come the disorder and dislocation of their environments, an idea carried over into the hard-boiled detective novel with its urban influence.

Each one of the early detectives appears fully-grown, all necessary formative experiences in the past. The Continental Op exemplifies this image, solid, strong, certain of his abilities. One learns a fact or two about his work in Baltimore, Buffalo, and New York. Apart from this, Hammett focuses the plot on whatever job the Op has. Not exactly a pre-Terminator man, nonetheless he presents a devastatingly empty image. That is why he fits well in Personville in *Red Harvest* even if he is not of it. Sam Spade offers little more humanity. In *The Maltese Falcon*, he goes well with the image of the dark alley in which his partner Miles Archer lies dead but unmourned. Other than fancy apartments and hotel lobbies, San Francisco never becomes a city filled with a variety of life. Corruption, greed, and murder committed by people from somewhere else dominate the action. Marlowe in *The*

Big Sleep reveals a hardness that his work and the people with whom he comes into contact have created. The decadence of the Sternwood sisters, Carmen and Vivian, and the image of Gen. Sternwood's disused oil pumps fit Marlowe's mood; in fact, they function as mutual interpreters of one another. Although not as morally flawed as the Sternwood daughters, neither Marlowe nor they can rejuvenate themselves. The paradoxical, Janus-like figure of Mickey Spillane's Mike Hammer looks back to the earliest hard-boiled detective novels in the portrayal of violence and a decaying environment in *I, The Jury* and forward to the Transitional Period through a greater revelation of Hammer's formative experiences, essentially World War II, and along with his ability to feel and love, his friendship with the dead Jack Williams and Cap. Pat Chambers. Michael Shayne in Brett Halliday's *Dividend on Death* (1939) and Mac in Thomas B. Dewey's *Draw the Curtain Close* (1947) enhance this image of the private investigator living on the edge. Both men exude a sense of being shaped by an ineluctable past that has left them hard and determined. Yet, they exert an independent will that does not always serve them well. Like his Los Angeles progenitor Philip Marlowe, Shayne lives on the dark side of a sunny world. By holding on to his own personal sense of order, he can help maintain or restore some balance to the social fabric. Phyllis Brighton, the beautiful nineteen-year old stepdaughter of a wealthy man, believes she is going to murder her mother. From the beginning of the novel, she introduces the twin themes of light and darkness. Shayne is a man who embodies both in his character, fitting the environment and, through Phyllis, the case. Halliday describes him:

> Michael Shayne slowly unlimbered himself and stood up. He had a tall angular body that concealed a lot of solid weight, and his freckled cheeks were thin to gauntness. His rumpled hair was violently red, giving him a little-boy look curiously in contrast with the harshness of his features. When he smiled, the harshness went out of his face and he didn't look at all like a hard-boiled private detective who had come to the top the tough way [*Dividend* 8–9].

Not just a description, this paragraph sums up his character. Halliday refers to Shayne's physicality and in the process underscores his place in the genre and suggests the way in which the genre unfolds. Miami and Los Angeles work well as settings that contrast the themes of light and darkness, emphasizing their physical and moral aspects.

Halliday particularly stresses the moral darkness inherent in the Miami setting, echoing Carroll John Daly's *The Hidden Hand*, when he describes Shayne's digging up Rufus Brighton's body. Shayne drives to within a quarter of a mile of the Brighton estate "taking deep breaths of the salt-tanged air, subconsciously delaying as much as possible" (*Dividend* 178). Using a steel rod, he probes the sand above the low-tide mark. Eventually, he finds something buried in the "wide expanse of sloping wet sand that glistened in the faint starlight" (178). Shayne uses a spade to dig up "a steel-banded trunk" (179) and after scraping away the sand opens the lid:

> A thick nauseating stench rolled up and struck him sickeningly in the face when he threw the lid back. He closed his eyes against it, turned his head to cough and spit the vile taste out of his mouth. The[n] he picked up his flashlight and turned its beam into the open trunk [179–80].

Inside was the corpse of a man who turns out to be Rufus Brighton. The beauty of the setting in daylight and darkness is evident, but the moral darkness that pervades the novel occupies that same space set on the edge of the Atlantic Ocean. Shayne's harsh demeanor well fits such a scene that pulls in contrary directions with no way out except through the imperfect machinery of the law.

As a fitting apex to a symbolic triangle, Chicago does not have the scenic effects of either Miami or Los Angeles, but in Dewey's Mac series, it rivals the darkness with only intermittent flashes of light. To emphasize the depth of corruption and moral decay, Dewey in *Draw the Curtain Close* creates the character of Warfield, born Luigi Scarpone. The Prohibition era serves as the source of Warfield's wealth. Cynthia Warfield, his estranged wife, knows something of her husband's depravity. When she was ten years old, he selected her for his future wife, had her educated to play the role of social hostess and forced her to marry him or see her father indicted for illegal manipulation in a savings and loan. She tells Mac that she agreed but has lived to regret being involved with him. Mac explains the gruesome limits to which Warfield would go when he tells her how Warfield took four of his lieutenants whose loyalty he suspected out on Lake Michigan, cut their heads off, dumped the remainder of their bodies overboard, and sent their heads "to four of his chief competitors. They went out of town the following day" (62). Mac, forced out of the police department by a corrupt politician but helped subsequently by his mentor then Sergeant but now Lt. Donovan, represents a core of veracity in the series. While there may be balmy summers on Lake Michigan, the cold winds of winter are more representative of the climate. Warfield, echoing the real-world corruption and violence of Al Capone, brings a darkness that only time can alleviate. He is universally hated and thus killed eventually by someone involved with him. Of course, just as neither Marlowe nor Shayne turn the physical light into a moral one neither does Mac. At most these and other hard-boiled detectives act as a defense against greed and corruption.

With such a character type as the early hard-boiled detective, one needs a striking environment like that indicated above. Decay, darkness, and gloom suggest as well as provide an atmosphere for harmful acts. Certainly,

James Fennimore Cooper's Leatherstocking tales employ the almost primeval forest, then receding rapidly westward, for their suggestiveness of hidden evil. Darkness and light are archetypal images of evil and goodness, respectively, and have become natural partners. Thus, Raymond Chandler's use of Southern California for his Philip Marlowe novels reveals a strong element of irony. Not only the Sternwood household in *The Big Sleep* but also many other aspects of the culture suggest that the bright light dazzles more than illuminates. The sun as the clarity of truth and hope, especially in the Christian tradition, functions in Chandler as the revelation of corruption, a corruption, to further intensify the irony, lying in Carmen's youth. General Sternwood's advanced age, however, distances him from his daughter's immorality. Hammett's *Red Harvest*, set in a medium-sized Montana town, is socially corrupt, beginning with Elihu Willsson, the father of Donald Willsson, the man who hires the Continental Detective Agency "to do some work for him" (14). Elihu Willsson controls the town and sets the moral tone that could hardly be lower. The physical image of Personville is the outward manifestation of the moral and social corruption of the city:

> The city wasn't pretty. Most of its builders had gone in for gaudiness. Maybe they had been successful at first. Since then the smelters whose brick stacks stuck up tall against a gloomy mountain to the south had yellow-smoked everything into uniform dinginess. The result was an ugly city of forty thousand people, set in an ugly notch between two ugly mountains that had been all dirtied up by mining. Spread over this was a grimy sky that looked as if it had come out of the smelters' stacks [*Red Harvest* 3–4].

The organized criminal elements that have threatened Elihu Willsson's power were originally hired by him to combat the unions. The number of deaths includes Willsson's son and many criminals, but in the end, Willsson and some of the remaining politicians make a deal and the status quo reasserts itself. Hammett could hardly have penned a more cynical finish to a story that cries out for some righting of the society, some recognition that if no supernatural force will intervene at least the human power brokers will understand that excess corruption and violence only lessen their ability to wield power.

John G. Cawelti and George Grella, as noted in Chapters 1 and 4, respectively, rightly focus on Mike Hammer's excessive and sadistic violence but overlook his cooler, harder moments. Grella additionally observes that Hammer "is convinced he is the hammer of God, free to torture, maim, or kill all who get in his way" ("Hard-Boiled Detective" 117). Yet, Spillane's hero, while tracking down Jack Williams' killer in *I, the Jury*, also works hard at following clues and thinking through the evidence. This process leads irrefutably to Charlotte Manning as the murderer, but rather than turning her over to the police, he shoots her in the stomach and watches her die. Sam Spade's conduct toward Brigid O'Shaughnessy in *The Maltese Falcon* comes to mind but in Hammer's case demonstrates a shift toward uncontrollable violence, a killing rage that he increasingly indulges. Possibly, it is more a return to the earlier violence of Daly, in many ways Spillane's mentor. Both Daly's *The Hidden Hand* and Spillane's *My Gun Is Quick* feature shadowy figures who manipulate most of the criminal element and whose serpentine paths the detectives follow to the formers' unmaskings. New York and Miami (Daly) and New York (Spillane) provide backdrops that weigh heavily on the protagonists. A moral gloom, with flashes of sudden death leading to a return and intensification of both the moral and physical darkness, pervade the novels. Williams and Hammer project a desperate futility regarding their ability, if not their desire, to control the evils they confront. Hammer kills sufficient numbers of communists in *One Lonely Night*, but his flailing in the darkness, while immediately effective, is ultimately futile. Superficially, one could say that it is a part of the genre that detectives need crimes, but more deeply, Daly and Spillane suggest profound reasons for the detectives' inability to lose their vocations. Violence, evil, and immorality will always be with us, they seem to say, and thus see this state as a continuing, inescapable reality. In the modern world, the city rather than the forest, is the ideal place for the above triumvirate. The detectives, at least in expectation, match the decaying environment.

Two detectives near the end of the early period, Shell Scott in Richard S. Prather's *Case of the Vanishing Beauty* and Brock Callahan in William Campbell Gault's *Ring Around Rosa* (1955), portray a mixed view of Los Angeles. The sun shines, the nights are warm, but there is an undertow to this beneficent image that reminds one, as it were, of the skull beneath the skin. In *Case of the Vanishing Beauty*, the various places emphasize the negative side of the city: El Cuchillo (The Knife), a bar with a knife-throwing act that is the hub of a drug ring; the Inner World Society of True Believers run by a con man, Walter Press, who uses the name Narda; sunrise services at the Inner World's temple at which guests are unknowingly given drugs to create a demand for them; the temple as a place to hold people who endanger their operation; the Lords and Ladies, a private gambling club where Scott meets Fred Vincent, an old con man who tells him about Press's cheating his partners out of their share of a scam in San Francisco; and Lucille Stoner's disordered home which apparently is the location of some other con. She tells Scott why she never returned to the Inner World after she was fired by Press and after he apparently died in a car wreck, "'No sense to. I got a deal, different deal now. Pretty soft'" (120). Two other characters add a special emphasis to this corrupt atmosphere: Margaret Remorse, the violent and grotesquely fat owner of El Cuchillo and the aforementioned Narda, the Wizard-of-Oz-like figure who manipulates his true believers, not only with drugs but with rhetoric that promises inner peace if they will only follow him. Scott attends one service and is impressed by the staging despite his misgivings. All the while, the life of the city continues, sunny and appealing on the surface but corrupt and deadly underneath. Three murders occur and Scott kills the Seipel twins, Margaret Remorse's enforcers as they try to kill him. Gault continues the deadly mixture of light and darkness in *Ring Around Rosa*. The deaths occur mostly because of jealousy or a desire for revenge — not drugs and con operations as in Prather's novel. Nonetheless, Gault depicts young lives lost. He begins the novel in a somewhat innocent setting: Callahan has set up office as a private investigator in Beverly Hills on South Beverly Drive. He is waiting for his first client, not knowing who it will be, when Juan Mira, an ex-boxer, enters. Mira darkens the office with his suppressed rage. He hires Callahan to find Rosa Carmona, his ex-fiancée. At that point she is still alive. However, when she later comes to Mira for help, he murders her in his Santa Monica home and buries her under a rose trellis in his backyard. Gault has Callahan describe Mira's neighborhood: "There were no new houses on the block, but the old ones were well kept up and the lawns were green. Clean, trimmed palm trees ran in symmetrical rows along both sides of the street" (185). Once inside Mira's empty house near the end of the novel, he gazes at the backyard: "From here, I could look out into a walled rear yard, the walls covered with bougainvillaea, the yard bordered with geraniums. And what were those in the middle, on the arched trellis? Yellow roses, big as small cabbages" (185).

Callahan notices, "The lawn was mounded almost imperceptibly under the trellis and the sod looked like it had been recently replaced" (186). Gault wisely ends the novel a few pages later. Along with the other murders; the motel blackmail operation of Roger Scott, the handsome lover of two beautiful women, one, Jan Bonnet, who becomes Callahan's on again and off again girlfriend; and the murderous violence of the gangster Red Nystrom, Rosa's death and burial threaten to leach away any possibility of a life-affirming tone. It is still Southern California, but Gault continues the tradition in the early hard-boiled detective novel of casting a cold eye, whatever the setting, on the human condition.

The detectives' natures and the often negative social environments within which they work affect their moral or professional choices. Race Williams and Mike Hammer, especially, announce their intentions to act alone though they maintain contacts with the police. They say they can do things the police, for political or legal reasons, often cannot. Of course, societal corruption lies below the surface of, and not so far below, these writers' novels and leads to the detectives' independent action and subsequent police support for it. A prominent sub-theme of Spillane's Mike Hammer novels is police restraint from above, not just to prevent police brutality but also to protect someone, however shadowy, from the discomfort or unpleasantness of disclosure. In *I, the Jury* and *The Big Kill* (1951), Cap. Pat Chambers rails to Hammer that his hands are tied; he cannot act to resolve some situation. This strains their relationship since Hammer is not shy in sharing his opinion regarding Chambers' position. However, after some threat that independent action will bring retribution, Chambers usually indicates that he will support what Hammer does. The latter thus becomes, at one level, Chambers' personal vigilante force. Of course, Hammer does not need much encouragement as he frequently has announced his intention to find and kill the criminal. However, Chambers cannot be absolved of culpability since his initially weak restraint shows his certain knowledge of Hammer's past violent tendencies. The decadent social and political environments, however shadowy the responsible forces remain, demand action that will remove the immediate source of evil and corruption but not lead to an amelioration of society's ills. The present evil presses so insistently that response is necessary but darkens even the good that ensues.

Both morally and professionally, the Continental Op's choices in *Red Harvest* narrow so much that in the end he just acts. Initially, the Op fulfills the role assigned with no hint that the situation will unravel in an orgy of violence along with the town of Personville. The Op asks questions, often acts predictably, but shifts into another mode not long after his employer, Donald Willsson, is killed. Not unfamiliar with death, the Op switches his activities to aid the father, but unlike Elihu Willsson, he is not in control of the events and, ironically, only plays an effective role as he loses options. This shift, the detective as instrument rather than intelligent actor, certainly resembles Mike Hammer's self-induced murderous frenzies but leaves the Op even less control than Hammer. Ross Macdonald's Lew Archer in *The Moving Target* seems to function in sharp contrast to either the Continental Op or Mike Hammer in the matter of choice. However, the Southern California environment is largely unchanged from Chandler's corruption under the sun, and Archer's investigation of Ralph Sampson's disappearance leads to the discovery that Albert Graves, Sampson's friend and an old acquaintance of Archer's, is the murderer. The more Archer investigates, the murkier the motivations that lead the protagonists to strike at others and destroy the lives of those closest to them. When it becomes personal for the detective, as it does later in Chandler's *The Long Goodbye* between Marlowe and Terry Lennox, one has nowhere to turn that allows positive choices. Archer and Marlowe are trapped by their own humanity in the corrupt environments in which they act. The deeper they probe the less chance that they will uncover any goodness. The only move is to turn away.

An underlying irony in the genre is that the detectives and others must make choices in this world of moral and social decay. The dominant image is that all participants stumble in the dark whether in New York, San Francisco, Los Angeles, Miami, or Chicago. This stumbling occurs on the detectives' part even when they can turn to their lawyers for help with the police as does Brock Callahan when he calls in Tommy Self. Beginning at least with Hammett's Continental Op and Sam Spade, police friends help the detectives even when the police, functioning as a bureaucracy and jealous of their jurisdictional authority, seem to prevent any enlightenment. In Gault's *Ring Around Rosa*, Callahan must deal with three police jurisdictions, i.e., Beverly Hills, West Los Angeles, and Santa Monica. Officials from each one suspect both Callahan's involvement and the interference of the other police authorities. After Callahan subdues Juan Mira in the latter's Santa Monica home, he calls Sgt. McCall of the Santa Monica police and Lt. Dave Trask in West Los Angeles, a man with whom his relationship varies moment by moment. Sgt. McCall warns him that he had better be right that Rosa's body is buried in Mira's backyard, and the Los Angeles police are also wary of acting on his information about Mira. In *Dividend on Death*, Halliday's Michael Shayne finds himself in an antagonistic relationship with Chief Peter Painter of the Miami Beach Detective Bureau, and only the help of his friend Chief Will Gentry of the Miami Detective Bureau prevents Painter from carrying out his threat to get Shayne. Shayne lives and works in Miami but often has cases in Miami Beach. Although Painter's constant misunderstanding of the events in Shayne's cases becomes too stylized, his real police power does attract Shayne's attention and desire, eventually, to offer some peace. In Dewey's *Every Bet's a Sure Thing*, Mac's case takes him from Chicago to Los Angeles, and only aid from his vacationing friend, Chicago Police Lt. Donovan, helps him out of his serious difficulties with the Los Angeles police.

From a distance these misunderstandings and dilemmas might seem comic, but in the detectives' lives they have dire repercussions. And, the detective protagonists are not themselves corrupt. They attempt to prevent miscarriages of justice and discover the real culprits. Of course, the police are by and large not corrupt either. They react against what often turns out to be the private detectives' correct actions, and their initial reactions to the detectives are usually based on incomplete knowledge. This sounds like the general human condition, but the effect of people acting at cross-purposes for even the best of reasons creates a sense of moral ambiguity and often despair. There appears to be no way out of this morass. Ross Macdonald's Lew Archer suggests a possible solution. Archer might be termed the reluctant detective, yet he and several other early private investigators act as bridges between not only the official police and private detectives but also the public and the police. Dewey's Mac served as a Chicago policeman but was fired, as mentioned above, when he resisted the city's political corruption. Archer, who did not like the "dirty politics" (*The Moving Target* 110), was fired from the Long Beach police and served in intelligence during World War II. He also did some work for Albert Graves in 1940 and 1941 when the latter was the district attorney. Gault's Brock Callahan worked three years for the OSS and his father was a cop. As indicated above, Mac and Callahan are not immune from conflicts and misunderstandings regarding the police, but they, and especially Archer, have a certain *gravitas* that at least deters the sometimes single-minded approach of the police from dragging the system through any more decadence than can be avoided. And, moral decadence is not the only sinkhole often avoided; the occasional failure of the police system through inertia and repetition contrasts to the dogged choices and actions of these and other private detectives. A final irony is that the very linear thinking of the police is what Poe's Dupin and Conan Doyle's Holmes feel superior to.

Post–World War II America presents an image that only partly fit the one that the early hard-boiled detectives show. However, both Spillane and Ross Macdonald grew up in the 1920s and 1930s and flourished as writers from the late 1940s through the 1960s, so some elements of their work reflect, if for no other reason than proximity in time, the more negative social pictures of the earlier decades. Yet, with changed economic circumstances, a more expansive view, however unreal, underlies the society the transitional hard-boiled detectives will portray. If no better, the society seems to offer a more varied array of possibilities, leading to their own complexities. The transitional detectives might not believe strongly, if at all, in social progress, but they pursue and engage more alternatives in coping with the dark side of humanity.

6

Work: Discourse and Danger

While Carroll John Daly, Dashiell Hammett, and Raymond Chandler especially focus the idea of work in the early hard-boiled detective novel, Edgar Allan Poe's C. Auguste Dupin and Arthur Conan Doyle's Sherlock Holmes loom in the background. The eccentric detective and his ever-reliable partner change in the early hard-boiled period into the detective largely working alone. However, the policeman as opponent and/or friend remains. No more than in Poe and Conan Doyle does the detective usually put money as the primary reason for action. In fact, Holmes only appears to take cases that interest him and will travel anywhere or nowhere as the spirit prompts. Carroll John Daly's Race Williams in *The Snarl of the Beast* and Dashiell Hammett's Sam Spade in *The Maltese Falcon* also investigate for reasons besides money, Williams to help the frightened Daniel Davidson and Spade to avenge his murdered partner Miles Archer. Work as thought dominates Dupin and Holmes, and the hard-boiled detectives, for all their reputations for physical violence, employ their minds as well. John G. Cawelti states: "[...] the creation of hard-boiled pattern involved a shift in the underlying archetype of the detective story from the pattern of mystery to that of heroic adventure. Of course, some elements of the mystery archetype remained since the hero was still a detective solving crimes" (*Adventure* 142).

The detectives react physically to clients and adversaries, but they also work through the evidence, interviewing and re-interviewing, remaining skeptical until the facts make sense. Few sit and ponder as does Holmes, but they carry the ratiocinative tradition into the private eye novel, deepening the idea of work in the process.

The conditions under which the detectives operate form an important part of the idea of work in the hard-boiled detective novel. As indicated, Poe and Conan Doyle create the image of the private detective accompanied by someone who participates in the action and listens. Their stories employ first-person narrators, an unnamed narrator and Dr. Watson, respectively, but the detective is the central focus. What he thinks and feels is paramount. No one considers either Dupin or Holmes as the partner. Rather it is the observer or narrator who functions as the partner, thus establishing the idea of partnership on an unequal level. In Daly's *The Snarl of the Beast*, Race Williams moves forcefully through the novel solving Daniel Davidson's dilemma over the murderous Ralph Dezzeia. Jerry, Williams' aide, drives him and looks after his home, but Daly has almost obliterated the idea of partnership. Part of this stems from Williams' dramatization of the self. The hard-boiled detective novel begins with a first-person narrator, the detective and not the partner, and this casts helpers into the shadows and expands the detective's presence. As business-like as Hammett's Continental Op is in *Red Harvest* and as methodically as he goes about his work, he dominates the action and sets the tone. George Grella describes him as "tough, unemotional, a thorough professional" ("Hard-Boiled Detective" 107). Near the end of the novel as the level of violence expands, the Continental Op sends for help from the Old Man who runs the San Francisco branch of the agency. Seemingly passionless and thus less dominated by ego, the Op nevertheless is everywhere present and renders the need for a partner problematic. In *The Hidden Hand*, Race Williams more dramatically forms a temporary bond with Gregory Ford to further his investigation, giving the sense of a needed balance, but these are only *ad hoc* connections that either the Op or Williams or circumstances beyond their control sever. For all the conflict and movement in Daly's first two Race Williams novels, the action unfolds from the narrator, and the illusion of the very limited partner employed in *The Snarl of the Beast* dissipates to be replaced by the partner competitor in *The Hidden Hand*.

Hammett briefly presents the idea of partnership in *The Maltese Falcon* but by the end of the first chapter has reduced the number of private detectives to one. Sam Spade and Miles Archer's uneasy working relationship ends abruptly when Brigid O'Shaughnessy shoots Archer in a San Francisco alley. But, Spade has previously violated their relationship by sleeping with Iva, Miles' wife. Fending off Iva after his partner's death, Spade attempts to restore some sense of professionalism by discovering Miles' murderer. When he finds out that Brigid killed Miles, he tells her, as mentioned in Chapter 1, that he is going to turn her over to the police. While this might seem forced, Spade at least bows to the necessity of acknowledging professional obligations if not pretending a friendship he did not feel. Mirroring this disintegrating partnership is the criminal trio of Casper Gutman, Joel Cairo, and Wilmer Cook. Conan Doyle earlier employs the idea of the criminal gang in the stories in which Dr. Moriarty appears. Daly continues this device with Dezzeia's gang. In the latter two cases, however, the master criminal dominates his subordinates completely. In contrast, Gutman and Cairo balance one another, with Gutman supplying the brains and Cairo the cunning and some of the violence. Wilmer is the odd man out as becomes apparent when Cairo shoots him. These criminal gangs supply a plot device by peopling the novel with adversaries. Their numbers are in sharp contrast to the detective, even the Continental Op, who usually contests the wrongdoers alone. The hierarchical nature of the criminal organizations pits their leaders against the hard-boiled detective, recalling the latter's origins in the Western gunfighter and the frontier hero. And, as the isolated gunfighter and frontiersman resolve threats against their respective societies, so does the private eye.

Raymond Chandler's Philip Marlowe represents a significant shift in the idea of partnership in the genre. Obviously foreshadowed by Spade's independent figure battling both police and criminal, Marlowe makes no pretense of needing a partner. He is the quintessential lone figure toward which the hard-boiled detective novel has moved. The ground was laid from 1923, the year of the publication of the first hard-boiled detective story by Daly followed shortly by Hammett's first story, to 1939 when *The Big Sleep*, Chandler's first novel, was published. He wrote Marlowe stories before this, publishing the first in 1933, but the novel, based on several early stories, dramatically projects Marlowe into the world from his isolated existence. His antagonists range from Carmen Sternwood to Eddie Mars, the gambler to whom Vivian, Carmen's sister, owes money. In addition, the corrupt society, especially the Sternwood family, and Marlowe's battles with his own sense of bleakness present near insurmountable obstacles. For, the hard-boiled detective has moved from clear victories to more muted and limited ones. The battles against both criminals and self recall another source for the hard-boiled detective, i.e., the medieval knight. To be worthy of fulfilling a quest is as important as knightly skills and courage. Marlowe's work tests both — and alone. He also refuses both Carmen's and Vivian's sexual offers. Mona Mars or Silver-Wig appeals to him, but the novel ends with him cut off from her. After leaving the Sternwood mansion where he reveals what he knows about the case to Vivian and after she tells him where her husband Rusty Regan's body lies, Marlowe says, "On the way downtown I stopped at a bar and had a couple of double Scotches. They didn't do me any good. All they did was make me think of Silver-Wig, and I never saw her again" (231). Coupled with his aloneness, however, is the memory of his twenty-five dollars a day speech to Vivian in which he tells her how much he does for so little reward.

Early in the hard-boiled detective novel, Hammett introduces the theme of conflict between the police and the private investigator. In *The Maltese Falcon*, his second novel, Hammett shows Spade arguing with Lt. Dundy and Detective Sgt. Tom Polhaus when they come to his apartment to question him about Archer's death. Spade resents their intrusive manner, and after Polhaus acts as the go-between for Lt. Dundy and Spade, they leave. Daly's Race Williams and Hammett's Continental Op, especially the latter, have essentially stable relationships with the police, but with Spade, Hammett couples conflict with the authorities and maintaining some type of communication with them. Brett Halliday's Michael Shayne continues this pattern through the conflict between him and Miami Beach Detective Bureau Chief Peter Painter and his friendship with Miami Detective Chief Will Gentry. Halliday inserts this into the first novel, *Dividend on Death*, when Painter comes to question him about the murder of Phyllis Brighton's mother. Gentry has to intercede to keep them from coming to blows. As mentioned in Chapter 5, this conflict becomes too stylized, but Halliday uses it in the second novel, *The Private Practice of Michael Shayne*, and subsequent works. In Mickey Spillane's Mike Hammer series, Hammer and Captain Pat Chambers' friendship is a staple. In Thomas B. Dewey's Mac series, Mac says to Cynthia Warfield in *Draw the Curtain Close* that Chicago police Lt. Donovan is like a father to him (40). Although Prather's Shell Scott's friendship with Cap. Phil Samson is important to him in *Case of the Vanishing Beauty* and later novels, Ross Macdonald's Lew Archer in *The Moving Target* establishes a more business-like approach to the police. In contrast, William Campbell Gault's Brock Callahan brings back Spade's and Shayne's confrontational encounters with the police. As Callahan tells Lt. Dave Trask in *Ring Around Rosa*, no matter how he has cooperated with the police they have treated him with hostility. And, he believes Trask is too small-minded to worry about.

If one asks why the Transitional Period reveals a return in some series to the partner tradition of Poe and Conan Doyle, the answer probably lies in the existence in the Early Period of the friendship between policeman and detective. Certain qualities in this latter group help define detective partnerships in general. First, both policeman and private detective have a degree of trust in one another and take risks together. When Chief Will Gentry comes to Michael Shayne's apartment in *Dividend on Death* to act as a go-between for Shayne and Chief Peter Painter, he vouches for Shayne. Painter is looking for Phyllis Brighton; he suspects her of killing her mother. However Shayne, while she is in fact in Shayne's bedroom, implies that she is not there. While Gentry suspects otherwise, he persuades Painter to accept

Shayne's statement. Gentry has gone out on a limb, but he believes Shayne must have a good reason for concealing her presence. Of course, the murder took place in Miami Beach so, technically, it is not Gentry's case, nor is their discussion in Shayne's apartment in Painter's jurisdiction. This example is symbolic of the trust-risk paradigm in the Early Period. Dewey's Mac and Chicago police Lt. Donovan, beginning, as noted above, in *Draw the Curtain Close* and continuing in *Every Bet's a Sure Thing*, exhibit the same kind of friendship. In fact, Mac conceals Cynthia Warfield in his office-apartment in *Draw the Curtain Close* soon after the police discover her murdered husband's body. Knowing that Mac was working for Warfield, Lt. Donovan comes to question him about the case. When Mac sees him outside his office-apartment, he takes him to a coffee shop across the street rather than ask him to come upstairs. Lt. Donovan had previously knocked on Mac's door and smelled coffee brewing inside but gotten no answer. When he tells Mac of this later, he says that he knew Mac had a legitimate reason for what he was doing. In *Every Bet's a Sure Thing*, Lt. Donovan, in a California setting and far removed from his area of authority, justifies Mac's opinion of him by taking equal risks. In a final confrontation with some of their adversaries, one of them shoots and seriously wounds Donovan. Another defining quality is that they share mutual interests. One of the most prominent is a visceral dislike of criminals, especially murderers. Spillane's Hammer and Captain Chambers also evidence real hatred for them, but Chambers, in accepting his legal responsibilities, shows more restraint than the often-mercurial Hammer. Dewey's Mac and Lt. Donovan served as policemen together. Donovan was Mac's mentor on the Chicago force. Ross Macdonald's Lew Archer in *The Drowning Pool* shares a desire to see justice done with Lt. Ralph Knudson of the Nopal police when they agree that the best solution to Olivia Slocum's murder is to let the sixteen-year old Cathy Slocum, her grandmother's killer, go to Chicago with her father Knudson, and not to reveal her act to anyone else.

A final quality that the private eye and policeman share as friends is a general willingness to work together, possessing an understanding of one another's motivations. As frequently happens, hostility exists between the private detective and some policemen. In Gault's *Ring Around Rosa*, Cap. Apoyan's more friendly manner counterbalances the often hostile attitudes of Lt. Trask, Sgt. Pascal, and Officer Caroline, the latter three, unfortunately for Callahan, having more contact with him than Cap. Apoyan. When it is in his interest, Chief Peter Painter is even willing to cooperate with Shayne, all the while threatening dire consequences if he makes him look more of a fool than he already appears. This happens both in *Dividend on Death* and *The Private Practice of Michael Shayne*. In the latter novel, Painter understands how much he will benefit if he agrees to go along with Shayne's tricky plan to expose Elliot Thomas as Harry Grange's real murderer. However, Painter quickly reverts to his earlier suspicious manner toward Shayne. Chief Will Gentry, understanding the different responsibilities and pressures that Shayne has, allows his friend to pursue his activities and approves of them when Shayne brings them in concert with the law. This combination of cooperation and mutual understanding rests on the first quality mentioned above of trusting one another. As events play out in Spillane's Mike Hammer series, Cap. Pat Chambers' greater hazard in trusting Hammer usually turns out well. Hammer's action, unknown to Chambers, of letting Berin burn to death at the end of *My Gun Is Quick* contrasts with his more defensible killings in *I, the Jury* and *One Lonely Night*. Lt. Donovan, on leave in California in Dewey's *Every Bet's a Sure Thing*, virtually becomes a private investigator as he moves in with Mac and works with him to rescue Roger and Bonnie, the two young children of the dead Harriet Mitchell. The police friendships that Halliday's, Spillane's, and Dewey's detectives have clearly presage the return of the partnership theme in the Transitional Period. Sharing the above qualities in varying degrees, John D. MacDonald's Travis McGee and Meyer; Robert B. Parker's Spenser, Hawk, Sgt. Belson, and Lt. Quirk; Bill Pronzini's Nameless and Lt. Eberhardt; and Stephen Dobyns' Charlie Bradshaw and Victor Plotz build on these early detectives' experiences and help return the genre to the partnership theme first introduced by Poe and Conan Doyle and even employed in Dickens' *Bleak House* in the active cooperation between Inspector Bucket and Esther Summerson.

Money is frequently a mystery in the hard-boiled detective novel. At the end of *The Big Sleep*, Marlowe tells Vivian how much money he could have made from his work, but he only gets $500 from Gen. Sternwood to deal with Arthur Gwynn Geiger's blackmail attempt. The general has offered him $1000 to find Rusty Regan, and Vivian will give him $15,000 not to reveal that Carmen shot Rusty. The honorable Marlowe counters the image of the corrupt private investigator who peeps through keyholes, an image in the genre beloved by policemen and some clients. For example, when Brock Callahan makes himself a drink in Juan Mira's house at the end of *Ring Around Rosa*, one of the policemen digging for Rosa Carmona's body in the backyard comes and remarks, "'You cheap peeper, drinking a citizen's booze'" (190). The partial separation of money and work generally allays any suspicion that only money, or rum and coke as in Callahan's situation, would drive the investigator. Authors set up situations that deal with work in ways that shift it into other planes, connecting the detectives' motivations to fundamental needs and desires. David Geherin says of Race Williams, "Unlike Holmes and his descendants who were amateur sleuths drawn to a case by the intellectual challenge it offered, Williams is a professional who makes his living by chasing criminals, and he demands to be well paid for his efforts" (*American Private Eye* 10). However, his emotional response to Davidson and Milly in *Snarl* counters his pecuniary motives. In *I, the Jury*, Mike Hammer vows to avenge the death of his friend Jack Williams. A danger, of course, is that by lifting the detective out of the every-day world of work for pay he loses a certain sense of professionalism, of someone hired to do a special task because he possesses special skills.

Among the early detectives, the Continental Op exhibits the most structured professional approach to his work. Partly this occurs because he seems to have no personal life. No wife, children, lovers, or friends distract him from his investigations. In Hammett's *The Dain Curse*, Owen Fitzstephan and the Op were on friendly terms in New York five years before the novel's commencement. Thus, it is a past experience, not a present one. Hammett organizes the Op's activities in *Red Harvest* so that he begins with an assignment through the Continental Detective Agency. It is true that Marlowe and Ross Macdonald's Lew Archer are hired before they start a case, but they assign themselves rather than being assigned. While it might seem ironical, the Op goes where he is told, but once there, he proceeds quite autonomously. And, he goes there alone. Only when things get truly out of hand does help arrive, and for the Op, things must go seriously awry before he cannot handle the situation. A comparison with the Dime Novel Western gunfighter is clearly relevant. Gangs, by definition have more than one member, but gunfighters act by themselves. The films *Shane* (1953), based on Jack Shaeffer's novel of the same name starring Alan Ladd, and *A Fistful of Dollars* (1964) starring Clint Eastwood parallel the role of the hard-boiled detective. Like them, the Continental Op takes on odds that threaten his survival. And like them, money is not an issue. However, this tends to subvert his professional stance as a man hired to work for pay.

Ross Macdonald's Lew Archer in *The Moving Target* and *The Way Some People Die* (1951) dramatizes this mixture of motives. Will he remain the professional earning his pay or the man controlled by his emotions and the need to do what he thinks is right? At the start of both novels, he states his rates and tries, in the latter novel, to get his client Mrs. Samuel Lawrence to let the police find her daughter. At some point, his involvement with people becomes more personal than professional. In *The Moving Target*, notwithstanding Elaine Sampson's assertion that money is power (194), Archer decides to give the money he recovers to Miranda Sampson, Elaine's stepdaughter. His compassion for her predicament, i.e., her husband Albert Graves is revealed as her father's murderer, and her youth move him toward actions not foreseen at the start. Similarly, Archer agrees to search for Galley Lawrence, Mrs. Samuel Lawrence's daughter in *The Way Some People*

Die, but after meeting Galley he also determines that he will help her. This is not identical with the job he originally undertook. He responds to her beauty and youthfulness. In addition, he believes, incorrectly, that like Miranda Sampson her husband Joe Tarantino has used and abandoned her. In essence, Archer, the seemingly remote detective, reacts to Miranda's and Galley's inexperience with a desire to rescue them. In this, his reasons resemble Marlowe's motivation in *The Big Sleep* and *Farewell, My Lovely*, though neither Carmen and Vivian Sternwood in the former novel nor Moose Malloy and Velma in the latter could be described as inexperienced. But, they do need help.

Brett Halliday's Michael Shayne appears to counter this shift from professional to more prosaic human concerns. He sometimes gives the impression that he only does his work for money, saying, in effect, what's in it for me? After accepting what appears to be a string of genuine pearls from Phyllis Brighton in *Dividend on Death* as payment to prevent her from killing her mother (13–14) and a $200 retainer from Dr. Joel Pedique, her physician, to do the same thing (18), Shayne adds, "'Now, if the old lady [Mrs. Brighton] would come around and hire me as her bodyguard, the setup would be perfect'" (18). Yet, his bemused responses to the young, beautiful, and wealthy Phyllis shift him from cynicism to attraction. He resents having his relatively stable life invaded by people who offer him nothing more than financial reasons to take a case. Phyllis, after telling Shayne she is thinking about killing her mother (7), adds that she is going crazy, "'I mean really crazy. Oh, I know I am. I can feel it. It gets worse every day'" (8). Shayne responds, "'Haven't you come to the wrong place? Sounds to me as though you need an alienist instead of a detective'" (8). Halliday states: "Mike Shayne didn't touch a case unless it interested him. Or unless he was dead broke. This case — if it was a case and not a case history — interested him. There was, the feel of beneath-the-surface stuff that set his nerves tingling in a way that hadn't happened to him for a long time" (13).

At the end of the case, Shayne returns Phyllis's pearls, but after again refusing to make love to her (220), he takes a "'slight fee,'" a kiss (221). He then sends "her away with a little push, closing the door behind her" (221). However, in the last paragraph he stands looking at a list of the money he made and thinking of Phyllis (221). This is a hard-boiled detective but one who stands balanced between the professional who works for pay and the man who acts on his emotional responses, thus painting a fuller human portrait. At the beginning of the Transitional Period, John D. MacDonald's Travis McGee will give away large sums of money, responding to the human concerns of his clients, their friends, and their families, while also adding to his secret cache aboard the *Busted Flush*.

Work as thought appears from the very beginning of the genre. Given the almost universal first-person narrative, the reader follows the problems as the detective confronts them. Although told in the past tense, the novels give an impression of unfolding in the present. Action and thought blend together in a continuous process that leads one inexorably to the end. However, the pace of action often prevents the detective from leisurely considering the evidence. The force of the moment thus dominates the narratives. Macdonald's Lew Archer in *The Moving Target*, influenced by Chandler's Marlowe, combines the flow of thought and action but with a possibly greater sense of self-examination than Marlowe. Elaine Sampson hires Archer to find her husband Ralph who has gone missing. Faced with a wife who may be crippled; a daughter Miranda in love with her father's pilot, Alan Taggert, who is not in love with her; Albert Graves, the family lawyer that Ralph wants Miranda to marry; and the mystery of Ralph's whereabouts, Archer thinks his way through the complications and dangers but with less need to act than his predecessors. Sherlock Holmes without the intellectual ostentation would be a good way to describe him. Uncovering Graves' perfidy also involves discovering things about himself.

Archer never loses sight of his job, but the experience of examining evidence, talking with those who might be involved, and reacting intellectually and emotionally to what he sees, hears, and learns affects him. The incident in which he first meets Fay Eastabrook in *Moving* is a good example of the sensory mixture that leads to doubts and self-reevaluations. Archer shows that going there and doing that and reacting and feeling those experiences change and shift him, however temporarily. Archer first sees Fay on a Telepictures movie set in Universal City. After watching her finish for the day, he describes her:

> In her dowdy costume — black hat with a widow's veil and plain black coat — her big, handsome body looked awkward and ungainly. It may have been the sun in my eyes or simple romanticism, but I had the feeling that the evil which hung in the studio air like an odorless gas was concentrated in that heavy black figure wandering up the empty fictitious street [30].

He drinks with her in several bars and then drives her home, "It was a lonely drive down the midnight boulevard with her half-conscious body. In the spotted coat it was like a sleeping animal beside me in the seat, a leopard or a wildcat heavy with age" (49). Later in the novel, he encounters Fay, Marcie Finch, and Betty Fraley, the latter two fighting. Betty has recently killed Eddie Lassiter, her brother and Marcie's lover. Archer carries Betty from the house but observes the other women, "Marcie and Fay were watching me from the corner. It seemed to me then that evil was a female quality, a poison that women secreted and transmitted to men like disease" (173). Even though he reacts strongly to the people involved in both

Sampson's kidnapping and Troy's smuggling of illegal immigrants, Archer never loses sight of his main responsibility to find Sampson.

Archer twice observes himself in the mirror in the downstairs bar at the Huntoon Park. Neither is gratifying. He notes that his face "was getting thin and predatory-looking" (43). He becomes even less flattering:

> The wrinkles formed at the corners of my eyes, the wings of my nose; the lips drew back from the teeth, but there was no smile. All I got was a lean famished look like a coyote's sneer. The face had seen too many bars, too many rundown hotels and crummy love nests, too many courtrooms and prisons, post-mortem and police lineups, too many nerve ends showing like tortured worms. If I found the face on a stranger, I wouldn't trust it [*Moving* 44].

However, he has an aversion to Betty Fraley's touching him as he carries her to his car. He also reacts negatively to Albert Graves when he discovers he killed Ralph Sampson. Archer's moral disgust with those who use and kill people resembles Marlowe's at the end of *The Big Sleep* when he tells himself, "Me, I was part of the nastiness now" (230). He has agreed that Vivian should take Carmen away and that if she does he will keep quiet about it. Neither Archer nor Marlowe is an armchair detective, and each one usually fills in details, follows up suppositions, makes mistakes, and corrects them as the cases unfold. There is a certain unerringness about their investigations that is inevitably a result of the literary form.

As the above "mirror" images of Archer show, experience prepares the detective to think through a case and follow leads. All the while, no matter the difficulties, hypotheses are tried and rejected. Archer's inductive approach is the only one compatible with human complexity. Readiness to think and act and the ability to understand people lead him to conclusions. Early in *Dividend on Death*, Halliday describes Shayne alone in his apartment, "The look of being withdrawn from what he was doing began to come over his face once again. It meant that Michael Shayne was beginning to add up the score" (35). Similar to Conan Doyle's Sherlock Holmes and Rex Stout's Nero Wolfe, Shayne's face reflects the inwardness required for thinking, for working through problems, and, at the very least, for realizing where one might have gone wrong and what other paths might be helpful in reaching a solution. When Archer is first hired in *The Moving Target*, he does not know what has happened other than that Sampson is missing. Eventually, the kidnapping plot emerges and $100,000 are demanded for Sampson's return. However, the illegal immigrant operation comes to light, and Archer learns that most of those involved work together on both cases. Eddie Lassiter and Betty Fraley kidnap Sampson with Alan Taggert's help as a sideline activity that leads to the men's deaths and Troy's anger at their independent actions that threaten and finally end the smuggling. Archer must keep his balance mentally and emotionally, especially with his attraction to the beautiful but too young Miranda Sampson. This precarious movement to hold on to his professional control is the essence of his thinking process and lends clarity to him in the midst of confusion. Although it might be too simple an allusion, he contends with the Scylla and Charybdis, the greed and sexual passion of human desire. Simple or not, the violence of those two monsters makes up for the two-part division of their forces and emphasizes that with which Archer struggles and through which he thinks his way.

The hard-boiled detective is his work. He expects to work; he is ready to work. His disillusion is not with going to the job every day but rather with the people with whom he must deal. He has had other lives and now has this one. Being up against life is both hard for him and the condition of his existence. He combines Hammett's practical image of him in his "From the Memoirs of a Private Detective" and Chandler's more dramatic one in "The Simple Art of Murder." Both images set the stage for the work he does and the work that other detectives will do.

7

Sexuality and Discovery

The early hard-boiled private detectives are aware of sexual overtones and undertones but are not always sexually active. Few have the Victorian image of women that Carroll John Daly's Race Williams demonstrates in *The Snarl of the Beast*, but Dashiell Hammett's Continental Op is curiously neutral toward women in *Red Harvest* while his Sam Spade sleeps with Brigid O'Shaughnessy in *The Maltese Falcon* because she attracts him even though he knows she is dangerous. Raymond Chandler's Philip Marlowe has a conflicted relation to overt sexuality in *The Big Sleep*. Richard S. Prather's Shell Scott, starting with *Case of the Vanishing Beauty*, is a playboy and minimizes through his many indulgences any sense of sexuality's value. Brett Halliday's Michael Shayne, though he marries, similarly pursues women beginning in *Dividend on Death* but without the exaggerations that fill Scott's portrait. Given his aura of violence, Mickey Spillane's Mike Hammer is, paradoxically, the principal early figure who mixes romance and sex, especially in *I, the Jury*. Finally, Ross Macdonald's Lew Archer, beginning with *The Moving Target*, depicts someone who stands aside from those he investigates, observing their various idiosyncrasies, sexual and otherwise, with little apparent inclination to participate. In effect, the portrait of the early hard-boiled detective reveals a contrast between the observer and the participant, between those whose investigative focus largely displaces sexual desire and those who indulge their lust or passion while solving their cases.

It may make little sense to ask of the origins of the affective life in the hard-boiled detective novel, but it is a temptation. With characters set in such extreme positions relative to sexuality as the above detectives, one is curious about their personal experiences even while knowing that they are bound up with literary ideas and conventions. If ever any characters sprang straight from the darkness into full adulthood, these men are the ones. They appear with fixed attitudes toward women and little or no intervening explanations regarding the sources for them. Hinted pasts suggesting clear presents indicate brief outlines within which they act. In *The Snarl of the Beast* and *The Hidden Hand*, Daly's Race Williams has what might be termed a displaced sexuality, one that circumstances have focused on the protection of young innocence. Whether it is Millie in *The Snarl of the Beast* or the even younger Betty, the General's daughter in *Murder from the East* (1935) or Alda Draymount, the senator's daughter from the same novel, Williams has targets of hate that command his immediate time and attention in order to provide that protection. Ralph Dezzeia and Mark Yarrow, respectively, represent extremities of hate and malice that brook no hesitation on the detectives' part in repelling them. In contrast, only a retrospective analysis of the Continental Op in *Red Harvest* reveals his varied passionate, if nonsexual, involvements. While his lust for killing at the end might be more than an alternative for sexual passion, the ambiguous death of Dina Brand, possibly at his hands, mixes one of the few emotional involvements he faces with a general violence that leaves echoes of each in the other. William F. Nolan remarks: "Although he drinks with the town's brassy playgirl, Dinah Brand, he does not make love to her; such entanglements leave a detective open to attack, and the Op wants no flaws in his armor" (76–77). Not of a prepossessing appearance, the Op has a massiveness hard to move but dangerous when in motion. It is this inner stasis that circumstances force into action and require him to hide from the Old Man in Ogden, Utah, as the massacre finishes in Personville. The killings are no surprise given the almost total corruption in every part of that society, from the official to the unofficial, but what does surprise even the Continental Op is his inability to control his responses. In Ogden, he seems to shake himself from a dream of indulged violence.

If Hammett's Sam Spade is a refreshing change with his almost "normal" expressions of sexual desire, Chandler's Philip Marlowe introduces a much darker source for sexual passion. Chandler leaves it undetermined to what extent the Sternwood sisters in *The Big Sleep* respond to something in Marlowe or the degree to which he reacts to something in them. The novel's ending equates Carmen's murderous reactions to Rusty Regan and Marlowe. Both men refuse her favors, and she shoots the former and intends to kill the latter as well. However, the novel does not explain her reaction to Regan in the same detail as it does her reaction to Marlowe. Marlowe disturbs her in more profound ways with his cold, but passionate nature. Something goes on beneath the surface of Marlowe that Chandler hardly bothers to hint at in Regan. Peter Wolfe states:

Despite his shaky self-image, Marlowe feels morally superior to almost everyone he meets. His sexual morals are higher; he does his job more honestly; he can also detect crime more quickly. Yet all this brings him little peace. He's forever showing off—his toughness, his piquant language and his ability to resist both bent money and beautiful women [*Something* 75–76].

Regan is Carmen's brother-in-law, and her apparent rage at his refusal to sleep with her is in inverse proportion to the effort needed to approach him. For Marlowe, Carmen reveals herself naked in his bed, expecting this to be a sufficient cause for his seduction. There is a disjoint between her desires and that of others, and she apparently only realizes this disjoint when someone rejects her, thus producing a violent reaction. Her sister Vivian, ostensibly protecting Carmen, ends up offering herself to Marlowe with the same expectations of success. Marlowe says no to her as well, and part of the rejections of both sisters lies in Marlowe's dual responses to General Sternwood. Marlowe both protects and condemns him. He protects him from the knowledge of his daughters' corrupt actions and morally condemns him for allowing them to act in the ways they do. Marlowe is thus conflicted, and desire for either woman is neutralized by their behavior and by who they are. Chandler's complex psychological portrait of Marlowe may have, as Wolfe argues, some of its source in the author's own relationship to women (*Something* 45, 49, 51), but Chandler more than adequately dramatizes Marlowe's emotional life and gives credence to its details.

Sam Spade's somewhat cooler portrait, as compared to Marlowe's, regarding his own relationship with women, has some facets illuminate his practical renunciation of Brigid at the end of *The Maltese Falcon* and her delivery to the police. First, Spade has an ongoing affair with Iva Archer, his partner's wife. In an act initially unknown to Spade, Brigid kills Miles in the first chapter, and Hammett presents Spade as desiring to put some emotional distance between himself and Iva. But what draws Spade to her and to Brigid? Danger and desire appear to influence him equally. Committing adultery with a partner's wife, especially a partner who also carries a gun, is a risky business. And, Hammett describes Iva as an unstable person attempting to hold on to Spade before and after Miles' death. At first, Brigid's danger is not apparent, but she does attract Spade and intends through her sexual appeal to use him as she does others. David Lehman observes:

The Maltese Falcon's Brigid O'Shaughnessy, in John Huston's film as in Dashiell Hammett's book, remains the foremost example of the type: the seductress whose fatal embrace tempts as it threatens the tough-guy sleuth. An acquired cynicism saves Sam Spade from succumbing to her romantic lure, which is that of Eros enhanced by Thanatos—and to which he is profoundly drawn [35].

Desire leads Spade to sleep with her before he realizes that she is willing to murder to obtain the Maltese Falcon. However, Spade maintains the ability to draw back from her once he satisfies his desire. Brigid cannot lead Spade up the alley as she literally does Archer. The latter's desire and her coldness produce his death. Spade thus has a fundamental control over his sexual instincts that allow him not only to draw back but also matter-of-factly renounce her, somewhat ironically, for killing his partner whom he did not particularly like and whom he betrayed with Iva.

Mickey Spillane's Mike Hammer and Ross Macdonald's Lew Archer present diametrically opposed views regarding the role of sexuality in their lives. One way to understand Hammer's passionate nature is to contrast his reaction to the murder of his friend Jack Williams in *I, the Jury* with Spade's reaction to Miles' death. The irony is that a woman killed Williams. That woman is Hammer's fiancé, someone he has refrained from making love to before their marriage because he wants everything to be perfect. As Max Allan Collins and James L. Traylor state: "Charlotte continues to give Hammer her moral support, and attempts, somewhat more subtly than Mary Bellemy, his seduction; but he is in love with Charlotte, and his code precludes his having casual premarital sex with a woman he loves" (47). Uncovering Dr. Charlotte Manning as Williams' murderer removes any illusion that Hammer would necessarily intuit her evil and could not then love her any more than he realizes that Juno Reeves in *Vengeance Is Mine* (1950) is really a man. His passion for Charlotte turns to rage, and he executes her as he intended. In another contrast to Hammer, Lew Archer's passion remains in the past. Or, one might say, it has been sublimated into finding solutions for other people's problems. These solutions, however, are to human tragedies, and Archer is relentless in discovering the guilty party. In *The Moving Target*, that person is Albert Graves, a lawyer and old acquaintance, but past connections do not deter Archer. As discussed in Chapter 6, Archer observes Elaine Sampson, the presumed invalid wife of the missing Ralph Sampson, her stepdaughter Miranda Sampson, and Ralph's pilot Alan Taggert. Graves is attracted to Miranda and Miranda to Alan. With the bitter Elaine and the missing and reportedly unbalanced Ralph, Archer has to deal with conflicting desires that eventually lead to murder. Appearances to the contrary, Miranda turns out to be the only sane one in the twisted relationships. Miranda is in love with Alan who has kidnapped her father. She decides to marry Albert who ends up killing Alan and her father. Miranda says to Archer at the end of the novel: "'Do you know what I wish at this moment?' she said. 'I wish I had no money and no sex. They're both more trouble than they're worth to me'" (*Moving Target* 197).

Elaine Sampson lies in her bed, seemingly removed from the immediate resolution of the novel. Miranda comes close to collapsing, and when Archer tells her to come with him, meaning to the district attorney, she interprets it as a romantic invitation. Archer remarks, "'Don't try to shift your weight to me, Miranda. You're a lovely girl, and I like you very much, but you're not my baby'" (*Moving* 198). Archer comforts her almost neutrally but walks away from her and the money she inherits.

Surprisingly, the females in the early hard-boiled detective novel present more typical patterns than the detectives. Of course, there are no hard-boiled female detectives in the early period if one discounts Velda, Hammer's secretary, who has a license and a gun. Discounting her is never wise:

> When it came to quick action she could whip off a shoe and crack a skull before you could bat an eye.
> Not only that, but she had a private op's ticket and on occasions when she went out with me on a case, packed a flat .32 automatic — and she wasn't afraid to use it. In the three years she worked for me I never made a pass at her. Not that I didn't want to, but it would be striking too close to home [*I, the Jury* 13].

Hammett's Brigid O'Shaughnessy sets the type for the early female of the genre in her mixture of sexuality and violence. She demonstrates an ability to "overlook" men in the sense of looking beyond them as people in order to see and follow her path to gain what she wants. Brigid projects a multitude of images, e.g., the siren, the corrupter, the presumed figure of virtue, the woman in need of help, each of which she assumes as needed to trap, deceive, or kill those men impeding her. Beginning with Carmen and Vivian Sternwood in *The Big Sleep* and Velma in *Farewell, My Lovely*, Raymond Chandler also emphasizes the potential deadliness of women. Like Brigid, Carmen is a killer. Mentally unstable and sexually driven, she lacks Brigid's sense of control in any situation though her unpredictability is her chief strength, for her several victims must have wondered before their deaths why she would kill them. Velma continues what becomes a major theme in the hard-boiled detective novel, i.e., a woman's equal ability with man to kill for what she desires. In an effort to conceal her identity, she murders Lindsay Marriott and Moose Malloy, the man who loves and desires her the most. But in reality, neither love nor desire prompts her to action. Partially, she kills to preserve her present life, but more than material possessions or social position motivates her. Velma kills to maintain her will in any situation in which she finds herself. This elemental presence disturbs the environments in which it acts. It has little connection to things, to human ambitions, or desires. It functions, as a primary explanation for the women it inhabits, for why they must do what they do. Heroines throughout myth and literature support this seemingly overbroad generalization.

Clytemnestra, Medea, Antigone, and Dido all arguably have this ultimate pursuit of their wills as a primary focus in their lives. In Virgil's *Aeneid*, Dido even turns away from Aeneas in Hades, stressing the point that no circumstance, either human or divine, will divert her from her purpose.

Dr. Charlotte Manning in *I, the Jury* has elements of two earlier women in the genre, Brigid O'Shaughnessy and Carmen Sternwood, demonstrating the way the hard-boiled detective novel builds on its progenitors. This idea of influence, without a marked anxiety, is important in its authors' generous acknowledgements of their forbears, e.g., Chandler for Hammett, Ross Macdonald and John D. MacDonald for Chandler, and many later male and female writers who allude to the methods, thoughts, and actions of earlier authors and investigators. Charlotte has Brigid's willingness to kill to gain her ends and Carmen's twisted sense of how to live with her fellow human beings. Hammer, who falls in love with Charlotte and wants to marry her, is essential to her portrait. Willing to have sex with the twins, Mary and Esther Bellemy, Hammer sees Charlotte as someone worth waiting for. This complete misunderstanding of her corrupt and violent nature has a possible source in his own unstable, violent tendencies. Mixed with their sexual attraction to one another and the strong sense of sexuality in their natures, the violent denouement in which he shoots the naked Charlotte before she can reach her hidden gun, a point seldom stressed by critics, to shoot him seems inevitable. Charlotte, like her two models, is someone who must be overcome, restrained, or killed. Spade hands Brigid over to the police, Marlowe arranges for Vivian to put Carmen under medical care, and Hammer kills Charlotte. These women represent physical danger and thus demand a physical response commensurate to it. No half measures will do for their type.

Women acting in the early hard-boiled detective novel, mixing sexuality, violence, and will, and the detective interacting with them as observer and/or participant do not comprise the only instances of females and detectives together. Thomas Dewey's Mac in *Draw the Curtain Close*, fundamentally an observer, but an acute one, says no to a relationship with Cynthia Warfield, the lovely heir to her gangster husband. Mac tells her that their worlds are too far apart to make it work. Dewey establishes that Mac is clearly attracted to Cynthia, yet he does not hide his attraction with a Marlovian cynicism. He simply closes the door to a future with Cynthia. Mac's no is not like Shayne's no to Phyllis Brighton in *Dividend on Death* and later novels. She offers herself sexually, and he tells her he is old enough to be her father. She repeats the offer. The difference between Brigid and Carmen and Phyllis is that Phyllis, knowing her physical attractiveness, is not guilty of any violence. If there is a symbol of sexual health in the early hard-boiled detective novel, she and Cynthia Warfield, forced into a marriage with Warfield to keep her father from going to prison, represent it. Ross Macdonald's Lew Archer in *The Way Some People Die* leans more toward an observer than participant in his relationship with Galatea "Galley" Lawrence. Never seriously tempted to have an affair with her, Archer responds to her beauty, independence, and apparent need for help. If not a corrupter, she is something of a siren, knowingly luring men to her. This is a somewhat simplistic description of her self-awareness and her awareness of others, but it partially derives from three descriptions Archer receives before they meet. First, Mrs. Samuel Lawrence hires Archer to locate her daughter. In telling Archer about Galley, she states, "'She's always been so fascinating to men, and she's never realized how evil men can be'" (*Way* 4). A few moments later she adds, "'Men have been after her since high school, like flies to honey'" (*Way* 5). Audrey Graham, a roommate of Galley's after she left home, counteracts this dependent image of Galley: "'When Galley was on a case she was spit-and-polish but in between she liked to break loose a bit, and she was crazy for men —'" (*Way* 8). Finally, a Mr. Raisch, the owner-manager of Acacia Court where Galley lived in Pacific Point, describes her, "'She was full of vim and vigor. I like a girl with personality. I've got a lot of personality myself and when I see somebody else that has it my heart goes out to them'" (*Way* 14). These three descriptions show Galley as being and doing. They revolve around her beauty and sexual attractiveness but do not yet include violence.

Another obvious clue to her personality lies in her first name, Galatea. In *Dictionary of Classical Mythology* (1964), J.E. Zimmerman recounts the story of Pygmalion and Galatea. He says that Pygmalion "A king of Cyprus, and celebrated sculptor [...] developed an aversion for woman and resolved never to marry" (224). The story comes from Ovid's *Metamorphoses*. Pygmalion created a marble statue of a beautiful woman and fell in love with it; Aphrodite answered his prayers to give the statue life. Pygmalion married her and named her Galatea. In Macdonald's novel, Galley Lawrence shares an important quality with Galatea. She exists as others' descriptions of her, e.g., her mother and Audrey Graham. In addition, she tells Archer that she married Joe Tarantine because he "'looked like something good for a little while'" (*Way* 110). Earlier, she says to Archer, "'You're something solid to hold on to, aren't you?'" (*Way* 107) Archer refuses to be her support but drives her to her mother's house (*Way* 112). However, Galley turns out to be a hard woman who murders three men. Archer reflects, "Only the female sex was human in her eyes, and she was its only really important member" (*Way* 173). Galley has isolated herself even from other females and males, from anyone who can define her. The twentieth-century Galatea reverses the original process and moves from the human to the inhuman. The last description of her comes from her mother. She tells Archer, "'My daughter is perfectly innocent, of course'" (*Way* 183). This is the last thing Galley says to him as well.

An additional, and illusive, point, is to ask what are the expectations, hopes, and goals that characters have in the area of sexual relations. What fulfillments, romantic or passionate or both, do they expect? The principal characters provide the main examples in this area, but minor ones are relevant as well. The layers of plot, with the minor characters slightly out of focus, deepen one's understanding of a theme such as sexuality. In *The Big Sleep*, Marlowe locates Eddie Mars' wife Mona, nicknamed Silver-Wig. Eddie Mars holds Carmen Sternwood's debts and disposed of Rusty Regan's body for Vivian after Carmen shot him (229). He is the hard businessman, and his relationship to Mona reveals emotional elements outside the central plot. Possibilities are that their marriage is purely physical, or merely expedient, on his side, that he expects nothing from her as a person. Captain Gregory of the Missing Persons Bureau tells Marlowe, "'Eddie Mars and his wife didn't live together, but they were friendly, Eddie says'" (122). Gregory also states, "'Jealousy is a bad motive for his type. Top-flight racketeers have business brains. They learn to do things that are good policy and let their personal feelings take care of themselves'" (124). However, to Marlowe, Mona denies going away with Rusty Regan, Vivian's husband (193), and maintains that she has cut her hair, donned a wig, and hid out because she "'loves [Eddie]'" (194).

Harvey Jones, a petty criminal on the edges of the plot, says to Marlowe that Eddie and Mona broke up because of Mars' criminal activity (165). Before Marlowe shoots Lash Canino, Mars' triggerman, Mona tells Marlowe, "'It's very funny,' she said breathlessly. 'Very funny, because, you see — I still love him. Women —'[.] She began to laugh again" (196). After Marlowe goes to the police and tells them about Canino's death, Mars comes for Mona, nonchalantly picking up the woman he used to divert suspicion from himself concerning Rusty Regan's disappearance: "Then the door opened and Eddie Mars came in and an abrupt smile flashed to his face when he saw Silver-Wig, and he said: 'Hello, sugar,' and she didn't look at him or answer him" (208).

There seems to be no hope or expectation on Mona's part for their marriage. She evinces no interest in him, and his presence stirs little emotional response. Ultimately in *The Big Sleep*, Chandler suggests no sense of sexuality's potential to draw people together and through an intimate contact renew a sense of life. Carmen and Vivian are takers in the physical realm and only givers in order to take. Aside from Vivian's involvement with the dead Rusty, she seems to put as little importance on the sexual act as Carmen. Even with Rusty, her feelings appear atrophied. She tells Marlowe, "'Rusty wasn't a bad fellow. I didn't love him. He was all right, I guess. He just didn't mean anything to me, one way or another, alive or dead, compared with keeping it from Dad'" 229).

It is quite clear that few of the early detectives expect much from romance or sex. Neither tempts the Continental Op from his work, but in *The Maltese Falcon*, Spade's affair with Iva Archer and, briefly, Brigid O'Shaughnessy brings sexuality into the genre while it also minimizes it. Neither the Op nor Spade does anything because of sexual passion or love. Yet, denying the possibility of love limits them. Even Marlowe's occasional sexual activities do not lend greater depth to his character, and his acceptance of an offer of marriage in *Playback* from Linda Loring of *The Long Goodbye* seems a reluctant act. However, Brett Halliday's Michael Shayne introduces the power of sexuality to shift people out of their self control. He tells Phyllis Brighton in *Dividend on Death* that if he kisses her he will not stop there. Her somewhat anemic desire to have sex in order to prove to herself that she is normal contrasts sharply with Shayne's remark. The degree of sexual desire and activity goes up with Spillane's Hammer and Prather's Scott but levels off with Dewey's Mac and Macdonald's Archer. Even with William Campbell Gault's Brock Callahan, romantic love or its reverse is not a strong factor in the detective's life. Sexually charged feeling, if not always romantic love, plays a role in the lives of some of the other characters. In Gault's *Day of the Ram* (1956), David Keene kills Johnny Quirk out of jealousy because Quirk possibly was going to marry Deborah Curtis, the woman Keene wants. Quirk had almost any woman he desired but to him, having them meant little. Juan Mira in Gault's *Ring Around Rosa* also kills his ex-fiancée Rosa Carmona out of jealousy. Velma Kills Moose Malloy in Chandler's *Farewell, My Lovely* to get rid of an annoyance, but he lets her shoot him, apparently out of love for her. If hopes for love do not always fail, neither do they easily find fulfillment. Brock Callahan and Jan Bonnet warily move toward some sense of love. They go with others at times but seem to relapse toward one another.

The above suggests that an anti-romantic attitude dominates the early hard-boiled detective novel. Thomas B. Dewey's *Every Bet's a Sure Thing* shows the reader what this looks like in the lives of his characters. The defeated Harriet Mitchell, married to Mr. Doyle, hopes she can live long enough to help her children. But, a description of Mr. London's two sons, Doyle and Anthony, who eventually kills Harriet on Mr. London's orders by squeezing her to death, does not encourage hope. When Mac begins his observation job in Chicago, his orders are to follow Harriet to Los Angeles without being detected. To keep her children, she has agreed to carry drugs for Doyle. London has her killed because he wants control of his grandchildren. Harriet is the archetypal figure without expectations, fulfillments, or romance. She has a faint hope she can save her children but soon after she talks with Mac, she tells him that she does not expect to live long. This is no bid for sympathy. Mac finds her body huddled in the closet of a Los Angeles hotel, her children gone. Paradoxically, this type of character may be too easy to employ and write about. Male or female, the disappointed, hopeless people in these novels sadly seem too familiar. Opposed to Harriet's melancholy portrait, Marjorie Fellows in Macdonald's *The Way Some People Die* divorced her first husband George because he bored her and then married Herman Speed, a soon-to-be-broken and dispirited criminal who suffers a gunshot wound over drugs and commits suicide by jumping off the Golden Gate Bridge. This leaves Marjorie free to respond to George after he reads about her in the Toledo newspaper, and the last Archer sees of them is the day they plan to remarry. The happy, overweight, but energetic Marjorie and the stooped, weak-looking George live out their romantic dreams with a careful eye for anyone from Toledo who might see them commit some act of impropriety. California, especially Los Angeles, is hell to Marjorie, but Toledo and being like everybody else are bliss. Macdonald's ironic portrait of love flowering at the Oasis Hotel in the desert outside Pacific Point is almost too difficult to face. Yet, this might be the apex of love compared to the nadir represented by Galley Lawrence and two of the men she kills, her husband Joe Tarantine and her lover Keith Dalling, the former an unsuccessful criminal and the latter a failed actor.

Between the extremes of sex for hire and the emotional and physical involvement with another, the early hard-boiled detective novel reveals a failure on the part of most detectives and many of the other characters to develop beyond passion or lust. If the former, it remains fleeting, unsupported by any emotional involvement. The detectives deal with some adults' grown children, but generally sex as procreation has no place in the genre. Only occasionally important, sexuality in these novels rarely deals with the future. A new generation of writers, especially John D. MacDonald and Robert B. Parker, partially solves the dilemma that arises when sexuality and love remain disconnected. However, neither writer creates a clear model that moves very far from the disparity between observer and participant.

8

Friendship:
The Absent Theme

The rhetoric of Carroll John Daly's Race Williams in *The Snarl of the Beast*, the melodramatic title of the first novel in the series, sets the tone for the detective's interpersonal relationships. David Geherin calls the private detective "this solitary brave man" (*American Private Eye* ix). For Williams, he needs little from anyone, his work in confronting the abounding criminal depredations in New York City absorbs him, and his strident assertions of these conditions push at the reader and allow some moments of sentiment to appear. Robert A. Baker and Michael T. Nietzel in *Private Eyes: One Hundred and One Knights: A Survey of American Detective Fiction 1922–1984* state, "Williams was tough, wise and often sentimental like the PIs of today" (2). The reader is, as it were, off balance in examining Williams' character. In a strikingly different manner but with much the same result, Dashiell Hammett's Continental Op in *Red Harvest* functions as an emotionally closed-off professional doing his job. Little of who he is or what he has done in life appears in the novels and short stories in which he goes about his work methodically and sometimes violently but with careful analysis of any facts he acquires. His personal life is nearly all in deep shadow. Two other early detectives expand the genre's limits in the area of friendship. Hammett's Sam Spade in *The Maltese Falcon* and Chandler's Philip Marlowe in *The Big Sleep* provide portraits of detectives with fuller, if still somewhat restricted, emotional lives when compared with Williams and the Continental Op. Spade's ironic, satiric manner and Marlowe's jaded weariness do not encourage friendship, but these characters engage in a broader emotional range with others. Mickey Spillane's Mike Hammer in *I, the Jury* and Ross Macdonald's Lew Archer in *The Moving Target,* among others, round out the idea of friendship as a theme more noticeable by its absence than its inclusion, thus establishing a complicated pattern that goes through many permutations in the history of the hard-boiled detective novel.

In a genre like the hard-boiled detective novel, predecessors play an important role. This occurs from the 1920s to the present through allusion, rhetorical effects, and plot patterns. Detective writers prior to the 1920s also influence the direction of the genre. Edgar Allan Poe's C. Auguste Dupin and Arthur Conan Doyle's Sherlock Holmes, along with Charles Dickens' Inspector Bucket in *Bleak House* and Wilkie Collins' Sergeant Cuff in *The Moonstone* (1868), create many aspects on the idea of friendship or its absence found later in the hard-boiled detective novel. Dupin's friend, as narrator, is present from the beginning of the stories, and Dr. Watson, as narrator of the series, relates how he meets Holmes. These ready-made friends, although Holmes and Watson's relationship evolves over time and reveals added depth, create assumptions regarding sharing and intimacy. Poe's few detective stories do not afford space to move beyond the relatively static nature of Dupin and his friend's relationship. However, the easy way the men relate and their common pursuits suggest a past adjustment successfully achieved. They appear to fulfill mutually felt needs. Each one answers unspoken questions: With whom can I live? With whom can I find a responsive temperament, intellectually, artistically, and socially? In contrast, Holmes and Watson present nearly direct opposites but nonetheless cohabit successfully in Baker Street until Dr. Watson's marriage. Their different personalities create responses in one another that hold them in a close bond even after Dr. Watson leaves Baker Street.

Dickens' Inspector Bucket and Collins' Sgt. Cuff are official detectives, appearing not long after the formation of the detective branch by Sir Robert Peel in London in 1842, but operate somewhat independently. Bucket, a clear predecessor to the Continental Op in his dogged, never-ending pursuit of wrongdoers, also, like the Op, has contacts and acquaintances but no real friends. He is married, but that has little restraint or effect on his work habits. Bucket admires Esther Summerson and John Jarndyce, her guardian, but his secretive habits and sense of moving on preempt any possibility of a private life and the diversion of friendship. He resembles Holmes in his manner of suggesting momentous business in many places and in knowing many people who help in his work, but one sees no time in suspension, no leisurely waiting, and no mundane moments like those that Holmes and Watson occasionally share. Like Inspector Bucket, Sgt. Cuff appears in his novel as an important but less than major figure. While Bucket gives the impression of moving among near equals, in power if not class,

Sgt. Cuff functions more as the state servant called in to do his job. Only his passion for roses raises him above the ranks of a police functionary. In contrast, Bucket works for Tulkinghorn and then Sir Leicester Dedlock, accepting the latter's generous fee, in addition to his official salary. Cuff investigates the theft of the moonstone and helps to solve the crime but lacks sufficient development to raise even the question of friendship's absence from his life.

The cohabitation of the detectives and their respective narrators in Poe and Conan Doyle referred to above deserves further attention. First, males rarely share apartments or houses with another male in the hard-boiled detective genre. Females might live near people who help or listen to them from time to time. This is the case in the Modern Period with Liza Cody's Anna Lee, Sara Paretsky's V.I. Warshawski, and Sue Grafton's Kinsey Millhone. Sandra Scoppetone's Laura Laurano lives with her partner-lover Kip Adams, but the latter dislikes her partner's occupation and its low pay. Second, in Poe and Conan Doyle, the detectives' narrators are their *ad hoc* partners in crime detection. The detectives ask them to come along and observe the investigations. Naturally, this allows the friend-narrator to be there from the beginning of a case. The narrators marvel at their friends' abilities to unravel seemingly unsolvable crimes. Having heard and seen all that the detectives have heard and seen underscores their surprise when informed of the solution. Of course, an audience is not unimportant to the detectives. And, their friendly audiences mitigate their former isolation. Taking away Poe's unnamed narrator and Conan Doyle's Dr. Watson leaves one with the same aloneness found in the early hard-boiled private detectives. Not a single one shares a home or apartment with a male friend or female lover. Several ultimately marry, e.g. Chandler's Philip Marlowe, Halliday's Michael Shayne, and Gault's Brock Callahan, but their initial conditions are possibly more like Dupin's and Holmes's are before the latter seek someone to share their home or apartment. Third, Dupin and Holmes discover that they share philosophical and/or scientific interests with their new roommates. Holmes' interest in chemistry and Watson's medical profession overlap while Dupin and his narrator-friend share a wider range of interests and a mutual curiosity about life. Finally, both sets of friends have a relish for danger, Doyle in his profession as a consulting detective and Dr. Watson as an army medical doctor in India and Afghanistan and later with Holmes. Dupin's acts to regain the letter from the powerful Minister D__ in "The Purloined Letter" and his and the narrator's nighttime ramblings through the dark streets of Paris show their willingness to take risks. These cohabiting friendships are almost never duplicated in the hard-boiled detective novel and especially highlight the near absence of friendship in the Early Period.

A defining aspect of the role of friendship in the hard-boiled detective novel is the substitution of other things for friendship. Writing of Chandler's Philip Marlowe, Peter Wolfe observes, "Marlowe's problem comes with his knowledge that, although he knows he needs other people, he also understands the difficulty he will have razing the wall he has built around himself" (*Something* 197). It might take a delicate bit of analysis to show that this substitution is more than compensation, that it has a force and a reason justifying it that rejects any scheme of values that gives priority of place to friendship. This seeming filling up of friendship's empty space with acquaintances rather than friends is one possible substitution. Marlowe's feelings for General Sternwood in *The Big Sleep* or Moose Malloy in *Farewell, My Lovely* are examples of brief acquaintanceships laced with feeling. Marlowe feels sorry for the General, given the nature of his two daughters, Carmen and Vivian. Adding to his interest in the General, even though he sees him as morally akin to the young women, is the General's liking for the absent but dead Rusty Regan. Marlowe realizes that the General hires him to find Regan because he cares for him. Marlowe responds to the General's feeling with feeling of his own. Marlowe is usually reactive, not proactive, when it comes to evincing an interest in someone. In *Farewell, My Lovely*, Malloy literally grabs him by the neck as Marlowe goes into Florian's. Malloy's action generates a response, initially no more than curiosity, which grows into a reluctant admiration on the part of Anne Riordan, Marlowe's temporary girlfriend, and even Marlowe that Malloy would let his Velma shoot him rather than protect himself. When Malloy steps from Marlowe's dressing room where he hides before Velma enters the apartment, he says, "'Hiya, babe. Long time no see.'" She points the gun she is holding on Marlowe at Malloy and states, "'Get away from me, you son of a bitch [...].'" Malloy drops his gun to his side, realizing, moments before "She [shoots] him five times in the stomach" (282), that she turned him in to the police eight years ago. Carmen, in *The Big Sleep*, represents the emotional danger towards which Marlowe drifts. She frantically searches for ways to feel while Marlowe waits for some outside force to energize him although he believes that nothing can fill his empty heart. Unlike Race Williams' many acquaintances and rivalries, criminal and otherwise, Marlowe's isolation as the principal figure of alienation in the hard-boiled detective novel's urban world puts him at greater emotional risk.

In *The Snarl of the Beast*, Race Williams involves himself emotionally with others as an aspect of the case. He cares or worries about Daniel Davidson and Millie, Davidson's girlfriend, and struggles with Raphael Dezzeia, Davidson's stepfather, as Dezzeia attempts to kill the young man. Since his interest in Millie and Davidson arises from the case, they easily dissolve into its resolution. This is Williams' defining relationship with others; he is passionately remote. In *The Hidden Hand*, a competitor extends Williams' emotional range, but the man does not grow to be a friend. Gregory Ford is as successful as a detective as Williams. Their rivalry dominates their relationship, especially in uncovering the identity of The Hidden Hand. Tina King, one of Williams' female interests, becomes more intellectualized than substantive. Williams has to see her as a certain type, controlled by the criminals with whom she is involved and thus absolved of responsibility for most actions. His susceptibility to women allows involvement but brackets her in such a way that she functions more as the type into which he places her than an individual. Williams apparently needs to maintain his preconceptions about people more than he needs living beings. Even when he embraces Tina at the end of the novel, he thinks of the money he lost by not getting payment the previous morning from Howard Quincy Travers, The Hidden Hand (260). The genre helps channel this categorization of people, with the detective's being the principal type. The concept of friendship, speaking to greater depths than formulas can easily reach, subsides in the early hard-boiled detective novels. Later writers will expand the formula in regard to this theme, a process that Chandler, ironically, will initiate.

Marlowe substitutes alienation for friendship in *The Big Sleep*. However, Marlowe's bitter, ironic attitude to others and to himself stays close, a needed "friend" in his lonely and dangerous world. Ross Macdonald, influenced by Chandler, expresses this idea in *The Drowning Pool*. Lew Archer swims a quarter of a mile out to sea: "I turned on my back and floated, looking up at the sky, nothing around me but cool clear Pacific, nothing in my eyes but long blue space. It was as close as I ever got to cleanliness and freedom, as far as I ever got from all the people" (21).

If the concept of alienation can substitute for friendship, then one needs to explore its paradoxical quality as a value to replace the reliance on others. Like Sam Spade and the Continental Op, Marlowe has harsh experiences to remind him of pertinent areas of human nature that, embodied in his clients and their friends, relatives, and acquaintances, not to mention the police and criminals he encounters, make alienation an almost welcome philosophy. This is an awareness that goes beyond the run-of-the-mill greed and corruption he sees. At the end of *The High Window*, after so much murder, avarice, and betrayal, Marlowe returns to his apartment:

> It was night. I went home and put my old houseclothes on and set the chessmen out and mixed adrink and played over another Capablanca. It went fifty-nine moves. Beautiful cold remorseless chess, almost creepy in its silent implacability.
> When it was done I listened at the open window for a while and smelled the night. Then I carried my glass out to the kitchen and rinsed it and filled it

with ice water and stood at the sink sipping and looking at my face in the mirror.

"You and Capablanca," I said [265].

Open windows reveal much that many want hidden. Louis Vannier fortuitously took a picture of Mrs. Murdock in *The High Window* as she pushed Horace Bright, her first husband, from a window. With this photograph, Vannier blackmailed her until her son Leslie killed him. Mrs. Murdock convinced the easily swayed Merle Davis, her secretary, that she pushed Bright. Marlowe's turn at the end from the window to the mirror in an act of self-reflexivity leaves only the long-dead chess genius Capablanca for a companion. His act of playing out one of Capablanca's games formally connects him to the latter's product, in which Marlowe finds more of himself than of the other man.

Lost friends and regret over their loss do factor into the genre, hovering both from the near and distant past. Of course, Marlowe's disappointment over Terry Lennox's deception in *The Long Goodbye* resurfaces in *Playback* when, appropriately, Marlowe hears from Linda Loring who first appears in the former novel. As mentioned in Chapters 3 and 7, she proposes marriage, and he accepts, more as a last resort than anything else. Wolfe speculates over the subconscious erotic aspects of Marlowe's final rejection of Terry in Mexico. If true, Marlowe may have needed to suppress his feelings in order to hold on to his image of himself. Wolfe states, "Because Marlowe can't cope with the impulses Terry has awakened in him, he denies their existence in favor of bringing moral judgment" (*Something* 207). In contrast, Macdonald is careful to place Albert Graves at a distance from Lew Archer in *The Moving Target*. Early in the novel, Archer tells his client Elaine Sampson that he "'did some work for [Graves] in '40 and '41. I haven't seen him since'" (4). At the end, Humphreys, the district attorney, speaks sympathetically of his friend Graves who has just confessed to killing two men. However, Archer counters each statement that rationalizes Graves' conduct with a hard practicality and a moral judgment that stresses Graves' desire to profit by his actions (198–99). He acknowledges to Miranda Sampson, formerly Graves' fiancée and the daughter of Ralph Sampson, one of the men he killed, that Graves "'was too honest to bluff it through'" (199). Archer holds aloof from others' sorrows but does his job nonetheless.

Some authors use a distancing device, e.g., death or a profession, to separate their detectives from friendship's involvement. As corrupt as *I, the Jury's* Charlotte Manning turns out to be, it says little of Hammer that he detects nothing out of order about her until he works through all possible murderers and she alone fits the facts. Williams' death conveniently frees Hammer from all obligations to him except the need for vengeance. Richard

S. Prather uses the same plot device in *Dance with the Dead* (1960) when Shell Scott's friend Webley Alden is killed a little more than twenty pages into the text (29). Captain Pat Chambers is friendly to Mike Hammer, and circumstances suggest that only a friend would be given the breaks that Chambers gives him, but Chambers' profession presents itself as a barrier to full support of Hammer on various occasions. In *Farewell, My Lovely*, Marlowe calls Red Norgaard "'a very nice guy'" (288) and mentions to Anne Riordan that Norgaard "'has got his job back'" (288). Norgaard is a policeman, and regardless of the possibilities for friendship, private detectives and policemen, existing in a state of tension, are often an unstable mix. In the Early Period, private detectives use and abuse the police who in turn use and abuse them. The line separating them might sometimes be faint but proves difficult to cross into trust. The tension also suggests loss and regret, if not always overtly. However, whatever the distancing device used, the genre convincingly adapts it. Later periods in the hard-boiled detective tradition also demonstrate friendship's appeal and some writers' structural rejection of it.

Detective writers also use other professions as distancing devices. Halliday dramatizes the conflict between Michael Shayne and Larry Kincaid in *The Private Practice of Michael Shayne* by using their past friendship. This is a common technique in the hard-boiled detective genre, one generally so forward focused, to give added depth to the detectives' character. Hammett employs it in *The Dain Curse* by including the past close acquaintance, if not actual friendship, between the Op and Owen Fitzstephan five years before in New York City. This is striking largely because of the paucity of personal details about the Op's former life. In addition, Hammett brings Fitzstephan to San Francisco and into the novel's plot through his central role as the killer. Although the tension might be less between Shayne and Kincaid, it develops in a similar fashion. In the past, Shayne was friends with Kincaid and his wife Helen. But now, Shayne and Kincaid have an acrimonious split. Kincaid wants Shayne to work with him to take evidence by force from an extortionist who is using it to blackmail his client Elliot Thomas (7). Shayne not only refuses to take the case but also tries to convince Kincaid that involving himself in such shady operations will hurt his reputation. He admits that he was once in Kincaid's shoes and took money but now regrets it (12). This dispute over ethics in the legal profession and his own embitters the struggling Kincaid more than it does Shayne. Kincaid makes matters worse by accusing him of wanting to sleep with his wife, in the past and now. Shayne, especially, regrets the loss of Kincaid's friendship. Halliday, ironically, makes the split permanent, first by showing Shayne's intense dislike of Helen Kincaid and the ruinous effect she has had on her husband and second, through Kincaid's murder. Shayne is left with no chance to restore their shattered relationship. In William Campbell Gault's *Day of the Ram*, bookstore owner David Keene murders star Rams quarterback Johnny Quirk from jealousy that Quirk's wealth and his new-found athletic fame will persuade Deborah Curtis to marry him. Their respective professions hover in the background and suggest a fear in Keene, Quirk's high-school friend, that he will never be able to compete with Quirk for Deborah's affections. Clearly, Quirk's sudden football renown pushed Keene to act when he did.

If a theme is important enough to be present through its absence, one might expect to find aspects of the theme in defining some parts of the characters' personalities, especially the private detectives. Of the principal human relationships, friendship's absence especially requires one to take notice, to fill in what is missing, to ask questions why something so basic cannot easily be included in the hard-boiled detective genre. In Western literature, friendship has operated as a sustaining aid to defining character. Achilles and Patroclus, Aeneas and Achates, Roland and Oliver, these friends impress one in their sustained feeling for one another while tragic figures in Aeschylus, Sophocles, and Euripedes present a disquieting aloneness. Archetypal characters reverberate in Western literature and spread into most genres. Homer's Odysseus, struggling along with companions and without them, sustains himself, of course with Athena's help, in all situations. As discussed more extensively in Chapter 3, the hard-boiled detective has antecedents through the centuries in the classical and medieval heroes. One defining aspect of their influence on the genre is the concept of will, discussed in Chapter 7 in relation to women, exerted regardless of obstacles, human or nonhuman. Achilles, the preeminent classical hero, acts for his friend Patroclus when he avenges his death at Hector's hands. But, he also acts for himself, knowing that if he kills Hector he will die. The absoluteness of his will surfaces after Patroclus's death, after friendship no longer is possible. Nothing else brings him and his Myrmidons out of his tent once again to confront the Trojans.

While the presence of will may not signal friendship's absence, either in classical literature or in the hard-boiled detective novel, the latter genre displays numerous examples of this dynamic. Even in *The Aeneid*, Aeneas's desertion of Carthage's Queen Dido and his fight to the death with Turnus in Italy signal exertions of will that displace love and friendship. Aeneas's actions, apparently destined to occur, move from the realm of human influence to that of the divine. Hammett describes Sam Spade as a "blond Satan" (3) in *The Maltese Falcon*. His ironically expressed will at the end of the novel when he turns Brigid O'Shaughnessy over to the police for murdering his partner indicates a modernist sensibility since he cares little for Archer. He says to Brigid, "'When a man's partner is killed he's supposed to do something about it. It doesn't make any difference what you thought of him. He was your partner and you're supposed to do something about it'" (226). This is Spade's first of seven reasons. His last is, "'Seventh, I don't even like the idea of thinking that there might be one chance in a hundred that you'd played me for a sucker'" (227). He reiterates the last idea again before the police arrive, "'I won't play the sap for you'" (228). Marlowe rejects Terry Lennox at the end of *The Long Goodbye* with some of the same hard willfulness but without the irony. The alienated hard-boiled private detective more easily exerts his will when other considerations recede in importance. Effie Perine, Spade's secretary, recoils at what Spade has done regarding Brigid, representing a more "normal" perspective, but Spade does not defend his actions except to say that Brigid killed Miles (*Maltese* 229). It is possible that Effie's reaction expresses an understanding that Spade turns in Brigid as an act of will only, Miles' death functioning as a reason that is no meaningful reason for Spade. Spade, the blond Satan, acts like his namesake, exerting his will for the sake of exerting it.

One would imagine the hard-boiled private detectives to have or have had friends. It would be a normal expectation for, admittedly, a sometimes-abnormal character type. Starting with the "have had" part of the first sentence above, one draws a decided blank. One might say that this derives from generic conditions in creating the hard-boiled detective. Generally, the early detectives have almost no revealed pasts. If not people, literary characters are like people, and so it is proper to assume a past, largely unknown though it may be. For example, stories and films attempt to recount the youth of Sherlock Holmes, though never of Dupin or hard-boiled detectives. The closest instances of this are when scholars suggest parts of the authors' lives underlie portraits of their creations. Raymond Chandler is a case in point. He was a noted Anglophile, and although he does not place Marlowe in Dulwich College, his south London alma mater, some of his mannerisms and ways of looking at the world, influenced by his years in England, appear in Marlowe. Apart from this latter avenue of insight into the characters' early lives, the writers in the Early Period give almost nothing of the childhood or teenage years of their detectives. One generally reads of some earlier work experience in another context or as a hard-boiled private detective. For instance, Gault's Brock Callahan not only played football for the Los Angeles Rams but also for Stanford. His father was a policeman, he was raised in Long Beach, and he served three years in the OSS. This is the extent of what Gault provides of his life before one sees him in his office in Beverly Hills in *Ring Around Rosa* waiting for his first customer. Neither childhood friends appear nor ones from his late youth. The same pattern occurs for Daly's Race Williams, Hammett's Continental Op and Sam Spade, Chandler's Philip Marlowe, Halliday's Michael

Shayne, Spillane's Mike Hammer, Dewey's Mac, Macdonald's Lew Archer, and Prather's Shell Scott. One notices the hole in the detectives' lives, the general lack of having friends as adults. The policemen with whom they have established friendships always have their legal responsibilities looming, and occasionally, as previously suggested, this interferes with their relationships with the detectives. Even Michael Shayne's friend, the reporter Timothy O'Rourke in *The Private Practice of Michael Shayne*, wants a story and will not sit still for being scooped, friend or not. Thus, the early detectives have no friends unconnected to their professions and generally remain unmarried; friendship's ironic absence dominates their personal portraits. The writers in the Transitional Period will gradually expand the detail about and the influences from their detectives' earlier lives and begin to include friends as necessary components.

Given its origins in the classical epic hero, the medieval knight, the American frontiersman, and the Western gunfighter, it is not surprising that friendship does not generally fare well as an important theme in the early hard-boiled detective novel. However, stasis is not long a possibility in life or literature. Change occurs as time unfolds, inevitably providing new conditions. The transitional hard-boiled private detective does not completely lose the sense of aloneness introduced in the Early Period, but from John D. MacDonald's Travis McGee on, new social circumstances and new writers and their characters expand the possibility that the friendless can experience friendship. Without necessarily seeking or expecting them, detectives incorporate others, friends and lovers, into their lives. In these areas, the transitional hard-boiled detective crosses a watershed in the genre. The Modern Period, the locus of the subsequent major changes that open the detectives to an even greater extent to others, will take only half as long to appear.

TRANSITIONAL PERIOD

9

Character in Conflict

A new generation of private detectives opens up rich possibilities for the genre. John D. MacDonald's *The Deep Blue Good-by* introduces Travis McGee, a more laconic, offbeat detective than most of the detectives from the Early Period. McGee is a prototype for the shift in focus of the new private detectives of the 1960s and 1970s. Brett Halliday's Michael Shayne and Richard S. Prather's Shell Scott have some of McGee's satiric mindset but lack his rich, socially focused portrait. In addition to the different tone and social analysis, MacDonald makes women central to McGee's self. They hire him, sleep with him and even love him, and immeasurably enrich his life, educating him and being educated by him. Other detectives during this period follow McGee's example, significantly increasing the number of love relationships in the genre. The almost ruthless expansion into other American cities than New York, San Francisco, Miami, Chicago, and Los Angeles also alerts one to the fundamental character shift coming. Robert B. Parker's Spenser in Boston, John Lutz's Alo Nudger in St. Louis, Michael Z. Lewin's Albert Samson in Indianapolis, and Stephen Dobyns' Charlie Bradshaw in Saratoga Springs vie with the Los Angeles of Arthur Lyons' Jacob Asch and Roger L. Simon's Moses Wine. The San Francisco of Bill Pronzini's Nameless and Marcia Muller's Sharon McCone along with the New York of Michael Collins' Dan Fortune and Lawrence Block's Matthew Scudder also refocus these traditional cities in the genre. Inevitably, new places and new detectives and their personal and social experiences create conflicting images of the detective's role and character and deepen and expand the narrative possibilities.

Generational shifts are a staple of ancient and modern literatures. With the rich possibilities sketched and developed in the Early hard-boiled detective Period, thematic continuances and variations in the next generation multiply, countering any chance that the form will dry up. One image of a generational shift is that posed by a contrast of Race Williams and Mike Hammer with Stephen Dobyns' Charlie Bradshaw. The two former detectives work in New York City and Bradshaw is a policeman in Saratoga Springs, New York, when his series starts in *Saratoga Longshot*. Williams and Hammer begin as private detectives, untroubled in their choice of careers and the direction of their lives. However, as his novel opens, Bradshaw's life, discussed briefly in Chapter 1, is about to change drastically. After his activities in New York where he locates Sam Cheney, the son of Gladys Cheney, a high-school girlfriend, Bradshaw's resignation from his job clears his way to become a private detective, and his wife divorces him. Like many of the transitional figures, Bradshaw goes through a crisis in order to know in which direction he will focus his energies. In addition to these disruptions which catapult him into a new world, Bradshaw stays in Saratoga Springs where his family either attempt to direct his energies or loom as successful, at times unspoken, examples of what one can do with one's life. The early detectives have only minimally examined pasts that ostensibly dominate their presents. MacDonald's McGee is similar to them in the small amount the reader learns of his early life but closer to Bradshaw in that his past hovers over his present. McGee's refusal to tell Lois Atkinson in *The Deep Blue Good-by* what the experiences are that have so deeply marked him clearly illustrates this. McGee has only recently saved her life after Junior Allen's brutalizations. Lois is falling in love with him, and McGee, though later than she, seems to move in that direction, but he never opens himself up to her legitimate questions about his character. At the least, she dies before McGee would have to confront that eventuality. Paradoxically, Race Williams' boasts about who he is and what he has done, a pattern echoed to some extent by Mike Hammer, emphasize the generational change. For, neither Williams nor Hammer, for all their boasts, have extensively explored pasts that strongly intrude into and/or dominate their presents.

Arthur Lyons' Jacob Asch in *The Dead Are Discreet* (1974) and Lawrence Block's Matthew Scudder in *The Sins of the Fathers* (1976) experience difficulties on their jobs which shift them into careers as private detectives although Scudder is not licensed as his series opens. Asch worked as a crime reporter for the *Chronicle* in Los Angeles. He refused to reveal his sources while doing a story on a trial and spent six months in jail. When released, he begins work for lawyer Paul Ellman as an investigator. Ellman is impressed by a series of articles that Asch wrote about one of his cases that resulted in Ellman's client being found not guilty. Scudder's reason for changing jobs is even more dramatic. He served as a New York policeman for nearly sixteen years. One night while drinking in a bar, two kids held it up. Scudder killed one and wounded the other after they killed the bartender. However, these actions did not make him resign from the force. In the shootout, one of his shots hit and killed a seven-year old girl named Estrellita Rivera. He tells his client Cale Hanniford in *The Sins of the Fathers*, "'There was no question of culpability. As a matter of fact, I got a departmental commendation. Then I resigned. I just didn't want to be a cop anymore'" (11). While early detectives do other things before becoming private investigators, many transitional detectives start their series with reference to their change of careers. This gives a sense of newness to what they do even if they have been private detectives for some years. These shifts also signal the possibly unintended, but certain, movement from the Early to the Transitional Period beginning with MacDonald's McGee.

Other detectives also go through significant changes before they begin their careers as private detectives. Two in particular have strange pasts for someone theoretically now responsible, as licensed detectives, for upholding the law. Collins' Dan Fortune was a teenage petty thief who lost an arm while trying to steal cargo from a ship. Older, he returns to Chelsea, the New York neighborhood in which he grew up, to start his career. *Act of Fear* takes place in that area and involves people he knew as a youth. Some detectives in the Early Period work in the same city or county in which they grew up, e.g., Brock Callahan — Los Angeles and Long Beach, but none in such a restricted area as Fortune. He will range wider in later cases, but the first novel identifies him as intimately connected to part of the whole. By handicapping Fortune, Collins establishes both a physical limitation (one arm) and a state of mind (fear of losing or injuring his other arm). He cannot do certain things, and he worries about the danger in what he does. When someone threatens to injure his other arm, he is nearly paralyzed with apprehension. While his example of a generational shift is not so drastic, Roger L. Simon's Moses Wine is a lingering sixties radical as *The Big Fix* opens. No other private eye makes quite the same feckless appearance as does Wine. He states, "I was at home playing solitaire Clue, trying to get a hit on my crusty hash pipe" (2). In addition to mocking his profession, Wine is alone and if not high, at least not unhappy. He is listening to a stereo wearing headphones when Lila Shea, an old girlfriend, knocks on his door bringing him a case. He last saw her in 1967 when they "were making love in the back of a 1952 Chrysler hearse parked across the street from the Oakland Induction Center. Tear gas was seeping through the floorboards and the crack of police truncheons was in our ears" (1).

While Lila hopes to get him to work for the presidential campaign of Democratic Senator Miles Hawthorne, Wine ultimately asserts his professionalism by reminding Lila and other campaign workers, "'But I do this for a living, of course. I'm not a volunteer for Hawthorne'" (12). "'People's Detective'" (12) or not, Simon establishes Wine's position in the developing private detective tradition. He may be offbeat, but he knows how to work and knows how to set limits. This is just a case for him, not a cause.

As part of the wider emotional and intellectual range in the Transitional Period, Joseph Hansen's Dave Brandstetter and Marcia Muller's Sharon McCone introduce the ideas of sexual identity and gender as relevant to the detective's character. First, Brandstetter is gay. Commenting on the quest by hard-boiled detective writers for "a credible individualizing feature," David Geherin states:

> But no one in the history of the genre has had the daring to do what Joseph Hansen has done: make his private eye a homosexual. With skill and subtlety, he has created a unique individual who is both a first-rate investigator and one of the most interesting series characters in the recent history of the genre [*American Private Eye* 177].

One recalls Philip Marlowe's harsh stereotyping of homosexuals in Raymond Chandler's *The Big Sleep*. In contrast, Hansen describes his detective as someone who has a respected reputation as an insurance investigator. He works well with the police, e.g., Cap. Jesus-Maria Campos in *Death Claims* (1973) and Lt. Yoshiba in *Troublemaker* (1975). Second, Brandstetter is someone who is only complete when he is in a love relationship. For most of the early hard-boiled detectives, they seldom find someone to love, to fulfill their lives. Brandstetter's feeling of isolation and aloneness is reminiscent of the images of a Race Williams, a Continental Op, a Philip Marlowe, and a Lew Archer, but his actions in seeking someone to love and risking involvement are profoundly different. Dashiell Hammett's Continental Op in *Red Harvest* also illustrates this difference. The Op manifests himself in his work, coming into clear focus only when he does something or thinks through a problem. Hammett describes almost no self apart from the Op's actions. His absorption of the blood lust dominating "Poisonville" in *Red* Harvest is somewhat of a shock since he previously operated to maximize the violence. Of course, the admission that Brandstetter has a fully developed emotional life does not prevent him from pushing investigations past people's resistance to have their secrets revealed. He is a hard, trained investigator that will not stop merely because someone's feelings are hurt.

With Sharon McCone, Marcia Muller introduces the first major female hard-boiled private detective in *Edwin of the Iron Shoes: A Novel of Suspense*. McCone appears several years before a number of other American and British female detectives. Liza Cody's Anna Lee in 1980, Sara Paretsky's V.I. Warshawski in 1982, Sue Grafton's Kinsey Millhone in 1982, and Gillian

Slovo's Kate Baeier in 1984, along with numerous male writers and detectives, introduce by their numbers, variety, and extensive settings the modern development of the hard-boiled detective novel. In discussing Muller's McCone, Kathleen Gregory Klein states, "McCone runs into the usual array of reactions to the combination of her gender and profession" (*Woman* 207). McCone sets the tone for women hard-boiled detectives by her silent reaction to a brief exchange between her and San Francisco homicide detective Lt. Gregory Marcus. He asks her, "'You're the woman who's been investigating the arsons and vandalisms down here?'" (*Edwin* 2) After saying she is, she thinks: "Marcus hesitated, the corner of his mouth twitching, and I braced myself for one of the variants of the usual remark, along the lines of 'what's-a-nice-girl-like-you-doing-mixed-up-with-an-ugly-business-like-this?'" (*Edwin* 2).

This, of course, is not the first instance of gender's role in detective fiction as a whole, but Muller quickly marks out the woman's path in the genre while including McCone in the range of activities of male detectives. McCone asks Lt. Marcus if she may look around the shop of the victim, Joan Albritton. Once inside, she wanders about, touching "some of Joan's beloved objects" (5), remembering her, sorrowing at her death, but also observing as a good detective should. In the Modern Period, it is sometimes difficult to distinguish female, male, and shared perspectives, but with the opening of different character aspects in the Transitional Period, one expects a complex intermixture that exists side by side with older character types.

Macdonald's introduction of Travis McGee provides another example of the deeper affective life that expands the hard-boiled detective novel and in McGee's interplay with Meyer, his economist friend, adds a real intellectual to the genre. McGee lives on the *Busted Flush* at Bahia Mar in Ft. Lauderdale, Florida. As *The Deep Blue Good-by* begins, McGee is planning to leave Ft. Lauderdale. Almost no hard-boiled detectives change their base of operations though, like McGee, they take cases that involve extensive travel. McGee's planned move introduces a sense of instability about his character that MacDonald carefully and realistically develops. Balanced against moments of emotional crisis, MacDonald shows McGee as a hard-boiled detective (He calls himself a salvage consultant.) strongly in control of his life. In preparation for his character's role as the friend of an intellectual, MacDonald reveals that McGee reads, responds to painting and music, and possesses curiosity about how the world functions. McGee also has the necessary physical attributes to survive his dangerous profession. He played college and some professional football, is a Korean War veteran, and keeps in superlative condition through rigorous exercise. Only Parker's Spenser, an ex-boxer, follows McGee in this strenuous habit. However, it is McGee's openness to the emotional life that sets him apart from most other detectives in the Transitional Period. Others fall in love, but none in love so thoroughly and so often. Spillane's Mike Hammer, of course, shows the way in incorporating the affective life into the hard-boiled detective genre. And like Hammer, McGee remembers his dead lovers, never fully recovering from each successive loss. When real people are strongly stirred, they do not just forget when they lose a loved one. It stays with them, working its way into their lives. MacDonald was intelligent enough to show McGee evolving in this way, living, loving, suffering, and aging with none of his experience ever truly lost.

The greater degree of introspection in the transitional hard-boiled detective versus its lesser amount in the early detectives indicates another direction in which newer writers explore the character type. References to or reports of past events and emotional experiences do not necessarily represent an introspective quality in a character. Many of the early detectives make these kinds of statements. The laconic Sam Spade in Hammett's *The Maltese Falcon* is presented in the third person, and this allows an easier distance than first-person narration. Many novels in the genre are told in the first person, but in the Early Period, possibilities for introspection are seldom used or even expected. More than Sam Spade, the Continental Op in *Red Harvest* and *The Dain Curse* effaces his personality, leaving the reader with an unknown, if strong, presence. The question for Spillane's Mike Hammer is whether or not he stands mute before his own life or whether he stands on his hardness as representative of his inner world. Certainly, he does not often question the direction of his life whether in regard to his feelings, thoughts, or actions. He tells the reader, and Cap. Pat Chambers, what he is going to do to the killer of his friend Jack Williams in Spillane's *I, the Jury*, but these expostulations do not substitute for a private sense of loss; this comes when he remembers those he has loved or for whom he has cared. As Max Allan Collins and James L. Traylor note, "Hammer has a swell of emotion as he sees the dead body of his friend, the one who lost an arm to a Jap soldier in World War II saving Hammer's life" (44–45). No one expects to see a stereotype of the modern, sensitive male, but it is important to note the difference in this respect between the early and transitional detectives. Bill Pronzini's Nameless, especially in *Hoodwink*, inverts the role of the alienated detective who exists in isolation into one who wants to end his isolation and loneliness. The reader learns of Nameless's sorrows and emotional losses while he pursues his career as a hard-boiled private detective.

Chandler's Marlowe and Macdonald's Archer reflect the most extensive use of introspection among early hard-boiled detectives. However, in *The Big Sleep*, Marlowe, though experienced and somewhat world weary, has relatively little to say of his condition. He reports on his thoughts, reflections, and reactions toward his client, Gen. Sternwood, and his two daughters, Carmen and Vivian. In one sense, as the reader sees Marlowe undergo one experience after another, one disillusionment after another regarding the truth and honor of people, he gradually displays the emptying of his life. Peter Wolfe remarks, "He sees his prepackaged ideas about right and wrong and about appearance and reality go smash in nearly every case he takes" (*Something* 89). Betrayals, not only of him, but especially of the friends and loved ones of those with whom he deals, dredge up his lonely, despairing comments and introspections that feature principally in subsequent novels. Frank MacShane suggests a reason for this attitude: "[...] in *The Big Sleep* he points his finger at those who are responsible for the corruption of society or who live off it, often unaware that they are parasites" (71). In that novel, Marlowe confronts Gen. Sternwood's daughters, both of who are corrupt and one, Carmen, murderous. She kills her sister's husband, Rusty Regan, a man her father admired. In turn, her sister protects her, knowing of her actions. Both act in mockery of their father, weakened with age, who cannot command their adherence to a more "normal" lifestyle. Marlowe can only walk away from the degradation he finds among the Sternwoods, and other murderous, greedy actors in the drama. He symbolically throws his hands up. But, there is a sense in which he finds what he knew would be there. This cynical expectation weakens his ability to stand against the corrupters. Velma's murder of Moose Malloy in *Farewell, My Lovely* is an expected occurrence given her past depredations. She shoots him in Marlowe's presence, and though Marlowe finds her later, at the time he cannot stop her killing Malloy. His feelings of betrayal by Terry Lennox in *The Long Goodbye* are confirmatory of a larger betrayal, one that involves his own hope for a different life in which loyalty and truth can be found.

In *The Moving Target*, Lew Archer begins his removal of self that acts as a witness to a world come undone. Except for Ralph Sampson, the husband of Elaine Sampson, and Miranda, his daughter, Archer observes a perversion of love, hope, and trustworthiness by the wife and Alan Taggert, Sampson's pilot, that extends to the other characters. And the most significant of these betrayers is Albert Graves, Archer's former friend and colleague. Like Chandler's Marlowe, Archer is a witness to their actions and adds up and records their crimes and the toll on himself. In Brett Halliday's *A Taste for Violence* (1949), Michael Shayne exhibits a strikingly different kind of "healer" of social wounds. Called in by Charles Roche, the endangered Centerville mine owner, Shayne arrives to find him murdered and later proves that George Brand, a corrupt labor organizer, is responsible. In the process, Shayne witnesses the chief of police murder one of his subordinates. Subsequently, Shayne forces Seth Gerald, the manager of the Roche mines, to assist him in becoming police chief for six months in order to clean up the town. The novel parallels Hammett's *Red Harvest* in its townspeople's lack of any moral center. Only the outsider Shayne, along with his secretary Lucy Hamilton and Tim Rourke, a Miami reporter Shayne sends for to run the *Gazette* for the duration, can put the town on a better course. Archer and Shayne resemble one another in that helping others does not lead to overmuch self-reflection on their part. Neither man can heal himself, and though Archer implies an awareness of the effects of others' troubles on his psyche, Shayne seldom raises the issue. Archer leads people to a better understanding of their actions while Shayne forces them to reform, however temporary such reform might be.

Given the general paucity of introspection in the early hard-boiled detectives, MacDonald's extensive exploration of McGee's thoughts and feelings in a first-person narration comes as a marked shift in the development of the hard-boiled detective. MacDonald admired Chandler's novels and states, "What Chandler did, I think, is to move closer to the classic novel form though he retained the structure of the detective novel" ("Introduction" 72). McGee is reminiscent of Marlowe in his occasional bouts of loneliness, isolation, and lack of purpose in his life, but MacDonald enhances McGee's reflective moments by allowing him to explore his weaknesses and true sense of desperation when he cannot hold onto a firm sense of who he is. Karen VanderVen remarks, "Travis McGee interestingly does not have a strong sense of self, despite the consistency of his responses and activities from book to book" ("Psychological Genesis" 33). Although McGee's hint to Lois Atkinson in *Blue* of a hidden, emotionally damaged past is never directly explored, McGee reveals the effects of this past. McGee uses an analogy to an astronomical disturbance, suggesting an undiscovered mass, planet or otherwise, that will account for the observed anomalies. Of course, MacDonald avoids limiting McGee's actions and emotional life by telling too much about his past. A series character must be open to change, and McGee experiences many emotional and physical changes while maintaining a recognizable personality. In *The Lonely Silver Rain* (1985), his newly discovered daughter Jean Killian tells him that he is nothing like the sybarite who supposedly abandoned Puss Killian and her expected child because they might disturb his lifestyle. McGee's disclosure that he still has Puss's letter to him, originally revealed in *Pale Gray for Guilt*, and pictures of some of his relatives in a bank safety deposit box shows that he is someone with a lived past, someone whose memories are part of his life in what he has lost and what remains. McGee's self-reflective moments join with his thoughts about people and the world around him. His friend Meyer supplements his knowledge and reasoning skills, but McGee supplies the orientation of someone burdened with self-knowledge and memory but not crippled by either. Through his introspections, one knows that his interior life affects his world, leaking out, as it were, into both his dangerous cases and times of idleness when nothing distracts him from unbidden thoughts.

In addition to the generational shift in character, a gender and sexual identity expansion, and an introspective quality, there is also a lessening of the detectives' sense of certainty about themselves and their profession, a growing tentativeness about what they do. Of course, exceptions exist and Robert B. Parker's Spenser is a striking example of someone who shows little doubt or reflection concerning his actions. He is a good example of the mainly unexamined life and is reminiscent of some early private investigators. It appears that at some point in his life every question settled into a clear pattern and he knew without much reflection what he thought about things and what to do in most situations. Pronzini's Nameless is clearly different in that he experiences challenges to his sense of who he is and his abilities as a detective but recovers through asserting his true nature or proving people wrong about his mental acuity. Erika Coates, Nameless's lover in *The Snatch* (1971), becomes dissatisfied with their relationship and leaves him. She is testy and quarrelsome. She represents a disturbing challenge to Nameless in *Blowback* (1977) when she attacks his whole way of life. He disagrees with her and asserts that his life is not a lie. Deceived by George Hickox, secretary to his client Clyde Mollenhauer in *Scattershot* (1982), Nameless's professional reputation is attacked, and he determines not only to find out who stole the expensive ring he was guarding but also to solve a murder. When these two cases end successfully, Nameless, if no one else, congratulates himself, realizing that he is a good investigator. Nameless's stubborn refusal to accept Ivan Wade's poor estimation of him as his daughter Kerry's lover in *Hoodwink* and his difficulties with her own refusal to hear any complaints about her parents' attitudes trouble him but ultimately do not deter him from pursuing a relationship with her. He is older than Kerry and overweight, and though these two factors give him pause, he persists in his avowals that he loves her and later that he wants to marry her.

Michael Collins' Dan Fortune in *Act of Fear* and Michael Z. Lewin's Albert Samson in *Ask the Right Question* also illustrate the tentativeness and self doubt that encompass some of the transitional hard-boiled detectives. Both men are competent investigators who stick to their cases, going through the necessary process of discovering something or someone that evades detection. However, both detectives exude a sense of reduced expectations. For example, the clients in their cases are young. Fortune thinks of Pete Vitanza as a "kid," a "boy" (Collins, *Act of Fear* 5). Samson learns that Eloise Crystal is fifteen, not the sixteen she claims (Lewin, *Ask the Right Question* 26). Fortune has only one arm, a limitation that affects him physically and emotionally. When he views Pete in the hospital after he has been beaten up, Fortune reflects, "There was something like a cold breath that went through that room and along my spine. I only have one good arm; I want to keep it in one piece" (*Act of Fear* 45). This thought returns to him, functioning as an outward manifestation of his doubts about his abilities as a detective. Rather than unlimited potential, the Marlovian image of the man come to put things right, Fortune gets along but projects no sense of transcending normal human abilities. Samson creates this same image in a different way. As *Ask the Right Question* opens, he has no clients, and one learns that he supplements his income writing crossword puzzles. Appropriate for the cerebral activities of a detective, this avocation suggests that physically one should not expect much from him. The novel takes place in Indianapolis, Samson's hometown, where his mother runs a luncheonette. Pasts hinted at, pasts hidden, pasts expected as far as biological and parental roles are one thing, but a living mother interacting with the protagonist signals that the detective is moving from the mythic world to the everyday even if every transitional detective is not from a city like Indianapolis. Collins and Lewin have created more modest, uncertain, unsure detectives than ones from the Early Period; they discourage major expectations but immeasurably enrich the genre with their portraits of detectives enmeshed in life's complexities.

John Lutz's Alo Nudger in *Buyer Beware* and Lawrence Block's Matthew Scudder in *Sins of the Father* physically manifest their unsure career choices as their series start. Nudger's wife and children were killed in a car wreck a few years earlier. Gordon Clark contacts him to find his daughter Melissa. His wife Joan has taken her to Florida and thus prevented him from exercising his parental visitation rights. Clark gives Nudger the paperwork showing that Joan violated the judge's order ruling that she not take Melissa out of state, but though it is technically legal to recover her, Nudger is uneasy about taking the case. He shows this by regularly taking anti-acid tablets. His problems compound when Dale Carlon, Joan's father and a wealthy businessman, hires him to find Joan. Nudger (the name suggests a physically weak man) finds himself pulled between two strong men. He demonstrates his rightful place in the detective tradition by carrying through his investigations to generally successful conclusions. However, he never stops taking the anti-acid pills. Block's Scudder, discussed above as an example of the generational shift from early to transitional hard-boiled private detectives, suffers a massive dislocation from accidentally shooting a child and resigning from the police force. In addition to leaving his family, Scudder moves into a hotel across the street from his favorite bar and begins drinking heavily. Although his actions do not stem from his occasional work as an unlicensed private investigator, they signify a perilous beginning as a detective. He refrains from taking a license because he cannot see himself believing in any future in which that suggestion of permanence would play a role. He has left only his relationship with Elaine Mardell, a prostitute; his friendship with Mick Ballou, a dangerous career criminal; and his few police contacts. Not a propitious start to a new life. However, Scudder demonstrates that he can perform his job as a private detective. He solves his cases and ultimately obtains a license. In the vein of many transitional private investigators, his life takes on a better balance when he stops drinking and marries Elaine after she retires from her profession.

Character, generic or individual, reveals much about these transitional figures, some still isolated and alone but frequently only temporarily. However, when they do lose someone, through death or altered affections, they reflect human emotions, not emotions to type. Parker describes Spenser as enduring Susan Silverman's temporary hiatus from their relationship. He does not cover up the loss; Spenser has no flippant remarks about that experience. McGee ages and fears the world that closes in on him in his isolation until he discovers a new reason for living with the sudden appearance of his teenage daughter and her acceptance of him as a real father. One can feel Nameless's sadness in his lonely existence and the desperation that he experiences in holding on to Kerry and her love. Alteration and development show that the writers have much to explore in their examinations of the hard-boiled detective genre.

10

Pervasive Violence

The definition of the hard-boiled detective novel is subject to change over time but, paradoxically, remains the same or nearly the same while adapting to new developments. In one area, violence, the hard-boiled detective novel would appear to be limited in its ability to shed its nature. John G. Cawelti writes:

> While the classical writer typically treats the actual apprehension of the criminal as a less significant matter than the explanation of the crime, the hard-boiled story usually ends with a confrontation between detective and criminal. Sometimes this is a violent encounter similar to the climactic shootdown of many westerns [*Adventure* 142–43].

Violence makes up an essential part of the genre's early works. Along with the character of the detective and the urban environment in which he operates, violence is *sui generis*, and each work repeats patterns of violence or creates new ones. However, in the Transitional Period, a subtle movement in the use of violence both employs and surrounds violent acts with other responses, altering, intensifying, even vitiating the violence displayed. Robert A. Baker and Michael T. Nietzel observe generally of PIs "the complexity of their personality, a mixture of roughness and sentimentality. Their terse, laconic exterior belied a much more complicated soul that was troubled with the unfairness and inequality that plagued life's victims" (5).

In the early hard-boiled detective novel, action violence predominates in which the events propel the narrative to resolve some aspect of the plot or push it into greater complexities. In varying degrees, all the early detectives represent this pattern. John D. MacDonald's Travis McGee series continues this early use of violence. However, not only MacDonald but subsequent transitional hard-boiled detective novelists such as Michael Collins, Arthur Lyons, Bill Pronzini, and Robert B. Parker add personal elements, physical limitations, emotional relationships, and an introspective expansion first initiated by Chandler's Philip Marlowe and continued by Ross Macdonald's Lew Archer that change not so much the impact but the feel of violence in their narratives.

Limitations surround or control the occurrence of violence in the Transitional Period. From 1964 to the mid to late seventies, the shift in its use is not overly apparent, but there is a growing lack of exuberance in the detectives' reliance on violence. Contrasting the transitional detectives with the extremes of Daly's Race Williams and Spillane's Mike Hammer, one clearly sees the shift. Williams and Hammer have a certainty about their actions. Mark Timlin's Nick Sharman in the 1980s and 1990s resembles them, but in his work violence often functions more as a caricature of the early practitioners than an integrated element. And, with the restrictions on gun ownership in England, Timlin is less convincing that his character bears any resemblance to real-life actions than would be the case in the United States, which may well be the author's intent. In *The Deep Blue Good-by*, McGee kills one man, Junior Allen, and that only accidentally. However much he might have intended to kill him, it was sheer, desperate luck that the anchor McGee threw at him on the dark ocean lodged in his throat. McGee reveals his desperation after making the toss but finding Allen apparently still alive:

> I could not move or think or speak. The known world was gone, and in nightmare I fought something that could never be whipped. I could not take the light off him. He rolled again. And then I saw what it was. His throat was wedged in that space between the flukes of the Danforth, and the edges of the points were angled up behind the corners of his jaw, the tension spreading his jowls into that grin [240].

What additionally marks this incident in *Blue* is how close Allen comes to murdering McGee. Of course Allen does kill Lois Atkinson, after having mentally, physically, and sexually abused her, leaving her near death before McGee initially saves her. Clearly, MacDonald has left violence as more potential than actual, but its psychological and emotional effects color the work. McGee tortures George Brell and breaks his spirit; the latter also happens to Lew Dagg when he forces McGee to fight him in front of Angie, Brell's daughter and Dagg's girlfriend. At the end, Cathy Kerr, the woman who originally hired McGee to recover what Allen stole from her and her family, nurses McGee back to health. In *Nightmare in Pink* (1964), McGee accidentally kills several people while in Dr. Varn's sinister Toll Valley

Hospital outside of New York City. McGee protects Nina Gibson and Terry Drummond by his quick thinking and quick actions. The ominous tone in these two novels conceals the shift from violence leading frequently to death to violence that explores a greater range of human emotions than does some early examples from either Daly or Hammett.

Michael Collins' Dan Fortune introduces a different kind of limitation to the hard-boiled detective novel. Having only one arm reduces Fortune's ability to commit violent acts. As he admits in *Act of Fear*, the first novel in the series, "Not that I investigate much that is big or dangerous" (2). As a teenager, Fortune injured his left arm so badly while robbing a ship that it was amputated. As stated earlier, the shift in the level of violence is not consistent, but the symbolic disarming of Patrolman Stettin on the first page of the novel and, in a more complete sense, Fortune, signals that while nothing revokes violence's sway it is shaken. Of course, as the police and the private detective lose a certain image of potency, Andy Pappas adds a balance to the novel. Pappas is a gangster who grew up with Fortune in New York's Chelsea district. People are rightfully afraid of Pappas, even Fortune, but Pappas never interferes with Fortune. He even tolerates Fortune's rejections of his overtures. Although the first person point of view continues to be the dominant narrative mode, Collins de-centers the detective as a principal source of violence and shifts it more broadly to society.

Robert B. Parker's Spenser initially presents an image reminiscent of the early detectives. An ex-boxer, Spenser projects a very physical presence in his series, lightened, in the manner of Philip Marlowe, by his flippant manner. The advent of Susan Silverman and Hawk in *God Save the Child* and *Promised Land*, respectively, pulls the series in two directions at once. He wants to have a relationship with Susan, thus from the early part of the series broadening his character. But with Hawk, the violence escalates. Parker demonstrates certain self-consciousness about Spenser's display of violence. Both Susan and Hawk comment on instances of its use. Susan, a psychiatrist, accepts him for who he is and acknowledges that he acts from a certain code of honor or responsibility. This is not a direct diminution of Spenser's violence, but it is startling in its difference from the early detectives. Spillane's Mike Hammer, always an exception, cannot let go of his killing of Charlotte Manning, and in *Vengeance Is Mine*, he dreams of violently wanting to shoot her again. He is full of anger and doubt and certainty about this past action, but he does not change his deadly manner of resolving his cases. In Parker, Hawk, a remorseless killer, chides Spenser in *Early Autumn* when he does not shoot a man that tried to kill them. He tells Spenser that he will eventually have to shoot him and proceeds to kill him himself. If not completely, Parker uses Hawk to separate Spenser from his deadly responses to adversaries. Hawk is a flat character that never changes or evolves. Always loyal to Susan and Spenser, Hawk is the odd man out in the series who functions to save Spenser from himself.

Arguments for the diversion of violent impulses or the delegitimatizing of violence in the transitional hard-boiled detective novel seem difficult to make if the writers are still to be included in the genre. Yet, if there has been a shift to a new phase of development starting with MacDonald's Travis McGee, then the reduced frequency of violence could signal the change. The variety of transitional detectives makes detection of any shift in this category difficult. One notes—in Lewin, Pronzini, and Simon for instance — gaps in the detectives' reliance on violence as well as a general, growing reluctance to use it. Initially, Parker's Spenser seems to continue the earlier tradition of violence as catharsis. While even its use in the Early Period might be overstated, Daly's Williams and Spillane's Hammer along with Hammett's the Continental Op do employ it as a necessary element in their profession.

Spenser, much like McGee, slows, with some notable exceptions, the degree to which he resorts to violence and eventually threatens more than acts. Even Hawk, at least while working with Spenser, uses less violence as the series progresses. This is not to suggest that either the detectives have become shells of their former selves or that the antagonists are any less given to violence. McGee might be the best model, for those who have often relied on their physical abilities, to suggest that an underlying desire to achieve their goals rather than vent their passions is uppermost as a motive for action. Edgar W. Hirshberg states that McGee is out "to right wrongs that have been perpetrated against weak, helpless, and usually good people by strong, powerful, and usually bad people" (*MacDonald* 71). As physically capable as he is, McGee often tries to con people out of their ill-gotten gains rather than kill them. Parker's Spenser, a former boxer, displays his pugilistic skills in *The Goodwill Manuscript* (1973) but only after Dennis Powell, later the novel's first murder victim, forces him to defend himself. A similar pattern occurs when Spenser beats Sonny, one of Joe Broz's thugs. Printing's Nameless uses his steady, determined investigative skills to avoid violent encounters with those who resent his questions and actions.

In MacDonald, the use of the amoral killer is one method employed to draw the specter of violence away from the detective. Earlier, Daly and Spillane utilize the master criminal but with different effects than McGee's villains achieve. Conan Doyle's Professor Moriarty is possibly the source for Quincy Howard Travers, Daly's eponymous Hidden Hand, and Spillane's Arthur Berin-Grotin in *My Gun Is Quick*. In addition, Ralph Dezzeia, the Beast in Daly's *Snarl of the Beast*, presents a gothic figure that has few direct descendants in the genre. The equable but essentially blundering Gutman in Dashiell Hammett's *The Maltese Falcon* is more a satire on the idea of the master criminal than any attempt to develop him as a figure of evil. But with the entirely believable Junior Allen, twisted by nature, MacDonald can locate society's image of aversion outside the detective and call forth the latter's occasional use of violence as a necessary stop-gap when clever tactics or the police fail. Thus, MacDonald's description of McGee as a last resort for people who have been wronged justifies his salvages and for the most part his defensive violence. Searching for the Allens, Waxwells (*Bright Orange for the Shroud*), Brindles (*The Turquoise Lament*), and Pittlers (*Cinnamon Skin*) is a dangerous business, and it is often kill or be killed. As MacDonald and Collins initiate a different direction toward violence, other detectives like Lewin's Albert Samson and Simon's Moses Wine introduce even more factors of diversion and delegitimacy.

The structure of Lewin's *Ask the Right Question* pushes the figure of Albert Samson, the detective protagonist, close to the edge of the genre. Formerly known as Officer Happy to school children, his ironic surname emphasizes Samson's rather mild approach to inserting himself into other people's lives. He does not carry a gun since once while working as a security guard, he shot a man: "So I plugged him. Not dead, but dead enough to kill something in me" (52). In addition, Samson's first client in the series, Eloise Crystal, a minor and the daughter of a wealthy couple in Indianapolis, at the very least disturbs the image of the detective receiving his mysterious but beautiful female client in his rundown office. In Samson's case, his office is also part of the seedy apartment in which he lives. While he is the detective and the adult, Eloise urges him to take the case after turning up at his office/home without calling. Samson has a young daughter to whom he writes, and he wonders at times if Eloise is becoming more than a client. Samson is good at discovering things and, like many private investigators, uses his contacts to get around official barriers, but one never senses that he will use physical violence to forward the case. However, he is on the receiving end when a security guard at Leander Crystal's second, secret office knocks him out as he surprises Samson going through Crystal's files and, more violently, when Fleur Crystal, Eloise's presumed mother, stabs him six times at the end of the novel (184).

In *The Big Fix*, Simon's ex-hippie Wine has slipped the bonds of peace and love, but he attracts violence more than dispenses it. David Geherin states,

> A writer of his generation who aims at recapturing the traditional hard-boiled atmosphere might easily be swayed by the temptation to parody the forties style. Simon avoids this by capturing the essence of the hero and retaining the conventions of the genre, then recreating and filtering both through his (and his generation's) cultural consciousness [*Sons* 87].

Hired by Senator Hawthorne's reelection committee to find Howard Eppis, an ex-activist who threatens to expose Hawthorne by endorsing him through the Free Amerika Party (10–11), Wine loses an old lover who is murdered because of her connection to the case. Lila Shea suddenly comes into his life after many years and leaves it just as quickly. Moses is attacked at a local market, threatened by a woman with a leather whip and two German shepherd dogs, kicks a man in the face, and is shot at. Wine lives in an aura of violence but one with few murders. As Simon demonstrates, Wine floats along, his surname a suggestively buoyant, intoxicating medium. Wine's ex-wife Suzanne and two children live with Madas, her guru, and once Wine spies on his children, Jacob and Simon, watching television in one room while Suzanne and Madas make love in another. If there is a limited aura of violence in the novel, Simon also suggests a general lack of permanence, blurring the landscape and suggesting that the very temporariness of relationships and life-styles limits the possibilities of or need for violent solutions.

An analysis of the victims in the Transitional Period reveals no significant reduction in their number but rather a partial shift in who does the killing and the identity of the victims. One factor that stands out in Hammett, Chandler, and Spillane is the prominence of female killers. Especially in Chandler, murder is frequently a female prerogative. Carmen Sternwood (*The Big Sleep*), Helen Grayle/Velma (*Farewell My Lovely*), Mrs. Murdock (*The High Window*), and Muriel Chess (*The Lady in the Lake* [1943]) dominate the violence in their respective novels, and neither Marlowe nor any other male competes with them though Marlowe uncovers their violence. And, men are usually their victims. Daly's Williams, Hammett's Continental Op, and Spillane's Hammer parallel females who kill but, even in the case of Hammer, are more often reactive than proactive. However, in the Transitional Period, except for MacDonald, women do not act so often as the killer. In fact, they frequently appear as victims and for nontraditional as well as traditional reasons. The former reason occurs because their roles in society are more important than heretofore. At the beginning of Marcia Muller's *Edwin of the Iron Shoes*, someone stabs Joan Albritton, an antiques dealer. In Muller's *Ask the Cards a Question* (1982), Molly Antonio, a retired department store clerk is strangled. She does not lose her life because of the prominence of her former position but rather because of the special knowledge she has about retail operations. To indicate part of McCone's self-protection, Kathleen Gregory Klein notes her independence, someone to be taken seriously and difficult to control:

> McCone, just under thirty when introduced, is staff investigator for the All Souls Cooperative, a legal and residential commune in San Francisco working with middle-class clients. This alternative to the corporate model of litigation

parallels Sharon's apparent disdain for rigid, official systems [*Woman Detective* 206].

In Simon's *The Big Fix*, Oscar Procari, Sr., causes the murder of Lila Shea because she has knowledge of his gambling operation and his attempt to fix the California Democratic presidential primary. Working for Sen. Hawthorne against Gov. Dillworthy, Lila knows things about the campaign and knows people involved that make her dangerous to Procari. Lila is approximately Sharon's age, but of course, Sharon is the protagonist in her series and thus immune from being eliminated.

Some women are killed for who they are or for whom they know; they also die because of those with whom they are involved. These are the more traditional reasons. And most are killed by men. In addition to Junior Allen's murder of Lois Atkinson in MacDonald's *The Deep Blue Good-by*, one of Dolores Estobar's half-brothers kills Mona Fox Yeoman in MacDonald's *A Purple Place for Dying*, Miguel Alconedo cuts Almah Hichin's throat in *A Deadly Shade of Gold* (1965), Boone Waxwell kills Wilma Ferner in *Bright Orange for the Shroud* after crippling her during rough sex and then feeds her body to the alligators in the swamp behind his house, and Griff and others throw Vangie Bellemer in front of a car in *Darker than Amber*. Saul Gorba probably kills his wife Gretchen, Dr. Fortner Geis's former teenage lover, in *One Fearful Yellow Eye* (1966). This only lists some of the women who die through MacDonald's eighth Travis McGee novel. In Parker's *The Godwulf Manuscript*, Professor Lowell Hayden murders his lover Cathy Connelly to protect himself from being discovered as a drug dealer. Sheila T. Warren in Lyons' *The Dead Are Discreet* is murdered before the action begins, and the police charge her husband John Warren. Warren's lawyer contacts Jacob Asch to prove his client's innocence. In Lawrence Block's *The Sins of the Fathers*, Matthew Scudder investigates Wendy Hanniford's death when her father becomes suspicious of the circumstances surrounding it.

Of course, women are not exempt from murder in the Transitional Period, and MacDonald rivals Chandler in the number of female killers. He is nearly an equal opportunity author in this category. Not only do women commit murder in this period, but they also kill other women. Cara Ingalls kills Joan Albritton, mentioned above, in Muller's *Edwin of the Iron Shoes*. In MacDonald's *The Quick Red Fox* (1964), Ulka M'Gruder kills her husband Vance, his ex-wife Patty, and photographer D.C. Ives. Mary Alice McDermit kills her fellow worker Jane Lawson in *The Scarlet Ruse* (1973). Dolores Estobar in *A Purple Place for Dying*, Anna Ottlo in *One Fearful Yellow Eye*, Vangie in *Darker than Amber*, one of the victims above, and Lilo Perris in *The Long Lavender Look* kill for various reasons, usually for gain but also for revenge. Estobar's and Perris's fathers spurn them, refusing to recognize them as their daughters. Like Ulka, Anna, Vangie, and Lilo are multiple killers with Anna topping the list as a former Nazi concentration camp guard along with her husband Perry Hennigan. While no one includes so many female killers in the Transitional Period as MacDonald, others employ them effectively. In Bill Pronzini's *Undercurrent* (1973), Bianca Tarrant kills her husband Keith to avenge his murder of her lover, Walter Paige. In Lyons' *The Dead Are Discreet*, Gloria Pilsen kills Christopher Ruane after sending him to kill her sister Sheila Warren and Randy Folsom. Her hatred for her sister lies behind her actions. Just as Chandler does, writers in this period place the females' motives for murder squarely alongside the males' in the complex lives of humans.

Children or youths also become victims in the Transitional Period. Youths, especially, suffer violence in the Early Period, but in MacDonald and Collins they become even more vulnerable to predators. In *The Deep Blue Good-by*, Junior Allen attempts to rape eighteen-year old Patricia Devlan whom McGee rescues. In *Act of Fear*, Pete Vitanza kills Nancy Driscoll and "'tried to get Jo-Jo [Olsen] killed too'" (148) according to Marty, Dan Fortune's girlfriend. Collins shows youth turning on youth through desire and fear. Both Devlan as victim and Vitanza as criminal function outside their experiential limits. Andy Pappas or one of his henchmen might commit murder and remain silent under questioning; Vitanza, however, becomes a child as Fortune pressures him. And, Devlan does not know what kind of person Allen is and is completely unprepared for his sexually violent behavior. Symbolic of the vulnerability of the child in the genre is Matthew Scudder's memory in *The Sins of the Fathers* of accidentally shooting seven-year old Estrellita Rivera while he was a cop.

For all that violence may be somewhat limited and diverted in the transitional period, the focus on its victims demonstrates that it still remains important to the genre. Yet, the feelings evoked by acts of violence and the doubts that arise with its use add another factor in the period's changed attitudes toward it. As Alo Nudger says in John Lutz's *Buyer Beware*, "The problem with homicides was that there was always someone else involved who was a murderer" (46). Properly fearful of the unknown killer of David Branley, Nudger reveals an aversion to murderous environments that bespeaks, not something flawed in his character, but rather a sensible human reaction. In Lutz's *Nightlines* (1984), Nudger's nervous stomach has more reasons to act up. In addition, to his client Jenine Boyington's posing as her dead twin sister Jeanette and her mother Agnes Boyington's self-righteousness leading her to murder an unknown woman in the same fashion as her daughter was killed, Nudger has to deal with Hugo Rumbo, a massive, slow-witted former boxer who follows the mother's instructions whether to assault or intimidate Nudger. Finally, the murderer Luther Kell attacks Nudger when he surprises Nudger in his client's apartment. Though not needing more trouble, Nudger almost loses his lover Claudia Bettencourt when she tries to hang herself. If one does not have a knight-complex as do MacDonald's Travis McGee and Parker's Spenser, why not let the police handle the investigation? And, this is especially good advice if one lacks the physical capabilities of the above two detectives. In Bill Pronzini's early novels, Nameless solves mysteries that involve murders but which do not begin as murder investigations. The focus frequently is on Nameless's analytical abilities, abilities that he convincingly demonstrates in *Scattershot* in the face of his employer Clyde Mollenhauer's disparagement. He hires Nameless to guard his daughter's wedding presents. When a valuable ring is stolen, Nameless shows that it could not have been a job from within the building, with him as the chief suspect, but rather, someone broke into the room from outside. Mollenhauer's assistant eventually admits his guilt. Nameless tops this by proving that Joe Craig shot the actress Bernice Nolan. For all his love of the pulps and his army and military intelligence backgrounds, one senses a desire for peace in Nameless. His search for love in the series might be the best evidence that he has no feel for or need of violence to show his manhood or his abilities as a detective.

The abatement of violence in the Transitional Period may be too amorphous to pinpoint easily. Certainly, Timothy Harris's *Kyd for Hire* (1977), at the end of the Transitional Period, belies the idea that violence has abated. Nearly every main character and some minor ones commit acts of violence, past or present, or become the victims of it. Incest, blackmail, suicide, murder and baby selling — Thomas Kyd deals with all of these and feels his life hardening in the process. Hired by Joe Elevel to find his missing daughter Charlotte after his wife commits suicide, Kyd quickly learns of the daughter's murder and the father's past family betrayals. Death occurs and amoral killers flourish, especially in MacDonald, before receiving their just deserts. Yet, even in MacDonald, the reaction to their depredations plays a significant role. There is not just moral revulsion but also the graphic depiction of personal loss. Focusing on those who endure and sometimes survive violence intensifies one's awareness of its effects. One sees the bodies fall in Daly and Hammett, but as early as MacDonald's Lois Atkinson in *The Deep Blue Good-by*, Dana Holtzer in *The Quick Red Fox*, and Vivian Watts in *Bright Orange for the Shroud*, the author emphasizes the physical and emotional pain suffered and the change brought to the victims' lives by their harsh experiences.

This realistic examination of loss moves the events from counters in a game, somehow bloodily bloodless, to one in which the suffering might be, and often is, too much to survive. Boone Waxwell's rape of Vivian Watts and the promise of more to come while her husband lies drunk in a living room chair forces her to kill herself and Crane, her lawyer husband. No one, not even McGee, who barely escapes with his life, seems able to stop Waxwell until McGee later frames him for the death of the Wattses.

MacDonald's most extensive examination of the effects of violence occurs in *Cinnamon Skin.* Cody T.W. Pittler murders Meyer's niece, Norma Greene Lawrence, his last relative, and two other people when he blows up the boat on which they are traveling. Norma is only one in a long string of women Pittler has killed and done so for little gain. During the novel, Meyer suffers his niece's loss and achieves catharsis only at the end when he buries Pittler alive under a ledge that he separates from the wall of a Cancun ravine where McGee, Meyer, and a group of Mayan Indians have trapped him. The symbolic use of earth and an ancient race releases Meyer to some sense of recovery.

This 1982 novel and the 1985 *The Lonely Silver Rain* are a start in the move away from violence if not a complete abandonment of it in the hard-boiled detective novel. The Modern Period will provide examples of both violence and the further lessening of violence, the latter especially by the introduction of a large number of female detectives following in the footsteps of Marcia Muller's Sharon McCone and the continuing direction taken by other detectives that reduce violence's profile in the genre.

As the hard-boiled detective novel continues to develop, responding to the central aspects of the genre created in the Early Period as well as a changing society, the principal themes and character types remain as fundamental, defining elements. The idea of violence is one of the most important of these themes, going to the heart of this literary form. Along with the use in any analysis of its most immediate literary antecedents, one must also include its broader reaches, primarily into English and American literature.

The knight motif generates new inflections, especially in MacDonald's frequent use of Don Quixote as an image of knightly intentions and abilities. This post-heroic figure becomes what one would term today a postmodern image of human aspirations and the ability to reach them. In addition to McGee's self-mocking references to Don Quixote, Parker's Spenser counterbalances this with the more traditional image of the medieval hero, an image contained in his name and the suggestions of *The Faerie Queene's* (1590, 1596) Redcross Knight as a man of courage, fidelity, and honor. Raymond Chandler's Philip Marlowe introduces this theme with his musings on the knight in the stained-glass window in the Sternwood mansion in his first novel, *The Big Sleep.* George Grella states, "Raymond Chandler embellishes the toughness of his Philip Marlowe with compassion, honesty, and wit, and a dimension of nobility that Spade and the laconic Op lack" ("Hard-Boiled Detective" 107). The presence of the knight demands his opposite, in Edmund Spenser's usage his Archimago, one who violates all standards of honor, morality, and decency. This binary opposition prevents any final resolution of the age-old conflict between good and evil, and on this the structure of the hard-boiled detective novel rests.

11

Expanded Space

Definitions of setting and place stress that both interior and exterior spaces figure as locations for actions. R. Gordon Kelly states in the introduction to his *Mystery Fiction and Modern Life* that there is "a pervasive pattern of incident and consequence characteristic of mystery fiction generally. That pattern relates mystery fiction to intrinsic features of our experience of modernity" (xv). Not only the physical space in which actions occur in time but also an individual's inner space matters. Dreams, reminiscences, and ponderings sometimes create different settings for characters than the ones they occupy at any particular moment. Inserting past locations or new, imaginary ones into present circumstances can also dramatically alter the characters' physical conditions. Of course, unbidden dreams, nightmares, and mental associations also transform immediate situations. Beginning with the Travis McGee series in *The Deep Blue Good-by*, John D. MacDonald's Ft. Lauderdale strikes one in its immediacy, but in that and subsequent novels, past experiences and the textures and places in which they occur are not long in intruding. Authors create solid, anchored settings as well as ephemeral ones. The Los Angeles of Arthur Lyons' *The Dead Are Discreet* and Roger L. Simon's *The Big Fix* testify to the sense of the real world's solidity equal to Raymond Chandler's depiction of the same city in *The Big Sleep* and Dashiell Hammett's San Francisco in *The Maltese Falcon*. In the transitional hard-boiled detective novel, nearly every place reverberates from experiences undergone in modern cities and towns or transferred from other real or imagined settings, giving them added depth and significance.

Naming, describing, and acting create occupied space. Without these events, particular spaces do not exist in the genre. Just as the Big Bang theoretically creates space and time in the universe, the use of San Francisco and its environs, Los Angeles, Montana, New York, and Miami in the early hard-boiled detective novel makes them occupied rather than empty spaces for the genre. Maurice O'Sullivan argues that

> [...] Dashiell Hammett and Raymond Chandler did more than remove murder mysteries from the harmoniously hierarchical world of quaintly placid British villages to the mean streets, sterile architecture, and dysfunctional families of urban America. They also created a ravaged social and and physical environment as the perfect elegiac background for their tales of the bleakness enveloping the postindustrial world [119].

Some cosmologists argue that the universe expands like a balloon, thus implying there is no space or time outside the balloon. There is only space inside which increases in diameter as galaxies move away from each other (Pasachoff). For the hard-boiled detective genre, New York, paradoxically, does not exist until Carroll John Daly's *The Snarl of the Beast* creates and employs it. For that or any other hard-boiled detective novel, neither Philadelphia nor Richmond nor Houston exists unless named, described, or acted in. As the genre grows in its three main phases (i.e., the Early, Transitional, and Modern), more and more of the United States becomes occupied, approaching the country's real-life dimensions. In Daly's *The Hidden Hand*, Miami and the Atlantic Ocean appear as part of the action. Dashiell Hammett's *Red Harvest* illuminates the sordid world of Personville (Butte, Montana). His *The Maltese Falcon*, set exclusively in San Francisco, gives a vivid picture of crime and betrayal in that city. Raymond Chandler's *The Big Sleep* brings Los Angeles to life and Ross Macdonald's *The Moving Target* adds to the city's portrait. Mickey Spillane's *I, the Jury* expands the image of New York City. Thomas B. Dewey puts Chicago on the genre's map while Brett Halliday and Richard S. Prather and William Campbell Gault add more on Miami and Los Angeles, respectively.

Occupied space increases rapidly in the Transitional Period, both in more detailed portraits of cities such as New York, Los Angeles, and San Francisco and an increased number of them. Boston, St. Louis, Indianapolis, Saratoga Springs, and Ft. Lauderdale represent the new spaces. Small-town Montana, again makes an exotic appearance in James Crumley's *The Wrong Case* (1975). Milo Milodragovitch lives from within the town of Meriwether. Unlike the Continental Op, Milodragovitch does not come to Montana to correct problems and restore order before moving on. He exists in a space that can neither achieve harmony nor lose its life. He has his office in a building inherited from his grandfather (3). In other words, he lives in the everyday world of passing time in which the succession of events produces changes. T.S. Eliot's image of the banality of modern life in such poems as "Preludes" (1917), "The Love Song of J. Alfred Prufrock" (1917), and *The Waste Land* (1922) is an intensification of the inevitable production of dull and ordinary moments in any age. The effect from the focus on autobiography, in whatever genre, creates the exotic quality in Crumley's novel. The mixture of the characters' actions and motivations for actions, past and present; their thoughts; and their feelings generates the exotic quality experienced in the novel's totality.

Several aspects of both the new and repeated spaces deserve attention. For example, MacDonald's Travis McGee resides in Ft. Lauderdale just as all the major cities in the early period are on the edges of the continent. McGee resides not only on the east coast of Florida, but he lives in a houseboat. McGee goes frequently into the city, so his position is not one of retreat. However, he takes no necessarily permanent share of Ft. Lauderdale's space. Slip F-18 at Bahia Mar could be empty at a moment's notice. Of course, McGee remains there throughout the twenty-one novels of the series and also in *Reading for Survival* (1987), MacDonald's posthumously published work on the absolute necessity for humans to read, thereby engaging their world at a deep level. Michael Collins' *Act of Fear* introduces Dan Fortune, a one-armed private investigator who has returned to New York and his old Chelsea neighborhood. Certainly, memory comes into play over the years for any series detective, but Collins uses the idea to capture Fortune's mood at returning to a space he occupied as a child. This is one of the first times that a hard-boiled detective writer has utilized space in this way. Spade and Marlowe have lived and worked in San Francisco and Los Angeles, respectively, but have not experienced childhood there. Every one of the early hard-boiled detectives dribbles out bits of their past lives, infrequently mentioning their early years. In the Transitional Period, Michael Z. Lewin's Albert Samson and Stephen Dobyns' Charlie Bradshaw rely on some aspects of their youth spent, respectively, in Indianapolis and Saratoga Springs to complete their characters' portraits.

Samson and Bradshaw have made their cities occupied spaces. To date, no other hard-boiled detective novelists have set series there. In effect, every description and every incident bring these spaces into the genre, demanding, as it were, that any analysis of it include them. The detectives' adult experiences initially concern the critic. Lewin's *Ask the Right Question* and Dobyns' *Saratoga Longshot* establish the protagonists and present a first sketch of their cities. Almost immediately in each novel, the past becomes important to the plot. For Samson, it is not at first his past but, ironically, the past of Eloise Crystal, his client. The irony lies in the fact that she is not yet sixteen-years old, and Samson is unsure he can represent her without her parents' consent. It is their past that sends her to Samson since she is convinced that she is not her father's daughter and wants Samson to find her biological father. As a parallel, if subdued, story, Samson's own youth gradually appears. He was booked as a kid for joyriding in other people's cars along with Jerry Miller, a black friend who later becomes a captain in the Indianapolis Police Department. Readers are also faced with a largely untold story, i.e., his childhood relationship to his mother through her presence in his adult life as the owner of a diner where he frequently eats. Bradshaw's client's past is bound up with his. Gladys Cheney, now missing her teeth and overweight, asks Bradshaw, a twenty-year veteran of the Saratoga Springs Police Department, to find and help her son, Sam. Rumors are that Sam is his son, but Bradshaw knows that he is not. In a rather complicated emotional relationship to Gladys, Bradshaw somehow feels responsible for her. He lusted after her in high school, and this figures in his sense of obligation, but he also knows this is a ridiculous reason for going to New York to look for her son, especially since once there the Saratoga Springs police chief threatens to fire him if he does not immediately return. Mixed with this is his poor relationship with his family and his memory of a father who gambled on horses and committed suicide. One can see the past memories overlaying and complicating his present occupied space.

At the beginning of the hard-boiled detective novel, one senses the belief that there are no new spaces, no frontiers remaining, and no hope of progress if it is dependent on inhabiting a new place. David Geherin observes of Collins' Dan Fortune series, "The early novels make especially effective use of the Chelsea neighborhood, where Fortune is as much at home as Natty Bumppo in the wilderness" (*American Private Eye* 161). James Fenimore Cooper's Natty Bumppo, depicted by William Ruehlmann as one "who flees the sound of the ax" (5), disappears into the Plains in *The Prairie* (1827) while Fortune burrows into New York. Fortune's space narrows, a recovered space that allows him to operate in memory and in the present. Similarly, Lawrence Block's Matthew Scudder, first introduced in *The Sins of the Fathers*, retreats to a Manhattan hotel, of which Donna R. Casella says, "The only thing in Scudder's one room is his bed and his booze [...]" (37), and nearby bars such as Armstrong's. Paradoxically, the genre continually produces new spaces, spaces to be occupied by the people and action. Additional cities and regions as plot locations do not, however, remove this sense of a narrowed or reduced space as an *a priori* concept. Historians of the United States describe this as a sense of loss of national direction. The westward physical expansion reaches the Pacific Ocean and rebounds into the interior. LeRoy Lad Panek notes "the widespread American prejudice that the country has somehow been tilted toward the Pacific and all the freaks have rolled into California [...]" (*Introduction* 167). A country that supposedly believes in its Manifest Destiny to occupy land between the oceans needs to create a new purpose regarding the idea of space when the old one is achieved. Outer space as the new frontier in the 1960s is one response to the demand for a new place to occupy. It might seem inevitable that a country that partially achieved its identity through a determined filling of the continental space, a space already generally inhabited, would be drawn to illimitable space as a project that presents no end to movement. In contrast, the Continental Op, a San Francisco detective whose career has traversed the continent, goes in *Red Harvest* to the dead-end city of Personville. The city is a sink of corruption, worse than most other locales in the genre. It is only an ironic frontier that beckons to no progress, only death of the good and the bad.

When the Continental Op retreats to Utah, a neutral corner, after the slaughter in Poisonville, he wants things to be over, to die down so that he can continue his career. What is missing is a moral aspect to what happened in Personville. A lack of continued violence and a restoration of some order dominate the city, but there is little sense that good has triumphed rather than evil. George Grella says of the hard-boiled detective novel, "Its central problem is a version of the quest, both a search for truth and an attempt to eradicate evil" ("Hard-Boiled Detective" 104). However, the corrupt Elihu Willsson, not his crusading, now-dead son Donald, remains to rebuild the city he rules and which he ruined. Race Williams brings a personal code of right and wrong to his novels, but no over-arching moral structure either. And, nothing that he does affects the larger society even though particular individuals can no longer harm anyone. Yet, a personal moral quality, like that also found in Hammett, Chandler, Spillane, and Macdonald, generally lies behind any possible broader moral framework. Individuals, of course, are the sole moral agents, but they can participate in living up to or supporting an application of moral concepts broader than their own separate lives. In *The Big Sleep*, Marlowe conceals information from General Sternwood about his daughters, though he suspects the worst, and turns the murderous Carmen over to her sister Vivian instead of the authorities. Marlowe makes a moral decision which may not be generally acceptable but which is based on more than his personal preferences.

Travis McGee and Robert B. Parker's Spenser continue this pattern of a private moral code not always known, accepted if known, or accessible by others and its effect on the world around them. One reason the idea of progress is problematic in the McGee series is that progress is often tied to the idea of development. Edgar W. Hirshberg states:

> Eventually Travis McGee takes up Jimmy Wing's [hero of MacDonald's
> *A Flash of Green* (1962)] losing battle against the uglifiers and spoilers and
> asphalters and tree-haters, with no better success. But, rather than taking an
> active part, he functions as a commentator and observer, looking at what they

already have done not only to Florida but to much of the rest of the world as well, and speculating about what the results of their depredations inevitably will lead to [*MacDonald* 81].

McGee does have a corrective in Meyer whose worldview includes the necessity of moral action in a social context. McGee's dark side affects the new spaces that he and Meyer occasionally inhabit through the former's cases, but Meyer continually opens up the new, closed space of McGee's world. Introduced in *The Godwulf Manuscript*, Spenser generally lacks this corrective in that Susan Silverman, his lover, acknowledges his personal moral code without adhering to it herself while with one exception Hawk is, as Spenser and Susan agree, amoral. All of them, along with Spenser and Hawk's former boxing trainer Henry Cimoli are loyal to one another, loyal in absolute terms. Within their private space, their moral code works, but the larger world of Boston looms bleakly, a new space that is reduced by the lack of a generally accepted and shared moral code.

The concept of unregenerate space, a space that needs to be recovered, helps clarify the paradoxical position in which new spaces, lacking an over-arching moral framework for those who inhabit them, create a sense of narrowing, of closing down, a cessation of a progressive social movement. MacDonald's many buried spaces especially illuminate these difficulties. In novel after novel in the Travis McGee series, death and burial symbolize the closing in of a world that seems to beckon otherwise. In *A Purple Place for Dying*, two characters, Mona Fox Yeoman and John Webb, are murdered and their bodies hidden away. Jass Yeoman sexually abused his illegitimate daughter, Dolores Estobar, and she avenges herself by having Jass's wife and the wife's lover killed. Yeoman destroyed the space in which his daughter wanted her father to love her as a daughter. Dolores murders him herself. Isobel Webb, John's sister, attempts suicide but later leaves Esmerelda with McGee and in the process becomes his lover. MacDonald ironically offers the American Southwest as a dark space that marks an area of intense struggle to recover life. Joseph Hansen uses sunny Southern California in a similar fashion to locate a narrowed, morally darkened world. Of course, Chandler's Philip Marlowe in *The Big Sleep* portrays an unregenerate space narrowed at the end of the novel to the empty oil well in which Rusty Regan's body lies buried. A moral decay, as strong as the stench of death, pervades the Sternwood world.

In many of the McGee novels, MacDonald seems obsessed with images of unregenerate and seemingly unrecoverable space, an effect of what O'Sullivan calls "the human capacity to corrupt both society and nature" (119). Slightly less graphically, Joseph Hansen's Dave Brandstetter's and Marcia Muller's Sharon McCone's novels do the same. In *Darker than Amber* and *The Turquoise Lament*, MacDonald uses burial sites in two different ways.

In the former, Griff, a member of the so-called Drowner's Inc., forces McGee to go to a deserted Florida beach where he plans to kill him and bury his body. McGee's moral position, even though he winds up killing Griff in self-defense and burying him in the grave Griff forced McGee to dig, is far more positive than in the latter novel. Morally, McGee nearly crosses the line between acceptable and unacceptable behavior in *The Turquoise Lament*. He abducts Tom Collier, Pidge Brindle's corrupt lawyer, and takes him to a remote section of his own ranch. As Griff does to him in *Darker than Amber*, McGee forces Collier to dig a grave and threatens to bury him alive unless he reveals Howie Brindle's plans for killing his wife Pidge. When Collier stalls, McGee throws the already bound man into the grave and proceeds in a business-like manner to fill it. Collier then quickly tells McGee what he wants to know concerning Brindle. However, the argument that the ends justify the means is a morally dangerous one even though in this case McGee manages to save Pidge's life with the information he obtains from Collier.

Hansen's use of an unregenerate space in *Fadeout* (1970) does not quite have the same impact as the threat of someone's being buried alive, but it dramatically presents an arena nearly out of man's control. An "arroyo" down which "water pounded, ugly, angry and deep" (1), "a bad road" (1), a strong but slippery bridge (2), and an approach to it angled and steep (2)— these elements of a box canyon above Pima, California, presumably contributed to the death of Fox Olson that Dave Brandstetter comes to investigate for Medallion Insurance. Coupled with Brandstetter's struggle with a desire for death during the previous six weeks, this forcefully presented space produces strong feelings of recoil in what Landon Burns labels "'things-as-they-are' observing" (181). Hansen suggests that at certain times death will control the spatial environment in one fashion or another. In Muller's *Edwin of the Iron Shoes*, Sharon McCone investigates Joan Albritton's murder in her Salem Street San Francisco antiques shop. McCone remembers the first time she met Albritton who pointed out her favorite objects: Clothilde — a headless dummy, Edwin of the Iron Shoes— a mannequin in a sailor suit, Edwin's playmate — a cloth doll with long yellow braids, and Bruno— a stuffed German shepherd (33–35). Albritton is vibrantly alive, but later, after McCone uncovers her criminal conduct, she sees Albritton in her shop in a different light:

Again the silence, deepening around me.
I understood how Joan could have become slightly unbalanced, spending her days in this dark shop with its echoes of the past. No wonder she talked to Clothilde and Bruno and the little boy in a sailor suit, trying to coax life out of them. I went down the aisle to Edwin of the Iron Shoes, alone in his gloomy corner.
The mannequin, as always, stared at the wall [195–96].

In an interview conducted by Frederick Isaac, Muller says, "'The characters depend on their surroundings, and the reverse is also true'" (27). Recovering these spaces in Hansen and Muller is problematic since the forces of nature and/or death are so omnipresent and permanent.

Interior space, expansive like the exterior world and its new cities and places, grows somewhat differently, using repetition and difference, e.g., in the areas of themes, emotional reactions to the outside world and experience, and formal patterns such as first-person point of view, to enlarge possibilities and present a new social matrix. Kelly asserts the connection between a genre's formal elements and the outside world: "Historically stable elements of mystery fiction [...] are systematically linked to constitutive features of modernity involving issues of knowledge, trust, risk, and power that arise in the course of everyday social interaction" (xi).

The accumulated experience of new characters creates a different feel for the world. In *I, the Jury*, Mickey Spillane's Mike Hammer adumbrates the direction that war experiences lead in the Transitional Period. Jack Williams lost an arm protecting Hammer during World War II. Rather than the more remote references to the world wars in Hammett, Chandler, and Ross Macdonald, John D. MacDonald's *Nightmare in Pink* also employs the theme of war sacrifice. Mike Gibson gets McGee to swear that he will help his sister Nina who is in despair, believing that her murdered boyfriend was a criminal and not the honest man she previously assumed he was. Gibson once volunteered to fill in for McGee, allowing him to go to Japan during the Korean War for rest and recuperation. Gibson is severely injured, and McGee feels, at times, that his friend took his place in injury. Hammer's response to Williams' murder is to cry vengeance. MacDonald shifts the direction of the theme of war sacrifice by having McGee save rather than kill someone.

Simon uses the Vietnam War as the backdrop for the many protests, now in the past for the thirty-year old Moses Wine, private investigator and divorced father of two. In *The Big Fix*, Wine recalls a sexual tryst with Lila Shea, a fellow 1960s activist, in a car near a demonstration: "The last time I was with Lila Shea we were making love in the back of a 1952 Chrysler hearse parked across the street from the Oakland Induction Center. Tear gas was seeping through the floorboards and the crack of police truncheons was in our ears" (1). The personal and the political blend in this intimate moment, through memory imploding the decade's anti-war activism, before jumping four years to the present. Published one year after *The Big Fix*, Lyons' *The Dead Are Discreet* barely refers to the Vietnam War in a novel in which Asch is hired to establish the innocence of John Meyer Warren, accused of killing his wife Sheila and her lover Randy Folsom. Sheila's brother, Jimmy Toppinger, stepped on a mine in Vietnam and died. Since

Sheila is also dead before the novel begins, Lyons uses her husband John and her sister Gloria Pilsen to reveal Sheila's emotional attachment, termed by Asch as "'sick'" (211) at the end of the novel, to Jimmy. Rev. James Harnell acted as Sheila's medium to contact Jimmy. He states, "'She wanted to contact her dead brother who was killed in Vietnam. She was curious about the Other Side, as are all people who come here'" (35). John Warren previously tells Asch:

> "[...] Sheila was quite upset about [her brother's death]. She started consulting some charlatan medium that some of her friends used to get psychic readings from, to try to contact Jimmy. [...] She started going to séances. She claimed to me that it was just entertainment, but I knew she was really starting to believe in all that crap" [18].

Equally skeptical about contacting the dead (29), Gloria tells more about her sister's inner life. She states that her sister and Jimmy were "'very close'" (28). Their parents' divorce resulted in Sheila and Jimmy's living with their father and Gloria's with the mother. However, Gloria claims her father had little time for anything besides his business, and that consequently "'[...] they were thrown that much closer together'" (28). Sheila's nervous breakdown over Jimmy's death resulted in her decision to employ a medium (28–29). While Lyons does not use Sheila as a symbol for the grief over the death of a loved one in war, the event and her subsequent loss open the dead woman's emotional life to the reader. John Warren, Rev. Harnell, and Gloria Pilsen reveal parts of Sheila's interior world, and Asch's investigation uncovers her sister's "'cold hatred'" (212) for her and Gloria's successful plan to have her and Folsom killed (212).

The use of space as a metaphor to explore characters' inner lives allows an indirect focus through which an accumulation of characteristics, statements, and actions thickens one's experience of the genre. Both Simon's Wine and Lyons' Asch are Jewish and divorced; Joseph Hansen's Dave Brandstetter is gay and loses a lover to cancer; Bill Pronzini's Nameless is initially unmarried and Swiss Italian; Parker's Spenser is unmarried but becomes permanently attached to Susan Silverman and later adopts a boy named Paul Giacomin; Lawrence Block's Matthew Scudder has an occasionally abrasive relationship with his ex-wife and son; Stephen Dobyns' Charlie Bradshaw is divorced but, like Nameless, is open to a relationship and, also like Nameless, occasionally succeeds; John Lutz's Alo Nudger's wife, son, and daughter die in a car crash; Michael Z. Lewin's Albert Samson is divorced with a daughter he seldom sees; Marcia Muller's Sharon McCone is single but lonely; and MacDonald's McGee never marries but has several serious relationships during the series and learns in the last novel that he has a daughter. This lengthy catalog of some of the detectives' private lives indicates sources for the emotional thickening that complications bring. The frequently used first-person point of view opens their lives to some scrutiny but closes it to others. Only what they reveal to themselves or in dialogue is available. Generally, no omniscient narrator ties together separate strands for the reader's convenience. Pronzini's Nameless is called Bill on at least one occasion (*Twospot* 72) but has no last name in the series. Hansen's Brandstetter and Muller's McCone work for others, Medallion Insurance and All Souls Cooperative, respectively, and Dobyns' Bradshaw and Pronzini's Nameless take on partners, but most detectives work alone. In the more expansive emotional space of the Transitional Period, the detectives reveal something of their private lives as they go about their cases. While in the Early Period the Continental Op works and thinks about work, the later detectives live into fuller human possibilities.

The concept of interior space names an element largely missing from the Early Period. Except for Race Williams' boasts, Philip Marlowe's bitter asides on society, and Mike Hammer's rages, the early hard-boiled detective writers care little to explore their characters' interior lives even while using the first person point of view. Since the early detectives are such powerful models for their successors, they sometimes pull them into their orbit; regression, therefore, does occur in the Transitional and Modern Periods. However, the developed emotional and intellectual space can be seen as restored space. The genre asserts its demands through its models, but later writers, by what they add, indicate what is earlier absent. If nothing else, other literary traditions arguably portray more complex characters, and hard-boiled writers gradually replicate and contribute to this ongoing development. What is paradoxically "restored" is a series of possibilities in the revealed motivations for actions and the emotional and intellectual responses to them. In *The Deep Blue Good-by*, Cathy Kerr helps McGee recover from the loss of Lois Atkinson and his confrontation with the amoral Junior Allen. When emotionally healed, he goes back to his regular life in Ft. Lauderdale. Cathy repeats this action in *The Scarlet Ruse* when Frank Sprenger nearly kills McGee and his friend Meyer, the academic, has to bring him to Cathy's and clean up the final scene of action. These are new events in the genre, and what is "restored" to the genre comes partially from an adaptation of the method of character portrayal found in novels of manners and morals. The unacknowledged possibilities in the form, suggested through McGee's need for help, come also as a restorative power that regenerates it. Later writers can move from the early models to new examples and back while remaining recognizably hard-boiled.

The detective novels' place, space, or setting — physical, emotional, or intellectual, exterior or interior — dominates plot and character and is dominated by them. While not making it as important as plot and character,

Aristotle's *Poetics* sees spectacle as an integral part of tragedy. Space acts as a frame as do other significant literary features, e.g., beginnings and endings with certain events, speeches, or emotional situations. David Lehman in *The Perfect Murder: A Study in Detection* writes, "Go back to the detective story's origins, however, and you'll find that its characteristic landscape is the big city with its crowded thoroughfares, its factories, and its slums" (117). The city as space looms large, but other venues expand the image of space as it operates to encircle, engulf, and enclose the story it supports.

12

Needed Work

Detective work in the Transitional Period is not markedly different than in the Early Period. People refer clients to the detectives or clients come to them; clients are emotionally involved or not; clients worry about the cost or not, etc. Except for Joseph Hansen's Dave Brandstetter and Marcia Muller's Sharon McCone, and they go on their own in later works, the detectives work for themselves and thus are able to reject cases or are forced to accept them when short of money. John D. MacDonald's Travis McGee in *A Purple Place for Dying* does not think the case is right for him but goes to Esmerelda in the Southwest to talk to Mona Fox Yeoman, his potential client. He is about to say no when someone shoots her. This action assures that McGee will investigate her death. Thus, in addition to independence, the personal, not just money, becomes an important ingredient in whether or not the detective will work for someone. In Roger L. Simon's *The Big Fix*, Moses Wine's old girlfriend Lila Shea appears one night at his apartment while he is playing a solitary game of Clue, and he agrees to work on a case involving a presidential primary race. Her death commits him even more. Some detectives also see themselves as part of the everyday world of work. More often than not middle class, they avoid the hint of upper class pretensions. In one sense, they might be seen as outside of class boundaries. Their varied experiences reinforce this concept and allow them to move between classes. The transitional hard-boiled detectives, however, see themselves mired, placed, enveloped by the complexities of the world, not above it, and practicing their profession as more than a means to an end.

Albert Samson in Michael Z. Lewin's *Ask the Right Question* has an office in his house. With this arrangement, he builds his own rhythms and living patterns. David Geherin observes, "[...] an offer of fifty-thousand dollars to drop the case he is working on [...] fails to dissuade him. His indifference to such financial incentives allows him to continue behaving like an 'indigent anachronism,' a man compelled to seek the truth before money" (*American Private Eye* 174).

Samson could maintain his independence with other living and working patterns, but with this one, he establishes a self-contained, daily routine. At home or work, he is always there, at that point of choice without need to change his environment to operate professionally. In the genre's tradition, the private investigator's office is in a seedy part of the city and is drab in its furnishings. It therefore contributes to the image of alienation often associated with the detective. Not sumptuous, Samson's home projects a sense of wholeness when Eloise Crystal arrives and attempts to hire him to find her biological father. He has no one else to convince that the delicate circumstances of being hired by an almost-sixteen-year old girl fit within his professional activities. Probably no more quixotic in the cases they take than the detectives from either the Early or Modern Periods, the transitional detectives do have some peculiar clients whose cases appeal to their sense of independence. In *Saratoga Longshot*, Stephen Dobyns' Charlie Bradshaw creates his path to freedom while, paradoxically, remaining in some measure of contact with those, mainly his family, from whom he frees himself.

Independence can be achieved with enough money on which to live, but even this condition is not finally determinable of the detectives' actions. Like Philip Marlowe in Raymond Chandler's *The Long Goodbye* who, for a time, keeps the $5000 bill given to him by Terry Lennox, but not to spend, MacDonald's Travis McGee has an emergency fund, hidden in an unfindable location on his boat *Busted Flush* and generally unused. He adds to it but seldom removes any money. The source of the detectives' independence is character, not cash, and some of the transitional hard-boiled writers as well as the early ones strongly focus their novels on the detectives' character. Leroy Lad Panek argues, "[...] academic hard-boiled writers have discovered facets of tone and character glossed-over, ignored, or unimagined by the inventors of the form. And by exploring these, the new writers have sought to make the hard-boiled story relevant to the seventies and eighties" (*Introduction* 199).

Chandler's insight into the detective's character in "The Simple Art of Murder" reveals a portrait of a figure who stands alone if not always apart. This condition results from his never losing sight of himself as a separate person even when with others. This aspect of independence does present a dilemma when the aloneness comes crowding in, urging the need to merge with others, however temporarily. Yet, even with Bill Pronzini's Nameless who wants to, and does, marry Kerry Wade, he still remains the detective, indigestible in his stolid pursuit of his career. Nameless admires the pulp detectives who first appeared in 1920s magazines like *Black Mask*. He aims to model his actions on theirs. This way of thinking may not be popular, but it reflects who he is. Nameless is unapologetic for himself or for what he does, even when a case seems to go awry as in *Scattershot*, discussed below.

After MacDonald's Travis McGee, Parker's Spenser is probably the most independent-minded private investigator in the Transitional Period. He differs from McGee primarily in having a license and in establishing and maintaining good police contacts. McGee avoids the police and does not like to join anything. In *The Long Lavender Look*, he tells Betsy Kapp:

> "I am a lot more conspicuous and memorable than I would like to be. It's a handicap in my line of work. If they ever make me on the front pages, with picture and with colorful account of how I make a living, that is the end of the living, honey. I would never get a chance to get in close enough to make a recovery, and I would have the law keeping a beady eye on me from that point on" [115].

At the end of *Mortal Stakes* (1975), Spenser lays out the code by which he operates. Parker largely derives this from Chandler's Philip Marlowe and his discussion of the code in "The Simple Art of Murder." However, Parker adds a realistic element to the idea of a code in a discussion with Susan. He is troubled by the inadequacy of the code to meet life's contingencies. Spenser tells Susan, "'I don't know if there is even a name for the system I've chosen, but it has to do with honor. And honor is behavior for its own reason'" (189). Susan adds, "'And' [...] 'two moral imperatives in your system are never to allow innocents to be victimized and never to kill people except involuntarily.'" She goes on, "'[T]his time you couldn't obey both those imperatives. You had to violate one'" (189). If Spenser wanted to help Marty and Linda Rabb, he had to kill Frank Doerr and Wally Hogg who were blackmailing them and would not stop. Spenser realizes that his dilemma has "'got to do with being human'" (189). He cannot gloss over what he sees as a failure in his code, and this lessens him somewhat in his own eyes. Spenser's independence in this aspect of the novel is that his awareness of the implications of his actions arise from his particular beliefs and the experience in trying to live by them. While he shares this with Susan, he does not expect her to make it any better. What is, is. During his explanation of the above to Susan, Spenser speaks of Linda Rabb's independent actions to save her family. After Doerr and Hogg are killed, Bucky Maynard and Lester Floyd remain to be dealt with. Bucky, the Red Sox play-by-play announcer, owed more money to Doerr than he could repay. He blackmails the Rabbs by threatening to reveal that Linda was a New York prostitute and appeared in a porn film. Even with Doerr's and Hogg's deaths, Maynard will not stop his blackmailing scheme. Wally Rabb has been throwing some games or innings for the gamblers. This is Maynard's price for his silence about Linda's past. Linda decides to reveal her past, and this eliminates Maynard's leverage. He cannot say anything about Wally without indicting himself. Spenser tells Susan, "'[...] I couldn't save them and her husband couldn't save them. She saved herself and her husband'" (187). Like Spenser, Linda's tough, independent mind derives from herself and her beliefs. In her case, she loves her family and believes they are worth the sacrifice.

Aside from his past connection to Lila Shea and his subsequent anger over her murder, Moses Wine in Simon's *The Big Fix* has no reason to go to work for Senator Miles Hawthorne in the Democratic presidential primary or to stay on the case. He tells Nate Sugars and Sam Sebastian, "'[...] I kind of owe it to a friend of mine in your campaign'" (12). Wine generally supports Hawthorne's positions as a Democrat, but this is not enough to motivate him. Robert A. Baker and Michael T. Nietzel describe his attitude toward work: "Now he's a long-haired, in-debt, denim-draped 'people's detective' who spends as much time stoking his hash pipe as he does investigating his cases" (264).

Simon provides Wine with a personal life, not only a professional one. He has an ex-wife, two sons, and his Aunt Sonya. Although he is a former sixties activist, Aunt Sonya is from an older and more radical generation of leftists. From this web of commitments, Wine works through the death of Lila to a public encounter. Of course, Wine is a private investigator, so he engages with the public, but Simon emphasizes the personal as a source of his actions. He watches the returns on election night with his two sons, arguing with Jacob, the older boy, about the value of television news and elections. Jacob is only four years old and Simon one. He thinks, "Being a father was a tough gig" (197). Sitting up all night watching the returns and the victory celebration for Hawthorne, Wine the detective merges with Wine the father; his public persona fades and one is left with the private man watching an event that the investigator in a small way helped bring about.

It would seem normal to believe that the personal element would figure largely in whether or not a detective takes a case. From the first hard-boiled detective novel, Carroll John Daly's *The Snarl of the Beast*, the detectives' emotions and desires have controlled not only their accepting cases but have influenced their handling of them. Even as cool an investigator as Sam Spade gets involved with his client, the murderer Brigid O'Shaughnessy, until he comes to his senses. Sexual desire temporarily clouds his judgment and almost puts him in her place, i.e., charged with murder. Miles Archer, Spade's partner, is not so fortunate when she earlier lures him into the San Francisco alley and kills him. The personal can be dangerous to other detectives as well when Philip Marlowe in *The Big Sleep* and Mike Hammer in *I, the Jury* narrowly escape death at the hands of Carmen Sternwood and Dr. Charlotte Manning, respectively. Given these progenitors, MacDonald's Travis McGee and Lawrence Block's Matthew Scudder easily seem to accept the personal response to a client, rather than a straight business arrangement, as a natural way to conduct their cases. McGee's clients sometimes come as a dead friend which occurs in *The Girl in the Plain Brown Wrapper* (1968) when he receives a letter and a check for $25,000 from Helena Pearson asking him to go to Ft. Courtney, Florida, and keep her daughter Maureen Pike from committing suicide. His memories of Helena and loyalty to the family make him decide in the affirmative. Scudder, a former policeman living across the street from Armstrong's, his favorite bar, operates solely on the personal in Lawrence Block's *The Sins of the Fathers*. He tells his client, Cale Hanniford that he is not a private detective: "'I do favors for people. They give me gifts'" (2). Initially, Scudder resists taking the case because the young man the police arrested for Wendy Hanniford's murder, Richard Vanderpoel, hanged himself in his jail cell. The police apparently believe that his death closed the case. Scudder reluctantly takes the work but not before thinking to himself: "I had not wanted the job. I work as infrequently as I can. I had no present need to work. I don't need much money. My room rent is cheap, my day-to-day expenses low enough. Besides, I had no reason to dislike this man. I have always felt more comfortable taking money from men I dislike" (4). Hanniford's plea that he needs to know why Wendy died convinces Scudder to work for him.

James Crumley's Milo Milodragovitch, Meriwether, Montana, private investigator is a descendant of a wealthy family and must wait until his fifty-third birthday to receive his inheritance. At thirty-nine years old, his heavy drinking and distinct lack of success as a P.I. do not bode well for his immediate future. The state has just ruined his divorce business in *The Wrong Case* by changing the law. Milo states, "Now we have dissolutions of marriage by reason of irreconcilable differences" (3). At the request of his friend Rick Diamond, an English professor at the local university, he agrees to take Helen Duffy's case. Her family has not heard from her brother Raymond Duffy for three weeks. He came out west two years before to work on a master's in history but recently dropped out of school. Helen is an assistant professor in English at Buena Vista College in Storm Lake, Iowa. Milo tells her that he is not very successful at finding people but that it can be costly to look. He suggests she should go to the police: "'The bastards are corrupt but they're cheap. I'm expensive and corrupt. And not very good at my job'" (18). After pressing him to take her case, she suddenly decides to leave. Milo, explaining the mess he has made of his life, asks her to stay. He suggests a deal, "'I'll look for your brother in exchange for your nights . . . my days for your nights'" (21). Helen rejects the bargain and leaves his office. Not only idiosyncratic, Milo stretches the idea of the private investigator taking cases for personal reasons. After her brother appears to have died of a possibly self-inflicted drug overdose, Helen hires Milo "'to look into the details of my brother's death'" (70). Not as far gone in drink as Old Pierre and Simon Rome, Milo's friend and a disbarred lawyer, he careens through the case and his life to a marginally successful conclusion. For Milo, the personal and professional so mix that he cannot disentangle them.

David Lehman in *The Perfect Murder: A Study in Detection* states, "Dupin has what Poe himself never enjoyed: enough of an inheritance to make it unnecessary for him to join the workaday world. He is free from the exigencies of making a living, free to indulge his genius only when and if it pleases him to do so" (65).

Dupin and to a certain extent Holmes, whose cavalier attitude toward compensation suggests some other income, differ greatly from their hard-boiled descendants who need to make a living. The latter are almost never working class, but they have a work ethic, however idiosyncratic, that would earn them at least an honorary blue collar. Not only do they spend long hours on the job, but they get their hands dirty, a phrase that blue-collar workers use to separate them from white-collar employees and which suggests they do "real" work. Parker's Spenser best fits this mold. Raised by his father and two hardworking uncles holding blue-collar jobs, Spenser becomes a boxer until he realizes that he cannot be the best. Jersey Joe Walcott, one of the best, knocks him out. After working as an investigator for the state's attorney's office, Spenser resigns to operate for himself. Well read, Spenser keeps in shape for those dangerous times that require the dirty work. However, he plays down any cultural or intellectual attainments in order to function on a work level at which a minimum of pretension is required. His first job is for a university. In *The Godwulf Manuscript*, he quickly becomes involved in a murder investigation and has to deal with the Boston mob. The man behind the murder and the theft of the manuscript turns out to be a professor at the university. Spenser's actions leave him in a position morally superior both to the university administration and the professor. He has endured the danger and put in the effort to achieve his goals.

The detectives operate in the real world, and this gives them the appearance of being part of the workaday environment however unusual their profession. The strangeness of the latter to the ordinary citizen appears time and again when people express amazement that they are talking to a "real" private detective. One of those who projects the most "real" attitude toward his work is Bill Pronzini's Nameless. Part of this attitude comes from Nameless's low-key approach to his cases. He is thorough but undramatic in the attention he gives to every aspect of a job. In addition, he feels a responsibility to his clients, not always reciprocated, that forces him to put in any extra effort needed to solve the problem before him. Nameless always shows a professional dedication to his job. Although Nameless cannot prevent the theft of the expensive ring in *Scattershot*, he does solve the case. Just as George Hickox, the actual thief who works for Nameless's client Clyde Mollenhauer, sets up the detective and steals the ring, so Louis Martinetti in Pronzini's *The Snatch* hires Nameless to deliver the ransom money to his son's kidnappers, a kidnapping he arranged, and subsequently asks him to investigate the crime. Nameless figures out the deception and the murders that occur. The contrast between Nameless's application to his work and life and his clients' absurdities, moral and otherwise, stands out strongly.

The image of the detective called in to bring order to a madhouse goes back to the earliest figures in the genre. Hammett's Continental Op in *Red Harvest* and Sam Spade in *The Maltese Falcon* and Chandler's Philip Marlowe in *The Big Sleep* and *Farewell, My Lovely* cultivate the figure of the cynical, disillusioned detective with sufficient reason for his cynicism and disillusionment. Similarly, Paul Ellman, John Meyer Warren's lawyer, asks Jacob Asch in Arthur Lyons' *The Dead Are Discreet* to clear Warren from charges that he murdered his wife Sheila. From what seems a straightforward case, Asch soon becomes aware that pornography, the occult, and family murder dominate the investigation. Asch, an ex-reporter once jailed for refusing to reveal his sources, sifts through the violent events to a conclusion that, as he leaves the home of Gloria Pilsen, one of the murderers and a woman whom he has had the misfortune to sleep with, unsettles him: "The air was warming up and it felt like it was going to be a hot summer's day, but that didn't help. Something caught the base of my spine and ran up my back with cold little feet. I shivered as I opened the car door and stepped in" (213). Asch's shiver is obviously more moral than meteorological. He has turned the pornographic film over to the police, implicating Pilsen, and knows they will soon come for her, but he cannot avoid the sense of hatred and evil emanating from her. Marlowe's leaving Gen. Sternwood's mansion at the end of *The Big Sleep*, having done the best he could in a desperate situation, comes to mind and suggests that one cannot completely escape the evil encountered.

Alo Nudger in John Lutz's *Buyer Beware* is the prototypical working detective. Nudger takes Gordon Clark's case because he needs the money (16). It is as simple as needing to pay the bill for his trailer-park home and office (11). Unpretentious fits Nudger well, especially when he admits he was, yes, Mr. Happy for three years on television: "'That was me,' I admitted. 'The clown cop who introduced safety cartoons for the kiddies'" (14). His former profession and his nervous stomach combine to give him a non-threatening image. Snatching a child from one parent to give it to the other, even when the latter has legal custody, will always be problematic. When Clark leaves his trailer after their first meeting, Nudger states: "Already I could feel the heavy pulsing in my stomach that I felt every time I took a new case. Clark had asked if there might be trouble. There might always be trouble in the taking of a child from its natural mother. I didn't allow myself to dwell on the kinds of trouble that were possible" (16). After the wealthy Dale Carlon cheats him of $35,000, he resigns himself, silently accepting the fact that the check for $5,000 and his $10,000 in the bank represent significant money to him (187). Even MacDonald's Travis McGee gets to reject Lysa Dean's offer of sex in *The Quick Red Fox*, an offer made in lieu of the additional $40,000 she owes him.

A final category of work in the Transitional Period involves its dangers. Are there still serious threats of bodily harm in the detecting business some forty years after Daly's first novel? The answer is yes, and it takes no real stretch of the imagination to accept the violence as realistic. The media steadily report the expansion or contraction of the American murder and violent crimes rate. If imagination fails a writer, there is no dearth of examples from which to choose, rather a plethora from the many incidents that shock and appall even those used to their constant occurrences. One knows of the innocent civilians harmed in the detective literature, but even the detective continues to be threatened. Michael Collins' Dan Fortune in *The Brass Rainbow* (1969 finds himself without a client but police pressure to stay out of the investigation of the death of the wealthy Jonathan Radford III. Sammy Weiss comes to Fortune for an alibi that he was with Fortune and not at Radford's apartment earlier in the day. Fortune says no. The next morning Detective Sgt. Bert Freedman, a bad cop according to Fortune, comes to his apartment and attempts to force him to reveal Weiss's whereabouts, something Fortune does not know. After Fortune later goes to Radford's apartment, Cap. Gazzo stops him on the street and tells him to stay out of the case. Fortune says, "I felt very alone" (17). However, Fortune's danger at this point is more situational than immediate. Michael Z. Lewin's *Ask the Right Question* starts off innocuously enough when Samson's too-young client hires him, as stated earlier, to find her real father. He begins asking questions and doing research. Before the novel ends, Samson uncovers a brutal sixteen-year-old murder and suffers six stab wounds from the woman who participated in that murder. How could he foresee such an eventuality? Yet, as *The Way We Die Now* (1973), the second novel in the series, begins, Samson has spent three months recovering from his near-lethal wounds and can barely raise his right arm above his shoulder. Not every detective is as physically capable as MacDonald's Travis McGee and Parker's Spenser, but even they are at times seriously endangered, especially McGee. Starting with *The Deep Blue Good-by*, McGee has to be nursed back to health after both physical and emotional losses. Cathy Kerr, his client in *Blue*, performs the task twice, the second time in *The Scarlet Ruse*. In that novel, Frank Sprenger beats him severely, but in the process, McGee manages to shoot and kill him.

Victims come in all shapes, sizes, and ages in the genre. If there is danger, sometimes there will be violence with all its possibly bloody consequences. As a reader, one is privy to the events, and all one needs is the imagination to know that this not only happens in the book but also could happen in real life. It takes Coleridge's suspension of disbelief to be there but not there. It may be difficult to accept that some parents could make their own children victims whether out of indifference or in an effort to use them to gain something. In Parker's *God Save the Child* and Pronzini's *The Snatch*, referred to above, one sees an example of each kind of parental abuse. Roger and Margery Bartlett come to Spenser to hire him to find and return their troubled teenaged son Kevin. It does not take Spenser long to realize that the parents' self-absorption is the reason for his disappearance. He has gotten into trouble at school and become involved with Vic Harroway, a gay bodybuilder, who actually loves him. Spenser meets Susan Silverman, a counselor at Kevin's school who helps him understand the dynamics of Kevin's family and his relationship with Harroway. Susan goes on to become Spenser's lover. Kevin's life is not in much danger in *God Save the Child*, but one cannot say the same for Louis Martinetti's son Gary in *The Snatch*. The father, as stated above, arranges the kidnapping of his son for monetary gain. In this novel, people involved with the kidnapping die. Apparently, Gary becomes an object to Martinetti who puts him in the danger that he should have expected would occur. Children are not often used as pawns in the hard-boiled detective novel, but it occurs, and when it does, few of the adults show the concern that Albert Samson reveals in his worry in *Ask the Right Question* as to whether he can take the fifteen-year old Eloise Crystal as a client.

Many victims' pasts leave them open to coercion, and there seems to be no lack of those who pressure them against their will. In Lewin's *The Enemies Within* (1974), Martin Willeston and Melanie Baer Kee's troubles begin when they are born. Freeman Baer sleeps with Mildred Willetson, and she bears Martin. He knows that he is illegitimate but not who his father is. Melanie is supposedly Freeman Baer's legitimate daughter. Unfortunately for all, Martin and Melanie fall in love, and not aware that they are half-brother and half-sister, they make love, and Melanie becomes pregnant. She runs away and does not tell Martin that she is pregnant. She meets and marries Edmund Kee, but her child dies before it is a year old. Melanie aborts the child she later conceives with Kee, but in revenge, Kee changes the computer records to indicate a live birth. Martin and Melanie are living together when Martin hires Samson to get Arthur Bartholomew, another private investigator, off their backs. No one in Indianapolis knows of his and Melanie's past, and in fact, she dresses as a man, and Bartholomew thinks Willeston is gay. It turns out that Freeman Baer is not Melanie's father, but rather she is the daughter of Robert Goger, Baer's lawyer. Both Melanie and Martin then, are illegitimate, their life of incest becomes no incest. Their subsequent marriage lasts only a short time. What Lewin and other writers argue from these complicated examples is that they are inescapable. Things happen to people at an early age when they do not think ahead and do not have sufficient control of their lives to believe that the inevitable consequences will occur.

For these detectives, work represents the condition in which they chiefly experience their lives. McGee is somewhat different in that he sees himself as permanently retired, at least until circumstances intervene, and on more than one occasion, he speaks of the excitement of the hunt that a case brings. Most of the detectives pursue careers that do not often involve violence, but it is the exceptional circumstances that give them their identities as hard-boiled investigators. On their own, they head toward the violence, a direction that those special, dangerous cases demand they go. The workaday world often encapsulates them, but it is an illusion that the sharp edge of danger shatters.

13

Love and Sexuality

Through an ineluctable process of change, love and romance seep into the hard-boiled detective tradition. Archetypal figures such as the Continental Op and Philip Marlowe argue against the possibility for this intimate human relationship. The Continental Op usually avoids this type of personal interaction. In *Red Harvest*, Dinah Brand, the woman he symbolically "stabs," interests him, but his customary method of investigation and his general focus on work leave him no time for love. Casual sexual contact seems also beyond his range. For Philip Marlowe, either a set dislike to the complex involvement required in a romantic meeting or an aversion to the kind of women he meets, e.g., Carmen and Vivian Sternwood in *The Big Sleep* or Velma in *Farewell, My Lovely*, early in the series prevents his seriously pursuing any possible love interest. But with John D. MacDonald's introduction of Travis McGee in *The Deep Blue Good-by*, the hard-boiled detective novel recreates itself in new directions. McGee shows a propensity for love and romance. Admittedly, he is outwardly reluctant to get involved and stridently rejects any idea that he is a candidate for the stability of marriage. Yet, Lois Atkinson draws him into an involvement that seems to grow without his acceptance, or even awareness, of future consequences and entanglements. Robert B. Parker's Spenser, beginning with *The Godwulf Manuscript*, appears a slightly updated version of Brett Halliday's Michael Shayne without marriage. With the introduction of Susan Silverman in *God Save the Child*, Spenser changes, a change quite unlike any of which Mickey Spillane's Mike Hammer or Ross Macdonald's Lew Archer are capable of sustaining. Along with Michael Z. Lewin's Albert Samson and Bill Pronzini's Nameless, the hard-boiled detectives in the

Transitional Period, while keeping their credentials for toughness, significantly alter their images through the intimacy of love and sexuality.

In a sequence of relationships in *The Deep Blue Good-by*, interspersed with more casual sexual contacts, MacDonald sets in motion a new attitude toward love and sexuality in the hard-boiled detective novel. LeRoy Lad Panek notes of the women in the Early Period that they "have no principles other than self-interest, whether it is sensualism like that of the Sternwood women or greed like that of Brigid O'Shaughnessy" (*Introduction* 163). Chookie McCall, Lois Atkinson, and Cathy Kerr are the three women through whom MacDonald initially explores this relatively new convention for the genre. Chookie is an old friend of McGee's and asks him to help Cathy, a dancer in her troupe. At the beginning of the novel, she is working on a dance routine on the *Busted Flush*, McGee's houseboat. After her exercise, she takes a bath in the boat's oversized tub. Asking McGee to bring her a drink, she makes sexual overtures. He responds by saying that he once approached her but that she said no. Now, he wants to know whether she wants to accept the conditions of friendly sex with no commitment. Chookie admits that she is fighting with her boyfriend and that she is not serious about beginning an affair with McGee. While McGee's desire for a sexual involvement with no strings is not that different from some early hard-boiled detectives, what is significant is the discussion about involvement, the clarification of sexual goals and boundaries. Some critics have remarked that MacDonald becomes preachy about the new sexual mores developing in the 1960s and which he incorporates into the hard-boiled detective novel. The dilemmas that intimacy brings to male-female relationships are a consistent theme throughout the Travis McGee series, and MacDonald's serious exploration of it in the hard-boiled detective novel adds considerable weight to his work.

Another dimension to MacDonald's examination of love and sexuality occurs before McGee begins searching for Junior Allen, Cathy Kerr's former lover, who has stolen something valuable that her father brought back from World War II. Sgt. Dave Berry died in Leavenworth before revealing what he returned with and where he hid it. Prior to his salvage for Cathy, McGee attends a party on the boat of the Alabama Tiger. His expressed purpose is to find an attractive sexual partner for the night. This is one of the few times in the series in which McGee approaches sex on such a purely physical level. His carnal binge in *The Turquoise Lament* is a later, rare exception exacerbated by his separation from Pidge Brindle and her decision to sail to Pago Pago with the murderous Howie, the husband whom she plans to divorce. McGee brings Molly Bea Archer in *Blue* back to the *Flush*, and they have sex. McGee's self consciousness about the act and his awareness of its essential meaninglessness when personal affection and caring are absent set this episode apart from other instances of casual sex in the genre. MacDonald appears to alter the whole direction of sexual activity in the hard-boiled detective novel with this scene. Mike Hammer regrets succumbing to the temptations of the twins in Mickey Spillane's *I, the Jury* since he is engaged to Charlotte Manning, but McGee's ruminations on his contact with Molly Bea and later his feeling of being sized up by a friend of Molly Bea's and passed on to her, an offer he declines, add other dimensions to the scene. Molly Bea and her friend become overt appraisers of sexual partners. Their more aggressive manifestation of a part of the age-old sexual dance is an aspect of the changing cultural climate. MacDonald dramatizes this change and makes the very masculine McGee feel skittish about the women's behavior. A similar appraisal and attempted handing over occurs between Deeleen and Cory after McGee has rescued Lois Atkinson and found Junior Allen. Deeleen and Cory are coarser versions of Molly Bea and her friend, but they show the same attitudes toward sexual accommodation.

While searching for Junior Allen, McGee finds Lois Atkinson, the second of Allen's current victims. She lives on Candle Key, and recently suffered from Allen's emotional and sexual abuse. When McGee appears at her door, she collapses, fearing that McGee has come to replace Allen and unable to endure more abuse. Specifically, she believes that Allen has passed her on to McGee and is too unwell to endure another predator. MacDonald adds another dimension to the themes of love and sexuality in the hard-boiled detective novel with McGee's love affair with Lois. When McGee realizes how sick Lois is, he calls a doctor, nurses her back to health, and when she can travel, takes her to the *Flush*. MacDonald implies that some significant shift in McGee's life has occurred and that he and Lois will stay together, with marriage not an impossibility. As will happen with later detectives in the Transitional Period, notably Parker's Spenser, genuine intimacy develops between Lois and McGee. Gone for the moment are the hard, lonely, isolated images of the detective who cannot connect in a basically loveless world. When Lois dies and McGee chases and kills Allen and rescues the young Patty Devlan, Cathy Kerr becomes McGee's aid and comfort and offers a warm body if he needs her. MacDonald pictures McGee suffering and needing succor. Cathy and her young son give him a sense of life again. Well once more, McGee remarks to himself that Lois changed him and her death shifted his life in irremediable ways.

The general direction of male-female relationships in the Transitional Period is toward monogamy. While Travis McGee is a problematic figure in this regard, an underlying motif of his romantic contacts is a desire to make some emotional connection. He may not be consistent in this, but he does keep coming back to it and rejecting the image of the libertine. In *A*

Tan and Sandy Silence (1971), he confesses his self-disgust to Meyer that his many affairs and even more casual contacts leave him with the paramount desire to escape from any more intimate entanglements. However, this revulsion does not lead to a cynical rejection of the possibility of love. Unlike Chandler's Philip Marlowe, McGee sees his own failure in establishing a mature relationship with a woman. In contrast, Parker's Spenser begins with an almost casual sexual indulgence in *The Godwulf Manuscript*. When Mrs. Marion Orchard and then her daughter Terry offer themselves to Spenser on the same day, he accepts with hardly any awareness of the odd-ity, if nothing else, of his actions. And, this is the wife and daughter of the man who hired him. The Continental Op's and Sam Spade's sense of pro-fessionalism are completely lacking in Spenser at that point. However, a shift in the direction of valuing love and a monogamous relationship occurs in Spenser's life when Susan Silverman becomes his primary romantic focus starting in *God Save the Child*. He values her above all and generally for-sakes other women for her. When she has doubts concerning their future together and has an affair with a friend in *Valediction* (1984), Spenser also begins an affair but waits for her. He has committed himself, and that ends the matter for him.

The desire for one person with whom to have a romantic relationship, at least one at a time, is a clear sign of maturity. McGee often makes this observation about himself and is at his most self-critical when he indulges in sex with no sense of emotional involvement. He does not always need a lifelong commitment such as those that appear to be developing in *The Quick Red Fox, Pale Gray for Guilt, The Turquoise Lament, The Empty Cop-per Sea* (1978), and *The Green Ripper*. Each relationship in the above nov-els has a different dynamic, but McGee wants to be with the woman and something intervenes rather than his indifference. Each affair grows from a case, and McGee's orientation toward some sense of permanence is the most interesting aspect of the affairs. It is as if he were destined for mar-riage or some relationship resembling it in terms of duration and commit-ment. There is an absence of doubt regarding the direction of his life in each instance. When Puss Killian in *Gray* leaves him and writes that she has returned to her husband, McGee's seeming dismissal of her rings hollowly. While Dobyn's Bradshaw has several relationships in the series, each woman is important to him, and the breakups come from the complexity of living, the result of choices made because of changes in interests or goals. And, the women feature prominently in these types of changes. They are not helpless victims of the man.

The image of the hard-boiled detective as a womanizer is frequently overstated. Brett Halliday's Michael Shayne and Richard S. Prather's Shell Scott come closest to this pattern though Spillane's Mike hammer, as noted above, is susceptible to seduction. But, the detective as womanizer is not the same as a description of the detective with sexual partners. Charlotte Manning, the murderer Hammer unknowingly seeks, is the woman he wants to marry. In his early idealization of Charlotte, Hammer's response to her resembles Race Williams' reaction to those women he believes are pure. Hammer refuses to sleep with Charlotte before marriage. The Op, Sam Spade, and Philip Marlowe are the archetypal figures who resist romantic commitment. But, Spade and Marlowe have relatively few affairs, and the Op's life is devoted primarily to work. What distinguishes these detectives and Ross Macdonald's Lew Archer is their sense of emotional isolation. This isolation extends to love relationships as well as friendships. And they have difficulty relying on friendship. In *The Dain Curse*, the Op encounters Owen Fitzstephan, a friend from his days in New York. He seems genuinely glad to see him. However, Fitzstephan turns out to be the killer the Op seeks. Lew Archer experiences the same thing with Albert Graves, a man with whom he struck up a friendship during World War II, and whom he discovers kills his client's husband and the husband's pilot/chauffeur.

Lewin's Albert Samson, like Archer, is divorced. Marriage is rare in the early hard-boiled detectives' lives, but either marriage or some form of commitment becomes the pattern in the Transitional Period. Shayne, an early exception, marries Phyllis Brighton in *The Uncomplaining Corpses* after a varied romantic life. Samson has a permanent love relationship and also has a daughter whom he writes to and occasionally sees. In addition, his mother lives in Indianapolis, and he occasionally eats at her luncheonette. Along with the permanent love affair, the addition of family members underscores the idea of the emotionally whole detective that develops in the Transitional Period. Samson's lover does not appear in *Ask the Right Question*, but she is so much a part of his life that no doubt arises as to their loyalty to one another. This assumption of a needed and desired permanence is what most strikes the reader. The detective, as it were, comes in from the cold. Of course, Lawrence Block's Matthew Scudder, a divorced ex-policeman who resigned after accidentally killing a young girl, initially lives alone in a Manhattan hotel. His relationship with his former wife is a cordial one in the early novels. However, Scudder gives the impression of a man who belongs elsewhere; he is someone set adrift from the kind of emotional relationship that would give greater meaning to his life. Scudder spends his evenings drinking in nearby bars and becomes better known to bartenders than friends. Gradually his real needs assert themselves, and from a casual affair with Elaine Mardell, a call girl who operates independently, Scudder grows to love her, and after she abandons her profession, they begin a serious, long-term relationship. In *The Devil Knows You're Dead* (1993), they decide to move in together and Scudder proposes to Elaine.

Block emphasizes the maturity in their commitment to one another in the earlier novels: both know their weaknesses and past actions, accept them, and acknowledge their need for a loving partner. Beginning from all the "wrong" bases, Block draws a picture of a fundamentally healthy adult relationship. Although their pasts do create stresses, they recognize that their mutual love and regard can help them overcome any difficulties. Reflecting this future-oriented direction of their lives, Scudder eventually stops drinking and attends AA meetings.

Bill Pronzini's *Scattershot* is as much about Nameless's love affair with Kerry as it is about the cases on which he works. Although the notoriety he gains from several of them affects their relationship, most of the novel dealing with their affair centers on their disagreement regarding marriage. And, throughout the novel, from the first pages to the last, Nameless and Kerry struggle over his attempt to pressure her to make a decision about their future. Kerry asks, "'Why is it so important to you that we get married? We've got a good thing going as it is.'" He replies, "'I'm old-fashioned, that's why' ... 'Where I come from, people who love each other get married'" (129). In his inimitable way, Pronzini portrays Nameless's single-minded attitude toward Kerry, a manner she describes as "'relentless'" (130). Part of this is because of his fear of it not working out. Fifty-three and overweight, jogging as the novel begins (1), Nameless worries that he "was going to lose her" (9). Pronzini underscores the shift in *Scattershot* in the areas of love and sexuality by emphasizing his admiration of the pulp detectives (133). However, he contrasts his behavior unfavorably with the supposed reaction of Philip Marlowe but then thinks, "The hell with Phil Marlowe [...] I'm not Phil Marlowe' I'm me. I'm me, damnit, and I love that lady" (23). Nameless, and the tradition, have changed.

Another shift in the ways that hard-boiled detective novelists deal with love and sexuality is in the detectives' desire for love and kindness, a need for sympathy on a deep human level. In addition to the general predilection for a monogamous relationship, this reaching out tends to humanize the men, moving them even further away from the figure of the unconnected, lonely private investigator whose life excludes closeness almost by definition. In *The Killing Floor* (1976), Arthur Lyons' Jacob Asch, a Los Angeles-based private detective, has no close romantic involvement, but he does reveal his need to be with someone that denotes more than having sex. After informing Barbara Fein, his client, that her husband, David Fein, is dead, Asch returns to his apartment. He makes himself a drink but realizes he cannot be alone: "My insides were seething, churning, and the thought of facing the plasterboard walls of my apartment for the rest of the night intolerable. I needed a kind word and the touch of sympathetic hands" (93).

Asch calls a young woman he is seeing named Sarah whom he awakes. He tells her, "'[...] I just needed to talk to somebody, that's all'" (94). Asch says, "Not that we had grown close. In many ways we remained almost total strangers. But we did fulfill certain immediate needs in each other, needs that went beyond sex, although that was good, too" (95). This acknowledgement of need and reaching out to fill it illustrates the kind of shift that occurs in the transitional hard-boiled detective novel. Asch remarks on the one other occasion in the novel that he visited her, after making love and talking most of the night, that he has "a feeling of utter isolation" (228). There is no elaboration as to why he experiences this emotional switch, but he does not deny the previous "feeling of sanctuary" (228) he had.

Michael Collins' Dan Fortune in *Walk a Black Wind* (1971) and Lewin's Samson in *Ask the Right Question* have regular girlfriends who do not appear in the above novels. One can infer a closeness from these relationships, but it is Robert B. Parker's Spenser in *God Save the Child* (1974) who establishes a romantic atmosphere comparable to Travis McGee's archetypal relationships in *Blue* and later novels. After Spenser's lack of close attachments in *The Godwulf Manuscript*, Parker introduces Susan Silverman into the series and begins the long love affair between her and Spenser. David Geherin states, "The intimacy that develops between the two arises naturally and is used by Parker to reveal a dimension to Spenser's character he would be unable to portray through his professional activities or narrative style alone" (*Sons* 26). While Spenser might not be as open about his feelings as some other hard-boiled detectives in this period, Parker leaves no doubt about his love and desire for Susan and that she supplies what his life is lacking. The Bartletts hire Spenser in *God Save the Child* to find their fifteen-year old son Kevin who has disappeared from home and school. After talking with the assistant principal at Kevin's school, Spenser speaks with Susan who is the school's guidance counselor. Spenser observes, "When she shook hands with me, I felt something click down back of my solar plexus" (36). He notes that their "two coats overlapped on the rack. It wasn't much, but it was a start" (36). In addition to the banter between them, the above quotes testify to his immediate orientation toward Susan, a shifting that does indeed forecast important changes in their lives. Spenser later calls Susan at 5:30 PM one night and invites her to dinner at his home. He tells her that he is "about to cook a pork tenderloin *en croute*" (69). Parker interrupts the story for a thirteen-page romantic interlude in which he briefly questions her about Kevin and asks her to elope with him (75) before they kiss (80). Susan does not make love with him, saying, "'Not the first time. Not in your apartment'" (81). She invites him to dinner at her home "'next Tuesday evening at eight'" (82). Arriving late and unable to call before, Spenser manages to explain what has happened, and they, after Spenser says, "'*je vous aime beaucoup, je ne sai pas* what to do'" (170), make love (170–71). Spenser involves her in the case and is even relaxing at her house when he calls Lt. Quirk in Boston and learns something concerning Smithfield's Chief Trask that subsequently ends the case. Spenser's earlier fight with Vic Harroway, Kevin Bartlett's apparent lover, establishes Spenser's hard-boiled credentials (188–93). However, the love affair that he begins with Susan is a true continuation of the inclusion of romantic intimacy in the hard-boiled detective novel that MacDonald's Travis McGee series initiates.

Unlike Parker's Spenser, McGee's progress toward a full, loving relationship in the last half of the series is uneven at best. At the end of *A Tan and Sandy Silence*, as stated above, McGee appears to recognize his inadequacies as a romantic partner. That is until Jeannie Dolan comes to the *Flush* and reminds him of his offer to take her on a cruise. As mentioned above, McGee suggests to Meyer, immediately prior to her arrival, a trip to the islands in an effort to purge his shallow attempts to connect romantically. Meyer seems edgy when Jeannie arrives and quizzes her about her level of emotional stability. She assures him that she is a simple, fun-loving girl, and Meyer hurries off in relief. This is one of the rather rare comic episodes in the series. However, it is the prelude to a three-novel sequence in which McGee moves "sideways" toward Gretel Howard in *The Empty Copper Sea* and *The Green Ripper*, identifying himself in the latter novel as he visits her in the hospital before her death as her "common-law husband." Remembering his statements in *The Deep Blue Good-by* regarding his lack of interest in marriage, McGee seems like another person. Following *Tan*, his feelings and actions in *The Scarlet Ruse* begin the process of change. McGee agrees to help Hirsh Fedderman find out what has happened to his missing and valuable stamps. He also begins an affair with Mary Alice McDermit but becomes impotent with her. He slowly realizes that he knows she not only is the thief but also Jane Lawson's murderer. McDermit and Lawson work for Fedderman, and Lawson confronts McDermit over her culpability and the latter kills her. McGee is not in love with Mary Alice, but he genuinely likes and is attracted to her. He is shaken that he could have misjudged her so badly. In *The Turquoise Lament*, Pidge Brindle rejects him and chooses her therapist at the end of the novel. She feels guilty because McGee has saved her life. He accepts the situation, but it is another personal loss. Cindy Birdsong in *The Dreadful Lemon Sky* not only rejects him but also tells him that he lacks the ability to give himself to another. Thus, when he meets Gretel in *The Empty Copper Sea*, he could not be made any more emotionally ready for a better love relationship than going through these difficult experiences. Unlike his normal emotional distance hidden behind a genialness, McGee tells her, in essence, that he cannot live without her. MacDonald has not surrendered himself to sentimentality in *Copper*. Rather, McGee has cured himself of whatever made him what he was as he told Lois Atkinson in *Blue*. The vengeance McGee takes in *Green* on those responsible for Gretel's death is a measure of what he knows he has lost.

A final area to explore in the Transitional Period regarding the relatively new roles suggested for love and sexuality is whether or not a balanced relationship giving importance to love, sex, and the emotional life suggests it as an oasis in the hurly-burly of modern life. Andrew Bergman's *The Big Kiss-Off of 1944* (1974) takes sexuality in a different direction when Kerry Lane comes to Jack LeVine's office to hire him to retrieve some pornographic films she made when she was an aspiring actress in Hollywood. Trying out now for a role on Broadway, she realizes her mistake, and not only does she want to recover the films, but she also wants to keep a man named Duke Fenton from blackmailing her over them. It turns out that her real name is Anne Savage and that the blackmail is directed at her father Eli Savage, president of the Quaker National Bank in Philadelphia and a principal supporter of Gov. Thomas Dewey in his 1944 presidential race against President Franklin Delano Roosevelt. Periodically in the novel, Levine and Kitty Seymour make love. Bergman describes these occasions in the most relaxed terms, "In the sack we made the sweetest of discoveries: that we really *were* friends, great and royal and generous friends. That stuff you don't get in the books" (40). Few of the detectives in this period reject intimacy outright though some authors position their protagonists so that the personal contact needed in a love relationship may be hard to achieve. James Crumley's Milo Milodragovtich in *The Wrong Case* has too many memories through which he sees each new person he meets. These distance his view of them. His memories are not just of past lovers but of a broken family. Crumley seems purposefully to have given Milo a client whose family life is and remains to the end as chaotic as his. Chandler's Marlowe comes to mind as the earliest prototype for this heaviness of past emotional losses. But, just as Marlowe shows even in his lowest moments, Milo knows himself and knows what he is doing. With not quite the same noise level, Lyons Jacob Asch, especially in *The Dead Are Discreet*, also rejects love as an oasis, a safeguard against the world. What both Milodragovitch and Asch discover is that people's real lives are sometimes so hidden from others that one surmises, rightly or wrongly, that they are equally in the dark about themselves. When Helen Duffy's mother explains her daughter's character to Milo, it comes as a revelation that much that has brought her to Meriwether is her passion for Rick Diamond, Milo's friend and a local college professor. Her mother tells Milo that Helen is strongly sexed and that all the women in the family have been. *The Wrong Case* does not resolve all the questions this raises about her actions in the novel, but the idea of hidden motives matches her nearly complete subservience to her mother's wishes. One can only imagine that, however obedient she is in complying with her mother's request that she return with her to Storm Lake, Iowa, rather than remain with Milo as he desires, she will break out again. For both Milo and Helen, stasis, ironically, equals a turbulent emotional life.

Arthur Lyons presents no more of an oasis for love and sexuality in *All God's Children* (1975), the second novel in the series, than he does in the first. Cynthia Haynes hires Jacob Asch to look for her daughter Susan Gurney Haynes. Her money is the only thing that appears to hold her marriage to Robert Haynes together. In fact, Haynes displays more concern for Susan than her mother does. He adopted her after the marriage and wants her found and returned safely even though she is eighteen-years old and an adult. Eric Gurney, Susan's father, has remarried and with a wife and children he tells Asch that he cannot take Susan in even if she returns home. Human weakness is at odds with any desire to see love, either romantic or between parent and child, as a safe haven in the world. For Lyons, people uproot the oasis and fill in the pools, thus destroying any potential to be found for life with mutually supportive others. Yet, these and other writers in the Transitional Period do not eliminate the idea that love has a special quality, in fact, to create a safe world. Steven Dobyns' Charlie Bradshaw goes from one disappointing relationship to another, but never loses the hope that he will match with someone in a permanent way. To all intents and purposes, Bradshaw is a failure in life, but he does not think so. Short, overweight, and even-tempered, he does not inspire romantic thoughts. However, he thinks them, and this attitude, connected to his compassion and tolerance for others, helps Bradshaw find several women who value him over the life of the series beginning with Doris Bailes in *Saratoga Swimmer* (1981). Bill Pronzini's Nameless with Kerry Wade and Lawrence Block's Matthew Scudder with Elaine Mardell share that trait in Bradshaw that moves toward a stable, loving relationship. One thing that all three men have in common is that, even with unpropitious beginnings, they and their women learn to know one another. This knowledge develops into love and trust, and thus, they create their oases without closing out the world. Marcia Muller's Sharon McCone, however, foreshadows the independent, relatively isolated female hard-boiled detectives in the Modern Period. Love and sexuality do not disappear in the latter period, either for males or females, but the influence of Hammett, Chandler, and Ross Macdonald resurfaces at times in the area of private relationships. McCone leaves her job as an investigator for All Souls Legal Cooperative and establishes a private practice. Independence is in the air, and ideas about romantic love subtly shift from the looked-for partner to one who will fit into the private investigator's lifestyle.

The broadening and deepening of the affective life in the transitional hard-boiled detective is a genuine change. Love and sexuality, the emotional life leading to romance, are not unknown in the Early Period, but from MacDonald on, the writers have developed this aspect of human experience, a development that extends into the Modern Period. Their narrative choices largely close off past directions. Some few, especially Jonathan Valin's Harry Stoner in that period, hark back to the work-oriented, isolated detective. Others, like the Modern Period's Loren D. Estleman's Amos Walker and the Transitional Period's Marcia Muller's McCone, experience moments when they establish contact, however fleetingly, with another and are drawn into an emotional relationship. These types of characters can live in that world of romance, may temporarily even believe they need to stay there, but, in the manner of Sue Grafton's Kinsey Millhone, they eventually withdraw into their own environments and for a while shut out lovers.

14

Friendship: Faint Stirrings

Friendship and the hard-boiled detective novel do not easily cohere. The concept seems both innocuous and improbable for the world of violence and danger that the detective inhabits and from which he occasionally escapes. The early hard-boiled detectives have employees or acquaintances but few friends. Carroll John Daly's Race Williams employs a chauffeur and maintains an uneasy truce with the police who admire and suspect him. Dashiell Hammett's Continental Op at times works with other operatives, notably in *Red Harvest*. Hammett's Sam Spade has a secretary but quickly loses a partner in *The Maltese Falcon*. Both Spade and the Op have functional relationships with the police. Raymond Chandler's Philip Marlowe remains outside of most personal connections. As a consequence of this background, the tentative inclusion of friends as well as lovers in the Transitional Period seems an almost necessary development. John D. MacDonald does not introduce Meyer into the Travis McGee series until the third novel, *A Purple Place for Dying*, and waits until the seventh work, *Darker than Amber*, for any lengthy involvement between Meyer and McGee. Michael Collins' Dan Fortune, Robert B. Parker's Spenser, and Bill Pronzini's Nameless slowly move into the lives of others outside the confines of their cases. Lawrence Block's Matthew Scudder finds two friends when he is a policeman, Mick Ballou (bar owner and criminal) and Elaine Mardell; he eventually marries Elaine, an ex-prostitute. Michael Z. Lewin's Albert Samson, John Lutz's Alo Nudger, and Arthur Lyons' Jacob Asch are friendly without establishing strong attachments in their series. Asch is probably the more irascible of this group, but Samson and Nudger either have or have had some strong family connections that possibly predispose them to some involvement with others. Thus, the idea of friendship operates in the Transitional Period in ways that expand the image of the hard-boiled detective into one who is, if only occasionally, more accommodating to other people's lives and concerns.

One might have feared that the "insidious" growth of friendship in the Transitional Period would mark the end of the hard-boiled detective novel whose protagonist John G. Cawelti describes as "a marginal man, a loner" (*Adventure* (151). The fear would have been logical since few early detectives experience or seem to want that kind of relationship, and thus its introduction would shift the genre towards other mystery and detective patterns. It would then become something else. However, this fear discounts the genre's ability to change and its hold, while operating within its literary conventions, on the real world. A vital tradition is not easy to confine within *a priori* boundaries, and the hard-boiled tradition is a major example of this. While Meyer fulfills MacDonald's narrative requirements by supplying McGee with an auditor, he also broadens his personality and adds depth to his character. McGee not only remains a figure thrown into and emerging from violent cases; he shifts his perspective in various areas, adapts to growing older, and experiences a deep love relationship with two women over four of the last five novels in the series, especially Gretel Howard in *The Empty Copper Sea* and *The Green Ripper*. The lasting friendship with Meyer is partly responsible for these developments in McGee's life. He needs Meyer and shows this need in their day-to-day interactions. Strains sometimes develop, but they never repudiate their friendship. But, MacDonald also subtly demonstrates the genre's strong pull by drawing Meyer into McGee's activities, endangering him in the process, and in *Cinnamon Skin* providing him with the opportunity to eliminate his niece's killer. MacDonald also emphasizes the importance of this by not fundamentally changing Meyer's personality. He is a man too sensitive to others, honorable, and above all nonviolent. When Desmin Grizzel forces him to betray McGee in *Free Fall in Crimson* (1981), Meyer is devastated by his actions. The Grizzels and Pittlers (*Cinnamon Skin*) of the world slash through people's lives, and the reality is that people like McGee are needed, officially or not.

It is important to remember the seeds of friendship's growth in the Early Period. Four private investigators have close relationships with senior police officers. Only twelve years elapsed from the time Carroll John Daly's *The Snarl of the Beast* initiated the hard-boiled detective novel until Brett Halliday published *Dividend on Death* featuring Michael Shayne, but Dashiell Hammett's Continental Op and Sam Spade and Raymond Chandler's Philip Marlowe dominate the Early Period so greatly that it later comes as a surprise to realize that the idea of friendship between private investigator and policeman becomes such a fixture. Shayne and Miami Chief of Detectives Will Gentry are not only good friends, but they also join forces, however subtly, against the new Chief of Detectives of Miami Beach Peter Painter. Mickey Spillane's Mike Hammer almost unconsciously assumes that his friendship with Captain Pat Chambers comes first in a case. Chambers has to remind him occasionally that he is a cop, but he never betrays Hammer. In this, Spillane truly stretches credulity and in this regard accentuates the distance between the three earliest detectives and Hammer. Thomas B. Dewey's Mac lowers the volume as it were but continues this variation on the hard-boiled detective tradition. Lt. Donovan is a friend and father figure to Mac. He worked with Mac for fifteen years on the Chicago police force, serving as his mentor. Finally, Richard S. Prather's Shell Scott, somewhat surprisingly given his dramatic appearance and yellow Cadillac convertible, befriends Cap. Phil Samson and speaks of his virtues as a policeman and a person. These four detectives have another peculiar aspect in common; the policemen seem to be their closest friends. The convention supplies at least one good reason for this since friendships with police facilitate their actions, but it nonetheless pulls against the image initiated by Daly, Hammett, and Chandler of the hard, lonely private investigator, isolated and at odds with society.

Neither a friendship like that between MacDonald's McGee and Meyer nor the relationships between private investigators and police noted above are easily duplicated in the Transitional Period. A tension creeps in between investigators and police that echoes that between William Campbell Gault's Brock Callahan and Lt. Dave Trask. Callahan's repudiation of Trask at the end of *Ring Around Rosa* strikes an ominous note. Certainly, Michael Collins' Dan Fortune treads warily with Cap. Gazzo since the latter knows of Fortune's past criminal activities. And, the dismissive manner of official policeman to private detectives occasionally found in the Early Period resurfaces. It is the unsure professional versus the assured amateur that first appears in Poe and Conan Doyle and partially reverses itself in the hard-boiled detective novel. In both Poe's and Conan Doyle's work, police come to the detectives with cap in hand, as it were. Dupin and Holmes then generously solve their cases. Hard-boiled detectives generally have to prove themselves, working against an assumed reputation that they are both ineffective and corrupt. Very few of the transitional detectives have close friends either among police or civilians. MacDonald sets the bar so high with McGee and Meyer that it is hard for another friendship to match it. The detectives have girlfriends or boyfriends or relatives, but finding a friend and maintaining the relationship becomes difficult if not impossible. Joseph Hansen's Dave Brandstetter is a good example of one who seeks a lover/partner for a permanent relationship but seems to have few other friendships. His relationships with the police resemble those that Hammett's

Continental Op establishes in *Red Harvest* and *The Dain Curse*. Both men represent big organizations, the Op the Continental Detective Agency and Brandstetter the Medallion Life Insurance Company. Brandstetter, especially, by his specialty as a death claims investigator and the Op by his long experience are extended a tolerance and respect from the police that is rare for hard-boiled private detectives. If not friendship, it is an unacknowledged attitude and belief that they know what they are doing.

Strong, lasting friendships in the hard-boiled detective tradition defy the odds. Philip Marlowe's response to Terry Lennox in *The Long Goodbye*, and much has been made of its possible homosexual overtones, is an important example of friendship's vulnerability and potential for disintegration. The very existence of a friendship between two men in the Early Period is worthy of observation. What anchors Marlowe and Terry's relationship to reality is the unequal role that Marlowe plays; he cares more and suffers from the loss of admiration he felt for Terry after he discovers the latter's duplicity. For every situation like Marlowe's and occasionally Spillane's Mike Hammer, whose friends die in the early novels, Dashiell Hammett's Sam Spade and his conflict with the false world of Gutman, Cairo, Wilmer, and O'Shaughnessy are the most common examples of the impossibility of trust and friendship. The relationship between Meyer and McGee, noted above, is one of the first in the Transitional Period. MacDonald seems reluctant to introduce Meyer, and his first important appearance does not come until the seventh novel. In Collins' *Act of Fear*, however, Dan Fortune comments, "Joe Harris is my oldest friend. He never left Chelsea, the way I did over the years, but we always kept in touch. Next to Marty, my woman, Joe is my best friend" (1). This novel, the first in the Dan Fortune series and coming one year after the publication of *Darker than Amber*, reinforces the idea that emotional relationships, e.g., friendship and love, are now legitimate themes for a genre that traditionally shunned them.

Friendships exist in the Early Period, especially as noted between private detective and policeman, but the diminution of examples in the Transitional Period suggests that the concept is still somewhat antithetical to the tradition. Instances occur, but they do not seem inevitable until the advent of large numbers of female hard-boiled detectives in the Modern Period. However, even from 1980 on when Liza Cody's Anna Lee, Sara Paretsky's V.I. Warshawski, Sue Grafton's Kinsey Millhone, and Gillian Slovo's Kate Baier open up the genre to women, many female detectives have characteristics of the early and transitional detectives that pull against community and bonding. Families could be sources of friendship or learning how to be a friend, but so many of the transitional detectives have few or no family members with whom to interact. Ex-wives or ex-husbands tend to predominate, and when, as in Dobyns' Charlie Bradshaw's case, a family appears and stays, it works against the detective. Most of McGee's, Spenser's, and Crumley's Milo Milodragovitch's relatives are dead or too distant to matter. Milo specializes in ex-wives and has an adopted and a natural son. His drunken friend Simon Rome dies in *The Wrong Case.* Simon is dependably dependent, needing strong drink more than anything, but Milo resembles him in that pastime, and they lean toward one another with Simon's helping Milo with information on cases as a recompense for his greater reliance on him. Milo is a man with a past, personal and family, but not much of a future as the series starts. Yet, if loyalty and dependability help define the idea of friendship, Milo and Simon exhibit these qualities. Crumley thus shows his paradoxical approach to the idea and revives interest in it.

It may be that presenting friendship as a paradox is the only way to dramatize it in the genre. Certainly, no friendships between civilians, such as McGee and Meyer, exist long without real stresses and strains. The police-private detective friendships noted above have boundaries much like the bar that stands between Michael Collins' Dan Fortune and his good friend Joe Harris. Parker's depiction of the friendship between Spenser and Hawk pushes even the limits of paradox. One asks, what could possibly draw them together? First, they knew one another as boxers years before. This and a common interest in staying in shape, e.g., sparring, weightlifting, and running, keep them in contact. They further this by training at Henry Cimoli's various gyms, a man they have known and respected from the start of their careers. But, are these past and still current activities enough to maintain a friendship? Hawk refuses King Powers' order to shoot Spenser in *Promised Land* simply because he has known Spenser a long time. In answer to Susan's question as to why he did not shoot him, Hawk says: "'Me and your old man there are a lot alike. I told you that already. There ain't all that many of us left, guys like old Spenser and me. He was gone there'd be one less. I'd have missed him. And I owed him one from this morning'" (218). However, Hawk is a professional killer, and Spenser, as discussed in Chapter 13, lives by a code that generally excludes this activity. Yet, they and Susan demonstrate a loyalty to one another that ignores Hawk's profession. They might disagree with his actions, but they do not condemn him. In fact, Spenser asks for his unpaid help whenever a case demands it. They protect one another and Susan, and what Hawk does in his other life is not their affair. The paradox lies in the fact that this relationship does not make psychological or moral sense. Spenser and even Hawk kill people in self-defense. However, Spenser never goes on murder contracts with Hawk. Susan has an approach to life that is even further removed from Hawk's than Spenser's. She is a psychoanalyst and is in the business of healing, not killing. Hawk's stance is, never complain, never explain, and one either takes him or leaves him. Yet, it is incongruous to imagine that either Susan or Spenser would say to Hawk that it is no longer possible to associate with you given your lifestyle.

The paradox in the friendship between Dobyns' Charlie Bradshaw and Victor Plotz that begins in *Saratoga Longshot* with a chance meeting in a New York bar and continues in later novels lies in the inexplicableness of Plotz's following Bradshaw back to Saratoga Springs. Also, the completely different pasts mystify one as well, i.e., small town and big city backgrounds. Bradshaw has spent twenty years as a policeman in Saratoga Springs, and Plotz has lived by his wits in New York. One answer is that both men are a puzzle to one another. Bradshaw is easy-going and seemingly stable and surprises even himself when he takes a sudden unauthorized leave of absence and goes to New York to look for Sam Cheney, Gladys Cheney's son. Plotz, however, appears to thrive on doing the unexpected. Yet, when he comes to Saratoga Springs, he acclimates quickly and finds an easy acceptance by a wide range of people. This must puzzle the once-again stable Bradshaw who, as Lew Ackerman's head of security at Lorelei Stables in *Saratoga Swimmer*, hires Victor as a guard. However idiosyncratically their relationship develops, Plotz fulfills an early literary convention going back to Poe and Conan Doyle by acting as Bradshaw's *de facto* partner. At bottom, Bradshaw welcomes his presence in Sarasota Springs, describing Plotz as his best friend, but Plotz has an irritating habit of asking Bradshaw questions about the progress of the investigation into Lew Ackerman's death, an investigation that Chief Peterson warns him to stay out of; Plotz's questions strain even Bradshaw's patience. Outside of the policemen with whom some private detectives work, the partnership tradition in the genre, as far as the hard-boiled detective is concerned, falls into abeyance until MacDonald and Parker revive it in the Transitional Period. In addition, the detective is no longer the sole source of deductive brilliance as the Holmes-Watson partnership establishes. Archie Goodwin, a hard-boiled detective with office skills in Rex Stout's Nero Wolfe series, shows his above-average detective skills when the duo separate for a time, but Wolfe re-establishes his role as the thinker when he returns. In MacDonald, Meyer is the brain and McGee, a more-than capable investigator, acknowledges his superior analytical skills. Parker's Spenser does not outstrip Hawk by much however the latter might mockingly refer to him as the detective. Bradshaw and Plotz are thus closer to Spenser and Hawk than McGee and Meyer as to who thinks and who acts even if the recognized detective is the final arbiter in each series of the course of action.

As in life, friendship often has difficulty competing with the demands of love, passion, and desire. When Chookie McCall apparently attempts to seduce Travis McGee in *The Deep Blue Good-by*, he offers honest lust with no ties, and she confesses that she is having problems with her boyfriend.

McGee and McCall remain friends, and she eventually marries one of his clients, Arthur Wilkinson, at the end of *Bright Orange for the Shroud*. McGee is not above casual sex, and he does not reject McCall in *Blue* because of their friendship. His position is more problematic than this and reflects some of the complexities that hard-boiled detectives confront in their relationships, especially in the Transitional and Modern Periods. McGee does not have sex with every woman with whom he becomes close. However, Bill Pronzini's Nameless seems programmed either to fall regularly in love or maintain a professional relationship with women. He does report that he is close to his friend Lt. Eberhardt's wife, but Eberhardt is the special friend, and when he and Dana separate in *Hoodwink* (161), Nameless attempts to console Eberhardt more than her. It is clear that the psychological makeups of McGee and Nameless produce effects in their lives. McGee does fall in love, but he is ultimately more fatalistic than Nameless about the possibility for love to last. Nameless is a romantic. Love or the hope of love fills up his life, and if it does not necessarily give him a reason for living, it brings color and vitality to his world. Never before married, he plans to ask Kerry Wade to marry him at the end of the novel (304). More the image of the confirmed bachelor than even McGee, he slips into the role of the husband-to-be with greater ease than he could have expected. After Gretel Howard's death in *The Green Ripper*, McGee experiences needs that no one can fill and that are not amenable to change. Other than Meyer, no close friends enter his life. For McGee and Nameless, their relationships with women lead to romance or nowhere until his previously unknown daughter Jeanne Killian appears in *The Lonely Silver Rain*, the last novel in the series.

The effects of the growth of friendship and the efforts to make lasting friends obviously differ from similar efforts in love relationships. If characters in the genre's early novels become romantically involved, they generally love or leave their partners. Some exceptions occur but not many. In the Transitional Period, Nameless's ex-lover Erika Coates in Pronzini's *The Snatch* leaves him but still seems bitter about his failure to measure up to her standards. She reminds him of his inadequacies over several novels, and these seem to center around his profession as a private investigator. However, this is one area in which Nameless feels no inadequacy and which helps define him as a person. The question especially arises as to why feelings of love so often inspire an either-or attitude and whether or not some shift occurs as the genre develops. Nameless admires the private investigators that begin to appear in the 1920s pulps. These are hard, tough, isolated men. He says at one point that he wants to model his conduct on theirs as they investigate a case no matter the threats and difficulties. This makes for trouble in any personal relationship requiring stability and security. As late as *Blowback*, Nameless disagrees with Erika and tells her that his life is not a lie. She probably cannot reconcile his desire for a love relationship with the dangers of his work. Nameless and Kerry Wade eventually adopt Emily Hunter. Both Nameless and Kerry are strong people and show that they can adapt to new circumstances. In the Transitional Period, at least five detectives are divorced or have lost a spouse or partner through death. Michael Z. Lewin's Albert Samson, Roger L. Simon's Moses Wine, Arthur Lyons' Jacob Asch, James Crumley's Milo Milodragovitch, and Lawrence Block's Matthew Scudder fit the first category and John Lutz's Alo Nudger loses his wife and children in a car wreck and Joseph Hansen's Dave Brandstetter has lost his lover/partner Rod Fleming to cancer as *Fadeout* begins. The model of Race Williams, the Continental Op, Philip Marlowe until *Playback*, Mike Hammer until *The Snake*, Lew Archer, and Shell Scott as having little room for permanent love relationships thus begins to change in the Transitional Period. Some of the detectives have children and some find other long-term love connections. MacDonald's McGee is the prime example of the either-or model in the Transitional Period until *The Empty Copper Sea* changes him. However, this either-or image fades as the specific circumstances affect individual choices, and while the detectives remain detectives, their lives expand to include others.

One important question is whether or not friendship is valued in the hard-boiled detective novel. And, what is its connection to other emotional bonds? Classical images assert the idea of the virtue of friendship, e.g., Achilles and Patroclus, Aeneas and Achates. The Christian idea of no greater love than laying down one's life for another certainly can be understood in terms of friendship as well as other relationships. The archetypal image of the hard-boiled detective as friend is that most passionate private investigator Mike Hammer. In *I, the Jury* and *My Gun Is Quick*, the violent deaths of friends, Jack Williams and Red, respectively, command his life for the duration of the novels. Long-term in the case of Williams but only a brief encounter involving Red, the friendships are intense as only the absence of the characters can reveal. Uncommon as friendship is in the Early Period, it enters the genre increasingly in the transitional years. In addition to MacDonald's Travis McGee and Meyer, Charlie Bradshaw in *Saratoga Longshot* gains a friend, Victor Plotz. Lawrence Block's Scudder's friendship with Mick Ballou and Elaine Mardell, both outsiders, emphasize the unusualness of this idea. It exists alongside and often complements other, briefer relationships. The combination of friendship with other emotional involvements often deepens both. Scudder and Mardell project a sense of duraton and desire. Only an unusual combination of events could dislodge and redirect their lives so that the other would not remain an important focus. One does not say "in friendship" as one says "in love," but Robert B. Parker's Spenser, Susan Silverman, and Hawk are in a state that admits few qualifiers.

Parker has created this absolute condition between the three characters that replays throughout the novels. Both trust and dependence hover over their lives as friends, and they gain novelistic depth from this posited condition. This paradoxically static image mutates under the dynamics of their individual and collective lives and the social pressures with which they deal. They exhibit the endless permutations of the picaresque hero as the idea of friendship tests itself in their lives and demonstrates its value.

The loss, change (weakening), or absence of friendship at times marks the hard-boiled detective. George Grella remarks on the character type, "Finding the social contract vicious and debilitating, he generally isolates himself from normal human relationships" ("Hard-Boiled Detective" 106). At one level, for all three of the above conditions to occur merely reflects social and personal reality. Both within the self and between the self and others, modifications and adjustments continually appear, however minor, and ultimately reveal themselves. Arthur Lyons' Jacob Asch operates in Los Angeles, a city in which the individual can feel or become lost or isolated in the geographical spread and cultural complexity. David Geherin observes, "Asch's world is harsher, more perverse, more threatening than that portrayed by any of Lyons's predecessors" (*American Private Eye* 184). Asch knows numerous people and becomes relatively friendly to many over time, but this is not the same as feeling close to them. He has developed contacts, relationships, and involvements with people of various ages, occupations, and regions of the city. He is often separate but not with the aloneness and alienation of a Philip Marlowe. Rather, Asch more resembles Sam Spade, though the latter functions in a narrower geographical area, than either Marlowe or the Continental Op. Asch does not have the Op's focus on the job to the exclusion of almost anything else. Because of Asch's activity, his busyness at various levels, one does not immediately note the absence of friends. And, Lyons does not portray Asch as affected by this state in the manner of Marlowe's emptiness of desire. Like Spade, Lyons' reflections are linked to activity, whether social or work-related. Nameless's loneliness is in marked contrast to Asch's absence of loneliness or any shift in mood, except for rare instances, that would reveal depression or low-spiritedness. Of course, Asch feels, thinks, and acts, but the question arises as to the range of feelings, thoughts, and activities and whether a narrowness in these ranges, if it exists, equates to a shallow personality or character. Does a fairly consistent even-temperedness mask an emotional blankness?

MacDonald makes it perfectly clear over the twenty-one McGee novels that his protagonist is full of contradictory impulses and actions about belonging and about the changes his friendship with Meyer undergoes. More stable emotionally than McGee, Meyer nonetheless needs McGee's friendship as much as the latter needs his. Meyer is saddened when McGee's personal demons strain their bonds and welcomes McGee back when he is able to deal with himself and others in a way that conduces to interaction. If one uses McGee as a touchstone, does Lyons' Asch demonstrate any similar complexity of reaction to himself, to others, and to life's vicissitudes? In *The Dead Are Discreet*, he has four encounters that connect him to others on a personal or at least semi-personal level. Gloria Pilsen, sister to the murdered Sheila Warren, sleeps with Asch not long after they meet. Lyons portrays her desire to be with Asch as springing from both a physical and emotional base. However, she turns out to be responsible for her sister's death as well as that of several others. In addition, Asch speaks with Charlie, an elderly elevator operator in a police building. He expresses a certain friendliness toward the older man. Lt. Herrera, the policeman Asch is on the way to see when he meets Charlie, is an old acquaintance. Partially, he fulfills one of the standard roles in the hard-boiled detective novel, i.e., the police friend and contact. Both men, while not necessarily close friends, have a mutually beneficial relationship — official help from Herrera and information that would help the policeman from Asch. Finally, Asch contacts Mike Sangster, a man he has known since he worked as a reporter. If not a friendship, their meeting is friendly. Asch, thus interacts with these people more intimately than with any others in the novel, but the emotional paucity of these interactions, stresses the absence in his life of love or close ties. Gloria's hatred and murderous manipulation, combined with his earlier sexual contact with her, symbolize his aloneness. Asch states, "Her eyes were empty and black. I had the feeling I was looking all the way to the back of her skull" (*Dead* 212). His mistake in sleeping with her emphasizes a certain flatness in perception if not in emotional response.

The twists and turns of the idea of friendship in the hard-boiled detective novel, like the unexpected shifts of more traditional novels that look closely at the surface of the real world, lead the genre in unusual directions. The formula ironically strains at the very idea of boundaries and leads its practitioners to pull their work away from the safe moorings of the customary paths while the novelists use the formula when and if they wish, e.g., the hero always survives. MacDonald, as stated earlier, pushes the genre's boundaries in ways that enrich it. Certainly, one sees a freedom to explore character and thematic boundaries in the transitional hard-boiled detective novel, an exploration that foreshadows the vastly increased use of new themes and other literary devices in the Modern Period. The writers look around them, as it were, rather than only back to what the form requires. This novelistic change and the publication of Hammett's and Chandler's work in the Library of America, have helped push the mystery/detective novel to its present acceptance as part of the canon.

15

The Quality of Change: Individual Lives and Social Transformation

The idea of a Transitional Period is by nature an *ex post facto* creation, and anyone who recognizes it at the time has, at most, the reputation of remarkable prescience. Thus, to call the early sixties to the late seventies the Transitional Period in the development of the hard-boiled detective novel is only possible with any certainty in the early twenty-first century. Implied by this concept is a straddling (spatial) and Janus-like (time) reaching, standing, and viewing of two periods, i.e., the early hard-boiled and the modern hard-boiled detective novels, both as unstable as the transitional focus from which one attempts to comprehend them. Later decades will collapse and rearrange these working fixities into other frameworks. The present sees clearly but dies off, leaving only ambiguous reports of what it knew. Characters in the hard-boiled detective novel from the Transitional Period change to varying degrees while the genre also shifts in a time of social transformation, symbolically, metaphorically transposed to fiction, both seen and not seen in its new venue. Aristotle's definition of plot (and, partially, tragedy) as an imitation of an action underlies this idea of representation, not life but like life, the value and significance lying in the uneven join between the two. From John D. MacDonald's Travis McGee to Marcia Muller's Sharon McCone and Timothy Harris's Thomas Kyd, the hard-boiled private detectives project and reflect a sense of uneasy adaptation to a new world while coping with the stresses this period provokes and, ironically, incorporates.

The hard-boiled detective novel as a literary genre creates patterns that writers extending the genre relate to, struggle with, revisit, or revive. Nothing, as it were, dies; it is either shelved or reused, in the latter case reappearing in its finery and startling even the cognoscente. The Los Angeles of Raymond Chandler's Philip Marlowe and Ross Macdonald's Lew Archer, the San Francisco area of Dashiell Hammett's Continental Op and Sam Spade, the New York of Carroll John Daly's Race Williams and Mickey Spillane's Mike Hammer, and the Miami of Brett Halliday's Michael Shayne are relatively stable social environments in which the novels' characters sometimes undergo dramatic changes. Elihu Willsson in Hammett's *Red Harvest* and Gen. Sternwood in Chandler's *The Big Sleep* symbolize paradoxical situations. Both old men, they and the detectives frame their novels through initial conversations and final resolutions. Between these poles, other characters experience shocks and even death. Yet, these physically fragile characters survive when a son, Donald Willsson in *Red Harvest*, or a son-in-law, Rusty Regan in *The Big Sleep*, die. Even the widespread violence in *Red Harvest* does not destroy the fundamental social stability. Corruption is exposed, some of the guilty are punished, but when the action subsides the social structure exists in a recognizable pattern. The novel projects an image of a town being picked up and dusted off with "new" people in charge. At one level, the detectives rely on this stability. Marlowe knows the police, he knows the criminals, and he knows what to expect from his occupation and where to look for answers to the questions clients bring him. In general, the rules do not change for either him or the Continental Op, whether the latter operates in Montana or San Francisco. As John G. Cawelti argues, the detective maintains his basic self in this world and contributes to its sense of an underlying order: "[...] the hard-boiled detective is a traditional man of virtue in an amoral and corrupt world" (*Adventure* 152).

The image of personal change in the early hard-boiled detective novel within an overall social stability is ultimately paradoxical. Prohibition, the Depression, and World Wars I and II cause too many dislocations and upheavals to be the bases for an unchanging world. If the hard-boiled detective novel is to maintain its reputation for the depiction of social and psychological reality, this gap in the expected pattern needs clarification. The first question to be asked is whether or not the genre does bear any relation to the everyday world. Numbers matter here. If most people in the population never actually experience crime, some do, and the intensity of the focus on their experiences produces an impression of wider criminal activity. Crime is real, and the effects on its victims are powerful. Even in Mickey Spillane's *I, the Jury*, Charlotte Manning's depredations and the corrupt world she inhabits affect relatively few people. Yet, from the first-person narrative of Mike Hammer, the reader senses the impact of his friend Jack Williams' murder, a murder which leads to all the others, and Hammer's emotional response dominates the novel in his unrelenting search for Williams' killer through New York's underworld. Yet, for all of Hammer's intensity, the underworld only appears clearly to the reader because of the social space separating it and the everyday world. Daly's melodramatic prose obscures this distinction, but even in his fiction there must be the dark, separate places in which crime and violence occur, thus implying the open, lighted spaces. This does not argue for the urban world as a pastoral reconfiguration. Only, within mass chaos there is little distinction between one personal tragedy and another. Social stability and expectation, even hope, of something better must be the norm.

MacDonald's McGee is a model in the Transitional Period for this mixture of change within an overall stable environment. He lives on the *Busted Flush* at Bahia Mar marina in Ft. Lauderdale, Florida, for all twenty-one novels. He is a salvage consultant from *The Deep Blue Good-by* to *The Lonely Silver Rain*. He maintains his friendship with Meyer from early in the series until the end. Celebrations of marriages and memorials for those who have died, along with various parties and cruises, have many of the same people in attendance. MacDonald lists them at Gretel's funeral in *The Green Ripper* and McGee's celebration in *Silver* of his daughter Jeanne Killian's graduation from high school and acceptance to college. McGee's hidden cache of money on the *Flush* never completely vanishes though he depletes and fills it during and after his cases. This is not to say that he is the nine-to-five career man that he tells Lois Atkinson in *Blue* he cannot emulate. In fact, though not independently wealthy, he only works when he has to but possesses a stable attitude to the everyday world for whose ordinary working people and high-paid executives, and many in between, he has great admiration. The question then arises, what does change in the world of Travis McGee? The answer is that McGee does. First of all, he ages, and this affects his ability to perform his work alone. In *Free Fall in Crimson*, he has to enlist the help of Preach, a Miami drug dealer, to keep Desmin Grizzel, a.k.a. Dirty Bob, from killing him. He tells Meyer that at one time he would not have needed help to deal with him. Second, McGee has a personality that can turn violent against the violent and that also can turn against himself. He says, after he learns in *The Green Ripper* who is responsible for Gretel's death, that he is going to California and kill them all. And he does. When he recovers his senses, he describes a chasm between his present self and his life before her death. He has left much, if not all, of that behind, on the other side of the chasm. This image of vast depth and broad width within which all the horror lies buried is problematic to say the least. Anne Renzetti in *Crimson* charges him with an inability to give of himself to another as other women have also claimed. If his passion for life has not died in *Cinnamon Skin* and *Silver*, it has leveled off. It seems appropriate that his career energies at the end of *Silver* now go toward working for his daughter's future, for whom he has put most of his money in trust.

While one may celebrate change, welcome it as a sign of vitality both in people and social institutions, its inevitability and unfailing appearance often produce a weariness that grows with age and creates a gap between those with little experience of change and others who expect the winter and darkness it ultimately brings. This is not only to suggest death and the final change but rather the continuingness of personal shifts and the variegations of the outer world. Parker's Spenser and Hawk are emblems of one kind of reaction to change's inevitability. Both men have reduced their lives to a narrow range of actions. Further, both have simplified their moral universes so that most decisions they make reflect an almost unconscious choice among their few, clear principles. In this case, Hawk reduces his reasons for action more than Spenser, and both men represent a continuum with Susan Silverman, Spenser's lover, who approaches a fuller life. Spenser's and Hawk's feelings and expectations function in a restricted area with, paradoxically, little sense of repression or the wish for a larger emotional life. David Geherin also suggests:

> By allowing Spenser to maintain a number of personal and professional relationships from one novel to the next, Parker avoids the gloomy air of loneliness that often haunts the Chandler and [Ross] Macdonald novels and gives his hero an anchor of stability and continuity in a world of loneliness and disorder [*Sons of Sam Spade* 45–46].

The Continental Op stands as the model for their emotional limitations. However, in contrast to Spenser and Hawk, the Op works for an agency and is controlled, tenuously, by its work requirements and by the Old Man to whom he reports. Spenser and Hawk work for themselves and, fittingly, together when needed. They have found one another. Susan's brief escape from Spenser in *Valediction* might reflect her need for a world beyond his fixities, both in what he believes and will or will not do and his love for her.

As a philosophical stance, Lawrence Block's Matthew Scudder might have imagined that sudden, devastating change was a likely possibility in his life. As a policeman, he wore a gun, he necessarily confronted violent people, and he even could have foreseen the likelihood that in New York a stray bullet would strike an innocent person, *even* a child. While he might realize change is a constant, Scudder does not confuse personal with social change. If nothing else, his police experience has prepared him for all the bad things that people do to one another, and his clients perpetually remind him of this. Like Scudder, MacDonald's Travis McGee expresses a sense of despair over the direction of the changes he undergoes. Loss and limitation dominate his world from *The Turquoise Lament* through *Cinnamon Skin*. In *Turquoise*, Pidge Brindle rejects McGee for her doctor who has helped her recover from Howie Brindle's violence. In *The Dreadful Lemon Sky*, McGee fails to sustain a relationship with Cindy Birdsong. Meyer connects McGee's feelings of devastation after Gretel Howard's death in *The Green Ripper* to a more general human and social decay. McGee's love affair with Anne Renzetti in *Free Fall in Crimson* dwindles to a mutual acceptance of their desire to separate in *Cinnamon*. McGee exemplifies the difference between a feeling of the continuity of evil and its oppression and corruption of individual lives. Only in *The Lonely Silver Rain* and the posthumous *Reading for Survival* do both Meyer and McGee appear to recover their spirits and to lose the miasma of despair. McGee's friendship with Meyer survives the inevitable shifts in focus and feeling to recover its vitality. In the dialogue in *Reading for Survival*, both men affirm a human constant through reading that manages and channels life's disruptions and disappointments.

Detective fiction offers the image of the individual detectives' leaping from silent, alone, desired, or undesired worlds into a social complexity that calls or demands their presence. The vainglory, the Cuchulain-battling-the-sea moment stands out with the added consciousness of the action's essential futility even if later occasionally successful. The moment's repetition and its memory underscore this futility even as the detectives' eventual survival, demanded by the genre and by their own perspective, dominates their consciousness. When Spenser drops Terry Orchard off in front of her house at the end of *The Godwulf Manuscript* knowing that he has, at least temporarily, saved her if not others, this represents a shift in that family's life. The dynamics demand that Spenser must remain near changeless to make change. The central focus and perspective of the genre's archetypal figures, e.g., Race Williams, the Continental Op, Sam Spade, and Philip Marlowe, as well as progenitors such as Natty Bumppo, Dupin, and Sherlock Holmes, create social and psychological space for those in need to approach them for succor. And in response to this sometimes importunate demand for help, the detectives' practiced leap into their clients' difficulties establishes the pattern of involvement and isolation. Any change that does occur in the detectives' lives stands in sharp contrast to their usual near immobility, a stasis that plays an important formal and thematic role in the genre. In contrast, Stephen Dobyns' *Saratoga Longshot* reverses the usual portrayal of change or lack of it in the detective's life. Bradshaw undergoes life-changing experiences in this novel. The structural patterns described above dominate the early hard-boiled detective novel from Daly and Hammett to Ross MacDonald and Thomas B. Dewey. Peter Wolfe's *Something More than*

Night: The Case of Raymond Chandler reflects Marlowe's consistent persona and the dramatic nature of any slight alteration in his behavior, especially with regard to motivations for conduct different than expected. However, Dobyns starts with a strongly modified pattern, alluding to Bradshaw's twenty years of police experience and a settled, if unhappy, marriage. The loss of his position and the subsequent divorce stemming from his freelance activity in New York city mark his return to Saratoga Springs and a new life. At the beginning of MacDonald's *The Deep Blue Good-by*, McGee thinks about moving the *Busted Flush* away from Bahia Mar, Ft. Lauderdale. Thus, the transitional hard-boiled detective novel, while thrusting the detective into his client's life and troubles, also energizes his background and life. Bradshaw searches for his client's son while dealing long distance with his own problems. The clarity of the Continental Op's reasons for acting contrast sharply with the uncertainties of transitional hard-boiled detectives as many nonetheless continue the traditional move into action from the silent office and the empty week.

Granting the more varied portraits of detectives when comparing those in the Early with the Transitional Period, what of the latters' abilities to affect positive change in their clients' lives or social environments? The situation is far more problematic for them in these two areas than the admittedly difficult experiences of earlier detectives. From the simplicity of Race Williams' victory over Ralph Dezzeia in Daly's *The Snarl of the Beast*, one moves to the chaos the Continental Op leaves in *Red Harvest* or Philip Marlowe's unsatisfactory solution to Rusty Regan's murder in *The Big Sleep*, unsatisfactory in what it reveals of Gen. Sternwood's family and Marlowe's inability to do much about it. When Mike Hammer shoots Charlotte Manning to end *I, the Jury*, he pleases his client, i.e., himself, but makes no dent in the unsavory urban world through which he tracked her. In the Transitional Period, one finds the same unyielding social structures, processes, and conditions. Travis McGee might retire to the Caribbean with Isobel Webb in *A Purple Place for Dying*, but what remains in Esmerelda? His client, Mona Fox Yeoman, is dead, and so are Isobel's brother John and Mona's husband Jass; Jass's daughter Delores is in jail and her two brothers are dead. Private versus public solutions to difficulties are endemic to the genre and connect the three periods, for in the modern hard-boiled detective novel, social intransigence affects the detectives as deeply as in earlier periods. Bradshaw's moving to Saratoga Lake in *Saratoga Swimmer* symbolizes this Candidean tending of one's own garden (184). Part of the reactions they have to the unsavory people with whom they must deal stems from the lack of effect from their private or public actions. Milo Milodragovtich tells the four women in *Dancing Bear* (1983) who tricked him into taking the case that one of the eight Montana toxic waste site mines is clean, and nothing more can be expected. However, he does not tell them which one. Milo can only withhold at this point.

The disastrous results from all the deception, violence, and death lead to the completion of the circle. For unless the detective awaits his very first client as Brock Callahan does in William Campbell Gault's *Ring Around Rosa*, his silent expectation of a client is the end of one phase of his or her investigative experience rather than the beginning. Even Travis McGee in MacDonald's *The Deep Blue Good-by* busies himself with charts as the novel picks up his career in *media res*. This raises the question as to where they find the necessary energy and will to leap into action. Many of the detectives are in their mid-thirties. By this point, life's illusions are frequently tarnished if not destroyed. Lt. Eberhardt leaves the San Francisco police and works for a short period as an investigator for Pronzini's Nameless. The latter is reluctant to hire a friend, and they quarrel and part. Eberhardt's bitterness over his life, especially his wife Dana's leaving him, prevent him from summoning up the necessary energy to do his share of the work. While Nameless might not possess the image of someone plunging into a case, he nevertheless is effective and pursues each one to the end. Rather than wasting away in isolation and despair over human foibles, Nameless rests up for cases in his downtime. In fact, most of the Transitional Period detectives have this quality of occupying their time between cases, and few want finally to end their careers. Lewin's Albert Samson creates crossword puzzles to supplement his income when business is slow. MacDonald's McGee either takes traditional salvage jobs or more of his retirement. Some like Dobyns' Charlie Bradshaw take security jobs for a while. Others do the less exciting work of a private detective that involves skip-tracing, checking information in city files for lawyers, or doing work for detectives who call from other cities. Of course, the genre still demands that the detective be ready to go when the occasion demands.

As in the real world, violence and the potential for violence temper and pervade social life in the hard-boiled detective novel. If, to paraphrase Aristotle, violence in literature is an imitation of an action, it is a pale imitation. Accepting this limitation, one looks for violence's literary merit more in its specific context than in its approximation to what humans actually do or can do. Literature cannot incorporate all of man's inhumanity to man but rather asks questions through narrative and other methods that contribute to an understanding. Michael Z. Lewin's *The Enemies Within* examines the effects of change in Melanie Kee's and Martin Bennett Willetson's lives. As discussed in Chapter 12, they believe they are kin, but Albert Samson's investigation shows that they are not actually related and thus that their child did not die from the effects of an incestuous affair (245). Samson travels from Indianapolis to Kokomo and Chicago, speaking with many people who knew Melanie and Martin. The many lines established as Samson moves from one city to another, interacting with private citizens and police departments as he attempts to unravel the characters' pasts and the lies they tell him, create a bewildering pattern and emphasize the potential impact of specific human action on social structures and individual lives. It is the symbolic nature of the paradoxically fragile human will that Lewin exhibits as it unleashes its transformative forces.

Positive change can sometimes develop from the most unlikely circumstances. Michael Collins' one-armed private detective Dan Fortune suffers more restrictions than the loss of his arm, but his determination is not one of them. In *Act of Fear*, Fortune searches for a missing young man, Jo-Jo Olsen, who appears to be involved with a criminal named Andy Pappas. Fortune grew up with Pappas and fears his potential for violence. However, when Pete Vitanza, Olsen's friend and the young man who hired Fortune, is severely beaten, Fortune, notwithstanding his awareness of the danger, feels compelled to act. Compounding Fortune's dilemma, Pappas has ordered him to stop his search for Olsen. Unknown to Fortune, Jake Roth, "Andy Pappas' best gun" (85), killed Tani Jones, Pappas' girlfriend. Roth is certain that Olsen can place him near Jones' apartment at the time of her murder and beats Fortune, possibly intending to kill him, so that Fortune will not find Olsen before he can locate him (86–88). However, the effect of the beating is to make Fortune more determined to find Olsen and warn him. Although raised in Chelsea, Olsen seems better than his surroundings and might make it out of the New York slum environment. Except for his younger sister Anna, Olsen's family is corrupted by its relationship with Roth, who actually turns out to be a cousin, and is willing to sacrifice their son for their own material comfort. Fortune responds to Jo-Jo Olsen's desire to better himself, apparently agreeing with him that moving beyond Chelsea is a laudable personal and social goal. Olsen is someone who can be rescued, and Fortune is his rescuer. Fortune, for all his hard-earned experience of human corruption, holds on to a vision of a better social construct.

Nate Bloom's sharp, anguished reaction to the shift from concealment to exposure in Arthur Lyons' *The Killing Floor* when Jacob Asch confronts him with David Fein's murder illustrates one kind of emotional change. At the beginning of the novel, the heavily symbolic odors of the meat-packing town of Vernon, California, underscore not only the possibility of human carnage, graphically fulfilled, but also the death of hope and feeling. Bloom asks Asch to talk with Barbara Fein who is worried about Dave Fein, her missing husband. Throughout the novel, she seems sad but controlled, in sharp contrast to the turmoil Asch undergoes. Bloom worked for Fein at Supreme Packing as a credit manager before Fein took on Steve

Tortorello as a partner. As it turns out, Tortorello has mob connections and possibly plans to loot the company. Fein's gambling compulsion has made him vulnerable to Tortorello's manipulations. Before Fein turns up dead in the trunk of a car in the parking lot of a gambling club, two men working for the bookie Chico Orduno beat Asch badly. Following this the violence escalates. After murdering Terri Wenke, a prostitute working for New World Spa, Orduno's two thugs take him to the packing plant where they have strung up Terri and plan to kill him as well, but Asch escapes. Lyons pushes Asch to the edge, but what is more important than the physical beatings are the emotional effects. Specifically, Lyons depicts Asch, as indicated in Chapter 14, involuntarily turning twice to Sarah, a twenty-four-year-old high school special education teacher at Hollywood High. The first time occurs at home after finding Fein's body. He says: "My insides were seething, churning, and the thought of facing the plasterboard walls of my apartment for the rest of the night was intolerable. I needed a kind word and the touch of sympathetic hands" (93). It is only a few minutes past 10 p.m., and he calls and she invites him over when he explains that he needs to talk to somebody. At her apartment, he detects a "faint hint of pity" (98) in her look but thinks, "But who was I to like or not to like? I was just thankful for Sarah and all the other Sarahs who had enabled me to make it to age 35" (98). After they make love, Asch reveals his emotional dilemma, "[...] the awareness of her next to me did nothing to lessen the feeling of loneliness—no, not really loneliness, but *alone-ness*—that filled me" (99). Asch's second episode happens near the end of the novel. Again, he is lying in bed with the sleeping Sarah after they make love. He observes, "A lonely restlessness crept up on me, a feeling of utter isolation, and I realized that whatever feelings of sanctuary I found here in the night had fled with the light" (228). Sarah is open and giving, but the emotional reactions he has undergone from the violence and death are too strong to be palliated by the often-soothing contact with another. This second time occurs after he turns Nate Bloom in for the murder of Dave Fein. The "cold" and the "chill" (227) that he feels when he arrives at Sarah's do not disappear completely. Asch's experiences seem to be pushing him beyond the help of human hands.

Like Asch, James Crumley's Milo Milodragovitch reveals a static quality to his life, a quality that derives from different sources in both men's lives. For Asch, it comes from being a private detective. This connects him to the detectives in the beginning of the genre who never raise the idea of changing professions. Their experiences as detectives begin to create ineradicable grooves in their personalities. Milo's static quality comes from a much different source. Although life has marked him as indelibly as it has Asch, he remains a detective out of default at other desirable or thinkable options.

In fact, after the roller coaster ride that working as a private detective for Helen Duffy in *The Wrong Case* produces, Milo quits in *Dancing Bear* and becomes a security guard for Haliburton. However, his past reputation as an investigator catches up with him, and he takes a case, with Col. Haliburton's consent, to find out for Sarah Weddington, a woman who knew and loved his father, the identities of two people she sees through her binoculars from her house in Meriwether. This seems an innocuous request, and he needs to do something while he waits until he reaches age fifty-two. At that time, he inherits his father's trust. The expectation of this has held him in suspension for years, not truly able to begin his life before the magic age. Yet, he has begun, and just as much as Jacob Asch, life and work mark and twist him. He does not wish to die before the trust matures, but he takes chances and participates in the violent resolution of his most recent case. At the very end of *Dancing Bear*, Milo has given up drugs and alcohol, has witnessed eight killings, some of which he performed, and forced the women who set everything in motion to establish trust funds for six children providing monthly payments until they are twenty-five and then arrange for them to get the rest of the money. This is the reverse of the trust fund for whose maturity he waits. On the last page, he becomes quite philosophical:

> I have learned some things. Modern life is warfare without end: take no prisoners, leave no wounded, eat the dead — that's environmentally sound.
>
> Fifty-two draws closer every day, and with it, my father's ton of money. So I wait, survive the winters, and when the money comes, let the final dance begin [228].

From the greater fixities and certainties of the early hard-boiled detective novel set in the 1920s, 30s, 40s, and 50s, the transitional period portrays the individual against the shifting world of the 1960s and 70s. While the writers do not structure their fiction as social protest works and only bring in specific historical events in an elliptical fashion, the positive and negative undercurrents of a period when basic cultural values are challenged affect individual behavior through ideas on how to live and choices made. The questionings and probings by characters who would seldom before thus have responded to their environments typify the shift in social attitudes and institutions. Whatever its result, change becomes a motivator for further change, and once questions are asked of basic social structures, others ineluctably follow.

16

Character and Wholeness

Although the idea of wholeness is illusory if it implies a rounding off or completion in any aspect of human affairs, nonetheless, the character of the hard-boiled detective has achieved a sense of fulfillment in the modern period, even if the fulfillment is no more than a prelude to an inevitable shift, an unforeseen destabilization in the character's image. The hard loners of the Early Period contain elements that indicate possible directions of openness in relationships and flexibility as to locales that are developed in the Transitional Period. Writing of Ross Macdonald's changes to the genre, David Lehman states:

> In bringing Chandler up to date, he altered the sociological rules of the game. Macdonald reduced the amount of physical violence and swagger in his work, increased the mental anguish, and shunned the milieu of racketeers and cheap hoods in favor of the respectable, discontented middle class. Less hooch was consumed, and more compassion openly displayed, by Lew Archer, Macdonald's private eye [169].

John D. MacDonald's Travis McGee most dramatically continues this development. However, while retaining and developing character elements of the early and transitional detectives, the modern hard-boiled detective from the 1980s to the present reveals a range of options, e.g., gender, race, sexual orientation, nationality, class, politics, and locales, that strain the formula with a dynamic urgency that leaves open the direction of the hard-boiled detective's future development.

Les Roberts' Milan Jacovich who first appears in *Pepper Pike* (1988) cannot fight Joe Bradac, his ex-wife Lila's lover and Milan's former high school acquaintance. Usually living alone, not far from his old home where

Lila and his two sons still reside, Milan is both drawn in and pushed away. His children stay with him somewhat regularly on the weekends. He is not emasculated, but there is a situational infringement on his independence. Divorce was inevitable. Slovene (he) and Serb (she) do not mix, as Milan notes on occasion. One of his strong acts of independence is to resign from the police force, something that his friend Lt. Marko "Mark" Meglich asked him not to do. Both as a realistic character and a representative genre figure, Milan is enmeshed in the social complexities of his situation. At moments, he aches for his children, but only time will handle that longing. As long as they live at home as minors, Milan will be the father and ex-husband, responsible for whatever he and Lila believe is his duty to perform. Not only is it interesting to analyze how the Continental Op's, Sam Spade's, and Philip Marlowe's successors get to this point but also necessary to speculate where the development of character will go. In the midst of one of the most creative stages of the hard-boiled detective and detective novel, one must question the direction if any of the character's development. J.K. Van Dover observes of the early hard-boiled detectives: "They can walk with confidence into tenements and mansions and talk with self-assurance to punks and millionaires. They know how cops' minds work, and how gangsters' minds work, and they know how to use this practical knowledge" (*You Know* 196–97). George Grella writes that Ross Macdonald's Lew Archer is the culmination of the hard-boiled character. However, nothing stays the same for long, and thirty years later neither an abatement of the form nor its hero's elimination is apparent.

For the male detective in the Modern Period, there is a confusion of roles, a confusion that not even all the female detectives avoid. Stephen Greenleaf's John Marshall Tanner who first appears in *Grave Error* (1979) has attitudes reminiscent of the early hard-boiled figures. Robert A. Baker and Michael T. Nietzel state: "Tanner is a straight-ahead practitioner of the Philip Marlowe work ethic. Not talking to people is one of the things he does best. He won't be bribed, he won't take money to fail. The client comes first, right after his own pride [...]" (216).

Early in the above novel, Tanner observes, "The investigator's trade is short of glamour and long on moral ambiguity. As proof of this: the California Business and Professions Code lumps it in with collection agents and insurance adjusters" (1). As he waits for Jacqueline Nelson, his prospective client, to state her business, he thinks, "Mrs. Nelson was babbling, avoiding coming to grips with whatever had brought her to see me. I didn't care. I didn't have any place to go or anyone to see" (9). This could refer specifically to business, but Tanner implies more, an emptiness and aloneness about his life. His secretary Peggy's silence about her private life only reinforces the image he projects that silence masks loss. One aspect of this confusion is Tanner's former profession as a lawyer. Almost no modern hard-boiled detectives have training as a lawyer. Paretsky's Warshawski was a public defender but got out of the business to work for herself. Being a lawyer does not disqualify Tanner from his new profession, but it does introduce elements of caution and control that change the image of the character of the hard-boiled detective more than occurs during the Transitional Period. Tanner has elements of the businessman about him. As he tells Jacqueline Nelson, he was suspended as a lawyer for contempt of court. Like Arthur Lyons' Jacob Asch who states in *The Dead Are Discreet* (1974) that as a newspaperman he refused to reveal his sources to a court, Tanner exhibits independence. But, this independence is qualified in his irritated response to Roland Nelson, the consumer advocate, that he hopes any information he digs up will be used responsibly. In addition, Tanner's relationship to Peggy, his secretary, is more like that of William G. Tapply's Brady Coyne, a lawyer and ad hoc detective, to his secretary than Sam Spade's and Mike Hammer's dealings with theirs. Tanner is not so much controlled by Peggy as he is reactive to her moods and ways. Rather than setting the tone of their interactions, he frequently follows her lead.

Loren D. Estleman's Amos Walker continues this image of the sometimes circumscribed modern detective. This is paradoxical in that Walker is even more like the early protagonists than Tanner and, for the most part, Jacovich. Estleman introduces Walker in *Motor City Blue* (1980). Baker and Nietzel write, "Walker is cut from lone-wolf cloth. Isolated and usually self-sufficient, he bears proud testimony to the independence of the Spade-Marlowe-Archer prototypes" (202). Chapter Two of the novel shares something about his past and his attitude toward his profession. Walker lives alone in a modest home near Hammtramck. He states: "It's not the lobby of the Detroit Plaza, but it's still more space than one person needs. Maybe when we know each other better I'll tell you about the person who used to share it with me. In any case, it will suit me until the taxes eat me alive" (9). This description has a wistful quality about a lost love or relationship and an expectation of a continuing contact with his auditor/reader. Of course, this is an authorial convention used to connect reader and character, but the hopeful note seems dominant and becomes almost a plea. Estleman ends the above quote with an image of impotence in which the overpowering state will consume, not just the house but also him. Walker certainly counters any image of weakness and lack of courage on his part in his series, but Estleman's lines rob him of a feeling of independence while making him more approachable as a man. He emphasizes this latter condition by having Walker remark: "I considered putting a 78 on the J.C. Penney stereo but vetoed it. My collection of jazz and early rock had been a source of some pride before the divorce settlement left me with just a bunch of records. I could do without the depression playing one would bring on" (10). Walker reveals an emotional depth in these few lines but also raises questions not only about his character but also about the hard-boiled detective in general. Can the detective maintain a hard edge with a continued series of revelations of human needs, feelings, and doubts?

A measure of the character's confusion of roles would be an extension of such behavior into his work. There, Walker generally falls into the hard-edged patterns of the early detectives. However, when Ben Morningstar has his bodyguard phone Walker, the latter's reaction is symptomatic of the shift in attitude discussed above. Walker observes:

> My grip didn't crack the receiver; that would be an exaggeration. But it came close. Ben Morningstar wasn't someone you spoke with on the telephone. He was a name in *Newsweek*, a photograph taken at a funeral by a G-man with a telephoto lens across the street, a pair of nervous hands fiddling with a package of Lucky Strikes in a Congressional hearing room on television in the early fifties [*Motor City Blue* 10–11].

Walker continues his awed monologue for nearly one-half of a page, ending with, "After a couple of seconds disguised as an hour, I found voice enough to say, 'I'm listening'" (11). This is a remarkable revelation, not of just a proper caution when dealing with a mob figure but of a loss of certainty. No further back in time than Spenser's introduction in Robert B. Parker's *The Godwulf Manuscript* (1971) would one note a completely different though maybe less realistic reaction to contact with a mob boss. In fact, Spenser clashes with Sonny, one of Joe Broz's men, in the above novel while in Broz's office. Spenser is aware of Broz's power to harm but does not let it control his behavior to the same extent that Morningstar's reputation initially affects Walker.

Marcia Muller's Sharon McCone is the only female hard-boiled detective in the Transitional Period. Although Mike Hammer's secretary Velda has a private investigator's license and undertakes cases on her own and with Hammer, she is the lone example in the Early Period. However, the gender of the detective is not a side issue in the Modern Period. Of the first seven detectives, beginning with Greenleaf's Tanner in *Grave Error*, three are women: Liza Cody's Anna Lee in *Dupe* in 1980, Sara Paretsky's V.I. Warshawski in *Indemnity Only* in 1982, and Sue Grafton's Kinsey Millhone in *"A" Is for Alibi* also in 1982. Afterwards, women appear regularly and help define the limits and characteristics of the genre. Kathleen Gregory Klein notes:

> The genre is now appreciably different from the examples offered by Edgar Allan Poe or Wilkie Collins more than a century ago. Yet the concentrated dialogue among writers and readers about the elements of the text has both

revised and reinforced the original and the contemporary shape of the genre [*Women Times Three* 8].

The question of character and gender thus becomes vitally important to any understanding of what defines the hard-boiled detective novel in the Modern Period. This question leads to answers in the area of male-female interactions and female-female ones. Given the numbers of female detectives created by female authors, one might say a critical mass (*Women Times Three* 11), to paraphrase Klein, has been reached. Approximately fifteen hard-boiled female private detectives operate in the modern period. Even if one accepts a basic human connection between men and women, it sometimes appears as if that were the last acknowledged point of contact between the sexes. One gender difference in character lies in the greater apparent need for some kind of community in women detectives than in most of the men. Klein writes, "Women, as recent feminist psychological studies have demonstrated, are taught to value relationships and interaction over abstractions" (*Women Times Three* 11). However, one observes the presence of this need in the modern male detective as well. Although it does not appear as readily in the men as in the women, the way is prepared for men by their male detective counterparts in the 1970s. Yet, Estleman's Walker and Valin's Harry Stoner exist alone much like the early hard-boiled detectives, e.g., the Continental Op, Sam Spade, and Philip Marlowe. Van Dover states: "The hard-boiled detective's aloneness testifies, primarily, to his alienation in a corrupt society; there is no moral community to which he can belong. But it also testifies to the absence of an intellectual community" [*You Know* 197]. In contrast, Cody's Lee, Paretsky's Warshawski, and Grafton's Millhone begin with full blown communities that sustain them throughout their series.

The female detectives' interactions with their separate communities are uneven at times. Lee, Warshawski, and Millhone live nearby but separately from people with whom they are close. Lee has a downstairs couple in *Dupe*, Selwyn and Bea Price, who both look out for her and do things with her. In *Indemnity Only*, Warshawski eventually obtains a downstairs neighbor as well, Mr. Contreras, who is very protective of her and with whom she talks. Millhone lives behind Henry Pitts' home in *"A" Is for Alibi*. He is a father figure to whom she is attracted even though he is in his eighties. He also shows his worry, at times more than she can easily accept, about her lifestyle and work. A common thread between all three detectives is that they expect contact and interaction with their communities. Even when irritated or wanting to be alone, they know they have to negotiate with their friends. No matter their expressed desires or opinions on interference or prying, they all expect it, sometimes literally or metaphorically tiptoeing to their apartments so as not to activate their friends' interest or curiosity.

Advice is freely given, and in the case of Warshawski, it also comes from her father's friend, Lt. Bobby Mallory and Dr. Lotty Herschel. R. Gordon Kelly states of Herschel and Contreras: "Both possess conspicuous integrity, and their faith and trust in Warshawski offer credible reassurance as to her essential trustworthiness, despite the dubious means she adopts on occasion to solve a particular problem" (*Mystery Fiction* 116).

Millhone gets advice not only from Henry but also from Rosa who runs a nearby restaurant she frequents. Lee's additional support and advice is found away from her home. Bernie Schiller, an ex-policeman who also works for Brierly Security, is a friend and mentor. The above communities function as replacements for lost or absent families. Lee mentions a mother, father, and sister, but they play no ongoing series role. She does speak of being an aunt with a three-year old nephew (*Dupe* 34). At Brierly Security, Anna has a friend in Bernie and acquaintances who only gradually, if grudgingly, accept her as an equal even though she served for five years in the police and is qualified to do her job. Warshawski's mother and father are dead. In the series, a hockey-playing cousin and an aunt appear. For Warshawski, memories of her parents, especially her mother, play the role of family, and she frequently refers to them. Millhone, though with an ex-husband who occasionally reenters her life, is devoid of family in the early novels. Raised by an aunt, she never learns until later that she has living relatives only several hours drive from her. Although they have known of her and finally contact her, Millhone has not suspected their existence.

Seeing the world through community affects character. This idea is prepared for in the Transitional Period, largely by male detectives, and modern male detectives continue this pattern even if they do not pursue it as intensely as female detectives. Composing the hard-boiled character thus requires an amalgam of gender roles which in the modern period realistically means reshaping the character of the detective in light of female experience and attitudes. Van Dover writes:

> The emergence of the female private investigator in detective novel series by writers such as Marcia Mulle[r], Sue Grafton and Sara Paretsky may raise the interesting and complex question of whether heroines of knowing differ in their ways of knowing from the heroes. These detectives are self-consciously female; the problems they encounter and their responses to the problems are often presented as in some degree different from those of the male detectives who defined the formulas which they now exploit and perhaps subvert [*You Know* 200].

The hard-boiled private detectives' characters are defined, severally and individually, by their actions. This general principle is established in the Early Period, continued in the Transitional Period, and generally maintained in the Modern era. If this is a truly established principle, then one can claim a strong connection between the hard-boiled detective, male and female, and the epic hero, for the epic hero's ties are forged by what they do. None wants to be different than what he is. Only after long struggle or advanced age do any of them retire. Menelaus and Odysseus fit the former description and Nestor the latter. Tennyson's "Ulysses" gives insight to the nature of the epic character for there the eponymous hero abandons his kingdom, wife, son, and Ithaca to sail to the western isles and rejoin his comrades. Only Achilles in *The Odyssey*, then a shade, claims that he would rather be the meanest peasant on earth than a prince in hell. However, in *The Iliad* Ajax chooses death when not given Achilles' armor, but Virgil's Aeneas leaves Dido and the comforts of Carthage to continue his adventures, adventures he is fated to perform. Character is destiny and destiny is character to the epic hero, and the hard-boiled detective follows a similar pattern. Many have resigned from other jobs or careers; some have been made redundant like Reginald Hill's Joe Sixsmith who lost his job as a lathe operator in a Luton factory north of London. However, private detectives do not wish to be something else. Once begun, that profession absorbs them, brings out their essential characters and gifts, and gives them a reason for living. From the earliest hard-boiled detectives, one hears that their work frames their lives, and thus one can argue it also defines them.

The early hard-boiled detective is quintessentially the man of action, and through his work carried out more in action than thought, his typical personality and character form themselves. Only late in the Early Period do detectives appear who predominantly reflect the analytical model of Poe's Dupin and Conan Doyle's Holmes while still functioning in the hard-boiled mold. In the Modern Period, as noted in the first section on confusion of roles, several hard-boiled detectives such as Greenleaf's Tanner, Estleman's Walker, and Roberts' Jacovich rely heavily on action as well as thought and through this combination reveal their natures. However, many other modern detectives, both male and female, rely on action to solve their cases and thus recall the early image of the hard-boiled detective as one whose character forms itself in action. Some of these evince an air of restless energy. Linda Barnes' Carlotta Carlyle who begins in *A Trouble of Fools* (1987) is always in motion, almost as a defense against the mental and physical exertions of her housemate Roz. Carlyle is not only a private detective but also drives a cab when she needs the money. She plays weekly on a woman's volleyball team and acts as a big sister to Paolina whose mother can hardly function as a parent. Carlyle has a personal life and of course is not always a blur of movement, but what she does reveals who she is as well as what she thinks and feels. Carlyle lives in this fashion while part of a community, as many of her actions involve others with whom she relates and not only clients and the people with whom she interacts on her cases.

Two other detectives especially portray character through action: Jonathan Valin's Harry Stoner who first appears in *The Lime Pit* in 1980 and Mark Timlin's Nick Sharman who debuts in *A Good Year for the Roses* in 1988. Stoner works in Cincinnati and Sharman in London. Stoner acts in a methodical, cumulative manner as he pursues his first case. He is a constant pressure on the principals and uses violence when necessary, either to help himself or others. Stoner is a loner in the fashion of the early detectives and has developed a hard personality through experience. Sharman, on the other hand, is laid-back but explosively violent in some novels in a way that echoes, if not caricatures, Spillane's Mike Hammer. Both men are hired in the above novels to find young women, Sharman by Patsy Bright's father, George Bright, and Stoner by Hugo Cratz who pretends to be Cindy Ann's father. Both girls are murdered, Patsy by her father's own men. The deaths of these young women mark these detectives even more than they originally are marked. Further action in their series etches lines in their characters as inevitably as breathing. Committed to their profession as most hard-boiled detectives are, they continue "developing" as people who are inextricably tied to society's most brutal venues and to the pursuit of those who inhabit them.

A final way in which the character of the hard-boiled private detective evolves occurs in the areas of race, ethnicity, and sexual identity. In the Transitional Period, Joseph Hansen's gay detective Dave Brandstetter opens the genre in a way that adds to the other representative figures. Marcia Muller's Sharon McCone, the first female hard-boiled detective, gives another focus to the character type in the same period. In the modern era, Walter Mosley's Easy Rawlins, a black private investigator, is a transplanted Texan who in *Devil in a Blue Dress* (1990), after working many years in Los Angeles, has recently lost his job and turns to investigation with no real professional intent. Rawlins' main purpose is to finish paying for his house. His bourgeois orientation is deep-rooted and drives his character. Lewis Griffin, another black private investigator, first appears in James Sallis's *The Long-Legged Fly* (1992). The novel ranges from 1964 to 1990 and covers Griffin's gritty detective work in New Orleans. At the latter date, he has started teaching and writing detective novels. Joe Sixsmith, mentioned above, a black man whose people originally came from the West Indies, chooses to pursue a career as a detective in Reginald Hill's *Blood Sympathy* (1993). Valerie Wilson Wesley's Tamara Hayle is a black private investigator whose series begins in Newark in *When Death Comes Stealing* (1994). With a teenaged son, an ex-husband, and many friends and acquaintances, she looks out from Newark, a city where she grew up and which she knows intimately. Bruce Cook's Antonio "Chico" Cervantes is a Mexican-American born in the United States. He starts his series in *The Mexican Standoff* in 1988. Cervantes has difficulties because he speaks Spanish with an accent but English without one. Working in the Mexican-American community in Los Angeles becomes difficult since he generates suspicion, apparently not clearly identified as being from one community or the other. Carolina Garcia-Aguilera's Lupe Solana begins detective work in *Bloody Waters* in 1996. Solano is Cuban-American. Living in the Cuban exile community in Miami and still residing with her parents while running a private detective business present her with many difficulties. However, she strongly sees herself as part of her family and community, and these, together with her Catholic faith, give her a solidity of interpretation regarding her cases and the people she encounters.

J.M. Redmann and Sandra Scoppetone employ lesbian hard-boiled private detectives from New Orleans and New York, respectively. Redmann's Michelle "Micky" Knight first appears in *Death by the Riverside* in 1990 and Scoppetone's Lauren Laurano in *Everything You Have Is Mine* in 1991. They are almost complete opposites. Redmann's Knight frequently indulges in one-night stands while Scoppetone's Laurano has had a monogamous relationship with Kip Adams for more than a decade. Knight is more of a presence in her hometown New Orleans than Laurano is in New York, largely because of the relative sizes of the cities. However, they both intensely insert themselves into their cases, sometimes endangering their lives. They do not see this in a markedly different way than the male detectives because danger is occasionally unavoidable in their profession. Laurano is very attuned to what it means to be a lesbian in a male-dominated society and seems constantly at war with those, usually male, who do not meet her standards regarding lesbians. Most of this war is internal but at times strongly expressed. Her manner is corrective for both men and women. This attitude gives a tension to the series that does not descend to a preachy political correctness though she often seems close to it. Knight is far more relaxed about herself and who she is, but since both women's perspectives are almost always outside the male's, and this can include gay men, and outside heterosexual women's as well, they add a position on character that constantly addresses societal givens and speaks for different interpretations in their lives.

The complex portrait of character and its ongoing evolution in the Modern hard-boiled Period owe much to the early and transitional writers and their detectives. Complicating things even more is the fact that many of the transitional detectives still appear in new works from the eighties on. Their writers continue to explore the genre and add to the character type to whose development so many new writers also contribute. However open-ended the genre appears, the hard-boiled private detective is easily recognizable as he or she moves into the initial cases and continues to pursue careers into the twenty-first century.

17

Violence: Echoes and Conversions

From Carroll John Daly's Race Williams and Dashiell Hammett's the Continental Op to Liza Cody's Anna Lee and James W. Hall's Thorn, the hard-boiled detective novel has undergone a profound change in the practice of violence. Part of this might be because of the introduction of the female hard-boiled detective. And yet, females also resort to violence to save themselves and others. Sue Grafton's Kinsey Millhone shoots Charlie Scorsoni, a former lover, in *"A" Is for Alibi* (1982) as he stalks her (214). Jenny Elizabeth Blade states, "Though she does progressively deviate from the male, hard-boiled detective, Grafton stays much closer to her male counterparts than do her female peers" (75). The difference between her and the typical male detective is that the shooting affects her in later novels. Maureen T. Reddy remarks, "The first time Kinsey uses her gun, strictly in self-defense, she kills a man who is trying to kill her, and the shooting haunts her [...]" (98). This helps to clarify Millhone's reaction. Les Roberts' Milan Jacovich and Loren D. Estleman's Amos Walker resemble detectives from the early period in regularly carrying guns, but changing social situations often diffuse and reduce the need for violence. People still die, and the detectives still experience violence, but many of the writers explore their worlds in such a way that violence does not dominate the action though it often threatens to do so. Has the genre introduced mixed aims since 1980 and thus lost its way in the world of detective fiction? For all that Mark Timlin's Nick Sharman may rival Mickey Spillane's Mike Hammer in his predilection for shooting people, the modern hard-boiled detective novel has successfully remade itself. Along with its larger variety of detectives and the expanded range of settings, the idea of violence undergoes a shift, attaching itself to a wide scope of themes without reducing them to its demands for finality.

While some people plan violent acts, others commit them under the pressure of some strong emotion. This, of course, sets aside the sociopaths, those for whom violence is a way to deal with life's complications whether it be assault or murder. A completely amoral person would not be squeamish about murder; he or she would see that as only one method to solve problems. Someone who commits a violent act under a strong emotional pressure differs from a sociopath who may not feel much fear or guilt. Although the comparison is somewhat mechanical, the power of the emotion appears stronger than any caution when extreme violence results. Both the sociopath and the person overcome by strong emotion are frightening images because neither one presents an example of control or restraint. Society may deal with them differently, but neither fits in any world in which civilized values reign. And no one knows who they are until they act. Hopefully, the sociopath is rare, but sadly, the person acting violently from an emotional compulsion might be anyone. John Baker's *Death Minus Zero* (1996) presents a striking example of the sociopath. Accidentally allowed to escape from prison, Norman Bunce carefully plans to track down his ex-wife, Selena White. He particularly wants to hurt her. Learning that she is somewhere in York and remarried, Bunce murders, assaults, and steals his way from Dartmoor to the North Sea before turning inland toward York. Realizing the difficulties in locating her, he comes to the office of Sam Turner, a local private investigator. Seeing Dr. Jennie Cosgrave, a research psychologist who previously worked at his prison, temporarily diverts him. Jennie will do as well as "Snow White," his ex-wife. Bunce is a cheerful opportunist when it comes to murder and violence and in this way reminds one of Howie Brindle's depredations in John D. MacDonald's *The Turquoise Lament*. In Benjamin Schutz's *Embrace the Wolf* (1985), Leo Haggerty tracks down the vicious pedophile Justin Randolph who specializes in torture and murder. Appropriately, a giant shark eats him off the coast of North Carolina (195). Neither Bunce, Brindle, nor Randolph has compunction or remorse in committing the most violent acts.

Emotional compulsion is by far the source of the greater number of violent acts in the modern hard-boiled detective novel. Possibly this is a largely unstated conviction on the writers' part that there are few true sociopaths and that a literary form needs the greater number of examples from which to choose. Thus Walter Mosley's series has only one Mouse but many who kill from fear, greed, or rage. Mouse stands apart, contributing little to *Devil in a Blue Dress* (1990) other than the fear he inspires in Easy

Rawlins, the protagonist, and the figure of the unpredictable killer. Calling him "the bad Black man" from black American folklore, Mary Young states that he is "uncompromising in his viciousness [...]. The reasons for his brutality are not readily apparent, but he blithfully [sic] enjoys his savagery" (147). While one may find a tenuous connection between Mouse's motivations and his acts in this regard, they do not provide grounds for a comprehensive discourse about them. One just stays away from him if one can. Rawlins cannot or, more accurately, Mouse will not stay away from him. Mouse even states, without reassuring Rawlins, that he likes him. Contrast Mouse with Joppy, the bartender and ex-fighter whom Rawlins knows from his visits to his bar. Rawlins is wary of him but understands his greed and the lengths he would go to satisfy himself physically or monetarily. Even Mr. DeWitt Albright, the rich white man who hires him to find Daphne Monet, represents human elements with which he can interact, i.e., power and desire. Joppy and Mr. Albright stand for comprehensible human emotions against which one can take precautions, averting their effects. But, Mouse functions outside of such motivations and introduces an alien atmosphere, an air of uneasiness that persists through all the permutations of the plot. With everyone except Mouse, Rawlins' ambiguity about his status as a detective and his focus on his home interject protective layers between himself and danger. Even the unstable Joppy can be handled at times, taming the image of raw emotion as the greatest danger.

The introduction of the female hard-boiled detective into the genre affects the kind and frequency of violence. Whereas women sometimes figure as the killers in the male hard-boiled detective novel, in the female writers' versions, they seldom kill or physically harm someone. Brigid O'Shaughnessy in Dashiell Hammett's *The Maltese Falcon*, Carmen Sternwood in Raymond Chandler's *The Big Sleep*, and Charlotte Manning in Mickey Spillane's *I, the Jury* represent striking examples of female violence in the early hard-boiled detective novel. John D. MacDonald continues this pattern in the Transitional Period with Lilo Perris in *The Long Lavender Look* and Mary Alice McDermit in *The Scarlet Ruse*. Not only do female writers in the Modern Period not often describe women committing violent acts, they more often portray them as the victims. Sandra Scoppetone's *Everything You Have Is Mine* is, however, an extreme case. Women are murdered, raped, and assaulted. Except for police, predators, clients, and family, Lauren Laurano, Scoppetone's lesbian private detective, spends the bulk of her time and emotional energy within the homosexual community, female and male. However, violence intrudes into the close love relationships and friendships depicted there. Laurano was raped and Warren Cooper, her date, killed when she was eighteen years old. She also accidentally shot and killed her lover and fellow FBI agent Lois when she was in her late twenties. During the course of Laurano's present investigation, Zach Ellroy tries to run her car off the road, hits her over the head, and tries to kill her near the end of the novel. In the struggle she shoots him in the kneecap. The rapes and murders spread in an almost Byzantine complexity and stretch back for two decades. Zach Ellroy, and to a lesser extent Bob Wise, are responsible for most of the violence with Harrison Webster playing a cameo role as Lake Huron's rapist. Ultimately, one learns that he confesses to more than seventy rapes across the country.

Together with the plot's convolutions, Scoppetone portrays the women's silences and concealments, especially with regard to the half-sisters Helena Bradshaw and Ursula Wise. Laurano with difficulty finds out the truth about their and Lake's background and discovers that Helena and Ursula's mother, Marion, did nothing to stop Bob Wise's sexual abuse of Helena and his own daughter Ursula. After Helena marries Ellroy, he abuses her and Ursula who has Lake by him. Near the end of the novel, Ellroy kills Lake in order to teach Helena a lesson (303). After Ursula finally clarifies much of the family relationships, Laurano reflects:

> I lie down on the bed again, overwhelmed by the amount of abuse in this case. It's like a diseased octopus. But why should I be surprised? This malady shows up everywhere: in the cavalier way men slap women around in movies and television; in the way they talk about them in comedy routines; in the easy portrayal of male-female violence in novels [*Everything* 283].

Scoppetone moves to the world outside the novel for her general, and accurate, statements, but her deeper analysis would be to reflect more on the ambiguities in her own work. Not only Marion and Helena, Ursula's being too young for any real responsibility for what was done to her, but also JoAnn Krupinski, whom Scoppetone remarks is complicit in Zach Ellroy's abuse of her, "a woman committed to being abused" (279), collude at different levels with their abusers. As Scoppetone shows, the failure to act immediately to protect oneself or one's loved ones prolongs and intensifies the suffering.

In contrast to Sandra Scoppetone's portrayal of women as victims in a world seemingly out of control, Val McDermid's *Dead Beat* restricts the level of violence against women while still depicting several instances of female victimhood. It is an important difference because one could look at the two main examples in *Dead Beat* and substitute male for female victims with little difficulty. Thus, one does not get the feeling that Moira Pollock and Kate Brannigan are attacked because they are weak women. On the contrary, they suffer violence because of the strong actions they take. Jett, a highly successful rock singer hires Kate to find his former songwriter Moira. Richard Barclay, Kate's lover, persuades her to take the case even though she and her partner Bill Mortensen only investigate white-collar crime. To establish her credentials in this latter area, Kate has a parallel case running while she looks for Moira. In that case, she spends long hours trying to obtain evidence that Gary and Jack "Billy" Smart are selling schneids, counterfeit products, in this case watches. In the end, she successfully photographs them shipping the merchandise. When the police close in, the two brothers flee and die in a car accident.

The accidental violence suffered by the Smarts is far different from the violence that leads to Moira's death. Soon after Kate finds her, someone murders her in Jett's home. Jett then hires Kate to find her killer. She discovers that in order to discredit Neil Webster's threatened revelation that Moira had aborted Jett's child after they broke up, Moira attempted to get Kevin Kleinman to push Webster out of Jett's entourage and thus dilute any subsequent accusation Jett's then-fired biographer would level. Kate explains Webster's violent outburst after Moira taunted him:

> "The prospect of being deprived of what must have been his last chance of a meal ticket was too much for him. He snapped and picked up the nearest object and thumped her with it. Like I said, I don't think murder was part of his plans but having done it, he did his damnedest to make sure he got away with it" [*Dead Beat* 206].

Kevin Kleinman attempts to strangle Kate when she mistakenly claims he killed Moira. He overpowers her, and only her precautions in having Bill Mortensen and Richard Barclay waiting in her home in case of an emergency save her. In both instances, Moira and Kate are acting rather than waiting for something to happen. Surprise makes the attack on Moira successful, but Kate's suspicions negate the element of surprise.

The modern hard-boiled detective novel employs violence in a controlled, directed manner. This rather sweeping generalization can be contradicted with many good examples. However, what lies behind it is a sense that the atmosphere of violence and evil in the genre has changed. It gradually shifts from a condition of casual, if frequent, violence to one in which it occurs in isolated, limited instances. From the dark and dangerous streets filled with menace in Carroll John Daly's *The Snarl of the Beast* (1927) to the smog of Dashiell Hammett's Personville in *Red Harvest* (1929) and the fog of San Francisco in *The Maltese Falcon* (1930) to the sunny decadence of Los Angeles in Raymond Chandler's *The Big Sleep* (1939) to the rough streets of New York in Mickey Spillane's *I, the Jury* (1947), violence pervades and corrupts these literary worlds. Both detective and killer are pulled into a sometimes melodramatic conflict between good and evil, sometimes clearly demarcated and sometimes not. Philip Marlowe might sit in his office staring at the walls with a sense of failure and waste about his life, but someone is also likely to come in and pull a gun on him. Unlike some modern detectives, Marlowe does not often describe his work as more involved in looking up records and filling out forms than action and danger. Klein states of Kinsey Millhone, "She notes that most of her job consists of tedious, monotonous, boring checking and cross-checking — plodding and patient routine" (*Woman Detective* 204). For Marlowe's successors, computers quickly locate people and information even though sometimes the information is outdated as initially happens to Mickey Knight in J.M. Redmann's *Lost Daughters* (1999) when she finds Lorraine Drummond through the internet only to learn that she has left that address. Office work, computers, fewer secretaries, and often more stable personal lives sometimes constrain violent encounters. Of course, these elements do not eliminate violence as Knight's struggle to overcome Bror, the serial killer she has been tracking, dramatically shows.

James W. Hall's Thorn in *Under the Cover of Daylight* (1987) and Janet Dawson's Jeri Howard in *Kindred Crimes* (1990) demonstrate how the expanded lives of the protagonists can limit and direct violence. It might seem ironic to speak of Thorn in terms of an expanded life. He lives on Key Largo south of Miami and ties flies for a living. Though Thorn is thirty-nine years old when the novel begins, the first in the series, the narrator actually starts with a flashback to the night twenty years before when Thorn avenged his parents' deaths. Nineteen years before that Quentin and Elizabeth Thorn left Miami for Key Largo. Elizabeth held the twenty-hour old Thorn in her lap on the trip home that would officially make him a Conch. Dallas James, drunk and showing off for his friends, forced the Thorns' car into Lake Surprise as he took his eye off the road. James briefly stopped and then quickly left the scene. Only Thorn survives. He learns the details of his parents' deaths from his step-father Dr. Bill when he is thirteen years old. Hall states, "It had simmered in him for six years, but he had finally done it" (17). The "it" is a reenactment of the crash except that Thorn drives with the abducted Dallas James in the passenger seat as Thorn steers the man's car at high speed into the lake near the same spot where his parents died. James dies and Thorn survives again, but this time he has to serve "an indeterminate sentence" (17), imposed by himself, for his act. What is important about this is Hall's careful positioning of Thorn's act of violence in which he takes an equal risk with James. The twenty-year old event is not an atmosphere of uncontrolled violence but rather the restricted use of it that sets it apart from the world of family, friends, and lovers and the daily cycle of life.

Phillip Foster hires Jeri Howard in Dawson's *Kindred Crimes* to find his missing wife. What unfolds is another case of past violence within a family that continues to bring harm to its members. But, the hermetic Willis family structure resists most outside influences. Society does not create the violence; society's members function with a variety of good and bad actions but with no sense of an ominous cloud looming over them. Renee Foster, i.e., Elizabeth Willis, killed her parents, and her brother Mark went to prison for it. Her sister Karen knew this and eventually blackmails Elizabeth. After prison, Mark attempts to make a life for himself, but his sister kills Karen and tries to kill him. In effect, Dawson creates a singular past if not an unique one. Friends and family of both Howard and the Willises envelop the action, and the plot resolves itself without more death. Howard saves Mark and captures Elizabeth, the latter event occurring in water and limiting Elizabeth's ability either to do further harm or escape. Elizabeth's relentless pursuit of her desire to erase the past sustains the violence. She removes Karen's blackmail attempt and tries to erase Mark's knowledge of the truth. The novel turns the violence inward, and when Howard captures Elizabeth, she limits the further possibility of violence in that family.

One does not expect there to be less violence in the Modern Period. After all, criminals and private investigators often come armed, and the police always are. In the United States, the criminals' knowledge that they usually will face no armed threat from a citizen emboldens them to use or at least to act as if they will use force. In the United Kingdom, except for Northern Ireland, police do not usually carry guns, but armed response teams are quickly available in cities like London. However, in the United States, with so many people possessing guns, the hard-boiled detective literature reflects this reality, and the threat of gun violence exists with few obvious solutions. In the Early Period, the detectives are not properly dressed without their shoulder holsters, and in dangerous situations they might wear a gun on their ankle. Loren D. Estleman's Amos Walker and Jonathan Valin's Harry Stoner replicate this early fashion in guns. Their worlds always threaten violence, and their answer is to be ready to counter it. Estleman describes the danger to policemen on a Detroit street in *Motor City Blue*

> where cops paired up on sticky August nights to patrol on raw nerve-ends, thumbs stroking the oily black hammers of the holstered magnums [...] ears tuned for the quick scuffing of rubber soles on the sidewalk behind them and the wood-on-metal clacking of a sawed-off pump shotgun being brought to bear just beyond the next corner [53].

For the lone private investigator, the danger would be even greater. In the United Kingdom, it is almost impossible to obtain a permit to carry a gun. Mark Timlin's Nick Sharman's ready use of guns is an aberration and stretches one's ability to accept this as bearing any relation to the real world as one might do in the case of Mickey Spillane's Mike Hammer in the New

York of the 1940s and later. The extent to which Hammer uses a gun is suspect but not its use. Occasionally, some detectives will not wear a gun if they do not think the situation warrants it. They often regret it, but the genre demands their survival, so something intervenes, or they manage to reverse roles with the criminal and wind up with the weapon. With Prohibition and the rise of the gangster in the 1920s and early 1930s, it would have been unrealistic for a private investigator not to come armed. And the detectives arm themselves against both males and females.

One apparent explanation for the different attitudes toward guns in the USA and the UK lies in divergent cultural expectations. The unspoken assumption in the UK is that there will be time to summon help, and thus the detective will not be in so much immediate danger that the situation always demands that he or she carries a gun. Dismissing for the moment the much-debated second amendment to the US Constitution and the individual's right to bear arms, in various periods of US history, the need for weapons, at least in the popular imagination, with the wilderness and frontier dangers, has at times prevailed. Even at the present time, several states have allowed citizens to wear arms as a right. Thus, in the States one gets the strong impression that no time will elapse between threat and execution. The modern US hard-boiled detective does not portray the role of violence in quite that way but does present the notion that the city is dangerous. Anna Lee in Cody's *Dupe* works for Brierly Security in London. She spent five years in the Metropolitan Police, and even Commander Brierly tells the Jackson family that she is experienced when they come to London to find out how their daughter Deirdre died. Unlike Bix Bowie's supposed death in MacDonald's *Dress Her in Indigo* (1969), Deirdre is really dead and apparently in an accident while driving alone. As it turns out, Deirdre blackmails several people, and one of three men kills her at a lab where they illegally copied films. Francis Neary, one of the three, commits suicide, and Raymond Brough and James Eady say he accidentally killed Deirdre. Cody observes, "They claim he thought he was scaring off an intruder, and she broke her neck by struggling" (234). Raymond Brough later attacks Anna Lee for her investigation, injuring her and himself in the process. No one uses firearms or knives, and Deirdre's blackmail activities go on for a considerable period before she dies.

None of this counters the fact that in the Modern Period bad things continue to happen, and people kill other people, both detectives and criminals participating. MacDonald's model of diverting danger by having McGee con people does not appear to be a dominant method during this Period. As depressing as it may sound, the writers reflect the belief that, while fashions in the hard-boiled detective genre might change with regard to the frequency with which characters use guns and the number of deaths, human tendencies toward violence, hate, and greed are eternal. Thus, detectives deal with ineradicable threats that arise from a basically flawed humanity. Reginald Hill's Joe Sixsmith is in his late thirties and reveals a life of rich experiences in *Blood Sympathy*. Yet, he is a neophyte as a detective and starts over in many ways. From being a skilled lathe operator, the company lays him off, and he becomes an unskilled detective in a world in which the criminals and the official police have an advantage. However, his knowledge of people and his ability to learn quickly and think clearly allow him to solve his cases. Sixsmith's girlfriend Beryl Boddington states, "'You're concerned about people. And this thing you got, that seems to steer you right even when you set out wrong, there's a name for it [...].'" Sixsmith replies, "'Serendipity [...]'" (209). This gift does not prevent him from being attacked by Carlos Rocca in the same novel, a man who kills four members of his own family, and beaten by Philip Frogat (Blue) and Timothy Orrel (Grey) who seize two kilos of heroin that Sixsmith discovered Soumitra Bannerje mailed to his wife. Beryl upbraids Joe: "'Where's it going to end for you? I mean, you can't go on for ever like this. I've only known you a couple of weeks and I've seen you with your face split open, and being attacked by a mad Italian with a knife, and knocked down by a goon in a car, and punched in the face by his partner [...]'" (218). Sixsmith's later response to himself is "a tumult of defiance he felt welling up inside him [...]" (220). His taxi-driver friend Mervyn Golightly earlier incongruously labels Sixsmith "Luton's answer to Sam Spade and Miss Marple in one" (34). While possessing some of Miss Marple's sagacity, this modern detective fits in the Sam Spade image of experiencing violence but continuing his work.

One serious but controlled threat to the hard-boiled detective in the Modern Period comes from the Mafia or smaller versions of it. The Mob examples in the Early Period generally are regional in nature. Still, one might assume that if a Howard Quincy Travers can operate in New York and Florida in Daly's *The Hidden Hand* his reach is national through other unnamed connections. Spillane's Arthur Berin, a Moriarty figure like Travers, plays a similar role in *My Gun Is Quick* though his activities are restricted to New York City and its environs. Dashiell Hammett's *Red Harvest* portrays the devastating effect organized criminals, if not organized crime, can have on one city. Yet, one man, Elihu Willsson, hires them, and one man effectively removes them in the person of the Continental Op. Similarly, Raymond Chandler's *The Big Sleep* uses local criminal Eddie Mars as a socially destabilizing force. In the Transitional Period, MacDonald employs parts of what are larger criminal organizations in *One Fearful Yellow Eye* and *The Scarlet Ruse* but makes organized crime, along with South American elements of the drug trade, crucial to the plot in *The Lonely Sil-*

ver Rain. Parker's Spenser confronts Boston elements of a larger criminal organization in his first novel, *The Godwulf Manuscript.* Throughout his series, the Mob has a sometimes distant, sometimes immediate presence with Spenser's becoming accustomed to using criminal acquaintances to aid him in his cases. The Modern Period accelerates this familiarization of the Mob's presence by introducing family connections. In Loren D. Estleman's first Amos Walker novel, *Motor City Blue,* an ailing Detroit mob boss hires Walker to find his wayward granddaughter. Jonathan Valin's Harry Stoner contends with a northern Kentucky crime figure in *The Lime Pit,* but other modern detectives also associate with members of the Mob. Carlotta Carlyle in Linda Barnes' *A Trouble of Fools* has an off-and-on affair with Sam Agnelli, the nephew of a Boston crime figure. In Les Roberts' *Pepper Pike,* Milan Jacovich becomes so enmeshed with the nephew of the Cleveland syndicate head that he attacks him. Dennis Lehane returns to the family relationships between a detective and the Mob in *A Drink Before the War.* Angela Genarro is the granddaughter of the head of the Boston mob but struggles to keep them out of her life. None of the detectives dies at the hands of the Mob, and occasionally they receive needed help, but on the whole, the criminal organizations disturb more than help the pattern of their work. For Barnes' Carlyle and Lehane's Genarro, the moral aspects become an issue that neither adequately solves. Carlyle cannot reject her lover, and Genarro cannot completely disown her family.

It is obvious that violence remains part of the hard-boiled detective genre in the Modern Period. Humans apparently cannot do without it whether in fiction or real life. If not entirely managed, violence takes a place but not the omnipresent place it formerly occupied. It is an integral theme, defining and exemplifying the genre without overshadowing other growths. Of course, violence naturally accompanies the hard-boiled detective. It is something that he or she expects to occur but that they, for the most part, feel able to handle.

18

Better Places

Given the nature of the genre, the hard-boiled detective novel always has the ability to inject evil, cruelty, and violence into the most outwardly placid and peaceful environments. John G. Cawelti comments:

> When we step from the world of the classical detective formula into the milieu of the American hard-boiled story, the vision of the city is almost reversed. Instead of the new Arabian nights, we find empty modernity, corruption, and death. A gleaming and deceptive facade hides a world of exploitation and criminality in which enchantment and significance must usually be sought elsewhere, in what remains of the natural world still unspoiled by the pervasive spread of the city [*Adventure* 141].

The modern hard-boiled detective novel continues this tradition but with notable attitude changes on the protagonists' part. Unlike the early detectives, modern investigators, while no more blinkered toward their cities' dark sides, operate with a broader appreciation of the urban worlds they inhabit. Speaking of the early detectives, George Grella states: "The hard-boiled novel's vision usually approximates the prevailing vision of American fiction. Its world, implied in Hammett's works, and fully articulated in Chandler and Macdonald, is an urban chaos, devoid of spiritual and moral values, pervaded by viciousness and random savagery" ["Hard-Boiled Detective" 110]. Les Roberts' Milan Jacovich in Cleveland, Reginald Hill's Joe Sixsmith in Luton, England, Sarah Dunant's Hannah Wolfe in London, and Janet Dawson's Jeri Howard in Oakland continue a shift away from the detective's traditional disgust and suspicion for his or her environment, a shift begun in the Transitional Period with John D. MacDonald's Travis McGee in Ft. Lauderdale and Robert B. Parker's Spenser in Boston. Thus, the modern hard-boiled detectives show a more positive, layered view of the societies in which they work and live than both sets of their progenitors.

So many cities appear in the modern hard-boiled detective novel that the idea of a special place no longer stands out as in the Early Period. The expansion from New York, San Francisco, Los Angeles, Chicago, and Miami to much of the United States begins in the Transitional Period and grows dramatically in the Modern era beginning around 1980. In addition, Great Britain easily accommodates the genre's special features. British hard-boiled detectives seldom live outside London, but Manchester, York, and Luton also provide the accustomed urban background. In America, large and small cities serve well, keeping the genre's basic form even when the city's size drops from a New York or Los Angeles to an Indianapolis, Cincinnati, or Saratoga Springs. Sacramento, Boston, small-town Montana, Detroit, Cleveland, Santa Teresa (north of Los Angeles), Oakland, and Seattle make this genre truly national by filling out the map of the United States. By extending the genre to all places, any place is a possible locus of the novels' special dangers. However, the peculiarities of each city matter, and throughout the history of the form, local knowledge, local situations, and local places affect the stories. Heat or cold, wet or dry, change or stasis— the weather enters into the lives of the detectives and, at the very least, accompanies the action and lends various tones and moods to its movements. San Francisco's fog and hills; Los Angeles' sun and freeways and the barriers of ocean, mountain, and desert; Boston's relative age and history; Chicago's, Cleveland's, and Detroit's ethnic neighborhoods and urban renewals; New York's buildings and masses; and Florida's heat, humidity, and sub-tropical suggestion of violence in a new-old loosening of moral focus— all resonate with disturbing visions and realities.

Roberts' Cleveland presents a complex picture of a modern urban environment that radiates tensions and possibilities. First, Milan Jacovich, a Slovenian, is divorced from Lila, a Serbian. Even in 1980s and 1990s Cleveland, the ethnic discords from the Balkans establish boundaries and loyalties that remain stubbornly resistant to change. Milan and Lila were high school sweethearts who bridged the weakening ethnic barriers but could not, even with two children, maintain their marriage. Ceaseless quarrels undermined any love they had, but they satisfactorily work out their parental responsibilities. Milan says, "[...] as we grew older she developed that Serbian aggressiveness that just didn't mesh well with my Slovenian mild manners, and we finally called it quits, fourteen years and two kids later" (*Pepper Pike* 11). Lila remains in the home with the children, but Milan cannot help but feel that it is still his home even though he moves south and east to an apartment in Cleveland Heights. Early in the series, Milan frequents Vuk's tavern, located in Slavic town where he grew up. With the different generations who drink and socialize there, Roberts injects a sense of time into his portrait of the city. Jacovich states in *Pepper Pike* that it was "Vuk, the bartender and owner, who had served me my first legal drink of alcohol when I'd come of age" (3). As Milan develops and changes in the series, he returns infrequently to Vuk's. Concomitant with this emotional withdrawal from past associations, Milan expresses a clear appreciation of the city and what it offers. Unlike many early private eyes who struggle with their cities and the people who live there, Jacovich comes to celebrate Cleveland's past and present. He even ventures west to the Cuyahoga and the Flats, "Cleveland's wine, dine, and dance center" (*Pepper Pike* 71), which represents a cultural shift from his working-class roots. For a while, he dates Mary Soderberg, a saleswoman for the local Ch. 12 TV, and takes her to the Flats on their first dinner date. Occasionally, Milan sees his old friend Marko Meglich, a lieutenant in the Cleveland Police Department. They joined the police together, but Milan left after four years. Marko ("Call me Mark"), also divorced, still resents Milan's departure and at times relates to him with a sharp edge.

At least five hard-boiled detectives work in Boston in the modern period. Of course, Robert B. Parker's Spenser, the first Boston hard-boiled detective, hovers in the background of any private eye operating there. Jeremiah Healy's John Francis Cuddy, Linda Barnes' Carlotta Carlyle, and Dennis Lehane's Patrick Kenzie and Angela Genarro bring different views of Boston to the genre, overlapping in interesting ways with Parker's. Cuddy, South-Boston Irish, Holy Cross graduate, and former investigator for Empire Insurance with a detour for service as a captain in the Military Police in Vietnam, loses his job and his wife before going on his own as a private investigator. In the first two chapters of *Blunt Darts*, Healy sketches in the city, connecting people and places. Surprisingly, Boston emerges with a small-town feel. The priest that married Cuddy and Beth also buried her, the restaurant where he meets an intermediary for a client, Mrs. Kinnington, is owned by a couple who lived above Cuddy and his wife's condominium, and he can walk to most downtown business meetings and to his office on Charles Street at the foot of Beacon Hill from his one-bedroom apartment. From his home, he can use the Charles River walkways for jogging. Most old East-coast cities have a sense of compression, and yet Cuddy also operates in a city that has spread, creating a feeling of distance between areas that includes miles as well as cultures. *Blunt Darts* takes him to the nearby town of Meade and subsequently to Western Massachusetts. Just as Spenser in his first two novels, *The Godwulf Manuscript* and *God Save the Child*, takes cases that develop in the suburbs away from his accustomed area of activity, Cuddy also must go out from his home turf to places in which wealth and/or class differences complicate his task.

Barnes' Carlyle, partly raised in Boston by her Aunt Bea, lives with her unconventional lodger Roz in the house left to her by her aunt. She inverts the perspective that Healy's Cuddy presents by living in Cambridge away from the downtown and, by virtue of her earlier part-time job as a cab driver, roving across the city. Her personal contacts, which include Gloria, the dispatcher for the same cab company; Paolina, the young child for whom she acts as a big sister; and Sam Gianelli, a lawyer and sometimes lover and the son of a Boston mob figure, change the shape of the city when compared to Cuddy's experience of it and bring her world closer to Spenser's. Of course, this similarity is more superficial than substantial. Kathleen Gregory Klein observes, "Little about her conforms with the traditional private eye out of Hammett and Chandler or even her Boston neighbor Spenser" (*Woman Detective* 237). Aside from Susan Silverman and Hawk, Spenser's lover and sometimes partner, respectively, Spenser is a loner. He does eventually adopt Paul Giacomin, introduced in *Early Autumn*, and maintains friendly contact with two policemen, Sgt. Frank Belson and eventually Lt. Martin Quirk, and Henry Cimoli, a health club proprietor and Spenser and Hawk's former boxing trainer. In contrast, Carlyle connects with people in more diverse and complicated relationships. Early in *A Trouble of Fools*, she reveals her Jewish-Irish ancestry, adding a Scots background too, and these different experiences function as sources for insights into and evaluations of people. Carlyle graduated from the University of Massachusetts—Boston with a degree in sociology and worked as a policewoman. Although independent, Carlyle has a web of relationships through which she lives in the city, emphasizing Louise Conley Jones's observation that the realistic depiction of society in "detective fiction continues in contemporary examples and is never more apparent than in those novels in which the detective, the hero, is a woman" (80). Carlotta says, "I used to love late-night walks. My ex-husband and I were great walkers. Boston's a walking town" (*Trouble* 35). Finally, she regularly plays on an 8 A.M. volleyball game at the YWCA.

Lehane's Kenzie and Genarro in *A Drink Before the War* are partners and develop a rocky relationship that at times explodes and leads to brief separations. Genarro is the granddaughter of a Boston mob figure whom she constantly pushes out of her business life. Worried about her, he sometimes assumes a paternal role that clashes with her idea of how she should work. Kenzie and Genarro resemble Carlyle in their involvement with the city. Both grew up in Boston and hung out with the same friends in their teens. Lehane gives a sense of Boston's different areas when he describes Kenzie's apartment directly across the street from his and Genarro's Dorchester office. The latter is different enough even for the hard-boiled genre: "My office is the bell tower of St. Bartholomew's Church. I've never found out what happened to the bell that used to be there and the nuns who teach at the parochial school next door won't tell me" (*Drink* 11).

One, Sister Joyce, grew up with him but is just as evasive as the older ones. Kenzie says, "I'm a detective, but nuns could stonewall Sam Spade into an asylum" (11). He says of his apartment, "I live directly across from the church in a blue-and-white three-decker that somehow missed the scourge of aluminum siding that overtook all its neighbors" (31). Lehane discriminates between white Dorchester and black Dorchester that the whites consider part of Roxbury. Given this sense of space and time, Lehane extends the narrative into the rest of Boston and surrounding suburbs. Boston becomes its many parts. Curiously, Lehane does not describe Genarro's home environment with her husband Phil. Other than the fact that she went to high school with Kenzie and shares an office and detective partnership, Genarro exists for the reader outside her home. Possibly this occurs because Phil beats her, sometimes severely. This mystifies Kenzie since she is otherwise an independent woman. He and Genarro dated and slept together when they were younger but married others. Once when Phil beat her very badly, Kenzie reciprocated, but this did not stop the abuse. Genarro says she loves Phil, and that seems to justify the beatings. Kenzie imagines them together, "Angie was home now, taking another few steps in that grotesque dance of pain she called a marriage" (79). Other than merging the physical abuse he received at his father's hands with Angie's, he gets little further in understanding her position or his father's actions.

With the expansion, in many senses, of the hard-boiled detective novel from 1980 on, the variety of detectives' offices and homes becomes positively exotic. Roberts' Jacovich and Loren D. Estleman's Amos Walker work and live in places reminiscent of those of Raymond Chandler's Philip Marlowe. Robert A. Baker and Michael T. Nietzel remark: "Walker's Detroit is a scary extension of Marlowe's LA: decadent, corrupt, evil. It is the American city gone bad, so bad that its treachery fails to shock much anymore. Its dark streets are full of predators, driven by paranoia, greed and hate" (199). For Jacovich and Walker, functional would be the most accurate description of home and office. Unlike Hammett's Sam Spade and Spillane's Hammer, neither have secretaries, and their offices are two plainly decorated rooms (Jacovich's is in his apartment) in which periods of boredom and violence are both likely to occur. Baker and Nietzel describe Walker's business address as a "dreary third floor office on Grand River" (201) that might account for Joseph Hynes' observation that "[...] Walker is nomadic within his particular urban setting" (121). Estleman gives brief descriptions of Walker's home and office in *Motor City Blue*. The office atmosphere is reminiscent of Marlowe's Los Angeles agency. Estleman states:

My office is a third-floor wheeze in one of the older buildings on Grand River, a pistol-shot from Woodward. The last time I scrubbed it, the pebbled-glass door, which always reminds me of the window in a public lavatory, read A. WALKER INVESTIGATIONS in flecked black letters tombstoned tastefully across the top and in need of touching up [51].

He says it used to be called "APOLLO CONFIDENTIAL INVESTIGATIONS" (51). He lists a "file cabinet," a "backless sofa," and a "desk with a bottom drawer deep enough to store a bottle of Hiram Walker's upright, suitable for tying one on" (51). Estleman includes the traditional elements for an environment that suggests danger and impermanence. Walker's home is a "little shack just west of Hamtramck" (9) in a "predominantly Ukrainian" (9) neighborhood. "It's a one-story frame dwelling, built during the great European famine in the 1920s, when refugees came here in droves and boasts a bath, a bedroom, a combined living room and dining area big enough for one or the other but not both, and a full kitchen, currently an endangered species" (9). The impermanence is illusory since he plans to stay "until the taxes eat me alive" (9). Roberts has compressed Jacovich's environment even more by working and living in the same place. Jacovich states, "It was nothing fancy, but there was a big front room I used for my business, a small parlor where I did most of my living, a closet-sized kitchen with a postage-stamp dining alcove, and two good-sized bedrooms" (*Pepper Pike* 4). Both men are divorced. This minimizes Walker's personal obligations but not Jacovich's since he has his two sons every other weekend.

Jacovich and Walker live and operate in sharp contrast to Sara Paretsky's V.I. Warshawski and Sue Grafton's Kinsey Millhone. The former lives in a North Chicago apartment building on Halstead that eventually comes with a downstairs, over-protective neighbor, Mr. Contreras. Warshawski is comfortable there, an impression reinforced by her action when Lt. Bobby Mallory and Sgt. McGonnigal leave her apartment in *Indemnity Only* after questioning her about Peter Thayer's murder and what she noticed about the crime scene when she found his body in an apartment near the University of Chicago: "I poured myself another cup of coffee and took it into the bathroom with me where I dumped a generous dollop of Azuree mineral salts in the tub and ran myself a hot bath" (33). However, her office is in a South-Loop office building verging on the gothic. A crumbling structure with balky elevators and electrical system, Warshawski meets clients there at night and sometimes with only the light from a Wabash Avenue street-lamp. Dark hallways and occasional violence on the premises do not deter her. Earlier in the above novel, her description of her office reflects her satisfaction with her own furnishings: "With the lights on my office looked Spartan but not unpleasant and I cheered up slightly. Unlike my apartment [...] my office is usually tidy." She has a "big wooden desk" and her mother's

"Olivetti portable." Along with a "reproduction of the Ufizzi hanging over my green filing cabinet, she has included "[t]wo straight-backed chairs for clients" (2). Millhone lives in Santa Teresa, California, in a converted garage behind the house of the retired baker Henry Pitts. She says, "Of all the places I've lived in Santa Teresa, my current cubbyhole is the best. It's located on an unpretentious street that parallels the wide boulevard running along the beach" (*"A" Is for Alibi* 13). She adds, "The room itself is fifteen feet square, outfitted as living room, bedroom, kitchen, bathroom, closet, and laundry facility.[...] It is to this cozy den that I escape most days after work [...]" (14). Unlike Warshawski's frequent irritation with Mr. Contreras, Millhone, though sometimes needing to restrain Henry's desire to help, often seeks out his company. She remarks, "I'm halfway in love with Henry Pitts" (14). Fortunately or unfortunately, Pitts is eighty-one years old. Like her safe home environment, she rents office space first from California Fidelity Insurance Company and later from a firm of lawyers. She writes of her first office: "I do a certain number of investigations for them in exchange for two rooms with a separate entrance and a small balcony overlooking the main street of Santa Teresa" (1). She repays the lawyers in the same fashion.

These homes and offices reflect Warshawski's and Millhone's personalities. Both detectives like to close off the world at times. For the most part, they live alone and like it that way. Close but not too close suits them for neighbors, friends, and lovers. Both have troubled pasts. Not only are Warshawski's mother and father dead, she also has few close relatives. However, she does have one close friend and Lt. Bobby Mallory who stick with her no matter how crusty her personality becomes. Dr. Lotty Herschel runs a clinic for women and children and is more an aunt- than mother-surrogate, but she matters deeply to Warshawski. Her clinic functions as a solid reminder that life matters and some people dedicate themselves to that ideal every day. Lt. Mallory cannot accept Washawski's sometimes dangerous profession. No matter how irritating he becomes with his many reminders that he is looking after her for her dead father, Warshawski does not sever the connection and finds a real family atmosphere at his home from his wife Eileen and their children. Millhone thinks that her aunt is her only living relative and that once she dies, she is alone in the world. Eventually, cousins and a grandmother turn up in *"J" Is for Judgment* (1993), cousins who know of her existence but not she of theirs. Apparently, Millhone's Aunt Gin wanted nothing to do with them and never apprised her of their living not far away. When they do contact her, Kinsey reacts warily to their desire to get to know her. Like Warshawski, Millhone's parents died some years before the first novel begins, but, like James W. Hall's Thorn in *Under Cover of Daylight*, they were killed in a car accident, and she was only a baby. Millhone also achieves independence in her work by depending on her own judgment. In a profession dominated by men, she and Warshawski establish firm boundaries that, for the most part, keep them secure.

Robert Crais's Elvis Cole uses a Los Angeles office that has the bare, dusty plainness of Marlowe's, in addition to an empty room representing his silent (literally) partner Joe Pike. Cole likes vistas from both his office and his home, "On a clear day I could go out [to the little balcony] and see all the way down Santa Monica Boulevard to the water. The view had been the selling point" (*The Monkey's Raincoat* 2). His home is a "rustic A-frame on a little road off Woodrow Wilson Drive above Hollywood" (20). He describes the view in the gathering night: "The rich black of the canyon was dotted with jack-o'-lantern lit houses, orange and white and yellow and red in the night. Where the canyon flattened out into Hollywood and the basin beyond, the light concentrated into thousands of blue-white diamonds spilled over the earth" (20). Cole descends into the city and, with Pike's efficient and deadly help, deflects most danger to his clients or himself. Harry Stoner's Cincinnati in Jonathan Valin's *The Lime Pit* presents a portrait, similar to Walker's Detroit, of a city in decay. As a result, many of the homes and apartments do not accommodate their residents well. Valin writes: "It's not that the houses don't look lived in; on the contrary, Clifton looks thoroughly lived in, richly historical in the clutter and detail of everyday life. But it is a sedate and melancholy clutter that smacks of decay" (9).

Hugo Cratz hires Harry Stoner to find his girl, Cindy Ann Evans. Cratz is over seventy years old and has fallen in love with the teenaged girl. The sadness that even overcomes Stoner, who has seen too much, derives from the physical and sexual abuse that Cindy Ann endures at the hands of two neighbors, Lance and Laurie Jellicoe, and they are just the first to use her. The moral corruption that Stoner sees in Cincinnati and across the Ohio River in Kentucky parallels the physical decay. Everything seems shoddy and rundown. Finding Cindy Ann's body in a lime pit seems like a natural progression for the events Stoner investigates.

Detectives vary in the way they fit into their homes, offices, and cities. Some seem to grow out of their immediate environments with a real sense of connection to place while others exist in their locales but are not equally of them. Mark Timlin's Nick Sharman and Janet Dawson's Jeri Howard, separated by six thousand miles, provide clear examples of this difference. Sharman, from South London, seems embedded in his world. He grew up in that area of the city and worked there as a policeman. After resigning from the police, and not voluntarily, he returns to the specific part of South London, Tulse Hill, that represents home:

The office I had rented was situated in a cul-de-sac leading to a railway station deep in South London. I had been born and bred in the area and when I was a baby, my mother had taken me for long walks across the grounds of a riding school which was now a council estate where two thousand souls lived. She'd bought our vegetables from a market garden where a used car lot now stood [*Good Year* 10].

Timlin also writes in *A Good Year for the Roses* that the shop in which Sharman sits "previously housed a coal-merchants." It contained "a large, high-ceilinged outer office," "a smaller, windowless inside room" and "a tiny, muddy, high walled yard which contained nothing but an outside toilet" (11). Sharman has returned to basic. Included is a pub across the road from his office from which he can keep an eye on the door for any chance customers. In the above novel, George Bright hires Sharman to find his missing eighteen-year old daughter Patsy. He saw Sharman's advertisement in a local paper and comes to his office at the start of the case. For all that London is a vast city and for all that Sharman ranges across it in pursuing the case, the start of the novel in the narrow area in which he works and lives, e.g., he can walk to work, reflects someone moving from the inside out. Sharman may have resigned from the police a step ahead of being fired and he may be divorced, but he is, inarguably, in his place.

One could argue that Dawson's Jeri Howard does not project the same sense of belonging due to the nature of the Bay Area. She lives in Oakland, the stepchild of San Francisco, and works in a larger range than Sharman. She even feels that she is somewhere when she is there, but except for Berkeley, what other bay city competes with San Francisco's rich, layered sense of both a past and a present that assumes an acknowledgement by others of its existence? Is it because it is a world city? Possibly so, but it is also a city that is not in recovery as a whole, a city that does not need to boost itself as thriving and dynamic. Parts of it might shift, change, deteriorate, blossom, etc., but that is the dynamic of a city which commands its space and the imaginations of those who encounter it on whatever level. These rather poetic and subjective ways of placing two spatial entities side by side in order to understand why they differ leads to some sense of Howard's life in Oakland. None of this, however, denies Howard's existence as authentic even while acknowledging her somewhat distant presentation of Oakland. Dawson writes with a strong sense of action rather than setting. *Kindred Crimes* begins with an interview in her office. Philip Foster's wife Renee has disappeared, leaving with him their child. Although the interview lasts for five pages, Dawson never describes her office. This and similar examples reinforce the idea that place seems less important than plot and character. Early in *Till the Old Men Die*, the second novel in the series, the action places Howard in her office and her home, but she describes neither one. Even the city gets scant attention though she is out in it. She briefly describes Alameda, "the town where I grew up" (39), and suggestively remarks, "In the distance the San Francisco skyline looked like the Emerald City" (*Till the Old Men* 39). If one does not accept Gertrude Stein's witticism on Oakland's ontological status, one still has the sense that for Howard Oakland exists partly as background rather than omnipresent foreground.

The spaces in which the detectives live and work are usually more than just background, more than unchanging locales for processes unaffected by people. Their cities and towns reflect, by definition, human purpose and intent, and as they add to their environments, they insert themselves into the places and become identified with them. Joe Sixsmith cannot be pulled from Reginald Hill's Luton, and Luton cannot be pulled from Sixsmith. While some detectives seem more connected to their locales than others, all take on their cities' effects and rhythms and form the images by which one recognizes each city and town.

19

Necessary Work

Thomas Carlyle is, or should be, the patron saint of hard-boiled detectives. Possibly no one extols the value of work more than he. In *Sartor Resartus* (1836) and *Past and Present* (1843), Carlyle enthuses about the nature of work, calling it religious. If the hard-boiled detectives have little obvious religious belief, work does almost function as a form of worship, at least regarding the time and energy that they allot it. The early detectives lay a groundwork of habits and attitudes for later writers in which work figures as a significant way to get through life. Both the transitional hard-boiled detectives and the modern ones continue this tradition. Work serves as a definer of who the detective is and hints at the limits of his or her personality. Work also reveals the detective's interests and aids in measuring the effects of his or her character on others. Across the spectrum of American and British hard-boiled detectives, work continues to be a preeminent life focus. Unlike John D. MacDonald's Travis McGee, few define themselves as retired. For the modern detectives, work provides a focus that unifies their reactions to the stresses and conflicts inherent in contemporary culture.

In the novels that introduce most modern hard-boiled private detectives, one finds them involved in cases from the start and set on the course of their fictional lives. What most also have in common is a background in some kind of police or investigative work. Les Roberts' Milan Jacovich and Liza Cody's Anna Lee are ex-policeman and policewoman. So are Sue Grafton's Kinsey Millhone, Linda Barnes' Carlotta Carlyle, Mark Timlin's Nick Sharman, and John Lutz's Fred Carver. This literary convention of past police or investigative work begins in the early hard-boiled detective novel with Raymond Chandler's Philip Marlowe, Thomas B. Dewey's Mac, and Ross Macdonald's Lew Archer and continues in the Transitional Period with Robert Parker's Spenser, John Lutz's Alo Nudger, and Lawrence Block's Matthew Scudder. Stephen Dobyns' Charlie Bradshaw is an exception in that one sees him actually moving from police to private detective work. One advantage to this kind of background is that it gives the detective professional contacts, however grudgingly the police extend any help. Even military police experience, as in the case of Loren D. Estleman's Amos Walker and Jeremiah Healy's John Francis Cuddy, is enough for the police detective to acknowledge some similarity in their training and practice. The ability to give one policeman the name of another when not working in one's city also helps solve some dilemmas and remove unnecessary suspicion from the private detective. Help and information at times are also more forthcoming, especially from a policeman who trusts the professionalism of the private detective.

John Lutz introduces an interesting variation in Fred Carver in *Tropical Heat* (1986) on the private investigator-policeman relationship. The author also, as mentioned above, of the Alo Nudger series set in St. Louis in the Transitional Period, Lutz develops Carver in striking contrast to his earlier detective. Nudger is a former policeman but one who becomes something of a laughing-stock, a policeman for children known as Mr. Happy, the clown cop in *Buyer Beware*. However, he keeps in contact with Lt. Jack Hammersmith, his former partner. Carver, also a former policeman, has kept in touch with Lt. Alfonso Desoto of the Orlando police. He left that force only after he suffered a smashed knee in the line of duty. Bitter and cynical, he can only walk with a cane. Since he lives in Del Moray, Florida, Lt. Desoto gives him more moral support than anything else. Thus, Carver is left on his own in his many conflicts with the corrupt, tricky survivor Lt. William McGregor of the Fort Lauderdale police department. Nothing changes McGregor's attitude toward Carver. Even after he wins promotion to captain at the end of *Scorcher* (1987) and then suffers a demotion to lieutenant in *Kiss* (1988) when he is forced to take a position with the Del Moray police department, McGregor stays true to character. Physically and morally revolting, McGregor keeps from becoming a stick figure by the surprising number of ways that he challenges the belief that a few people have some good in them. It is not that one looks for goodness in McGregor but that he sees immorality or corruption in every act performed by others. Carver's inability to contain his disgust at McGregor's actions and statements testifies to his belief, however bitter he might appear, that there are some positive things in the world. Even though Carver will not commit himself to a permanent relationship with a woman, he cares for several in the series. Far from using them, Carver seems to fear the consequences of fully giving himself. He recognizes that he is a hard man, and while this does not serve him well in his love affairs, it enables him to handle both the criminals and the impermeable Lt. McGregor.

The above kinds of past experiences are important because they convincingly imprint themselves on the detectives. War and police work, in effect, hammer the hardest kinds of human experience into people. One needs little convincing that the detective expects to deal with harsh reality and that his or her present occupation is a continuation, if in a civilian capacity, of this pattern. Private detectives seldom recoil from what they encounter though they may be saddened or disgusted at the recurring examples of man's inhumanity to man. Rather, they expect brutality and dishonesty from most people whom they question or investigate. The knight motif that occurs at least as early as Raymond Chandler's *The Big Sleep* is no accident, and Marlowe's general attitude implies the disillusionment that heroes and knights must feel while living out their ideals. In meeting Grendel, his mother, and the dragon, the eponymous Beowulf has no illusions about the quality of mercy he will receive if defeated. The knight and the epic hero especially prefigure the hard-boiled detective by enduring hardships and confronting adversaries. The latter define the detectives and give reality to the expectations raised by their own difficult pasts. Sara Paretsky's V.I. Warshawski grew up in a tough neighborhood, lost her mother and father, worked as a legal aid lawyer, and finally becomes a private detective specializing in business and financial crimes. Robert A. Baker and Michael T. Nietzel in *Private Eyes: One Hundred and One Knights: A Survey of American Detective Fiction 1922–1984* write: "She's a bit like her Monroe and Wabash office: solid, down to earth, almost blue-collar although she specializes in white-collar cases, peppered with the brutality and insistent violence that Chicago has inherited as an unfortunate trademark" (322). She does not have to pass through a crisis of identity when someone hires her to investigate some perfidy. Not everyone in her world is corrupt, but she meets enough that are, and her rough background has shaped her so that she successfully engages criminals.

Being a detective does not preclude marriage or a long-term relationship, but few live as long with their significant others as does Sandra Scoppetone's Lauren Laurano. She and Kip Adams own a home together in Greenwich Village. As the series begins, they have lived together eleven years. Laurano acknowledges some of the stresses her job brings to their involvement, but she does not seek another line of work. Detecting is her business, and by extension, it defines who she is as a person. However, the friction between the detective and those close to her or him is a constant theme in the genre. Some just are detectives, with a perfunctory transition to their real work from any other obligation. Loren D. Estleman's Amos Walker fits this category. Although formerly married, he is like the first generation of hard-boiled detectives in having no permanent relationships and no important areas in his life outside his work. Jonathan Valin's Harry Stoner also seems to exist to work. Generally, Walker and Valin are two modern hard-boiled detectives who can be traced directly to Raymond Chandler's Philip Marlowe who comes to life as a detective and is left in isolation when not engaged on a job. Usually, the modern hard-boiled detective's relationships have greater permanence than in Marlowe's case and must be dealt with because the detectives are people with fuller lives than those in the early period. Janet Dawson's Jeri Howard balances between her divorced parents; her mother wants her to change jobs, and her father accepts her more as she is. In addition, lovers have to be told that she has a profession that is not changeable just because it upsets them. When Alex Tongco wants to help her in *Till the Old Men Die*, she reminds him that she is the detective.

Some authors structure their novels so that the detectives have relationships, but they also keep some distance between them and their loved ones. In Gillian Slovo's Kate Baier series, Baier lives in London with Sam and his nine-year-old son Matthew. In *Morbid Symptoms*, this has lasted for seven years, but she still maintains her old flat. Kate Brannigan, Val McDermid's Manchester detective, shares a living arrangement in *Dead Beat* with her lover Richard Barclay — adjoining bungalows with a common rear conservatory. This together but apart arrangement satisfies their temperaments and acts as a safety valve without cutting off the other person. Brannigan narrates the series, and one hears about her frustrations and satisfactions over Barclay's conduct and personal qualities as well as her positive responses to him. Robert Crais's Elvis Cole, a Los Angeles private detective, shares a house with a cat but does not own the animal. In the series, he falls in love with Lucille Chenier, a Louisiana lawyer. They visit one another, but neither will move and, until she comes to Los Angeles in *Indigo Slam* (1997), they have the ultimate in separate living arrangements. In *Katwalk*, Karen Kijewski's Kat Colorado, a Sacramento private detective, begins a long-distance relationship with Detective Hank Palmer of the Las Vegas police. She meets him when she goes to Las Vegas on a case in this first novel in the series. While the protagonists adapt to their separate situations, the need for independent action deriving from their work is central for all of them.

Sam Turner in John Baker's *Poet in the Gutter* (1995) complicates his life and work as a detective and, ironically, thus makes it possible to live a more unified existence. Nothing, however, is simple and straightforward. His client's wife, Jane Deacon, turns out to be the one responsible for her sister's killing all the people in a Leeds communal house starting some years before. Sam first collects people by giving money to a homeless boy on the streets of York. Eventually, Sam wins his trust and brings him home in order to save him. When his business begins to expand, Geordie, the teenaged boy, has recovered enough for Sam to employ him. After Jane Deacon tells him the story of the communal house, he visits Celia Allison, a "nice homely old lady" (*Poet* 45) who taught English for forty years. She was friendly with various people in the communal house. She and Sam get along well, and when Sam returns to have a meal with her, he asks her to work for him as his secretary. Celia tells him that she never married, but says, "'I had a love affair with English, with teaching'" (66). Regardless of the difference in their ages, they realize how much they are alike. She tentatively agrees to work for him: "'I'm going to read Chandler again,' said Celia. "See if I can get into this detective business'" (67). When he offers to lend her some of Chandler's books, she replies, "'I've got a couple myself,' she told him. 'I'll read those first. Then I'll call you'" (67). Sam also turns to Gus, a barman at a snooker hall. When he offers to increase his present salary by fifty percent, Gus answers, "'When do I start?'" (63). Sam does not stand behind the scenes manipulating his new "family"; rather, he becomes as involved in their lives as they in his. He has stopped drinking and attends AA meetings. At a solo club, Sam meets Wanda, and even though he thinks early in the novel that they are not working out, she is still around at the end. Using Geordie's experiences on the streets as a guide, York is a dangerous place for the innocent. Few of Sam's family are as vulnerable as Geordie initially is, but together all of them hold one another upright and the means to do this are Sam's work as a detective, work that they make more valuable in multiple ways.

Baker sets Turner's people among the killers and surrounds the latter with them. In the process, they are endangered as well as empowered by their successful work. Jane Deacon wants to kill her husband Terry and sets up an elaborate scheme to accomplish this. She relates to Turner that her sister Frances Golding tells her that her lover Graham East "'wanted her to kill all the people in the communal house. I saw it as an easy way of getting rid of Terry. She'd kill him, I'd have you as an alibi'" (*Poet* 235). Jane tells Sam this near the end of the novel, after shooting but not killing Geordie and planning to kill Sam. He shoots her first. Jane has previously killed Frances, her little sister, after giving her her passport to travel to New Zealand and Sweden to kill two women from the commune. Frances also goes to London to kill Steven Bright who was Jane's lover in the commune. Baker contrasts this mayhem with the healthy vibrations emanating from Sam's group. In the last chapter, Sam, Celia, Wanda, Geordie, and Gus and his wife Marie are at a dance. Sam fills in the details of the case for Celia as they dance. Gus and Marie move past as Sam begins. Sam tells her, "'We kept it together. We're a real team'" (238). Meanwhile Geordie and Wanda talk about Sam's authorizing a car for Gus's work in the agency. Geordie plans to learn how to drive and also to get a car for his work. Wanda offers to teach him how to drive, and it turns out that Celia is helping him in the same way. Geordie, dealing with the past nightmares he suffered from his mother and brother's abandoning him and the abuse he endured on the York streets, says that he has moved upstairs in Sam's house to his own flat. He asks Wanda if she also wants to teach him how to dance, and she says yes. All of these mundane, homely details establish the framework for even believing that work matters.

Many detectives comment on the ordinary quality of their work — an overlooked factor. Sometimes a character will state that what the detectives do is exciting, only to be countered with the boring, often dirty work of checking records to find people or information about them: marriage, birth, property, business, each kind having its own specific problems. Deanna Daniels remarks to Thomas Black in Earl Emerson's *Nervous Laughter* (1986): "'Security work. That must be very exciting.' 'Mostly it's just work.' 'I can't help but think there must be an awful lot of adventure to it.' 'About once every ten years.' I was thinking about a pair of hoodlums who had tried to teach me to breathe under water six weeks before" [12]. This presents a difficulty for the writer of fiction since a novel is not a report even though Sue Grafton uses this device to structure her fiction. Reports to themselves serve as reminders that they run businesses and must make sense of what they do in order to present their findings in a coherent fashion to their clients and thus receive payment. To accomplish the latter, they must bill them and often more than once. While computers help, the secretaries that some private detectives employ are not just for decoration. Parnell Hall's Stanley Hastings in *Detective* (1987) takes this aspect of his work to another level. He works for a lawyer, Richard Rosenberg, whose work is predominantly on accident and negligence cases. Hastings takes statements from the clients and photographs that show the stairs, pavement, etc., that presumably caused particular accidents. Rosenberg's secretaries process this material and keep Hastings moving around the city in an efficient manner. Cody's Lee works for Brierly Security in London, and the novels emphasize the amount of paperwork needed to keep even a small security firm organized. In addition to the enigmatic presence of Commander Martin Brierly with his police background and mysterious contacts, Beryl Doyle, the office secretary, appears to have a form for every eventuality. The operatives spend a good portion of their time in the office filling them out. Kathleen Gregory Klein, contrasting Lee with her American colleagues, states that she

> leads a professional life which diverges considerably from that of her American counterparts. By comparison, it is boring, circumscribed, and controlled,

but it is also likely to be much more realistic. Her cases begin as small-scale investigations—an auto accident, child custody suit, business fraud, a missing person, and bodyguard duty; only two eventually involve murder [*Woman Detective* 158].

This practical focus looks behind the scenes with a vengeance, but Dashiell Hammett, as in so many other areas, also alludes to this aspect of the hard-boiled detective's work. The Continental Op works for the Old Man who runs the San Francisco office of the Continental Detective Agency and files reports with him on his cases. Hammett's Pinkerton background probably prompted the inclusion of this area of a real-life private detective's work.

Aspects of their cases that could become dangerous, but often are not, involve driving to crime sites, waiting — either in their offices or on stakeouts, and tailing someone. One effect of these activities is to inject a sense of real time into the novels without the reader's having to suffer through it. They give a practical break between moments of danger. In McDermid's *Dead Beat*, Kate Brannigan investigates illegal trading in schneids, copies of expensive watches and shirts. She tails people to warehouses and sits in her car for hours, taking incriminating pictures. However, this is not Mortensen and Brannigan's main case and is not even the principal method by means of which they solve their cases which is usually done in their offices sitting behind a computer. Once she starts looking for Moira Pollock, Jett's childhood friend and former lyricist in the same novel, she goes to Bradford, after interviewing people in Manchester, and traces Moira to a drug rehabilitation project. Returning to Manchester, she writes, "On the way back to Manchester, I'd dictated a report for Shelley to type up and fax to Jett so he'd know I wasn't just sitting around collecting my daily retainer" (*Dead Beat* 64). Earlier, Brannigan states her "hatred of paperwork" (61), but McDermid carefully inserts this mundane aspect into the plot, in this instance as a consequence of the previous questionings.

As becomes obvious, the hard-boiled detective novel thrives on the tension between concrete, known details of the detectives' private and business lives and the unexpected that often arrives in the guise of danger and conflict. One of the aims of these writers seems to be a desire to graft the former onto the latter. A major effect is a sense of substance, a feeling of reality in a fictional setting. William Ruehlmann comments on the everyday life of real private detectives: "He tends to behave himself because of the restrictions placed upon him. He does not make much money. In the main he is an innocuous figure unassociated with personal heroism and connected more closely with tedium than with romance" (4). In contrast, the danger and conflict experienced by literary detectives frequently drive the novels, but the works rely on Ruehlmann's above-mentioned aspects to fill out the characters' lives. The form has its own demands, but the novelists pack their fiction with novelistic material that pulls at its sense of cohesion. James Sallis's Lew Griffin novel, *The Long-Legged Fly*, divides into three time frames that cover twenty-four years. While other writers refer to the past, filling in the lives of protagonists and other characters, Sallis moves through Griffin's history, thus setting up social and psychological events which portray him over time. A black New Orleans private detective, Griffin is filled with racial animosity and must learn to deal with it. Solving the case in this novel involves attending to his personal problems, past and present. The detective does not function as a collection of abilities hired to investigate a problem but as a flawed human being who shifts and changes apart from and through his work. An even clearer, if more low-key example, of the mixture of past and present is Joe Sixsmith in Reginald Hill's *Blood Sympathy*. Sixsmith worked for twenty years as a lathe-operator in Luton, north of London. Laid off, he decides to become a private detective. However, his detecting occurs through a web of associations in Luton and particularly in his own area of that city. Family, neighbors, former work associates— all factor into the way he works and thinks about his work. For both Sallis and Hill, the danger stirs up their protagonists' lives as well as those who hire them. It creates complex problems and adds a measure of loss possibly not experienced in some other detective fiction. The young boy that Sixsmith discovers dead in a cardboard box in *Born Guilty* (1994) outside St. Monica's where he has rehearsed with the Boyling Corner Chapel Concert Choir, the South Bedfordshire Sinfonia, and St. Monica's Chorale does not remain as the body as necessary object for a mystery. The story develops from the lost life to those guilty in a rich association of danger and everyday life.

Walter Mosley's Easy Rawlins in *Devil in a Blue Dress* navigates between the dangerous rocks represented by companions from his Houston past. Characters like Mouse and Joppy Shag chart where Rawlins can go and what he can do in his newly chosen profession as private detective. They represent violence inside rather than outside his range of experience and consequently make it difficult for him to get away from them. The novel takes place in 1948, and the racial divide in Los Angeles exacerbates the tension that exists between the black characters. Originally having left Houston to escape Mouse's atmosphere of violence, he cannot shake him, and Mouse finds him and even lectures Rawlins at the end of the novel for thinking "'like you white'" (205). Easy attempts to carve out a private life safe from the temptations and desires of others. In *Devil*, his main desire is to keep his house. Laid off from Champion Aircraft, Easy accepts the case that Joppy arranges. Joppy is no more trustworthy than Easy's first client in the case, DeWitt Albright. However, Joppy is black and Albright is white and wealthy. Rawlins associates with Shag by coming to his bar. Although he distrusts whites, he takes the job though sensing trouble ahead. One way Rawlins manages to keep focused is by generally keeping his own counsel. In later novels, Rawlins marries and has a child, further increasing his sense of belonging but also his anxieties at the additional responsibilities. Adding to the latter is the risks he takes with women. In one sense, Rawlins is Everyman looking for his this-world salvation and hoping to find it regardless of his own liabilities.

Stephen Greenleaf's John Marshall Tanner approaches the dangers involved in a private detective's work from an entirely different angle. In *Grave Error*, one learns of the regular order of business in his office. His secretary Peggy sits at her desk outside his office doing the many tasks required to keep Tanner's agency profitable. Tanner insists on a client's observing proper procedures, so when Jacqueline Nelson is late for an appointment, he keeps her waiting in his outer office to show her his time is valuable. Tanner is a suspended, not disbarred, lawyer and presents a business-like front. However, the ironic gap between this orderly San Francisco professional life and what unfolds in the rest of the novel mocks any attempt to control events. Mrs. Nelson hires Tanner to find out where her husband Roland Nelson disappears to for up to a week and to discover whether or not someone is blackmailing him. At the end of the novel, she reveals her real reason: "'He's become impotent, did you know that? The great Roland Nelson can't get it up. That's what made me hire you in the first place, Tanner. I figured he was getting it someplace else and that was why he couldn't satisfy me'" (213). Nelson is a nationally famous consumer activist who runs the Institute for Consumer Awareness. When Tanner visits the Institute to begin his investigation, he agrees to pretend to scrutinize a chain of health clinics for them. All of this is straightforward enough until Tanner uncovers the complex personal relationships between the employees. It is not just the present relationships but also the past ones in Oxtail, California, that contribute to the confusion and danger as the novel develops. First, Roland Nelson and Jacqueline Nelson are using assumed names. They are really Michael Whiston and Angie Peel. They fled Oxtail when Michael hit her father and thought he had killed him. Alvin Rodman, another of Angie's lovers, killed her father and her mother. Claire Nelson, whom Roland thinks is his daughter, is, according to her mother Jacqueline, Alvin Rodman's daughter. Sara Brooke and Roland have loved one another for twenty years, but the killings prevent them from being together. In addition, Sara has killed Harry Springs, Tanner's friend and the man Claire Nelson hired to find her real parents; she was ten years old when Roland adopted her. To compound Tanner's difficulties in untangling what originally seems like a simple case, false assumptions about who killed whom lead him astray until he feels overwhelmed by the morass of their lives. At the end of novel, he apparently gives Sara several days before going to Sheriff Marks, during which she commits suicide. Tanner thinks about where to place the guilt:

> There was nothing else I wanted to say, about Claire or Angie or anyone else. I just wanted to get away from it, the curse that Oxtail had cast upon everyone who lived there. That was where the guilt lay, with the town, with the collective consciousness that twisted and bent and spoiled and soured the people who had grown up with it, breathing its vapors [229].

Focusing on various ideas about work in the modern hard-boiled detective novel reveals part of the base on which the writers construct their plots. Work as theme is possibly at the opposite end of the spectrum from what draws one to the genre. Suspense, danger, and conflict are staples that only increase in interest with time. Yet, the critic's questions concerning structure, language, and theme produce a necessary understanding of the way in which the novels operate and achieve their effects. Work, among other themes, is part of the suspense and enriches it in the end. It is that in which the suspense lies embedded and allows it to develop and resonate, using elements of mystery as well and achieving a novelistic wholeness.

20

Sexuality and Diversity

The dramatic shift in sexual attitudes and practices between the early and modern hard-boiled detective novels symbolizes both cultural changes and formal shifts in the genre. From a largely male-centered heterosexual expression in the 1920s to the 1950s, the genre expands from heterosexual to include homosexual and from male to female sexuality. The Transitional Period introduced Joseph Hansen's Dave Brandstetter in 1970, a homosexual claims investigator working for his father at Medallion Life Insurance in Los Angeles. Although no other male homosexual private detectives have appeared in the genre, two female homosexual investigators, J.M. Redmann's Michelle "Micky" Knight and Sandra Scoppetone's Lauren Laurano, operate in the Modern Period in New Orleans and New York, respectively. Black, white, and Hispanic hard-boiled detectives, male and female, also contribute to the theme's variety. British and American representatives suggest another cultural shift that creates internal and external complexities. For example, Carolina Garcia-Aguilera's Miami-based Lupe Solano was born in the United States but calls herself Cuban. However, Reginald Hill's Joe Sixsmith, working out of Luton, England, was born in England of black Caribbean parents and calls himself English. Solano is sexually adventurous while Sixsmith is not. From the detectives to the wider cast of characters, the modern hard-boiled detective novel experiments with various sexual situations, thus paralleling the genre's development of other themes, and gives little indication of limiting change, sexually or otherwise.

The combination of sexuality and danger makes a compelling focus. Whether a threat to one's life or peace of mind, professional standing, personal relationships, or living arrangements, sexual danger is constant for many hard-boiled private detectives throughout the genre. Walter Mosley's Easy Rawlins in *Devil in a Blue Dress* adds spice to his existence by sleeping with the wives and/or girlfriends of violent men. This is an unaccountable action on Rawlins' part given the way that Mosley describes his character. Rawlins basically wants a peaceful life, and that especially includes keeping up the payments on his house. The reluctant private detective needs the money when he lets Joppy Shag push him into working for DeWitt Albright. In the process of trying to locate Daphne Monet, Todd Carter's mistress, and Frank Green, Mosley has sex with Coretta James while her boyfriend Dupree Bouchard sleeps off a drunk in the next room. Rawlins' exterior passivity masks a rebellious spirit that takes risks up to a point. Mouse, Rawlins' unstable "friend" from Houston, would very likely kill him if he found out that he had ever taken his money but not if he had slept with his fiancée EttaMae (152). Mosley unequivocally states that Mouse is dangerous and that Rawlins knows it (48). What is equivocal is why Rawlins risks his life this way. The sphere of sexuality, more than any other, appears to beckon Rawlins with a power greater than lust. Rawlins killed German soldiers in World War II and has seen death since, but nothing tempts him to risk his life more than a sexual situation fraught with danger. However, few other male or female detectives come close to knowingly having sex with someone who might pose a danger to them. In *Just Another Day in Paradise* (1985) in A.E. Maxwell's Fiddler and Fiora series, Fiora, Fiddler's ex-wife and sometimes lover, becomes sexually involved with Volker who, unknown to her, kills her brother Danny and then threatens her and Fiddler. Joe Sixsmith in Reginald Hill's *Singing the Sadness* (1999) flirts with the seductive but violent Bronwen Williams. Both Sixsmith and Fiora thus learn of their precarious positions after having some sexual contact.

The avoidance of sexual contact with someone dangerous seems counterintuitive in regard to the hard-boiled private detective. By definition, both male and female detectives take risks in their investigations. From the beginning of the genre, the cases which they take on lead to someone's harm, and often theirs. Yet, an almost fastidious caution prevents a sexual involvement beyond their control. Dashiell Hammett's Sam Spade is having an affair in *The Maltese Falcon* with Iva Archer, his partner Miles' wife. Spade is becoming bored with her, but since Miles dies in the first chapter, she cannot seriously threaten him by hinting at a confession to Miles. It is only with Brigid O'Shaughnessy that Spade acts before he knows enough about her. They sleep together, but Spade's investigation, with Brigid as his client, reveals her culpability in several murders, including Archer's, and Spade turns her over to the police. In Mickey Spillane's *I, the Jury*, Mike Hammer falls in love with Charlotte Manning and wants to marry her. Hammer sleeps with several other women in the novel but decides to wait for marriage before having sex with Charlotte. Like Spade, Hammer's investigation into his friend Jack Williams' murder shows that the woman whom he loves is the killer. Instead of turning her over to the police, Hammer shoots her before she, unknown to him, can reach a concealed gun and kill him. Raymond Chandler's Philip Marlowe and Ross Macdonald's Lew Archer reveal a similar caution regarding sexual involvement in their cases. This attitude in the Early Period extends into the Transitional Era. Amidst extensive violence and danger, the detectives carefully maneuver their way through sexual traps that would cloud their judgments or dull their responses.

If John D. MacDonald does not introduce the theme of sexuality to the hard-boiled detective novel, he certainly develops it, employing humor, moral repugnance, and danger to reject certain partners. Connie Melgar in *A Deadly Shade of Gold* and Lady Rebecca Divin-Harrison in *Dress Her in Indigo* prove too much for McGee's sexual stamina. These two women have carved out lives of pleasure, and McGee, in addition to admitting to sexual limits, finds no room for sentiment with them, however deeply felt. McGee feels moral repugnance toward Vangie Bellmeer and Del Whitney in *Darker than Amber* and Lisa Dissat in *A Tan and Sandy Silence*. He especially rejects the offer of sex from the latter two because of their utter lack of remorse for involvement in their novels' murder schemes. McGee admires Vangie's courage in breaking away from the so-called Drowners Inc., but she still has the odor of corruption about her, and he is not tempted when she offers, as a reward for rescuing her, to sleep with him. Mary Alice McDermit in *The Scarlet Ruse* temporarily fools him, but her moral corruption gradually makes itself known, rendering McGee impotent with her. As he admits, he would not be able to trust her in any event, given her callous murder of Jane Lawson. She becomes one of the few women who pose a real danger to him. McGee has emotional problems with other women either because they reject him or because they threaten his independence. He usually sidesteps the latter group with ease, but one suspects that Mary Smith's sudden pursuit of the satyr-like Hero in *Pale Gray for Guilt*, in the midst of plans to accompany McGee on a cruise, must have left him more bemused than bruised.

Sue Grafton's Kinsey Millhone, early in the modern period, hides in a barrel as Charlie Scorsoni, her lover, stalks her. The barrel's womb-like associations at the end of *"A" Is for Alibi*, reminiscent of her garage-apartment behind Henry Pitts' home, suggest the protective nature of her hiding place and the danger outside of it. Millhone shoots Scorsoni but deeply regrets the unavoidable action. The multiple dangers of sexuality might be what lead her to abstain for long periods of time. While Millhone experiences physical and emotional risks from her affair with Scorsoni,

Jeremiah Healy's John Francis Cuddy appears in *Blunt Darts* only partially recovered from the death of his wife and lover Beth. His loss and his memory of her encapsulate him, drawing him away from other possible relationships. His statement to Valerie Jacobs that he is not drawn to her as he was to Beth is evidence of his still present sense of loss (138). Healy does not sentimentalize Cuddy's situation, but in depicting his conversations with his dead wife when he visits her grave, Healy suggests that he may not easily recover. However, his wife later "tells" him it is time to turn to the living, a not-so-subtle narrative device whereby he tells himself. While Millhone ends her danger with a justifiable shooting *"A" Is for Alibi*, neither she nor Cuddy can easily adjust to the quite different events they face. This suggests the moral bases of their lives but does not make future relationships any less problematic. Sexual engagements lead to risks, but both investigators eventually re-engage with life and experience the consequences.

The idea of a nurturing sexuality in the hard-boiled detective novel chiefly arises with John D. MacDonald's Travis McGee. Hard-boiled detectives in the early period do not connect the act of sex with nurturing. Daly's Race Williams may sentimentalize some women, Hammett's Continental Op and Sam Spade may generally deal with them either as somewhat sexless creatures (Op) or turn them over to the police after sleeping with them (Spade), Chandler's Philip Marlowe may be both harsh and hesitant toward their expressions of sexuality, and Ross Macdonald's Lew Archer may see them largely as clients, but only Spillane's Mike Hammer seems to be invested with an uncontrolled emotional life that leads to love, passion, and violence that shut out any act of nurturing except in the case of Velda, his secretary, who is sexually willing but whom he feels he cannot touch. His nurturing of her comes most often in acts of violence toward those who would harm her. MacDonald inserts the new tone into *The Deep Blue Goodby*. Not only does McGee nurse Lois Atkinson back to health, partly by being there for her when she can make love again, but Cathy Kerr succors him at the end of the novel. McGee as the emotional rescuer and the emotionally rescued appears many times in the series, sometimes, like in *Blue*, in both roles in the same novel. Once MacDonald's McGee shows the way, detectives in the Transitional and Modern Periods, especially the latter, begin to reveal a wider emotional life.

Paradoxically, the first detectives in the Modern Period, rather than a nurturing sexuality, seem to revert to the model of the early detectives but with hints that other sexual possibilities are open to them. Stephen Greenleaf's John Marshall Tanner, Liza Cody's Anna Lee, Loren D. Estleman's Amos Walker, Jonathan Valin's Harry Stoner, Sara Paretsky's V.I. Warshawski, and Sue Grafton's Kinsey Millhone exhibit a strong degree of caution, reticence, and restraint in the area of sexuality. The transitional detectives closest to them in chronology, e.g., James Crumley's Milo Milodragovich, Lawrence Block's Matthew Scudder, Stephen Dobyns' Charlie Bradshaw, John Lutz's Alo Nudger, and Marcia Muller's Sharon McCone do not follow McGee's lead to any great degree, but they generally are more open to sexual engagement than the above detectives, at least in the early novels in their respective series. Millhone's dangerous lapse in *"A" Is for Alibi* is an exception for the first modern detectives, possibly even a cautionary one. After Block's Scudder accidentally shoots Estrellita Rivera in *The Sins of the Fathers*, he drastically changes his life. The events are discussed above in Chapter 9, but what is important in the present context is the nurturing quality shown by the ex-prostitute Elaine Mardell with whom Scudder falls in love and the inevitability in this process that Block describes. Dobyns' Charlie Bradshaw follows a similar path, especially in divorcing his over-ambitious and overbearing wife. Seemingly on the way to permanent bachelorhood, Bradshaw later meets Doris Bailes in *Saratoga Headhunter* (1985) and begins an affair with her. Although she is an independent woman, Bradshaw has a quality of permanence about him, an immovability that both directs and inspires their affair. They nonetheless manage to reach out to one another in inescapable if subtle ways.

James Crumley's Milo Milodragovich acts like damaged goods in *Dancing Bear* but also demonstrates a strong desire to help, to make whole his sexual partners. The converse of a nurturing attitude in sex would be a manipulative or exploitative attitude. While love or desire leaves little room for harshness in romantic relationships, a nurturing sexuality would have some degree of love in it. McGee parses this idea of degree with Betsy Kapp in *The Long Lavender Look*. He does not love Betsy as he did Lois Atkinson in *The Deep Blue Good-by* or Dana Holtzer in *The Quick Red Fox* or Puss Killian in *Pale Gray for Guilt*, but he knows the sentimentally romantic Betsy needs some reassurance that she is more than a large pair of breasts. Similarly to Crumley's Milodragovich, Marcia Muller's Sharon McCone shows a desire for more than physical fulfillment. While she is not damaged goods, she feels a sense of isolation among the men and women with whom she works at All Souls Cooperative. McCone shows no desire for sexual conquests but rather a need for someone with whom she can share a physical and emotional relationship. In *Edwin of the Iron Shoes*, she begins an approach to Lt. Gregory Marcus that she hopes will develop further. Lutz's Alo Nudger commences the series in *Buyer Beware* with the widowed Nudger oriented towards a romantic relationship but presently uninvolved with anyone. Lutz does not present him as thoroughly domesticated or as emotionally devastated after the death of his wife and child in a car accident since enough time has passed for him to come to terms with their loss.

After an apparently happy marriage, Nudger exhibits no bitterness at the idea of having to try again.

Greenleaf's Tanner in *Grave Error* illustrates the above-mentioned caution, reticence, and restraint in sexual matters. To give his detective a plausible cover for his lack of sexual engagement, Greenleaf introduces Tanner as middle-aged. Common ideas of reduced libido, a transference of energy and attention to work, and reduced physical activity suggest themselves as explanations for his condition. Add to these a desire to maintain one's independence and an unwillingness to change habits and ways of living, and most of the six detectives who establish a shift in the genre that creates the Modern Period fit within some or all of the above categories. For Tanner, work consumes his time, and the desire to live in his customary ways shields him against any real temptation to make substantive changes to his life. In the early novels of the series, Tanner is no Nameless who in middle age longs for a solid relationship. Younger than Tanner, Cody's Anna Lee in *Dupe* nonetheless seems to have little room for romance. Of course, she works to establish her position at Brierly Security, and this effort squeezes out other possibilities in her life. Between Tanner and Lee in age, Estleman's Walker and Valin's Stoner present some of the above qualities as well as appearing morose, hard, and withdrawn. Sexual engagement for them is usually temporary, frequently because they do not want to encourage any attempt at permanence with their lovers. Paretsky's Warshawski in *Indemnity Only* and Grafton's Millhone in *"A" Is for Alibi* work to maintain their independence usually by avoiding efforts to lead them into a long-term relationship. Both often substitute friends for lovers as sources of emotional sustenance and rely on bad marriages to remind them of possible pitfalls. However, the Modern Period soon offers other models of a nurturing sexuality.

No uniform examples appear for the above idea, but consistent occurrences establish its validity. And, writers employ it in a variety of contexts. Linda Barnes' Carlotta Carlyle has several sexual partners in the series but, starting in *A Trouble of Fools*, often turns to Sam Gianelli, a man whose family has mob connections. Admittedly, their continuing, somewhat undirected affair evolves in a slightly skewed manner. Both are independent, strong people, but they give and receive pleasure to and from one another in a semi-permanent way. They do not constantly set up adverse reactions that would lead to estrangement. However, they are not dependent on one another in a way that a married couple would be after deciding fully to share their lives. Their specific solution works for them and allows affection to grow with desire. Barnes comes up with an answer to the dilemma of diverging personalities who nevertheless keep sight of one another. If hers is not a unique answer, it is one that works itself out in a convincing way. Paradoxically, they resemble Joe Sixsmith and Beryl Boddington's in

Reginald Hill's *Blood Sympathy*. Sixsmith is edgy over any idea that he should marry her, a goal that his Aunt Mirabelle commits herself to but to which Beryl remains aloof. In their initially unconsummated affair, Sixsmith and she, however, indirectly communicate their desire for one another and their mutual recognition of the other's importance to their lives. The sexual overtones in this dance to fulfillment have comic aspects, but both Sixsmith and Beryl hear one another clearly. Sandra Scoppetone also includes the idea of duration in her Lauren Laurano series. Lauren and her partner Kip Adams have lived together for eleven years as *Everything You Have Is Mine* begins. Several problems complicate their relationship — e.g., Kip earns more money as a psychiatrist than Lauren does, or can, as a detective, and Lauren's job exposes her to dangers — but they stick with one another through their physical and emotional crises. Love and sexuality fuse in these three couples' lives as the normal and not-so-normal pressures of life impinge on them.

Most ideas need a trial period before they gain general acceptance. For the modern hard-boiled detective novel, the idea of romantic love slowly expands from its base in the transitional phase. MacDonald's McGee and his relationship with Gretel Howard in *The Empty Copper Sea* and *The Green Ripper*, Bill Pronzini's Nameless and his pursuit of Kerry Wade in *Hoodwink* and *Scattershot*, and Robert B. Parker's Spenser and his passion for Susan Silverman starting in *God Save the Child* legitimize romantic love for the hard-boiled detective novel. After these writers, the theme fits naturally into a genre that in its initial phase alternately avoids or disparages it. MacDonald, Pronzini, and Parker focus on several things these lovers share: a strong physical attraction, an intimate emotional connection, and an irrevocable commitment, once commitment is made, to one another. It is primarily in this area of life that the genre's novels approach novels of manners and morals. This is not the only theme that suggests this approach, but it is an important element in the delicate expansion of the genre's ways of being. George Grella's and John G. Cawelti's ideas on the limited possibilities for the genre's development in the 1970s rely mainly on the omnipresent early developers of the form, especially Hammett, Chandler, and Ross Macdonald. John D. MacDonald, Pronzini, and Parker remake the genre, and if love does not conquer all, it sufficiently generates new excitement and interest.

Earl Emerson's Thomas Black, Dennis Lehane's Patrick Kenzie and Angela Genarro, and Michelle Spring's Laura Principal exemplify the importance of romantic love in the Modern Period. Through a strong physical attraction, an intimate emotional connection, and an unyielding commitment to the loved one, these four detectives help alter the form's sexual emphasis. Lehane's *A Drink Before the War*, in addition to the search for

Jenna Angeline and the documents she stole from a state senator, is the story of the developing love between Patrick Kenzie and Angela Genarro, detective partners. Friends since childhood, they have set up an agency but have gone separate ways romantically. Angela married Phil Dimassi, another childhood friend, who abuses her, and Patrick marries and divorces Renee, Angela's sister. From this unpromising start, Kenzie and Genarro move toward recognition that the other probably is more important in their lives than anyone else. Aside from a kiss, holding one another several times, sleeping in the same hotel bed for fourteen hours without having sex, and Genarro's taking Kenzie's hand at the end of the novel, there is at that point no other adult physical connection. However, Lehane's careful unfolding of their mutual love and trust is strongly suggestive of a real awareness of the romantic life. By the end of *Sacred* (1997), the third novel in the series, they become lovers, something they almost accomplish in *Darkness, Take My Hand* (1996), the second installment. In *Every Breath You Take*, Spring's Principal operates a detective agency with her lover Sonny Mendlowitz. They have offices in London and Cambridge, the latter where Principal has a home and frequently works. Spring presents the reader with an ongoing love affair that seems fragile in its periods of separation but which has lasted and which appears important to both. In one sense, outsiders have to accept their own evaluation of why they stay together when they are so often apart. Desire, intimacy, and commitment underlie the relationship and give it credence. Thinking about Sonny and his relationship with his two boys, Dominic and Daniel, Principal states: "Here was a man who didn't find the stuff of life distasteful. And made me feel that I could love and still be myself. Sonny, it was clear, needed a woman for many things, but he wouldn't depend on me to provide all the warmth and caring in his life" (22).

In Earl Emerson's Thomas Black series, the Seattle investigator and Kathy Birchfield, the woman who rents the basement apartment in his house, begin what is possibly the longest courtship in the genre. In *The Rainy City* (1985), Kathy has lived in Thomas's house for almost four years (9). Now a first-year law student, she and Thomas "[...] met at the university in a history course I was taking for the police department and she was taking on her way to a bona fide law degree" (9). The attraction between them is apparent from the beginning, but they wonder in later novels why they did not do anything about it. Thomas calls her his "best friend" (9), a condition that could be harmed by love and sex. Seven novels later in *The Vanishing Smile* (1995) they marry. The delay somewhat resembles that between Lehane's Kenzie and Genarro, but with entirely different emphases. By Emerson's second novel, *Poverty Bay* (1985), Kathy has passed the state bar exam and works for the law firm of Leech, Bemis and Ott. She hires Thomas when she needs an investigator, telling her clients that he is one of the best at finding people. This arrangement provides a new structure for fairly regular contacts since she has moved out of his house. Although they do not become lovers before *The Vanishing Smile*, they have a curious physical relationship. Occasionally, Kathy shares his bed, especially when she feels threatened as in *Rainy*. They do not have sex, but Kathy hugs and kisses him after someone breaks into her basement apartment and attacks her. Afterward, she and Black sleep together. He says, "It took me an hour to get back to sleep. It was the second time in my life I had slept all night with Kathy. We had never made love" (*Rainy* 55). This pattern continues as they have affairs with others, but nothing endangers their relationship until Kathy becomes engaged to Philip Bacon in *Yellow Dog Party* (1991). As the marriage looms nearer, Thomas asks her to break up with Bacon. He states that he loves her and wants to live with her but not marry her. Kathy ironically comments on his "romantic" offer (*Yellow* 286) but says she needs time to think about this new idea for them (287). Two novels later, they finally marry, and one might see a certain inevitability about this result, but Emerson develops their coming together with a believable sense of its necessity for both characters. LeRoy Lad Panek describes their relationship as "a third alternative" between the difficulties of childhood and adulthood, "the alternative of creating, insofar as they can, the spontaneity and joy that should belong to childhood in the midst of and around the edges of their adult lives and their adult burdens" (*Hard-Boiled* 140).

A final category of the idea of sexuality in the Modern Period lacks the others' sense of clarity, of boundaries, not so much in the concrete examples as in the centrifugal force they exhibit when one attempts to keep them in a category. Yet, they strangely cohere, if for no other reason than they do not fit well in other places. A few words suggest their centripetal as well as centrifugal movement: plurality, variety, diversity, difference. It is not that they do not have elements of examples from the other categories but that they fit so well together when placed side-by-side. Laura Lippman's *Baltimore Blues* (1997) exhibits many of the above four qualities. Tess Monaghan lives on the top floor of a building owned by her forty-one year old Aunt Kitty, the owner also of a bookstore on the bottom floor named Women and Children First. Sexually, Kitty likes variety. Sometimes Tess has breakfast "with her aunt and her aunt's man of the month, both usually in bathrobes and flushed" (15). Currently, "Her latest beau was one of the city's new bicycle cops, lured into the shop after Kitty saw his legs flashing by. Thaddeus Faudenberg. He was twenty-four, as big and cuddly as a Labrador, and only a few IQ points dumber" (17). Tess describes Kitty as "beautiful" (21). She apparently attracts men easily and sleeps with those she desires. Tess, on the other hand, possesses a body that "had not changed since she was fifteen when her mother declared it obscene and began the struggle to keep it from public view" (73). This suggests a lush sensuality but not one that Tess translates into frequent partners. Jonathan Ross, a reporter on the *Beacon-Light*, formerly lived with Tess, but they have separated while still occasionally sleeping together. Tess enjoys sex but does not see it as anymore connected to monogamy than does her Aunt Kitty. Ava Hill, Daryll "Rock" Paxton's fiancée, is a young associate at a prestigious Baltimore law firm, O'Neal, O'Connor and O'Neill, who has an affair with Michael Abramowitz, her boss at the firm. Ava later claims to Paxton that Abramowitz coerced her into having sex with him. He is short and unattractive with a giant head and much older than she. Ava uses sex with an impersonal attitude that attaches no importance to whomever she sleeps with. This apparently applies to Paxton as well as Abramowitz. Plurality rules her choices, not to count up the men she beds, but as an effect of her indifference to any significance the act might suggest of a shared intimacy. It is with relief when one remembers the healthy enjoyment that both Kitty and Tess have in the sexual act. Tess demonstrates this one night when she thinks how much better the act is with Jonathan the second time after he has given up the ineffectual attempt to glean information about Abramowitz's murder, a murder with which Paxton is charged and that he insists to Tyner Gray, his lawyer, that Tess investigates.

Carolina Garcia-Aguilera's Lupe Solano in *Bloody Waters* (1996) exemplifies most of the ideas encompassed in this category. First, she is Cuban-American, part of the exile community. She says, "Though my sisters and I were in Miami and had never been to Cuba, never for a day could we forget the island's impact on our lives" (7). She adds, "If you asked my sisters or me where we were from, we would answer without hesitation that we were Cuban, from Havana"(8). This is an important element when she specifically talks about her love life. Except for her sister Lourdes, a nun, the rest of her family is "in a complete state of denial" (101) regarding her sexual experience. Lupe explains this oddity, "This made us like the rest of the Cuban-American families in Miami. Girls were considered forever chaste and virginal, even after they grew into women, married, and had babies" (101). Early in the novel, Lupe says that she has had "plenty" (14) of boyfriends. However, she states, "Still, it's not as though I slept around randomly; in fact, for the past three or four years I hadn't been with a new man" (101). Lupe remarks that she does "sleep with former lovers" (101). One in particular appeals to her, Tommy McDonald. She and Tommy came close to marriage but "decided we liked each other too much. [...] I enjoyed his company better than most men's, and the sex wasn't bad, either" (99). Tommy is a successful white American lawyer who allows her to be herself. Lupe states earlier why she has never married, "I couldn't deal with the male ego on a daily basis" (85). Fatima, Lupe's other sister, has returned home with her two daughters after a bad marriage. Lupe discovered Julio Juarez having sex with "one of the caterer's assistants" (9) on the day of his and Fatima's wedding. Later, he works for and then embezzles from his father-in-law's company. Catholic or not, Fatima divorces him. Lupe says that watching Hadrian Wells, the investigator their lawyer Stanley Zimmerman hired, do his work led to her joining the profession (9–11). Lupe's independence is essential to her sex life and her work. Although she occasionally briefly returns home, she maintains her own apartment. Lupe's father keeps a boat ready to return to Cuba once Castro dies or someone deposes him. Lupe's experiences growing up in America, even if partially within the Cuban exile community, argue against her going permanently with him. Plurality, variety, diversity, difference. Lupe represents all of these in a paradoxically well-balanced life, especially in the sexual area. After the case is over, she phones Tommy McDonald, "'Tommy? It's me. You want to go out tonight? Tear up the will and buy some champagne. You're going to have great time, *querido*. I promise'" (292).

The varied sexual patterns in the modern hard-boiled detective novel indicate the genre's realistic development in this area of human experience. Danger, nurturing, and love — these constitute significant aspects of sexuality that challenge, comfort, threaten, and lift the people caught up in the physical and emotional turmoil of its power. Threading this theme into familiar plot lines and character types leads the genre into deeper imaginative explorations, reminding one of sexuality's eternal, generative force.

21

Surviving Friendship

Friendship is hardly an issue with the early hard-boiled detectives. Their work is their life. George Grella states, "Finding the social contract vicious and debilitating, he [the hard-boiled detective] generally isolates himself from normal relationships" ("Hard-Boiled Detective" 106). However, the transitional detectives, beginning with John D. MacDonald's Travis McGee, complicate the role of friendship in the genre. Some, like Lawrence Block's Matthew Scudder, undergo dramatic changes, entering into long-term relationships or even marrying and developing friendships that subject the detectives to the normal stresses of life. In the Modern Period, the distance between this group and the early detectives widens in this as in so many other areas. The genre enters this era with a vengeance and in the area of friendship raises new social possibilities with nearly every writer. Friendship, thus, acts as a prism to the detectives' actions, refracting the directions of the generic conventions and producing a dazzling array of possibilities—emotional, social, and work oriented.

One of the first, and possibly the most important, questions that the idea of friendship raises in this Period relates to its effect on the genre. If the hard-boiled detective develops as a lonely, alienated man in a harsh urban environment lacking love or affection, what role can friendship play if seen as a serious factor in a detective's life? The ghosts of Race Williams, the Continental Op, Sam Spade, Philip Marlowe, Mike Hammer, and Lew Archer ask this question. This might be rhetorical overkill, but one needs to address its implications. Fundamentally, one must decide whether or not the genre can develop. Some critics have thought that it had nowhere to go after the detectives listed above were introduced. In his essay, Grella writes:

"The private detective has had his day—the shamus, the dick, the peeper, the snooper, who became a powerful American hero in Hammett and Chandler, has descended to the bully, the sadist, the voyeur, no longer a hero at all, but merely a villain who claims the right always to be right" ("Hard-Boiled Detective" 118). The only possible answer is to turn to the new writers in the Transitional Period and determine whether or not they have succeeded in adding to the genre's forms and themes. One answer comes early in John D. MacDonald's assertion, as indicated in Chapter 1, that no one can say that he cannot write his mystery and detective novels as close as he wishes to novels of manners and morals ("Introduction and Comment" (73). This opens, for MacDonald and later writers, thematic possibilities that hardly matter in the Early Period. Rather than generically limited, cause and effect lead to outcomes that resemble those in more traditional novels. David Geherin states of Robert B. Parker's Spenser: "But he has grown significantly, especially in the area of self-knowledge, thanks in part to the frequent confrontations between his conscience and his actions, but more importantly because of his ever-deepening relationship with Susan" (*Sons* 81–82). Of course, convention does not disappear and, most especially, detectives have their dark moments. MacDonald's McGee, Lyons' Jacob Asch, Bill Pronzini's Nameless, and Joseph Hansen's Dave Brandstetter are just a few examples of detectives who feel their isolation, at times, from others even if they seek to end it.

Love relationships might be intense if brief for modern detectives, but friendships go through many difficult permutations. The admission of the theme of friendship into the Transitional Period and the continued development of it after 1980 demonstrate the expansion of generic possibilities. As portrayed, the aloneness of the early detectives admits no opportunity to develop friendships. In Dashiell Hammett's *Red Harvest*, the Continental Op appears to make friends with Dina Brand before her suspicious death, a death that circumstances link to him. Raymond Chandler's *The Long Goodbye* develops the idea of friendship between Philip Marlowe and Terry Lennox only to have him deceive Marlowe about his supposed death. Mickey Spillane's *I, the Jury* begins with the death of Mike Hammer's friend Jack Williams. Ross Macdonald's *The Moving Target* shows Lew Archer's discovering that Albert Graves, a man with whom he once had a friendly association, is the murderer of Ralph Sampson. Not only John D. MacDonald's Travis McGee and Meyer in the Transitional Period, but also Bill Pronzini's Nameless and Lt. Eberhardt, Marcia Muller's Sharon McCone and members of the legal cooperative for which she works as an investigator, Parker's Spenser and Hawk, and Stephen Dobyns' Charlie Bradshaw and Victor Plotz show the vitality of this idea for the genre. In the Modern Period, connected through direct allusion and example to the early and transitional detectives, friendship continues to operate thematically. Many detectives surround themselves with groups of friends. This modern development of the idea of friendship reveals itself as an organic concept in the genre. Given the right circumstances, it grows and matures bringing the genre with it.

As the tendency toward the novelistic development of the hard-boiled detective novel increases, the idea of friendship, among others, begins to demand serious development and incorporation into the plots. It is one thing to introduce this theme, as noted above concerning the Early Period, only then to decline to explore it in any complex way. In that case, friendship is a stylized concept that enhances the detective's isolation by its absence. However, the full-fledged exploration of the demands that friendship makes on people pulls at the overarching formula of the genre. Both the maintenance of and the challenge to the detective formula constitute the tension in the modern hard-boiled detective novel. The use of characters with acknowledged pasts who have the ability to change and are susceptible to the influence of others might turn the genre from its past strengths. Some writers take the risks in an expansive manner while others are more restrictive in the explorations of friendship as a theme. Linda Barnes' Carlotta Carlyle and Robert Crais's Elvis Cole are representative, respectively, of these types. Carlyle surrounds herself from the first novel in the series, *A Trouble of Fools*, with numerous people, some closer to her than others. One encounters Gloria, her taxicab dispatcher friend; Roz her tenant; Sam Gianelli, her sometimes lover and friend; and Paolina towards whom she acts as a big sister and who becomes a permanent part of her life. With these and the mostly anonymous women with whom she plays her weekly game of volleyball, Carlyle exists in an expanding series of relationships and interrelationships that Barnes fuses into her plot. Of course, it is principally the case that holds the novel in the genre while friendship and other themes risk immersing it in complexities that might make it a novel with a detective and a problem to solve rather than a detective novel.

In Crais's *The Monkey's Raincoat*, the friendship between Cole and Joe Pike seems containable. Cole and Pike are Vietnam veterans who meet after the war and who operate a detective agency together from the office of which Pike is nearly always absent. Pike is a partner on call, a call to which he always responds. Each case needs both their abilities and their trust in one another. Pike is a simplified constant and Cole the variegated character who supplies change and humor. In Crais's novels, the formula controls the plots more thoroughly than in Barnes. Since Cole and Pike's friendship is so unquestioned, it poses no threat that expected changes in close relationships nearly always suggest. Time brings little alteration to their friendship. Cole's romantic involvements, especially with Lucille Chenier beginning in *Voodoo River* (1995), pull at the formula but not strongly enough to shift it from its source in the Early Period. Crais presents an example of the careful introduction of a novelistic theme that does not undermine formulaic boundaries. Paradoxically, it is their loyalty to one another that limits generic breakdown due to this theme. John D. MacDonald's Travis McGee series provides an earlier contrary example on ways to minimize friendship's demands by focusing the emotional crisis mainly on one character. In *Free Fall in Crimson* and *Cinnamon Skin*, Meyer's problematic betrayal of McGee in the first novel and the former's recovery of his self-respect in the second when he avenges the death of his niece by killing her murderer Cody T.W. Pittler introduce difficulties that explore limits to friendship and personal responsibility under inhumane circumstances. Meyer's betrayal of McGee comes near the end of *Crimson*, so the integration of this plot element cannot direct much of the novel. However, *Cinnamon* centers on Meyer's guilt and the desire to make recompense for actions that he cannot see ways to change given who he is. This complex emotional situation dominates the novel and makes it different than others in the series. Whatever the dividing line between detective and traditional novels, *Cinnamon* comes close to crossing it.

One aspect of the idea of friendship that involves much of the hard-boiled genre as well as nineteenth-century detectives such as Poe's Dupin and Conan Doyle's Holmes focuses on the detective and police as "adversarial" friends or acquaintances. This somewhat ambiguous phrase nonetheless captures the uneven connection between these two groups, one unofficial and one official. John G. Cawelti goes so far as to state, "The hard-boiled detective's relationship to the police is inevitably competitive and hostile" (*Adventure* 153). Sherlock Holmes constantly shows up the inability of the police to solve difficult crimes. Nearly ninety years later, Dobyns' Charlie Bradshaw, a former policeman, frequently has conflicts with Chief Peterson of the Saratoga Springs police for the identical reason. Acquaintances but hardly friends, Chief Peterson accuses Bradshaw of trying to embarrass the authorities with his successes. Other transitional hard-boiled detectives have police friends, but their contacts are never simple either. Parker's Spenser is a good example of a private investigator whose friendship with certain policemen evolves. Sgt. Frank Belson and Lt. Martin Quirk, especially the latter, are at the very least nervous regarding what Spenser might do. As the series progresses, Spenser becomes like one of their own to help and protect. Of course, the early hard-boiled detective novel sets the tone for the possible varieties of friendships between private detectives and police. Daly's Williams, Hammett's Spade, Chandler's Marlowe, and Halliday's Michael Shayne clash with many of the police officials they encounter in their cases. Hammett's Continental Op and Spillane's

Mike Hammer have close relationships to some policemen, but even these interactions are not always smooth. Macdonald's Lew Archer lies between these two groups of early detectives in his contacts with the police. Possibly due to his calm manner, Archer disarms the potential conflict between private investigator and public official but does not create close friendships either. With the exception of Shayne's friendship with Chief Will Gentry in the Early Period, only the friendship between Thomas B. Dewey's Mac and Lt. Donovan genuinely removes the inevitable barrier between official and civilian.

Given this legacy regarding friendships between police and private investigator, the modern hard-boiled detective duplicates many of the past experiences and adds new ones. One in particular derives from gender differences. Sexual attraction complicates and frays some contacts between them. Sue Grafton's Kinsey Millhone has a sexual relationship with Sgt. Jonah Robb of the Santa Teresa police in *"D" Is for Deadbeat* (1987). With Lt. Con Dolan, Millhone has a more typical relationship between private investigator and policeman, a mixture of crustiness and friendliness. In *"B" Is for Burglar* (1985), she observes, "My relationship to Con Dolan has always been adversarial, remote, based on grudging mutual respect. He doesn't like private investigators as a rule. He feels we should mind our own business, whatever *that* is, and leave law enforcement to professionals like him" (47). Even more problematic is Janet Dawson's Jeri Howard's unavoidable contact with her ex-husband Oakland homicide detective Sgt. Sid Vernon. For the most part, they behave well with one another, but at times Oakland seems too small a town for both of them. Part of the difficulty between the men and women lies in the contrast in physical size. Sandra Scoppetone's Lauren Laurano is constantly aware of her diminutive 5'2". In addition, Laurano is a lesbian, and this disturbs some police and some civilians. For her, Sgt. Cecchi of the New York police is a welcome exception. Along with his wife Annette, Cecchi maintains close contact with Laurano and her partner Kip Adams. Sara Paretsky's V.I. Warshawski has an even more complicated set of circumstances to deal with regarding the police. Lt. Bobby Mallory of the Chicago police served with her now-dead father. Mallory sees himself as a father substitute, however self-appointed his status. Warshawski cares for him and his family, but she knows that she must keep some distance between them. She is a former public defender and now a private investigator and able to take care of herself. Patriarchal overtones thus dominate Mallory's attitude towards her, especially since he couches them in terms of protecting her as her father would have wanted him to do. The generational and emotional conflicts cause Warshawski to push Mallory away without at the same time making a complete break.

Several other modern hard-boiled detectives have close but difficult friendships with policemen. Les Roberts' Milan Jacovich inevitably must deal with Lt. Marko "Mark" Meglich, a childhood friend. Both played high school and college football together, both became policemen, but Jacovich quit the force to become a private investigator. This upset Meglich since it disturbed his vision of their rising together in the force. Roberts intertwines the strains in their friendship with the novels' plots, a strain that ultimately has no solution. Jeremiah Healy's John Francis Cuddy and Lt. Robert J. Murphy of the Boston police have an uneven relationship, sometimes friendly, sometimes with Murphy's irritation showing. Again, Cuddy must deal with Murphy, but there never seems the possibility of achieving a balance that would obviate the friction. Finally, Loren D. Estleman's Amos Walker and Detroit policeman Lt. John Alderdyce of the Detroit police resemble Jacovich and Meglich in the length of their friendship, but in Walker and Alderdyce's case, their fathers were in business together. Walker and Cuddy are white while Murphy and Alderdyce are black, but race does not appear to add problems for them. What lies at the bottom of these last three "adversarial" friendships is that the pairs of friends have different sources of power. For the police, their official powers give them an appearance of controlling their opposite private detectives. But, the latter have an independence of action that the officials both envy and decry. In consequence, policemen occasionally use a private investigator's freedom to act to further official cases or to undertake private actions for them, sometimes turning a blind eye to their friends' illegal measures. Cutting through the bureaucratic red tape is often the excuse, an action that the official police cannot publicly take unless they are willing to sacrifice their careers.

In addition to concerns regarding the effect that friendship has on the genre and the idea of policeman and private investigator as adversarial friends, ideas relating to friendship's effect on character reveal significant changes in the hard-boiled detective novel. Some of these effects concern the time given to friendship, the hope required for it, the emotional investments that it demands, and the stress that friendship brings. The stance toward others, mentioned above, that the early hard-boiled detective displays sets the stage for subsequent events in the genre. For if isolation and loneliness, if bitterness or even disgust with life and others, if cynicism and suspicion supposedly well-founded on experience are the original sources of the hard-boiled detective's character, where does one find a place for hope and emotional investment as well as the other aspects of a fuller human being in his or her character? The join between some modern hard-boiled detectives and earlier figures is not easy or smooth. With regard to time to give to friendship, isolated figures potentially have it in abundance but not in reality. There is neither time nor space in which Sam Spade or Philip Marlowe could place a lasting friendship. William Ruehlmann notes that Macdonald's "[...] Archer, surnamed after Sam Spade's partner in tribute to Hammett, finds empathy rather than rage the informing source for his actions. Like Spade and Marlowe, he is a solitary man without much money; but unlike them, his personal sense of guilt makes him more prone to pity than punishment [...]" (105). However, Archer is no more able than Spade or Marlowe to bridge the divide between himself and others.

Mark Timlin's Nick Sharman is a bridge figure in this area. Dismissed from the police for taking payoffs, Sharman sets up as a private detective in south London. He has an ex-wife, a young daughter, and assorted lovers. Slowly, Timlin brings in friends or friendly acquaintances against a backdrop of former contacts in both the police and criminal worlds. One limitation in this area is the defects Timlin draws in Sharman's character. However violently he might occasionally act, Sharman has an emptiness in him that comes not just from a reaction to the world's disappointments. In *Romeo's Tune* (1990), Teresa, an ex-girlfriend and former prostitute, tells Sharman that she sees a "cold streak" in him (12). However, neither the emptiness nor the coldness turns him into the kind of killer represented by Benjamin Ferrara, the Mafia figure who works for the Cassini family. Other modern hard-boiled detectives who resemble earlier figures, detectives such as Jonathan Valin's Harry Stoner and Estleman's Amos Walker, have a substance of character that Sharman lacks and seems to know he lacks. John Baker's Sam Turner is a character who effortlessly makes time for friendship. His recognition of the humanity of others, probably the lack of which is the source of Sharman's actions, creates time for them. Stoner's and Walker's generally unexplained isolation from others does not reduce their characters as does Sharman's. A generic stance might better explain their isolated lives. As Marlowe, Spade, the Continental Op, and Archer go, so go they. Sharman's self-absorption belies the possibility that he can develop much beyond the opening scene in *A Good Year for the Roses*. The upheaval in his resignation from the police has settled, but Sharman appears quite content with the result. He evinces little desire for growth and change.

As is apparent from the above question of time given or not to friendship, the absence of hope, emotional investment, and stress in relation to the theme is as significant for character as presence. Hope encouraged or dashed, desired or denied expands one's understanding both of the detectives and the characters who act out the fictions with them. John Lutz's Fred Carver generally denies the claims and possibilities of friendship. It is true that he maintains contact with Lt. Alfonso Desoto, a man with whom he served on the Orlando police force. Ironically, Carver's relationship to Desoto appears closer than it probably is, especially in comparison to his contacts with the abhorrent Lt. William McGregor of the Ft. Lauderdale and later Del Moray police. However, Carver's denial of any hope of close contact lies not in his relations with the police, friend or foe, but with the women with whom he sleeps. Carver retired from the Orlando police because he was shot in the left knee. His knee was fused at a thirty-degree angle that requires the use of a cane to walk (*Tropical Heat* 5). Only in the water is he physically on equal terms with anyone. It is not too much to suggest that his injury and the subsequent condition are symbolic of Carver's rejection of intimacy. The early hard-boiled detectives are emotionally isolated figures; Lutz depicts a physical representation of Carver's sense of isolation with no additional explanation for its causes. Matching Carver later with Beth Jackson, his tall, strong, black lover introduced in *Bloodfire* (1991), balances his portrait in an uneasy way since she seems even more self contained than he. One is left to observe, through a series of novels, that they at least remain together in some fashion, a bleak hope at best for friendship's survival.

In *Scorcher* (1987), Carver returns to his beach cottage north of Del Moray, Florida, after the murder of his son. He has been living with Edwina Talbot whom he met in *Tropical Heat* (1986), the first novel in the series. Whatever intimacy they temporarily have fractures in his withdrawal from Edwina and denial of her succor. In contrast to Carver's bleak world, G. M. Ford's Leo Waterman in *Who in Hell Is Wanda Fuca?* (1995) represents a scenario in which friendship, at multiple levels, expands and washes over his life. His father was a prominent Seattle politician, and the son inherits the father's recognition status. Four alcoholics, men who have descended from important careers, act as aids to his cases during which they manage to stay passably sober. Waterman exists in a world of expected friendliness; his father was liked, so he is liked. If he exudes a certain watchfulness, it probably derives from his being the target of so much unearned bonhomie. The hope for friendship is thus never challenged. When Tim Flood, a Seattle crime figure and an old friend of Waterman's father hires Waterman in the above novel to look for and look after his unwilling granddaughter, he presumes on his former relationship with Waterman's father. Seeing Flood as a problematic friend, Waterman nonetheless takes the case. His general struggle in the area of friendship will be to discover an opportunity to develop a closeness to someone. The genre does not easily position detectives for that, but some manage if they recognize the effort needed to achieve that condition.

The concept of the emotional investment needed to achieve and maintain friendship functions as an important theme in traditional novels of manners and morals. The hard-boiled detective novel accommodates this and other novelistic themes regardless of the ever-present pull of formula. The genre has many examples in the Modern Period of the adaptation of this theme and the repositioning of the genre to use it. Several British and

American detectives make credible efforts toward investing time and themselves in order to create an atmosphere of friendship within the larger social worlds they inhabit. John Baker's Sam Turner, a private investigator in York, England, assembles a group of people around him. Rather than as a sign of dependency or neediness, Baker suggests that this is what human beings do. The early hard-boiled detective tradition reveals that this is not what detectives do, but Baker carries it off and holds Turner within the tradition by having him assert a separate existence from the group while maintaining his connection to it. Turner attends AA meetings and solo clubs as *Poet in the Gutter* opens. Before the novel ends, he has a girlfriend, Wanda; Celia Allison, a retired English teacher who acts as his office assistant; Geordie, a homeless teenager whom he rescues and who lives in his home and eventually helps him with his cases; and Gus as an assistant investigator. Despite the many currents in this group, Turner maintains a separate sense of himself and keeps his developing detective agency intact.

Karen Kijewski's Kat Colorado also has a close circle of friends. Charity Collins, an advice columnist, appears in the first novel, *Katwalk*. It takes place predominately in Las Vegas, and there Kat meets Detective Hank Parker of the Las Vegas police. They become lovers who somehow maintain a commuter relationship since Kat lives in Sacramento. Kat bumps into a childhood friend in the Las Vegas Airport when she first arrives. He has become part of the scene in that city, a rough part and nearly winds up choking Kat to death but stops himself. Almost as a premonition, Kat says to him when they meet for drinks after she first arrives, "'You've changed a lot, Deck. I'm not sure I like it'" (19). In *Katapult* (1990), the second novel, Kijewski brings in Alma Flaherty, Kat's eighty-one-year old "grandmother." Finally, Lindy, a teenage prostitute wants to hire Kat to find out who killed Lisa, her friend and fellow prostitute. Kat rescues the fifteen-year old Lindy and gives her back her youth with the help of Charity and Alma. Alma took in the nine-year old Kat when her alcoholic mother abandoned her (*Katapult* 32). Kijewski creates as many crosscurrents for Kat Colorado as Baker does for Sam Turner. Similarly to Turner, Kat maintains her identity and her role as a hard-boiled detective while meeting the demands of friendship.

Walter Mosley's Easy Rawlins in 1948 Los Angeles defines the nature of stress coupled with friendship. In *Devil in a Blue Dress* (1990), Rawlins experiences half friendships and friendly acquaintanceships. While Odell Jones might be close to a friend, Joppy Shag, a bar owner, fits the latter category, and if he can be categorized, Raymond Alexander or Mouse, the former. All three are from Houston but eventually live in Los Angeles. Joppy is an ex-heavyweight prizefighter whom Rawlins is careful about trusting too far, and Mouse is someone that Rawlins hopes to avoid but cannot.

Mouse professes friendship to Rawlins, but Easy believes that Mouse would kill him without hesitation if the thought came to him. Mosley portrays Rawlins as the only sane man in an insane environment. Rawlins is a home-owner, a man with a mortgage, but he has been recently fired from his job at Champion Aircraft. Consequently, when the somewhat reckless Joppy loudly recommends Rawlins to DeWitt Albright for a job, Rawlins reluc-tantly takes his first case. Albright says to him, "'I need to find somebody and I might need a little help looking'" (*Devil* 5). The uneasy Rawlins states to Joppy after Albright leaves his bar, "'Thanks for thinkin a me, Jop,' I said, but wondered if I'd still be thankful later on" (10). Rawlins previously told Joppy that Albright reminded him of Mouse (9). Rawlins is black like Joppy and Mouse, and Albright is white, but Rawlins feels himself cut off from anyone who threatens his sense of stability and control. Writing of Rawlins' family conditions in later novels, Mary Young remarks, "Like the slave trickster, Easy represses his true feelings whether about his work, his money or his wife. The only emotions he allows himself to express are those concerning his baby daughter, Edna, or his adopted son, Jesus. But some-how this repression of feeling and lack of idealism allowed him to survive" (147). When he goes to see Albright in *Devil in a Blue Dress* that same night, another white man surprises him, and he forgets Albright's name. He thinks, "I hated myself for it but I also hated white people, and colored people too, for making me that way" (13). A beleaguered Rawlins exists in a world that continually threatens his place in it, an unassuming place but one that he determines to keep.

Reginald Hill's Joe Sixsmith in *Blood Sympathy* is a black man who endures stress of a different order. Although his family originally came from the West Indies, Sixsmith, who was born in England, indignantly proclaims himself English when any white person asks him how long he has lived there. Laid off like Rawlins, he has a flat and is unmarried; all of that and his new work as a private investigator furnish subjects for comments by his friends. In addition to their commentary, Sixsmith's friends are not the most restrained group, especially when generally discussing his affairs. In fact, between his Aunt Mirabelle, Rev. Pot, Major Sholto Tweedie, Detec-tive Constable Dylan Doberley, Beryl Boddington, and Mervyn Golightly, Sixsmith has difficulty asserting his right to privacy and having the asser-tion recognized and accepted. Each of the above people plays a part in his life and also attempts to arrange it. Sixsmith does appear acclimated to his world and the frustration of maintaining any sense of a separate life. He wants the involvement but also wants more independence from friends, family, and acquaintances. Mervyn Golightly, a fitter made redundant when Joe was, now drives a taxi and dumps Mrs. Bannerjee and her two children on Joe in *Blood Sympathy*, the first novel in the series, thinking to help him in his P.I. business. Unlike Mosley's Rawlins, Sixsmith's involvement with others presents a somewhat more friendly stress.

Friendship is a common human experience, and most cultures provide positive and negative examples of it. The latter comes from falling out of friendship or the participants' different understandings of their limits and needs. Mosley's Rawlins wants greater limits on his contact with Mouse, preferably none at all, but does not know how to accomplish this in *Devil in a Blue Dress*. The very ordinariness of the concept becomes strange with Mouse, and examples of friendships with people like him open up the concept, inserting tension, stress, and multiple levels into what seems a simple human relationship, thus adding greater complexity to the hard-boiled detective novel. An acceptance of difference such as occurs between Elvis Cole and Joe Pike in Robert Crais's series allows individuals to lead their separate lives and still stay connected. From the Early Period to the Modern, the hard-boiled detective genre "collects" instances of friendships, from the 1920s and 1930s when detectives had few or no friends to the 1980s onwards when the expansion of the genre works them into the detectives' lives and cases. This layered accumulation creates a depth against which the plots unfold.

22

Multiples of Change

The degree of change in the modern hard-boiled detective novel, even though foreshadowed by trends in the Transitional Period, is so great that one might justly call it a crisis of change. The crisis relates to the form itself. Can the genre hold to its sense of continuity with the past while expanding in so many ways, or will it fragment, going in numerous directions and creating new forms? R. Gordon Kelly observes, "In adapting the conventions of the hard-boiled private eye story, Sara Paretsky retains those elements that define the detective as socially and economically marginal" (*Mystery* 131). This sense of marginality appears necessary to the form's stability. David Lehman, writing on Paretsky's V.I. Warshawski and Sue Grafton's Kinsey Millhone, notes: "The recent emergence of such female gumshoes may be inevitable, given the course of contemporary feminism, but it is really quite startling when you consider the genre's initial ambivalence at best and hostility at worst toward its women characters" (*Perfect* 177–78). Female detectives, minority detectives, gay and lesbian detectives, and an expansion of the number of cities as settings, not only in the United States but especially into the United Kingdom — all of these make it difficult, though not impossible, for critics to connect detectives from the 1920s to the 1950s with those from the 1980s to the early twenty-first century. Paradoxically, the genre holds together, with each new development testing the form's boundaries and finding them elastic enough to contain the many alterations.

One of the first things to realize about the modern hard-boiled detective novel is that change has become the genre's natural state. Change, ironically, is the form's continuity and stability. David Geherin states, "The private-eye genre is a dynamic genre, capable of changing with the times, of adapting to everything from the Depression and World War II to the social and sexual revolution of the 1960s" (*American Private Eye* 200). This may augur poorly for the future of the genre, especially if the rate of change increases, the pace accelerating to pull into its narrative whatever will come. And, the pace of change has increased. One might argue that much of this is forecast in the changes inaugurated in the Transitional Period. Even accepting this, can the form hold together if even more elements are added? The seventy-eight year history of the hard-boiled detective novel is lengthy enough to make tentative early and late comparisons, especially with regard to the character of the detective. Choosing Carroll John Daly's Race Williams and Dashiell Hammett's Continental Op from the Early Period and Sandra Scoppetone's Lauren Laurano and John Lutz's Fred Carver from the Modern Era strains credulity when one is expected to think of them as part of the same genre. Williams and the Op are private detectives almost by nature. Williams has a generally antagonistic relationship with the police while the Op works well with them. Both men are asexual but aware of the opposite sex. In contrast, Laurano is female and a lesbian; she lives with Kip Adams in a somewhat uneasy relationship, but sexuality helps define it. Carver is an ex-policeman who was forced to retire when a criminal shot him in the knee. He has a police friend in Orlando, but a police antagonist in the area in which he lives. Carver also is sexually active, sometimes with a regular partner. Without his cane, Carver can hardly walk.

If one accepts the idea that change is the natural state for the genre, that it helps to create continuity and stability, then the apparent differences between the above two pairs of detectives are not the most important aspects on which to focus. Concentrating on change will record events but not catch the resistant elements in the genre, those that reappear over time. If the modern detectives are to be seen as descendants of those from the Early and Transitional Periods, then something must connect them even if that something is not at first obvious. Milan Jacovich first appears in Les Roberts' *Pepper Pike*. Roberts sets the series in Cleveland, bringing that large mid-western city into the forefront of the genre. The fact that Milan is Slovenian and his ex-wife Serbian features prominently in the series. A detective's ethnic background comes into the genre largely in the Modern Period. However, Rex Stout's Nero Wolfe's connection to Montenegro and Bill Pronzini's Nameless's Swiss-Italian heritage help define them. The major hard-boiled private detectives from the Early Period are for the most part Anglo-Saxon and thus, ironically, seen to be American. This Americanness, e.g., national identity, patriotic attitudes, expands in the Modern Period to include most races and ethnic groups. For Jacovich, it goes without saying that he is American even though he remembers and cares about his ethnic past. That ethnic past becomes American through the generations. Walter Mosley's Easy Rawlins never forgets that he is black and that whites are largely "others," outside his world. But, he gives no indication that he is any less American. His Houston past, his WWII Army experiences, and his struggles in Los Angeles fill out his American story. John D. MacDonald's Travis McGee is Scots-Irish-American, but by the time the first novel appears in the mid-1960s, being Scots-Irish-American is seen as American as anyone whose ancestors came solely from England.

If these various ethnic groups come to see themselves as American, the degree of national identification for those with immigrant family backgrounds who live and work in the United Kingdom is often different. Two of the eight hard-boiled detectives residing there comment on their ethnic backgrounds. As stated in Chapter 19, Reginald Hill's Joe Sixsmith lives and works in Luton. He displays an easy assumption of being where he is by right. Even though he encounters some negative reactions to his race, Sixsmith knows he is black and mixes with both blacks and whites in his hometown. Valerie Wilson Wesley's Tamara Hayle from Newark, New Jersey, comes closer to Sixsmith than other black American private investigators in seeing her life circumstances more in human than racial terms. Her son, her friends, her cases, and her ex-husband, among other possibilities, focus her attention on life as it unfolds. Gillian Slovo's Kate Baeier is originally from Portugal but lives and works in London. Somewhat inexplicably, being Portuguese-British or Anglo-Portuguese, if those phrases would even be used, does not determine how clients or friends see her. And, she considers her father's poor treatment of her more important than the ethnic aspect of their lives. The other six hard-boiled detectives in the United Kingdom, i.e., Liza Cody's Anna Lee, Mark Timlin's Nick Sharman, Sarah Dunant's Hannah Wolfe, Val McDermid's Kate Brannigan, John Baker's Sam Turner, and Michelle Spring's Laura Principal, do not raise the issue of ethnicity. It has for the most part merged into the general mass of the citizenry.

Since the Transitional Period, the role of family and children, if not marriage, has deepened. To go from mentioning a previous marriage to including it and any offspring in the narrative is a complicating factor that not only creates a greater sense of stability in what can be expected in terms of relationships but also appears to threaten the genre's identity with its predecessors, especially from the Early Period. And, the thematic influence becomes evident when formulaic expectations are weakened with regard to the protagonist's character and the flavor of novels of morals and manners intrudes, when one cannot assume a certain direction to the plot but is left to the complex interactions of cause and effect on humans. Parnell Hall's Stanley Hastings in *Detective* illustrates this modern dilemma. Is he a real detective? Is he a hard-boiled detective? Hastings has a wife of ten years,

Alice, and a five-year-old son, Tommie, who likes to play catch with him when he comes home from work. All the entanglements from marriage and a child enmesh him in a world other than the detective business. Stanley wants to be a writer but cannot find time to write. He initially doubts his abilities as a detective and sees himself only as an ambulance chaser for Richard Rosenberg, an accident claims-personal injury lawyer. Hastings gets ten dollars an hour and thirty cents a mile to sign up clients who call Rosenberg's television-advertised number. Hall thus gives Hastings the most mundane framework within which to work. In *Detective*, Hastings reminds himself once each that he is neither Philip Marlowe nor Sam Spade and twice that he is not Mike Hammer. Having failed as an actor and facing an uncertain future as a writer, Hastings unaccountably puts his life in danger for Walter Albrecht, a dead man who was almost a client. This bizarre shift forces him to consort with, trick, and cosh dangerous drug dealers and killers. Like the reader, Hastings can hardly believe that he is a detective and that he solved the case with, ultimately, no danger to himself and his family. His assumption of the generic role as a hard-boiled detective carries him through and keeps family and children as acceptable thematic elements.

As appears from the themes of family and children, what was a change in the Transitional Period has become an element of stability in the Modern Period. The same occurs with love relationships. Aside from Hammer's love for the murderous Charlotte Manning in Mickey Spillane's *I, the Jury* and his continuing and separate infatuation with his secretary Velda whom he finally makes love to in *The Snake*, the Early Period has, at best, only ironic emotional connections between the detectives and their women. Spade counters his admission in Dashiell Hammett's *The Maltese Falcon* that he cares for Brigid O'Shaughnassey with the fact that he plans to turn her over to the police for the murder of Miles Archer, his ex-partner. However, writers in the Transitional Period, once they admit the possibility of a detective's being in love, go all the way in this area. Rejection, heartbreak, the death of a loved one — most variations enter the generic mix. Underlying this complex theme is the idea that it will become as important to the hard-boiled detective novel as it has become to more traditional novels.

The suddenness of change in the modern period must be part of any analysis of the concept. For example, with only one major female hard-boiled private detective up to 1977, Marcia Muller's Sharon McCone, the next seventeen years witness thirteen new series featuring females, two of whom are lesbians. Lehman states, "What Paretsky does—and does brilliantly—is turn the hard-boiled novel's original masculine-feminine hierarchy upside down" (179). This is even more accurate when applied to the female hard-boiled detectives as a whole. Joseph Hansen's Dave Brandstetter is the first overtly homosexual hard-boiled private detective. Determinedly monogamous and occasionally thwarted romantically, Brandstetter contrasts sharply with J.M. Redmann's Michele "Micky" Knight in New Orleans who in *Death by the Riverside* (1990) tries to distance herself from her reputation for one-night stands. Sandra Scoppetone's Lauren Laurano in New York maintains an uneven relationship with her lover Kip Adams. Money differences and personality clashes pull them apart, but love keeps them together. Five of these new female detectives, as mentioned above, work in the United Kingdom: Cody's Lee, Slovo's Baeier, Dunant's Wolfe, McDermid's Brannigan, and Spring's Principal. The six other female detectives are American: Paretsky's Warshawski, Grafton's Millhone, Barnes' Carlyle, Kijewski's Colorado, Dawson's Howard, and Wesley's Hayle who is black. Along with three other British male hard-boiled private detectives, one of who is black, and three black American male detectives, all working by 1995, the sudden, undigested shift in the modern hard-boiled private detective novel is more than obvious. To borrow a metaphor from biology, a jump or mutation in development is significant, heralding new adaptations that are or could lead to new species. Have these sudden, new changes done something similar to the genre?

It would be foolish to argue that sudden, almost "explosive" moves in several directions would leave the genre unaffected. However, traditional strands continue in the Modern Period with only faint awareness registered by the detectives of the new world developing around them. Robert A. Baker and Michael T. Nietzel argue, "Walker could never be a cop just like Marlowe could never have been: they're not authorities" (200). In 1980, Jonathan Valin's Harry Stoner and Loren D. Estleman's Amos Walker appear in *The Lime Pit* and *Motor City Blue*, respectively. At first glance, one could place them squarely in the Early Period in terms of their personalities and attitudes toward work. LeRoy Lad Panek says of Estleman's Walker, "Estleman aims to re-create the wardrobe, office, house, and attitudes—especially attitudes—of the hard-boiled hero of the thirties and forties. Except his hero lives and works in the eighties" (*New Hard-Boiled* 49). Loners, with dashes of bitterness and alienation, and professionals in pursuing their cases, Stoner and Walker straddle the genre's time periods. Stoner, especially, like his name, is the hard man, emotionally shut down as he investigates the murky urban violence of Cincinnati and a world even more atavistic in the trans-Ohio Kentucky underworld. Baker and Nietzel write, "With the exception of Robert Parker's Spenser there is probably not a modern detective who is less hesitant to pass judgment and to kill for justice's sake than Stoner" (266). Estleman's Walker matches his portraits of a desolate urban landscape, decayed or destroyed or in peril of both, to those of Valin. Certainly the novels featuring the Continental Op, Spade, Marlowe, and Hammer support the images Walker and Stoner illustrate. As the stable elements are necessary to see the changes and support the idea of change as the Modern Period's natural state for the genre, so these and other modern hard-boiled private detectives frame the sudden expansion of character possibilities. Although the detectives' numbers do not always balance in terms of gender, from 1979 to 1982 the first six hard-boiled detectives include three men and three women. In addition to influences on character from the Early Period, these six detectives reflect elements that have come to prominence in the Transitional Period. Not only possessing a prickly independence, Cody's, Paretsky's, and Grafton's heroes experience uneven love relationships and form shifting but supportive friendships. Among the men, Walker is the most susceptible to romantic involvement but always draws back from any real commitment. His relationship with his childhood friend Lt. John Alderdyce is more than private detective and policeman. Valin's Stoner avoids most kinds of relationship while Stephen Greenleaf's John Marshall Tanner has developed into a bachelor more from habit than intention. He resembles Pronzini's Nameless in this though the latter works hard in the early part of the series to cement his relationship with Kerry Wade. However, by then Nameless is fifty-some years old.

The suddenness of change in the hard-boiled detective novel during the Modern Period reflects the microcosm against which the social, cultural, and political events nationally and internationally form the macrocosm. It does little good to focus at any length exclusively on this macrocosm. However, the selective use of ideas and events from the larger world deepens the effect the writers produce. John D. MacDonald leads the way in this category in the Transitional Period. He shows how it can be done. Some criticize McGee's ruminations on society, but many see the positive way MacDonald integrates these thoughts and comments into the series. First, McGee is intelligent, college-educated, and well read. Second his friend Meyer is an unpretentious intellectual, and their dialogues support the value of bringing aspects of the macrocosm into the microcosm. Third, the plots of the various novels mesh well with both men's intellectual interests and concerns. MacDonald saw the benefit of the dialogue form, as old as Socrates and Plato in its philosophical use, when he wrote *Reading for Survival* featuring McGee and Meyer with the latter providing most of the ideas on reading's importance to humanity. While no hard-boiled detective writer has yet extensively included the effects of the collapse of the Soviet Union and the end of the Cold War, Mickey Spillane's Mike Hammer demonstrates how one could bring such a large theme into the genre. Spillane began his series around the time Richard M. Nixon and then Senator McCarthy started fulminating against communists in high places. In *Hollywood and LeVine* (1975), Andrew Bergman later uses Nixon and the House

Un-American Coordinating Committee. Spillane's *One Lonely Night* rids the world of a number of communist agents in a dramatic and, in Hammer's expressed terms, heartfelt manner. Scientific and technological advances also show up in the genre in the increased use of computers and the Internet. Terrorists and serial killers have as yet made few inroads into the genre, being largely confined to thrillers and espionage novels. John Baker's *Death Minus Zero* does feature a serial killer who terrorizes York. Sexual abuse, always present in one form or another, appears in Baker's *Poet in the Gutter*. P.I. Sam Turner rescues Geordie who, abandoned by his family, has been sexually abused by others on the street and those to whom he has rented his body to survive. Turner gives him a home and a chance for a future. Of course, illegal drugs and all they imply figure greatly in many novels from this period. The detectives' cases sometimes involve the sale and distribution of drugs, but most often it is the individual damage to people's lives that concern them. Estleman's *Motor City Blue* and Valin's *The Lime Pit* include drugs as part of the evil they confront. Timlin's Sharman lost his London police position before *A Good Year for the Roses* begins because of his involvement with drugs. The destructive effect of drugs is not, of course, a new theme in the Modern Period, but it appears widely during these nearly three decades.

One reason that the general social changes in the Modern Period do not overwhelm the genre and relegate it to the margins is that the writers rely on human nature to act as a buffer. No matter what happens in the real world, human greed, cruelty, and violence and their opposites, act as touchstones to lead the form back to its main themes. Robert Campbell's *In La-La Land We Trust* (1986) introduces Whistler and employs a setting that suggests the absolute need for a cleansing of the social structure. Whistler maintains an office in Gentry's coffee shop on the corner of Hollywood and Vine. The jaded private investigator sits in his booth late one night when the actor Ernest Tillman crashes his car into a station wagon killing the driver and dumping a headless female body on the street. Tillman calls the pedophile Walter Cape for help, and Cape gets the police to squelch any reference to Tillman and Shiela Andes, an aspiring actress with whom Tillman engaged in sexual foreplay moments before the crash. The accident thrusts the jaded Whistler into a dangerous situation that, except for the dead woman, gets worse for everyone concerned. From the window Whistler looks on as the two vehicles, "a crippled station wagon" and a "silver 635 CSi BMW," converge: "Whistler watched with the melancholy calm of a man who knew the worst would always happen. There were only two cars on the road, and they were going to have a smashup. That's the way things happen on a rainy night in La-La Land" (13). Immediately before the accident, Whistler reads in *The Enquirer* of a woman's head found a few days previously on the edge of Lake Pontchartrain. The rain has temporarily washed the decadence and crime from the intersection, but the crash brings it all back, with the headless body being later identified as the one belonging to the head found in New Orleans. The swift change for Bosco, Gentry's one-armed counterman, and Whistler erases the peaceful late-night atmosphere of the coffee shop. Things settle down as the machinations of violence and retaliation work themselves out after New Orleans comes to Los Angeles in the form of the pornographer Nonny Barcaloo.

Shifts are endemic to the hard-boiled detective novel, whether in terms of action or ideas. With regard to the former, shifts swiftly develop from a quiescent to an active state. Much like the above example from Campbell, William J. Reynolds in *The Nebraska Quotient* (1984) opens the novel with a tense scene that disturbs the protagonist Nebraska with its past echoes. Nebraska says, "I was standing at the kitchen sink in my underwear and the dark, washing down the pills with cold, bitter coffee, trying to suck a breath of air through the screened windows over the sink" (1). Nebraska is both a private investigator and a free-lance writer up late that night working on "The Book" (1). Suddenly he hears a sound from the front of his apartment. He goes to investigate and sees the silhouette of a large man climbing over the railing to the terrace of his second-floor apartment. The man, who turns out to be Morris Coppel, Nebraska's ex-partner, crashes through the screen-door and dies from a gunshot wound on his living-room floor. Prior to his death, he gives Nebraska a set of negatives of Adrian Mallory, Senator Daniel G. Mallory's daughter, posing in the nude. This is starting a novel from a standing start. Reynolds has thrust Nebraska into a dangerous predicament that, coupled with his need for money and, eventually, a client who supplies it, unravels in more violence and death. Mickey Spillane portrays Mike Hammer usually in a state of compressed violence that explodes with ideas and events. In the first three novels in the series, someone kills a person that Hammer cares for, and he carries out acts of revenge against the perpetrators. He never seems to be in a state of rest. Usually the reason for Hammer's move into action comes from within the novel, growing out of the plot and his character. The Modern Period runs the gamut of possible reasons prompting the detective to go to work, from violence, greed, jealousy, and past, unresolved conflicts. People lie to the detective and pose as someone they are not, both acts committed by the same person in Sara Paretsky's *Indemnity Only*. Paretsky ironically shows the vulnerability of modern technology when V.I Warshawski meets a prospective client in her Loop office and the power goes out. The many sudden changes, almost before the novels begin, expected or unexpected, provide access for the genre's involvement with the larger society and draw it away from any tendency to repeat itself in nearly unchangeable patterns.

These changes also lead to crises both for the structure of individual novels and the genre's form.

The idea of crisis seems inevitably linked to change. Crisis implies events reaching a certain state so that something crucially important is about to happen or has just happened which will transform the present situation, a transformation that cannot be forestalled or delayed. It also implies that people, whatever their attitudes to the crisis, are not in complete control. Therefore, the results of the crisis may veer in unforeseen directions. James W. Hall's Thorn experiences a series of crises, some of which, paradoxically, are suspended in time, even a long period of time, before resolution occurs. After summarizing a list of crises, Harold Nugent and Susan Nugent state, "In each case, Thorn becomes the one who must solve the mystery" (86). Resolution, especially for Thorn, does not always have positive outcomes. In *Under the Cover of Daylight*, Thorn's parents die in a senseless accident that he survives. Thorn is then only a baby. However, when Thorn grows up, he tracks down the man, twenty-one years old at the time of the accident, and kills him in exactly the same way his parents died. Thorn drives the man's car and participates in the reenactment of the crime. Dallas James was drinking and driving dangerously fast when he forced Thorn's family into Lake Surprise on the road to Key Largo. This ritual eye for an eye and tooth for a tooth approach does not lift Thorn from his melancholy and depression. A sudden crisis on a Florida highway leading to death and a long-smoldering crisis which results in dangerous revenge and which arguably leaves Thorn still in crisis—these are the frames for Hall's series and leave open the directions that Thorn's changes may take.

This uncertain connection between crisis and change, in Hall and other writers in the Modern Period, raises another connection, that between order/disorder and change. Any shift in thinking or behavior may disrupt social patterns and initiate a cycle from order to disorder to order again. Of course, this presumed cycle imposes a seemingly positive outcome that bears little relationship to actual events in literature or history. Repetition in cycle content questions the very idea of change. John G. Cawelti's *Adventure, Mystery, and Romance: Formula Stories as Art and Popular Culture* suggests that the determinism of formula preempts change. The thesis of this book argues that change appears in the genre but that formulaic aspects do not completely disappear. Critical examination of novels from the Modern Period, as well as the Early and Transitional Periods, demonstrates this phenomenon. The private investigator usually restores order. Does he or she remain above the fray? Chandler's Marlowe suffers crises, helps others in like circumstances, and achieves some resolution, or at least some cessation of the previous violence, in each novel. Does Marlowe resolve the disorder that the novels uncover, assuming that they begin with an atmosphere of order? It might be accurate to say that he restores an order if not the order with which a particular novel begins. The order or hiatus between cases, always leaving the detective in a different emotional situation before another crisis creates a new sense of disorder, is not the same as a final order. And, it is within Marlowe, or any detective, that the shift surfaces.

Just as the disillusioned Marlowe at the end of *The Long Goodbye* is a very different person from the one who turns the murderous Carmen over to her sister Vivian at the close of *The Big Sleep*, so other detectives move from hiatus to hiatus or order to order, undergoing changes provoked by the crises in their lives. Chaos best describes the personal situation of Mark Timlin's Nick Sharman as he begins *A Good Year for the Roses*. Dismissed from the police force, taking drugs and drinking too much, Sharman works as a private detective. At that time, one apparently did not need a license to investigate cases though the police, just as in the United States, frowned on private detectives interfering in official cases. In the tradition of the private investigator from the form's inception, Sharman occasionally strays across the line and disturbs the authorities. Receiving little sympathy from them since he was a bent copper, Sharman handles his cases and personal problems but slips more and more into chaos as his life fragments. His ex-wife remarries and moves with her and Sharman's young daughter to Scotland. Getting away from Sharman and the dangers of his South London lifestyle figure prominently in this decision. Each hiatus between cases finds a diminished Sharman. At the beginning of *A Street That Rhymed at 3 AM* (1997), even his fifteen-year-old daughter senses that something is wrong in his life and worries about his safety and ability to cope although she has just learned that her mother, stepfather, and half-brother have died in a plane crash at Chicago's O'Hare International Airport. Women involved with Sharman die, and the course of his life and career raises doubts as to whether order is an achievable goal after so much loss and so many personal compromises. If he is to remain in a permanent state of crisis or semi-crisis, how does his character affect the genre? Of course, Sharman's is just one example, but his dangerous predicaments transcend those of some Early and Transitional Period investigators. Daly's Race Williams is often a hyperbolic instance of a detective's dangling on the edge of one cliff after another. However, Williams possesses a consistent personality. The sometimes-problematic Mike Hammer and the occasionally emotionally unstable Travis McGee also rediscover their sense of direction. In effect, other modern hard-boiled private detectives counteract Sharman's unstable example, notably among them Reginald Hill's Joe Sixsmith and his practical sensibility.

Where will the changes lead? That question interests writers, critics, and readers. One possibility is that a new genre will eventually emerge just as the hard-boiled form grew from the many strands starting with Poe and Conan Doyle and even earlier in the image of the lone frontiersman embodied in James Fenimore Cooper's Natty Bumppo, known as Leatherstocking. In the city, as the detective novel's prime locale, World War I and the gangsterism following Prohibition in the 1920s contributed to the form's development. This should temper projections of what will occur in the genre since any future major historical and social events are, by definition, unknown. It is also possible that the form will use its own past examples to build on future patterns as occurs in the Transitional and Modern Periods. Whatever the answer, it should be both interesting and compelling.

23

The Uses of Memory

The past plays a major role in much fiction. The hard-boiled detective novel is no exception. The detectives' previous activities, private and social, work their way into their present lives and affect them professionally. Usually, their training and experience, especially in the police or military, prepare them for their often-dangerous jobs. But, professional training does not always make their work easier. For example, most American private eyes function as licensed detectives. Stephen Greenleaf's John Marshall Tanner, Jeremiah Healy's John Francis Cuddy, Sara Paretsky's V.I. Warshawski, and Stephen Dobyns' Charlie Bradshaw have licenses but uneven relationships with the police. British examples of the hard-boiled detective represent even more ambiguous positions. Liza Cody's Anna Lee and Sarah Dunant's Hannah Wolfe are private detectives working for security firms. However, many hard-boiled characters are *ad hoc* detectives, best exemplified by Dick Francis's heroes, who find themselves in difficult positions and must act to clear themselves and/or friends. Jonathan Gash's Lovejoy, John Malcolm's Tim Simpson, and Jimmy Sangster's James Reed are examples of the British hard-boiled character who circumstances force to become a detective. Their various backgrounds—e.g., Francis's protagonists, horse racing; Lovejoy, antiques; Simpson, art and finance; and Reed, writer and ex–Scotland Yard investigator—indicate the possible areas of conflict, especially those deriving from the past. As Scott R. Christianson states, "[...] the impetus of much contemporary hardboiled fiction [...] is still an attempt to make sense through language of our modern experience" (147). From personal events in the protagonists' lives to important social events, the modern American and British detectives, licensed or not, react to the force of memory through which they judge the present and make decisions, fortunate or not, that impinge on those with whom they interact.

Personal memories play a large role in the lives of hard-boiled detectives. It is not so much that they remember violence performed or endured though this occasionally plays a role in some first-generation private eyes. Mike Hammer's disturbing recollections of a judge's condemnation of his violent actions as he walks across a New York bridge in *One Lonely Night* and his memory of shooting Charlotte Manning in *I, the Jury* demonstrate that even the hardest detectives cannot prevent the swirl and sway of memory. Even deeper are the memories and influences of their early lives, stretching sometimes to childhood. Two hard-boiled characters, one a licensed detective, though separated by time, gender, and culture, represent opposite poles in the degree to which personal memory affects their novels. Dick Francis's Alan York in *Dead Cert* (1962) and Sara Paretsky's V.I. Warshawski in *Indemnity Only* courageously face danger and, if not unscarred, manage to survive their ordeals. Both have positive views of their parents but the degree to which they refer to them is strikingly different. York almost never alludes to his mother and father though his father enters the novel after York suffers a serious racing injury. He is a Southern Rhodesian who looks after his father's business in London while pursuing a career as an amateur steeple-chase jockey. York's mother is dead, and he says nothing else about her. His sparsely recorded memories of his past usually involve his father and their activities together, e.g., crocodile hunting at the age of ten. Their relationship is one of expectation and fulfillment with no sense of the son's being forced into any mold and with a strong degree of his gratitude for his father's treatment of him. York resembles Hammett's Continental Op who makes no references to his family in *Red Harvest* and *The Dain Curse*. For all intents and purposes, he was born in a brown suit, with a brown coat and brown shoes. Of course, somewhere on his person he must have had his two guns. Hyperbole aside, it is astonishing the way the genre begins with the Continental Op and other early detectives in motion. However, the idea of human memory and its effects is not so easily pushed aside, literary convention notwithstanding, and writers in the Modern Period, especially, have included this important theme in their fiction.

In contrast, Warshawski frequently alludes to her Italian mother and Polish father, both now dead, and also feels a sense of gratitude for the way they raised her. Warshawski's memories of her mother Gabriella, symbolized by the eight cut-glass Venetian goblets she brought to America with her before the start of World War II, have a sharp immediateness. Referring more often to her mother than her father, but without minimizing his role in her life, she recalls her mother's love of opera and her desire that her daughter become an opera singer. Her father Tony, a sergeant in the Chicago police, was glad that she was tough enough to survive her neighborhood and school environments, and she grows up to be a lawyer for the Public Defender's office and then a successful private investigator specializing in industrial espionage. Lt. Bobby Mallory, her father's friend who knew Warshawski as a child, represents a connection to the past both in his concern for her and through invitations to his home. However, Mallory's friendship does not come without complications. Maureen Reddy states in *Sisters in Crime*, "V.I.'s family [her mother and father are dead], from whom she is estranged, shares Mallory's disapproval of her career and life-style, asserting their right to judge her by using the name she hates, Victoria" (92). Sometimes Warshawski suffers too much from memory come to life in the guise of Mallory. However, for personal and professional reasons she keeps the connection alive.

Personal memories in the novels function more as defining aspects of the characters' lives than as causes leading to specific actions. These memories are the effects from the past that tell one who they are more than what they will do. Liza Cody's *Dupe* shows the complexities of memory as a defining state. Thomas and Susan Jackson come to Brierly Security in London to find out more about their daughter Deirdre's death than the police have discovered. As becomes especially clear later in the novel, the Jacksons have different ideas about their daughter's character. Obviously, Deirdre is not only dead but has left little or nothing behind to oppose their ideas about her. One of the strongest arguments that Thomas Jackson makes to counter the police determination that she died in an accident is that he taught her how to drive and believes that nothing about the accident scene convinces him that she lost control of the car. Susan Jackson's statements about Deirdre at the first interview and at the end when Anna Lee goes to Wiltshire to disclose what her investigations have revealed about their daughter's blackmailing activities show a mother aware of her daughter's limitations and weaknesses. Through her memories of Deirdre, she shows herself as tolerant, supportive, and loving toward her husband, but resigned regarding her daughter's real character. Klein, who describes Anna "as resourceful and independent as her position allows her to be" (*Woman Detective* 159), also notes that at times "she is removed from cases because the clients refuse to work with a woman" (159). However, Susan Jackson is not one of them. Anna's statements only confirm Susan's intuitions about the directions Deirdre's life took and show her own wisdom in seeing her daughter whole.

Of course, past actions do have some causal connections to present events even though writers do not always provide enough detail to explain why something happens in a character's life. This occurs in much hard-boiled detective fiction. In Jimmy Sangster's *Snowball* (1986), ex–Scotland Yard Detective Sergeant James Reed agrees to help Katherine Long, a famous actress and his ex-wife, with her drug-dealing daughter Caroline. While they remain friends and while he acknowledges to himself, "Even when he knew what he was agreeing to was all wrong, he still went along with it" (22), his succumbing to her entreaties does reveal him as more malleable than weak. Thus, Sangster portrays Reed's character while stating a cause for his action. Don Henderson, the drug dealer responsible for Caroline's death, bewails the fact that Reed, known as someone who cared for nothing and nobody, has trapped him. The irony is that Reed had no more profound reason for his actions than to protect Katherine, the woman whose actions led to their marriage break-up and whose self-referential conduct continues to place him in situations from which he cannot escape.

Social memory, recent or distant in time, abounds in the hard-boiled detective novel. Characters in books and films, political allusions, specific references to other fictional detectives, and the use of metaphor, recalling early writers like Chandler, through which the past illuminates, expands, or clarifies the present, flow through and around the novels' events interacting with the protagonists' personal pasts. In Loren D. Estleman's *Motor City Blue*, Amos Walker refers to his experiences in the Army in Vietnam and Cambodia and as an MP stateside for three years (88), reminding the reader of his police training as well as that socially divisive conflict. This reference, only five years after South Vietnam fell to the communists and with the repercussions of that event, both in the United States and internationally, still vivid, is enough to stir unease or disquiet for those old enough to remember even if specific events of the war do not add to the memories. And, Walker is not the only hard-boiled detective with this experience. Jeremiah Healy's John Francis Cuddy in *Blunt Darts* and Les Roberts' Milan Jacovich in *Pepper Pike* functioned as military policemen in Vietnam. At one level, this type of service reinforces the image of the hard-boiled detective. They not only have served in the Army but also have acquired police training and experience. When Bingo Jefferson attacks Walker with a bat in *Angel Eyes* (1981), Walker disarms him and says, "'Never stick-fight with an ex-MP'" (8).

The cities in which the detectives operate provide a vivid environment while also allowing the detectives to establish links with their own and their societies' pasts. Susan Grafton's Kinsey Millhone in *"A" Is for Alibi* and Stephen Greenleaf's John Marshall Tanner in *Grave Error*, both of whom work in California, Millhone in Santa Teresa north of Los Angeles and Tanner in San Francisco, are very conscious of the history of their cities and others to which their work takes them. Both man-made and natural changes provoke comment. Millhone's work brings her into contact with wealthy people, but she, in keeping with most private eyes, has only her own income on which to live. She says at the beginning of *"A" Is for Alibi*, "I don't earn a lot of money but I make ends meet" (1). She observes of Santa Teresa:

> The public buildings look like old Spanish missions, the private homes look like magazine illustrations, the palm trees are trimmed of unsightly brown fronds, and the marina is as perfect as a picture postcard with the blue-gray hills forming a backdrop and white boats bobbing in the sunlight.... Even the frame bungalows of the poor could hardly be called squalid [8].

However, this idyllic description contrasts sharply with her, quite literally, snug apartment converted from a garage behind the home of her friend, Henry Pitts, the eighty-one year old retired baker. Rosie's rather plain restaurant bar in her neighborhood also suggests another, simpler California. Millhone notes, "Most of the homes in the neighborhood are owned by retired folk whose memories of the town go back to the days when it was all citrus groves and resort hotels" (13). This certainly echoes Marlowe's observations of the changes, mostly all bad, that have occurred in the Los Angeles area.

Grafton in *A Is for Alibi* gives Millhone a different sense of Los Angeles' and Las Vegas's pasts. The Glass's apartment building in Los Angeles, "set into the crook of the San Diego and Ventura freeways" (67), she describes as having "gone up in the thirties before anybody figured out that California architecture should imitate southern mansions and Italian villas" (68). She observes, "The season to be jolly, in this neighborhood, was long past" (68). This sense of a plainer and happier period connects with the unspoilt image of the earlier history of Santa Teresa; change does not lead to anything good. John Marshall Tanner in *Grave Error* not only uncovers murder and violence connected to the Whiston family but shows their effects on the present along with new instances of deadly violence. In Las Vegas, Grafton contrasts her present image of the city that "suits my notion of some eventual life in cities under the sea" (89) and whose main area she calls "the artificial daylight of Glitter Gulch" (89) with the immediacy of the desert that

> stretched away behind the motel in a haze of pale gray, fading to mauve at the horizon. The wind was mild and dry, the promise of summer heat only hinted at in the distant shimmering sunlight that sat on the desert floor in flat pools, evaporating on approach. Occasional patches of sagebrush, nearly silver with dust, broke up the long low lines of treeless wasteland fenced in by distant hills [91].

She senses the real past of that city, but human relationships pull her back into the present.

In *Grave Error*, John Marshall Tanner, like Kinsey Millhone, exudes a sense of place and time though San Francisco is not his hometown. Describing his office building, he says it was built "just after the earthquake" and is located in an "area [...] called Jackson Square. It's east of Chinatown and south of North Beach. A long time ago it was part of the Barbary Coast, but now it's an oasis of slick specialty shops that cater to interior decorators and wealthy collectors" (7). The description gives an effect of time being stacked, an effect that most cities produce for anyone who has seen change within a specific area. Both Oxtail and Rutledge, California, towns to which Tanner's investigation leads him, have a thinness about them as if only one thing has been built or has happened in a particular area regardless of how long ago it occurred. An exception is John Whitson's home outside Oxtail that the owner says "is over one hundred years old" (130). The ranch "predates the Treaty of Guadalupe Hidalgo" (130) and thus was in a different country at one point. In contrast, Tanner, trying unsuccessfully to get an address for Angelina Peel in Rutledge where she moved after leaving Oxtail, remarks, "In towns like Rutledge, ten years is forever" (151). "Southern California in microcosm" (145), Rutledge has the same bleakness Tanner found in Oxtail without the fertile soil.

Metaphor or simile lies at the heart of social memory in the hard-boiled detective novel. Of course, not all the writers discussed use the ironic, satiric comparison favored by Raymond Chandler. Estleman's Amos Walker is probably the best modern example of commentary on human behavior through metaphor. In the process, he draws examples from a wide range of elite and popular culture. The principal classical figure is the Homeric simile that contrasts with the hard-boiled comparisons in its generally loftier subject matter, e.g., the gods, heroes, nature. Stephen Dobyns' Charlie Bradshaw differs from Estleman's use of metaphor in asides that refer to nineteenth-century lawmen and outlaws. There is a didactic quality in the way that Bradshaw silently recalls these incidents or inserts them into conversation. After someone shoots Lew Ackerman in *Saratoga Swimmer* while he swims in the Saratoga Springs YMCA pool, Bradshaw speculates that other killers "had swum through blood. But [he] thought it improbable. More likely it was the victims themselves who swam through blood, unfortunately their own, as they made their futile attempts at escape" (9). Several people are in the pool with Ackerman, and by drawing this comparison, Dobyns places his characters in the role of innocent victims suffering that never-ending pattern of man's inhumanity to man. However, even the use of this universal theme does not outweigh the real-world atmosphere that Dobyns employs in his Saratoga Springs setting. The racing season, the training and year-long care of horses, and the changing city mix with the sense of lives altering and responding to events and of time passing. In

"Forms of Time and Chronotope in the Novel," M.M. Bakhtin argues that the Greek romance is set in "adventure-time" that "lacks any natural, everyday cyclicity — such as might have introduced into it a temporal order and indices on a human scale, tying it to the repetitive aspects of natural and human life" (*The Dialogic Imagination* 91). He adds, "In this kind of time, nothing changes: the world remains as it was, the biographical life of the heroes does not change, their feelings do not change, people do not even age" (91). One might argue that some detective series resemble this portrait, but, paradoxically, the comparison is at best superficial. Of course, not all writers of detective series purposefully age their heroes as John D. MacDonald does Travis McGee, and there is a sense of changelessness in some series, but the enormous amount of social references pull the characters into the times in which stories are set. Both current and antecedent references to events in cultural history give what might be termed a sense of realism to the action. For example, Sarah Dunant's *Fatlands* (1993), in addition to its topical use of the rights and wrongs of animal research, is replete with references to European and American culture, e.g., Eric Clapton, Chuck Berry, Stonehenge and Druids, Tess and Hardy, Polanski, Kingsley Amis, Lady Chatterley and D.H. Lawrence, Scarlett O'Hara, Mahler's *Requiem*, Abelard and Heloise, etc. Each reference more or less functions in some clarifying way and in the process adds up to a work centered in real time whether or not the protagonist Hannah Wolfe ultimately undergoes many character changes. Nowhere do the social events originate more clearly in personal experience than in William J. Reynolds Nebraska series. Literary allusions establish a past for *The Nebraska Quotient*, and through Nebraska, a private investigator and free-lance journalist and writer of detective fiction, other aspects of social memory play a role. Eighteen years before the novel begins, he worked on a senatorial campaign. As a Vietnam War veteran, he lived through one of the central dramas of his time. The city of Omaha also figures in Nebraska's narration. He has seen the changes in a city that functions both as a backdrop to the action and as a pressing reality to its citizens. Through time, experience, and memory, the city holds the people together.

Just as the detectives recall the layered pasts of the cultures, cities, and towns in which they operate, so they also remember and reveal their professional experiences, both cases and methods. Sheriff Benson Marks in Greenleaf's *Grave Error* observes that Tanner resembles him in that he does not let go once he begins to investigate a case. This dogged pursuit of leads and suspects, a quality that Tanner shares with most hard-boiled private investigators, is a fundamental aspect of the genre. Along with loyalty to a client, the detective will pursue a case to its end even when he or she is no longer being paid. Only a stronger moral claim will shift him or her in a different direction. After his friend Harry Spring is murdered in *Grave Error*, Tanner tells Jacqueline Nelson that he cannot continue working for her until he discovers who killed him. Friends with both Harry and his wife Ruthie, Tanner obligates himself to complete this task. In *Fatlands*, Dunant's Hannah Wolfe does something similar when someone blows up a car containing a young woman Wolfe is looking after for the day rather than the intended victim, the girl's father. These present attitudes and actions are indicative of past circumstances and suggest sure directions for future conduct. Of course, Greenleaf's and Dunant's detectives are not alone in having professional histories though Wolfe has only worked for Frank Comfort for two years at the beginning of *Birth Marks*. Consequently, Comfort, an ex-CID officer for the metropolitan police, initially provides the experience. In the detective novel, Sherlock Holmes is the best example of a suggested but never published past, and Dr. Watson's allusions to these professional incidents hint at intriguing possibilities. In the hard-boiled genre, Hammett's Continental Op and John D. MacDonald's Travis McGee also employ this narrative device. Even as the list of their novels and stories grows, this other professional life adds a layer of suggestiveness to the characters' identities. These unexplored cases produce a quite different effect compared to references to earlier published works. In the latter, characters and incidents referred to add a sense of reality to the protagonists' lives—they have a history that can be checked.

In *The Judas Pair* (1977), Jonathan Gash's Lovejoy, on the periphery of the hard-boiled detective novel, recalls two different kinds of work experience. First, he has the entire field of antiques on which to expand, and he seems to know something about everything connected to the subject. His recollections are not only of previous cases involving antiques but rather constitute a rich, never-ending background on antiques from which past and present deceit and criminality emerge. The antiques themselves have a history of their makers and their methods and of their owners. This latter group generate both peaceful and violent stories of how the antiques have changed hands. Adding to this rich mixture, while functioning as recorder, preserver, and reverent acolyte, Lovejoy reveals himself as a divvy, someone able to intuit the genuineness of the article before him by means of a sympathetic bell that goes off in his chest (3, 5). Lovejoy is thus the past incarnate and has only been wrong once. He thinks he made a mistake over his Armstrong Siddeley automobile to which he is nonetheless attached (108, 144). Somewhat separate from Lovejoy's experiences with antiques, which provide the context which gives his cases life, Gash slowly reveals earlier incidents involving Lovejoy and Tinker, his barker (2, 13), that connect to Lovejoy's role as an *ad hoc* detective and that also add a sense of danger and uncertainty to the present novel that obviously has no others on which to draw. Gash makes it clear that Lovejoy lives on the edge, whether involving women, his almost desperate search for antiques, or his sometimes uneasy relationships with other antique dealers. He remembers once helping to save Tinker from the police and at another time from the "Brighton lads" (99). Brighton and London are areas of great danger to Lovejoy in other novels. They represent important criminal venues in the antique trade. As a small, two-man group, Lovejoy's antique business is vulnerable to the combination of money and violence. However, Lovejoy is not above becoming involved in shady activities, activities that seem endemic to his profession. Two in particular illustrate this tendency. In a box gambit, a dealer reads of the death of a wealthy person likely to have a house full of antiques and rushes to relieve the surviving spouse of anything that the dealer can obtain (83). The other, ringing, is actual collusion between dealers not to bid on an item at an auction except for one person who then gets it cheaply and conducts a separate auction for those in on the plan (139). Lovejoy speaks of these activities in general terms, but along with his production of fakes that becomes an important source of income in later novels and at which he reveals himself to be a multi-talented expert, he apparently refers to actions of which he has intimate knowledge. To Muriel Field, the woman whose husband's murder he investigates while trying to find the Judas pair of flintlock duelers (25), Lovejoy says, "'We dealers are pretty slick. Some are all right, but some are not. [...] Some pretty boys, smart, handsome, looking wealthy. Cleverer than any artists, better than any actor. They'll pick your house clean any way they can and brag about it in the pub afterwards'" (85). When she asks if he is like all the others, Lovejoy replies, "'I'm the worst dealer there ever was, as far as you're concerned [...]'" (88). His self-flagellation relates to the occasional free divvying that he does and more deeply to his love of antiques.

John Lutz in *Tropical Heat* uses an indirect approach to reveal Fred Carver's work as a policeman in Orlando. Edwina Talbot, a client, repeats Lt. Desoto's opinions of Carver as a homicide detective. Afterwards, Carver states how he lost the use of his left knee. Desoto's portrait of Carver does not flatter, but it does interest Talbot. She wants Carver to find her lover Willis Davis, missing for about a week. Several elements of Carver's character especially attract her: he is tough, skeptical, and thinks like a criminal (15). She learns this from Lt. Alfonso Desoto, a man for whom Carver worked before his injury. Desoto also thinks Carver is a good detective (15). Carver presently has difficulty with two memories. First, Lutz says, "His divorce from Laura had been finalized just three days before he'd been shot. Two deep wounds in one week took it out of a man" (16). Second, Carver wakes up at 5:30 AM the morning after Edwina comes to ask Carver to look for Willis. It has been six months since he was shot, but he vividly remembers the two men who held up the all-night grocery store and being shot by the one hiding in the back. Lutz states, "The knee was ruined, locked at a thirty-degree angle for life" (5). When Carver goes to Orlando to talk to Desoto about Edwina Talbot and the missing boyfriend, Desoto sums up Carver as, "Almost like a split personality. Officer Jekyll and Mr. Hyde. It's rare, that quality" (36). This summation refers to Carver before the shooting. The literary allusion helps create a past that interacts, if true, with his memories of loss and injury.

Fred Carver lives in Florida when his troubles occur, but Lew Fonesca in Stuart Kaminsky's *Vengeance* (1999) comes to Sarasota after his wife dies in a Chicago car accident. The novel begins some three and a half years after this traumatic event, but it still dominates Fonesca's life just as Carver's past difficulties affect him. Both men's lives organize themselves around their emotional, physical, and psychological losses. However, the physical component of Carver's difficulty apparently makes it more bearable than Fonesca's. His wife died, and he remembers, bearing a seemingly greater psychological and emotional burden than Carver. When Fonesca serves a subpoena to Ann Horowitz, a psychotherapist, she asks him to come see her. She sees the pain in his eyes. When he goes to her, he cannot mention his wife's name, but he keeps the name plaque from her office door on his desk. When Dr. Horowitz asks, "'Why do you always say "my wife" instead of using her name?'" He responds, "'It hurts'" (31). As a result of her death, he also says, "'I don't get angry anymore'" (31). These are not memories of Fonesca's work, but they are memories that strongly affect him and in consequence his work. When Fonesca goes to see Sally Porovsky at Children's Services of Sarasota as he searches for Adele Tree, his client Beryl Tree's daughter, he finds himself attracted to her and asks her out to dinner. Before that he gives her a two-minute rundown on himself. While it is not as intimate as what he discusses with Dr. Horowitz, he is comprehensive. He speaks of his wife's death in Chicago, his work there for the district attorney's office, his education, his reason for being in Sarasota, his former wife's hopes to have children, his general health, his exercise pattern, his ethnic background, and his lack of religious belief. Fonesca surprises himself with the dinner invitation and his self-revelations. However, it indicates that he has his past memories under enough control to go on with his life and work.

David Geherin remarks at the end of *The American Private Eye: The Image in Fiction* that the private eye is best seen as a "Janus figure, an individual who looks backwards to a more noble past while at the same time staring open-eyed at the world before him" (201). This doubleness of vision especially characterizes the hard-boiled detective's focus on his sometimes dangerous present while both plagued and uplifted by the past. Lovejoy speaks approvingly of the Victorians and their use of memory:

Somebody once said you get no choice in life, and none in memory either. Judging by what the Victorians left in the way of knickknacks, they made a valiant attempt to control memory by means of lockets for engravings, 'likenesses' in all manner of materials ranging from hairs from the head of the beloved to diamonds, and a strange celebration of death through the oddest mixture of jubilation and grief [*Judas* 117].

Each one of the detectives discussed, whether predominantly through personal, social, or professional memories, deals with a past that will not go away but that may be managed. Jeremiah Healy's John Francis Cuddy visits his wife's grave and talks with her. The author even inserts in italics her imagined responses. Cuddy nearly always leaves the cemetery with a sense of peace if not the solution to whatever problem bothers him at the moment. In whatever fashion, this image of the hard-boiled detective enduring through and with memory remains as a central figure in the genre.

24

Lies and Deceit: Family

Family conflict is a staple in fiction. This central social relation provides much of the tension in the modern novel and has remained an important theme in the hard-boiled detective novel since its inception. Richard Slotkin states that part of the difficulty of solving a murder in the realist tradition, i.e., hard-boiled tradition, is that the investigation is "complicated by," among other social currents, "the cross-conflicts born of family psychology" (91). Carroll John Daly's *The Snarl of the Beast* and Dashiell Hammett's *Red Harvest* feature family crises. Sara Paretsky's *Indemnity Only* and Jeremiah Healy's *Blunt Darts*, among others, continue this exploration. One might argue that since the late seventies, family crises play an increasing role in the genre. Both detectives such as Stephen Dobyns' Charlie Bradshaw in *Saratoga Longshot* and characters like Stephen Greenleaf's Roland Nelson in *Grave Error* portray people in destabilizing family situations. And, few undergo these experiences without significant loss, either of life or relationships. Paralleling social trends, the prominence of this theme in the modern hard-boiled detective novel sets the stage for ideas of violence and betrayal and invests the fiction with a sense of precariousness during a period when, paradoxically, the detective has become increasingly integrated into society.

The extensive focus on the family in crisis in the hard-boiled detective novel is a reflection of the vital importance of that theme to the nineteenth and early twentieth century American and British novel. Daly's *The Snarl of the Beast* and Hammett's *Red Harvest*, two of the first three hard-boiled detective novels, construct their novels around family conflicts. Daniel Davidson hires Race Williams in *The Snarl of the Beast* to prevent his uncle O.M. Davidson and his stepfather Raphael Dezzeia from murdering him and stealing his inheritance. The superhuman Dezzeia, a figure from the gothic novel, ironically pulls this work in a different direction from what came to be the mainstream hard-boiled detective novel, but it still retains enough elements to be an identifiable progenitor. However, Hammett's *Red Harvest* sets the hard-boiled detective novel on a solid course. In this work, the Continental Op (and later Sam Spade in *The Maltese Falcon*) gives a stamp of clarity to the genre's tough professionals. In addition, Hammett's portrayal of the struggles and losses in the Willsson family add several dimensions to the exploration of the family theme. Donald Willsson, Elihu Willsson's son and presumptive heir, is killed early in the novel, and the Continental Op, initially hired by Donald, works for Elihu in the cleaning of Personville. This reversal of the expected succession of one generation by another adds a sour note to any sense of the future contained in the idea of the family. Jopi Nyman remarks, "Since in Personville even the family tie is shown to be based on betrayal and deception, not love and mutual respect, the family is shown to be corrupt and its importance diminished" (79). Paralleling this is the decay in Personville ("Poisonville") that requires cleansing, decay stemming from Elihu's own actions. As George Grella observes of the effect of this kind of social development on the detective, "Finding the social contract vicious and debilitating, he generally isolates himself from normal human relationships" ("Hard-Boiled Detective" 106). Hammett thus undercuts any image of the family as support and development with the Willssons as devastated as the town after the murderous violence. Summing up Hammett's work, John G. Cawelti states, "his stories are essentially about the discovery that the comforting pieties of the past — belief in a benevolent universe, in progress, in romantic love — are illusions and that man is alone in a meaningless universe" (*Adventure* 173).

In *The Maltese Falcon*, Sam Spade has no family and sleeps with his partner's wife. Iva Archer, Miles Archer's wife, is a clinging, unstable woman whom Spade attempts to ease out of his life. In the process, someone kills Miles in a San Francisco alley. Spade falls in love with Brigid O'Shaughnessy, Miles's killer, but turns her over to the police at the end of the novel. Caspar Gutman, Joel Cairo, and Wilmer Smith, joined to Brigid through the pursuit of the Maltese Falcon, have an ongoing connection based on greed and, on Gutman's part, his fascination with the supposedly valuable falcon's history and provenance. Hammett portrays an adult world with no room for stable personal relationships. No families with young children appear in this work or in *Red Harvest*. These are not novels that have a future marked out in generations. Spade does have a friendly relationship with Effie Perrine, his secretary, who lives with her mother, and he maintains a somewhat stable contact with Sgt. Tom Polhaus of the San Francisco

Police. At this early point in the hard-boiled detective novel, the authors make no room for a more three-dimensional social environment that includes the detectives. While their clients sometimes have family and other intimate relationships, the detectives more often do not and thus appear with empty pasts and, at times, less complex personalities than later protagonists reveal. Later, Mickey Spillane's Mike Hammer and Raymond Chandler's Philip Marlowe begin to fill out the portraits of the hard-boiled detectives.

Chandler's *The Big Sleep* continues the image of the patriarch's surviving the break-up of his family, the older generation contemplating the destruction of the younger one. General Sternwood's two daughters, Vivian and Carmen, suffer losses, one more grievous than the other. Carmen shoots Rusty Regan, her older sister's husband, and unknowingly shoots Marlowe with blanks before collapsing (219–20). Gen. Sternwood had grown fond of Regan before the latter's disappearance, and his reaction to the loss of his son-in-law seems close to that of a son's. But, the novel reveals the lack of any sense of direction in his daughters' lives. Noting the "unseasonal mid–October rains," Peter Wolfe says, "Relations among the Sternwoods are as unnatural as this out-of-season occurrence [...]" (*Something More than Night* 117). Chandler portrays the general as a decent man, and his age and fragility, by contrast, emphasize his daughters' air of corruption. Marlowe, the isolated detective who refuses to make love to both women since he was not hired for that (151, 156), sits in ironic judgment on their bad faith. His position argues for a family imperative that the younger generation should inherit the good, struggle against the bad, and develop in a positive direction. In the hard-boiled detective tradition, families seldom follow that hopeful path.

Spillane wastes no time in eliminating that possibility from *I, the Jury*. Jack Williams, Myrna Devlin's fiancé and Hammer's friend, is murdered, shot in the stomach. Before going off to World War II, Williams, then a policeman, saves Myrna from committing suicide, they fall in love, and they plan to marry. Setting up this romantic beginning, Spillane inevitably reverses the direction of the novel. In a world in which sex, drugs, and murder dominate, their mirror opposites, i.e., traditional family life and/or love relationships, have nowhere to gain purchase. Hammer, capable of strong emotion and idealizing the woman he loves, Dr. Charlotte Manning, Williams' killer, exemplifies the twisting strands of feeling in the early hard-boiled detective novel. Both Williams and Hammer want marriage and the stability of family life but do not live in a world that always offers it. And, falling in love with Charlotte is a further example of the difficulty in making one's hopes and life experiences coincide. The inversion of Hammer's strong feeling is complete when he shoots Charlotte in the stomach just as he promised to do to Williams' unknown killer. Hammer's feelings erupt time and again but frequently, until he marries his secretary Velda, they are in the service of vengeance against those who have murdered or caused the death of someone for whom he cares. In *One Lonely Knight: Mickey Spillane's Mike Hammer*, Max Allan Collins and James L. Traylor state,

> Since love and friendship are the two most important factors in Hammer's life, the internal conflict created by his having to shoot the woman he loved to avenge the death of his best friend almost drives him mad — and perhaps it does. Only in his later years, when he finally realizes that Velda is the love of his life, does he come to grips with Charlotte's death [46].

In *My Gun Is Quick*, Spillane introduces an example of Collins and Traylor's second factor. Hammer meets a young redhead in a coffee shop late at night and is impressed by her. He does not learn her name, and she leaves the shop. When she turns up murdered, Hammer vows that whoever is responsible will not get away with it. Arthur Berin, who seemingly has acted as a father figure toward Red, as she is initially known, hires Hammer to find her killer. In the manner of Daly's eponymous Hidden Hand, Berin turns out not only to be the behind-the-scene crime figure but also responsible for Red's death. Once again Hammer's strong feelings are poured into vengeance against someone who has destroyed an element of good in the world through a murderous betrayal of the innocent. Hammer says, when he learns through Cap. Pat Chambers that Red was murdered, "[...] I started cursing under my breath. It always starts that way, the crazy mad feeling that makes me want to choke the life out of some son of a bitch, and there's nothing to grab but air" (15). Although Hammer shoots Berin in a burning building before firemen arrive, the solution does not stop threats to the young and defenseless.

In *The Moving Target*, Ross Macdonald adds a new element to the idea of family. While Ralph Sampson's murder is another example of the outside threat to the family introduced by Hammett in *Red Harvest*, Albert Graves, Sampson's killer (196), further destabilizes any image of family harmony. He is Sampson's family friend and lawyer. His very closeness to them, composed of professional and personal trust, compounds his treachery. Just as the hard-boiled detective novel portrays a violent urban world, disjointed both socially and morally, so Macdonald adds further support to the idea that there is no wall separating family life from this enveloping danger, thus locating "evil," as David Geherin notes, in a "familial" context (*Sons* 22). And, Lew Archer, like the Continental Op and Philip Marlowe, has no answer to the deterioration he witnesses. Standing outside the family, divorced himself (Macdonald, *Moving* 15) while the two former detectives have no romantic and few personal relationships, Archer walks away from the shambles, like the Op and Marlowe, disclaiming any further role in their lives. Limited as his part is, his investigations and observations merely add a bleak coda to the sometimes-hopeless events. As Martin Priestman observes of Macdonald, he "takes the form's critical view of an increasingly acquisitive society as a starting point, but focuses most of his narrative ingenuity on the uncovering of buried family traumas which tend [...] to be overwhelmingly Oedipal" (176). This element of Freudian cultural determinism underscores the inability of the families to control and direct their lives.

The family dysfunction in *The Moving Target* is only a prelude to a worse family predicament in *The Drowning Pool*. In *Moving*, Elaine Sampson fell from a horse, and the accident either made her an invalid or she pretends to be one. Her stepdaughter Miranda Sampson believes the latter. Ralph drinks heavily and further estranges himself from his wife and daughter when he becomes involved with a religious cult. In addition, Sampson wants his daughter to marry Graves. However, she is interested in Alan Taggert, her father's pilot, who does not respond to her. *The Drowning Pool* multiplies the dangers to the family by locating nearly all of them within its structure. James and Maude Slocum live with Olivia Slocum, his mother, on the estate in Nopal Valley near Quinto, California. Olivia controls the purse strings and aside from a small income from an investment, James and Maude depend entirely on her. Lew Archer enters the case after Maude receives a letter threatening to expose her unfaithfulness. It turns out that their daughter Cathy wrote the letter. Cathy does not know that her supposed "father" is a homosexual and that she is the daughter of her mother's lover, Lt. Ralph Knudson, a local police chief. Cathy drowns her grandmother Olivia in order to hurt her mother. Archer gradually uncovers the details and agrees to let Cathy go with Knudson to Chicago after Maude commits suicide. Macdonald, in only his second Lew Archer novel, has completed the internalization of the danger to the family. Three generations mix and destroy any chance for the family to survive intact. Two generations of the women are dead, and Cathy has to live with the knowledge that she murdered her grandmother. Only an outsider who is in reality no outsider picks up what remains and, seemingly, starts over again. The family and the family place have been corrupted, and Cathy and Knudson need 2000 miles between them and the past.

John D. MacDonald begins *The Deep Blue Good-by* (1964) on what seems like a different note but which quickly reveals itself as a series of family crises. Cathy Kerr, through Chookie McCall, attempts to hire Travis McGee to recover whatever Junior Allen stole from her family. As McGee later learns, Cathy's father, Sgt. Dave Berry, hid some gems in the gateposts in front of their home. He dies in prison before he can tell anyone where they are, but Allen, in Leavenworth with him, has learned that he secreted something of value in or near his home and goes to Candle Key on his release from prison. Once again, the father figure sets in motion the conflict. When McGee arrives at Cathy's home, he discovers that her husband is absent. Cathy and her sister Christine struggle to support their families, and Cathy admits her sexual vulnerability to a predator like Allen. Lois Atkinson, like Cathy a victim of Allen's, had undergone a divorce before Allen entered her life, and McGee, attempting to find help for Lois, is rebuffed by her sister-in-law; her husband, Lois's brother, has had a heart attack, and no one can help Lois. The Travis McGee series, begun in the Transitional stage in the development of the hard-boiled detective novel, thus continues and varies the image of the family in crisis, elaborating a novelistic chronotope (Bakhtin, *The Dialogic Imagination* 425–26) that has yet to lose its force. Lewis D. Moore, commenting on McGee's attempt to help the Brell family in *Blue*, states, "[...] given the choices of speaking or doing nothing, he speaks, thus moving to hold together this core social unit as if it were as essential to him that they stay together as it is to them" (153).

Four of the above writers from the Early Period, Daly, Hammett, Chandler, and Ross Macdonald, set their detectives outside the family; they minister to families from some self-imposed distance. LeRoy Lad Panek comments, "With the exception of Nick Charles, almost all hard-boiled heroes of the twenties and thirties are unmarried, just as virtually all hard-boiled heroes of the seventies and eighties, except Spenser, are divorced" (*Introduction* 163). But for John D. MacDonald and, later, Robert B. Parker, the detective often becomes physically and/or emotionally involved with the families they encounter. McGee sleeps with Cathy and Lois; at the end of the novel, Lois, because of her love and concern for him, loses her life, and Cathy helps him recover from a sense of despair over Lois's death. It is through his merging sexually with Cathy and temporarily merging also with her family life on Candle Key, source of the major family crises involving Allen, that McGee recovers his sense of the future. This deeper involvement of the detective in the lives of the other characters signals one of the major shifts in the genre that continues into the Modern Period. Robert B. Parker's *The Godwulf Manuscript* involves Spenser in a sexual relationship with two of the main characters. Hired by Roland and Marion Orchard to find their daughter Terry, Spenser winds up sleeping first with the mother and then with the daughter. Although his involvement with the women is more superficial than McGee's is with Cathy and Lois, it continues the incorporation of the detective into their everyday lives even when, as Geherin states, "He is a man who understands guilt [...] because he has made love to Mrs. Orchard, mother of the girl he is trying to save and wife of the man who has hired him" (*Sons* 20). But, Geherin points out some pages later,

"At the end of *The Godwulf Manuscript,* Spenser returned Terry Orchard to her family but left her at her parents' door, unwilling to become involved in what he dismisses as 'family business'" (26). Thus, it is not a full incorporation, and detectives from the modern period such as Loren D. Estleman's Amos Walker, first seen in *Motor City Blue,* revert to a personal aloofness nearly the equal of the Continental Op's, Sam Spade's, and Philip Marlowe's.

The Transitional Period in the hard-boiled detective novel also witnesses the tentative introduction of the detective's family. Except for occasional references to family members, earlier hard-boiled detectives have no distinct pasts, no three-dimensional image of growth and development, of nurturing resulting in who they are as adults. This withheld past, of course, objectifies them in ways that clarify the hard-boiled detective in his early stages, setting him apart from other private detectives. Michael Z. Lewin's *Ask the Right Question* and Lawrence Block's *In the Midst of Death,* introducing Albert Samson and Matthew Scudder, respectively, provide this missing family dimension. Although divorced, both maintain contact with their ex-wives and children. Samson, "whose name," according to Geherin, "suggests his role as a lineal descendant of Sam Spade" (*American Private Eye* 172), writes to his daughter but does not see her in the novel. However, he focuses on his correspondence with her, giving it importance in his life. While little more than a ripple, this element is a harbinger of real change. Foreshadowing the even more profound shifts that Stephen Dobyns and, in the Modern Period, Les Roberts introduce with Charlie Bradshaw's and Milan Jacovich's families, respectively, Lewin also includes Samson's mother at whose luncheonette he occasionally eats. Bradshaw's waitress mother and Jacovich's Aunt Branka continue this inclusion of an earlier generation. Scudder's family relationships present a more bitter image. His ex-wife and sons later treat him with scorn when he visits his former home. Living in a hotel and spending much time drinking in bars, Scudder appears caught between his life's moments. A former policeman who resigned because he accidentally shot a child (*In the Midst* 36), Scudder makes a moderate living, in the hard-boiled tradition, but has no meaningful relationships. Thus, his contacts with his wife and sons give him a substance, which unlike earlier private investigators, does not come solely from his work and his attitude toward it. After fifty years, the Continental Op's suit of clothes, pistols, and a job no longer serve to define the hard-boiled detective. Whether because of post-sixties societal changes, the advent of feminism, or the problematic shift of the hard-boiled detective novel toward elements of the novel of manners and morals, marital and love relationships have assumed an increasing importance.

Joseph Hansen's Dave Brandstetter and Bill Pronzini's Nameless, superficially quite different men, illustrate the two major changes regarding the family in the Transitional Period, i.e., the involvement of the detective in the client's or at least an important character's family life and the introduction of the detective's own family or personal life as important to the novel's development. Pronzini's Nameless is slower to interact with a client's family than Hansen's Brandstetter, and it is not until the second novel of the series, *The Vanished* (1973), that Nameless becomes involved with Cheryl Rosmond and thinks that he might love her. Unfortunately, he exposes Doug Rosmond, her brother, as Roy Sands' killer, and she rejects him. In *The Snatch*, the first novel in the series, Nameless's lover Erika Coates leaves him. In *Hoodwink*, Nameless again falls in love with someone involved in the investigation, but this coming together lasts, though there are moments when both Kerry Wade and Nameless delay the possibility of a permanent relationship, yet they not only marry but also eventually adopt a young girl named Emily Hunter. Other facets of his original family come out in subsequent novels, and one learns in *Scattershot* that Nameless is Swiss-Italian and that he goes to watch older Italians play bocce, a game his father used to play. Lt. Eberhardt of the San Francisco police becomes something close to a brother to him as the series progresses, and Nameless interacts more on a personal than professional level with him, especially after Dana, Eberhardt's wife, leaves him. Both Nameless and Brandstetter want stability and love in their lives. As Joseph Hansen's *Fade-out* begins, Brandstetter is mourning the death of Rod Fleming, his lover, from cancer. Hansen immediately plunges one into the personal life of his protagonist. Brandstetter is an insurance investigator working for his father's company, Medallion Life Insurance. He goes to Pima, California, to investigate the puzzling absence of Fox Olson's body after his car plunges into a rain-swollen river. When he first talks with Thorne Olson, Fox's supposed widow, she brings Brandstetter into the family's life by telling Fox's story. It turns out that Fox was bisexual, and while Brandstetter solves the case, he is attracted to Doug Sawyer, Fox's lover, and they begin a serious relationship as the novel ends. Ernest Fontana states, "Unlike Marlowe Brandstetter is not afraid of love or tenderness" (90).

In the modern period, the families of both detectives and clients become more important. A contrast between Parker's Spenser in *The Godwulf Manuscript* and Sara Paretsky's V.I. Warshawski in *Indemnity Only* is instructive. Both detectives are called in to help find a family member of a client. Neither detective has any ongoing family involvement. However, Warshawski's mother and father are presences in her novel. Her memories and sense of them sustain her and, in part, motivate her conduct. Kathleen Gregory Klein states, "Although her father had been a cop, clearly her mother's drive was the more important influence in Vic's life; but, she believes, neither parent would have approved of her decision to become a detective" (*Woman Detective* 212). From the beginning, Paretsky also employs the idea of the extended family, something that MacDonald's McGee and Parker's Spenser work toward in later novels. With Dr. Lotty Herschel, Lt. Bobby Mallory, and in later books her elderly downstairs neighbor Mr. Contreras, Warshawski has emotional and physical resources to help in her life and cases. Louise Conley Jones, however, notes Warshawski's "ambivalence" toward help from her "extended family"; "To give in to such care indicates weakness, a denial of the loner status so important to the American hard-boiled tradition" (85). Sue Grafton's Kinsey Millhone (*"A" Is for Alibi*) and Linda Barnes' Carlotta Carlyle (*A Trouble of Fools*) also have extended families from the beginning of their series as well as vividly remembered aunts who raised them. Panek notes, "Grafton builds for her the pseudo-domestic circle of Rosie, Henry, and Henry's assorted siblings with whom Kinsey finds comfort and pleasure" (*New Hard-Boiled* 92). Millhone's landlord, Henry Pitts, a retired baker and creator of crossword puzzles, and Rosie, her stern, tavern-owning friend, both feed and encourage her. Millhone's womb-like garage apartment with the nearby Pitts acting somewhat as a sentinel for the independent detective especially reveals her structural connectedness to others. Similarly, Lotty worries over Warshawski's health and well being while Mr. Contreras, along with his dog, acts as her enfeebled protector. Carlyle's tenant Roz and her cab-dispatcher friend Gloria, along with her occasional lover Sam Gianelli and Paolina, her young friend, envelop her in multiple human situations. While Parker's Spenser, like the three female detectives above, works on a case in his first novel concerning family conflict, he has neither family nor friends himself. Initially, Spenser resembles the early hard-boiled detectives in this regard; Susan Silverman, Hawk, and Paul Giacomin lie in the future.

Detectives in the modern period not only take cases in which their clients' families suffer difficulties, but also become vulnerable themselves in this area. Milan Jacovich in Les Roberts' *Pepper Pike* and Jeremiah Healy in *Blunt Darts* no longer represent the objective professional whose personal life has no family depth. Now they must contend with the same pressures as their clients, helping them as they work out their own family problems. Les Roberts' Milan Jacovich significantly shifts the hard-boiled detective novel by bringing in his own children. Divorced when *Pepper Pike* begins, Jacovich has an ongoing relationship with his two sons Milan, Jr., and Stephen. While his marriage to Lila, a high school sweetheart, was a failure, his divorce is a success (11). Roberts limits Jacovich's freedom of action by having his children in his apartment on alternate weekends (4–5). Ex-wives are one thing, but present, nearby children add novelistic dimensions that the genre, however surprisingly, expands to include. And, Jacovich's children are not limited to names in the background but rather enter the story early and become endangered when Victor Gaimari, heir apparent to Giancarlo D'Alessandro, the Cleveland mob boss, implicitly threatens them. Widening Jacovich's family and personal circle, Roberts includes his Aunt Branka and two fellow Slovenians, Louis Vukovich and Lt. Marko Meglich, the former a tavern owner in his old neighborhood and the latter a childhood friend. Moving between family, friends, and the outside world, Roberts carefully balances the various plot demands. And, one of the most important demands in *Pepper Pike* involves another family. Richard Amber, a successful Cleveland advertising executive, hires Jacovich as a bodyguard but disappears before he can do the job. Subsequently, Judith Amber, with whom Richard has marital difficulties, hires Jacovich to find him. The detective becomes enmeshed with Walter Deming, Judith's wealthy uncle, and D'Alessandro, whom Richard owed $40,000 over a gambling debt. Rather than the traditional detective tale with the detective outside the family circles, Roberts constructs a triangle, i.e., the Ambers and Deming, D'Alessandro and Gaimari, and the Jacoviches. Marlowe, Archer, and McGee enter and leave the lives of the families in conflict, but Bradshaw and Jacovich have nowhere to go. They are held in stasis by their family roots, no longer the isolated detective who has no other life than what his clients need. While McGee does develop friendships, even a "brother" in Meyer, his home, a boat, symbolizes the possibility of impermanence even if the series does not offer it in any clear way. Even though Jacovich lives in a different home, Lila and his two children live in his old home in the old neighborhood, effectively tying him to his past, as does his relationship with his friends, notably Lt. Meglich.

Healy's John Francis Cuddy has a deep but necessarily limited relationship with his wife. Cuddy communes in *Blunt Darts* with his dead wife Beth when he visits her grave. He talks about both his cases and his life, and Healy includes her imagined responses in italics. However, rather than just the pathos of the scene, Healy in this way objectifies Cuddy's emotional life. This internal dialogue could occur anywhere, but Healy sets it in the cemetery, periodically throughout the year, and presents it without overstatement. Cuddy's visitations, set apart from the action and thus less immediate than Bradshaw's and Jacovich's family relationships, are nonetheless equally important in his life. However, his clients' family difficulties, about which he "talks" with Beth, more than make up for any presumed distancing of his own family. The missing fourteen-year old Stephen Kinnington, whom his grandmother hires Cuddy to locate, has killed his mother and later kills his supposed father and his father's bodyguard. In reality, Stephen is the son of his mother's husband's brother, Telford, who died in 1969 in Vietnam. The dead mother's sexual promiscuity, of which her relations with

Telford were only one instance; murder; Stephen's madness; and the grandmother's concealment of his actions even after he murders her son, all combine to present a family crisis for which there is no solution, a situation comparable to the Nelsons' in Greenleaf's *Grave Error*. Cuddy's thought about the case, "Something was wrong there" (127), after pondering what he knew about Stephen "with" Beth, is a fitting epitaph to the Kinningtons' story.

Two modern British hard-boiled detectives, Liza Cody's Anna Lee in *Dupe* and Sarah Dunant's Hannah Wolfe in *Birth Marks*, both with loose family relationships and both with the beginnings of extended families, investigate the deaths of young women with artistic leanings who broke away from family life (Cody) or a surrogate mother figure (Dunant). Although willful, neither young woman ultimately attempted to succeed in life through their art, and their deaths are pointless accidents springing from other people's plans and desires. The image of waste dominates both novels, an irony at the heart of the purposelessness of death for the healthy young. While Dunant's Carolyn Hamilton was somewhat remote from her family after going to live with Augusta Patrick in the hope of becoming a professional ballet dancer, Cody's Deirdre Jackson maintained a sporadic relationship with her parents who care enough about her death that they hire Brierly Security to discover the cause. Both women had the energy to go to London to pursue a career, Deirdre in acting and film and Carolyn in dance, but neither could focus enough on their goals to develop what abilities they had or adapt to what experience taught them. Ultimately, both women turned to their bodies, though in different ways, for a solution to their dilemmas, with Deirdre's relying on her physical presence, her personality expressed through a sense of determination to obtain what she wanted, and Carolyn on her generally good health and fertility. She agreed to become a surrogate mother for Jules Belmont, a French industrialist, and died pregnant while attempting to circumvent the contract. In future novels, Lee and Wolfe seldom discover more hopeful family possibilities, contending anew with waste and the recurrent belief that youth and resilience will find ways to salvage the family.

While Healy's novel might leave us stunned to silence in its stark portrayal of family disintegration, both artistic and everyday inventiveness give one a confidence that the theme is far from losing its potency. Just as life most often begins in a family setting, so the hard-boiled detective novel, with seeming inevitability, opens out from this dominant and dynamic social structure. The genre derives its most powerful tensions and conflicts from this basic source of human interactions, which both sustains and is sustained by the enveloping social world.

25

Conclusion:
Expanding the Word

Through the late 1970s, the hard-boiled detective novel is, in one particular area, homogeneous. It is largely male and white. Beginning with Marcia Muller's Sharon McCone in San Francisco, Sara Paretsky's V.I. Warshawski in Chicago, and Liza Cody's Anna Lee in London, females play an increasingly significant role in the genre's development. Also, Walter Mosley's Easy Rawlins and James Sallis's Lew Griffin introduce black American hard-boiled detectives and Bruce Cook does the same with Chico Cervantes, a Chicano. Joseph Hansen's David Brandstetter is gay, and J.M. Redmann's Michelle "Micky" Knight and Sandra Scoppettone's Lauren Laurano are lesbians. While Hansen first publishes his Brandstetter novels in the Transitional Period, Redmann and Scoppetone begin writing in the Modern Era. Reginald Hill's Joe Sixsmith debuts in 1993; Sixsmith is a laid-off black of West Indian descent, born and bred in Luton, north of London. George Grella's unhappy announcement in 1970 (see Chapter 21) concerning the death of the hard-boiled detective novel, ironically echoing Mark Twain's discovery of his premature demise, came while the genre was undergoing a rebirth; the expansion in numbers and kinds of hard-boiled detectives has continued to the present. The depth and variety of critical attention has also increased. The diversity in the kinds of hard-boiled detectives, replicating the changing demographics in the United States and to a lesser extent in Great Britain, inevitably expands the boundaries of attitudes and actions, leading to the dramatization of social, sexual, and racial tensions, both ominous and liberating. The genre's vitality thus marks its future direction in creative ways.

Sara Paretsky, Sue Grafton, Liza Cody, and Gillian Slovo begin their hard-boiled detective novels within a few years of one another in the early to mid 1980s. Val McDermid, Linda Barnes, Karen Kijewski, Sarah Dunant, and Janet Dawson follow in the late 1980s and early 1990s. Since women writers have figured prominently in the mystery genre from the late-nineteenth century, this appearance might not seem unusual. However, the early hard-boiled detective novel is not so much male-oriented as *terra incognita* to women protagonists. The heroes of most of the above series narrate their works, thus situating women inside looking out and in the central position from which to view the world and judge or evaluate events. The question that should occupy the critic, while not What is the world coming to?, is What does it all mean? This applies to female as well as male critics, and while it is probably unanswerable, it places the critic in the proper role of humble enquirer. Some critics maintain that being a hard-boiled detective precludes one from being a feminist—by definition. But, female hard-boiled detectives are feminists and, in part, so easily assume the previously male role that one wonders how it could happen. Kathleen Gregory Klein argues for a less certain adaptation of the female detective to the previously male genre: "When transferred straight from the male private eye to the female, the role fits poorly" (*Woman Detective* 162). However, the apparent subversion of gender roles demands explanation if not expostulation. Genres are not so lightly diverted; the momentum of tradition, if nothing else, would make it difficult to reshape the basic formula in such a drastic way.

The ghosts of Carroll John Daly, Dashiell Hammett, Raymond Chandler, and Ross Macdonald are probably protesting at this easy assumption of the role of hard-boiled detectives by the modern female protagonists. But not Mickey Spillane, the writer the critics love to hate. Of course, Spillane is still alive, but Mike Hammer, more than most of the early hard-boiled detectives, senses the power of women. This power is shown not only by Velda, his blonde secretary, but also by lovers and villains alike as well as those who reject him. The opening scene of *One Lonely Night* in which the young woman, fleeing from a man who intends to kill her, sees Hammer on a New York bridge but prefers to jump into the river rather than accept his help, stays in the reader's mind even more than Hammer's violent actions against her pursuer. While she is not a protagonist, it is her power to act in a moment of total, instinctive rejection that affects him the most. Thus, Paretsky's V.I. Warshawski lives the role of the hard-boiled detective with an inevitability that forces one to look for the joins but not easily find them. Louise Conley Jones writes, "Is then the P.I. code—empathy, physical superiority, and self-reliant isolation—so very far removed from modern revisionist feminism? I suggest that it is not [...]" (78). In assuming the role, the female hard-boiled detective changes it, but changes it to fit while leaving it for others, male and female, to live out and define it for themselves.

Cody's Anna Lee in London and Grafton's Kinsey Millhone in Santa Teresa north of Los Angeles appear at roughly the same time as Paretsky's Chicago detective with similar experiences defining their roles. They clearly see themselves as extending a tradition but slightly alter the boundaries. Like Warshawski, Millhone and Lee have neighbors on whom they depend to one degree or another. Their relationships are not always smooth, but they maintain contact and gratefully receive help when necessary. Dunant's Hannah Wolfe in *Birth Marks* remains close to her London family. Her sister Kate and her young niece are important emotional ballasts. One difference between these female detectives is that the British either work for a security agency, have a partner, or work alone and the Americans tend to act mostly on their own. This American sense of isolation partially occurs because the Los Angeles of Raymond Chandler and Ross Macdonald looms so large in Paretsky's and Grafton's work. Additionally, the detective as loner is not as easily established in Britain as in the United States. Yet, Gillian Slovo's Kate Baeier lives with her lover Sam and his son Matthew in London but still maintains her apartment. This refuge is important to her and possibly helps keep her with her "family." Baeir observes, "I loved my flat. I loved the quiet of it and the fact that it had been decorated without any of the compromises that came from sharing" (*Death Comes Staccato* 29). Val McDermid's Kate Brannigan shares a bungalow with her rock journalist lover Richard Barclay, but each has separate apartments connected by a rear conservatory. As *Dead Beat* begins, they have been lovers for nine months, and the aggravations stemming from their relationship make her ponder "why I broke all the rules of a lifetime and allowed this man to invade my personal space" (14). Nevertheless, they stay together. Michelle Spring's Laura Principal in *Every Breath You Take* lives in Cambridge and her partner/lover Sonny Medlowitz has an apartment and office in London. They both also stay with one another when they can work out the logistics.

One aspect of the advent of the woman hard-boiled detective is a tendency toward domestication. A tendency is not, of course, a settled habit, a confirmed direction, but this tendency does appear and suggests that female susceptibilities and concerns matter and contend for the definition of the norm. Grafton's Millhone is very sensitive to her place and after the explosion in *"E" Is for Evidence* (1988) has Henry remodel it to represent an even more secure extension of herself. For her, to admit or not admit someone to the apartment usually involves the decision to admit or not admit him to the body. Female detectives are occasionally attacked in or near their homes. In *Killing Orders* (1985), someone attacks V.I. Warshawski with acid on the darkened stairway landing outside her apartment door (100–01). Incidents such as this are not examples of adding to, rearranging, or creating the home environment, but they do suggest place as refuge even when violated, place as central to the self, and place as the expression of sensibility — sensibility that creates a new direction for action springing from intimate spaces that do not suggest an innate bleakness as the primal core for being. However messy Warshawski's apartment, the image that Paretsky suggests is that a sentient being lives there; it is her mess, "created" by her and is an example of life's variety, not an impersonal chaos. As she says in *Indemnity Only*, "[...] I'm messy but not a slob" (11). Domestication battles with the "hard" in hard-boiled and relentlessly dictates a change that breathes life into the home, the place of origin. Eating, sleeping, cooking, making love, hiding out, and recovering from injuries — these are more frequently aspects of the modern female hard-boiled detective than the male.

The appearance of the hard-boiled detective novel in Great Britain adds a geographical expansion to the form. This might be the genre's most surprising development. P.D. James' Cordelia Gray in *An Unsuitable Job for a Woman* (1972) comes close to being a progenitor though not a hard-boiled detective. Appropriately enough, five of the British hard-boiled detective novelists, as mentioned above, are women: Cody, Dunant, Slovo, McDermid, and Spring. Mark Timlin's Nick Sharman, Reginald Hill's Joe Sixsmith, and John Baker's Sam Turner are other notable additions. London is the preferred area for their work with the exception of McDermid's Brannigan who operates in Manchester, Hill's Sixsmith in Luton north of London, and Baker's Turner in York. While detective fiction is not new to Britain, the hard-boiled detective is new. It is such an American genre, in genesis and form, that one is initially surprised that it survives the transplantation. Violence and action, as early as the Sherlock Holmes stories, are present in various types of British mystery fiction. However, the focus on the individual loner and specific historical circumstances during which the form developed, e.g., Prohibition and the rise of the gangster, are not part of the British cultural past. Even American reactions to World War I and the Depression differ substantially from the British ones. In addition, over fifty years pass from the genre's commencement to its British start with Cody et al.

Geographical expansion of the genre is not limited to Great Britain. As early as the Transitional Period, hard-boiled detectives spread to many urban areas in the United States outside of New York, Los Angeles, San Francisco, Chicago, and Miami. Fort Lauderdale, Boston, Saratoga Springs, Meriwether, MT, Indianapolis, and Saint Louis serve as locales for private detective series. The Modern Period adds Detroit, Cincinnati, Cleveland,

Santa Teresa, Sacramento, New Orleans, Newark, Seattle, Oakland, West Palm Beach, and Omaha. The inclusion of these cities provides new settings for an old form that grew out of an older form — the detective novel — that was international with its most famous nineteenth-century detectives, Dupin and Holmes. The genre moves from urban to suburban to exurban with a relentless force. The jump to new cities like Cincinnati and Sacramento is a veritable setting mutation. And, wherever the genre lands, it seems to take root and flourish. This does not occur without an awareness of a curious pattern revealed in the genre's progenitors. Some new cities seemingly gaze at the original cities in the genre — Newark at New York, Oakland at San Francisco, and Ft. Lauderdale at Miami. Thus, without in every case a self-conscious distancing from the five principal American cities as in the case of Seattle, New Orleans, and Indianapolis, Newark and Oakland challenge and involve their more significant neighbors in a distinctly literary manner; image, repetition, and irony play off the cities across the water against their new, brash challengers. The use of these new cities also rejects the image of them as backwaters.

Development in the areas of family, love, and friendship represent nothing less than a paradigm shift in the modern hard-boiled detective novel. As with these and other ideas, the Transitional Period sets the tone for the Modern Era and, along with those novelists who continued writing into the latter period, examples abound of these ideas' development. For instance, John D. MacDonald's Travis McGee series begins in *The Deep Blue Good-by* with McGee's friendship with one woman and love affair with another, strongly implying in the latter case that marriage is in the near future. Paul Stanial, a private detective in MacDonald's *The Drowner* (1963), actually marries his client, so this thinking is not unusual for MacDonald. In the last novel of the series, *The Lonely Silver Rain*, McGee acquires a daughter Jeanne Killian, his and Puss Killian's child from *Pale Gray for Guilt*. Michael Z. Lewin, Bill Pronzini, Robert B. Parker, John Lutz (Alo Nudger), Stephen Dobyns (Charlie Bradshaw), and Lawrence Block explore situations that move their heroes away from the position of the isolated loner best exemplified by Dashiell Hammett's Continental Op, Raymond Chandler's Philip Marlowe, and Ross Macdonald's Lew Archer. Thus, the modern hard-boiled detective novel embraces the ideas of family, love, and friendship as natural components of the genre. With Paretsky's Warshawski, the memory of her mother and father and the occasional appearance of other relatives are significant elements in the series. While her love affairs are temporary, a pattern reminding one of the early hard-boiled detective novels, Warshawski maintains close friendships with Dr. Lotty Herschel, Mr. Contreras, and Lt. Bobby Mallory. They are close in different ways, but the relationships are continuous. Grafton's Millhone begins with only the memory of being raised by an aunt but has several important friendships: Henry Pitts and Rosie. In *"J" Is for Judgment*, Grafton later adds, as noted in Chapter 18, another aunt, a grandmother, and several cousins, who remain on the periphery of the series, to create a family. Linda Barnes Carlotta Carlyle, raised like Millhone by an aunt, surrounds herself with friends and engages in an intense, on-again off-again affair with Sam Gianelli. When one adds Roz, her somewhat strange tenant; Gloria, her cab company dispatcher friend; and Paolina, the young girl whom she nurtures through a big sister's program, Carlyle, except for her profession, seems like someone with aspirations clearly identified as middle American. Even her weekly participation in the volleyball games supports this image of someone staying connected with others in meaningful ways.

Of course, in the category of relationships, the modern hard-boiled detective novel has significant connections to the early exemplars of the form. Jonathan Valin's Harry Stoner and Loren D. Estleman's Amos Walker are important representatives of the hard-boiled detective's origins. Neither Stoner nor Walker form significant relationships, friends or lovers, that continue for an extended period in their series. And, family has no place in their lives, either in the present or the future. For Stoner, any commitment seems out of the question. Like the Continental Op, he predominantly focuses on his cases. Walker has brief affairs with some women but makes it clear that he has no intention of developing the relationships. Les Roberts' Milan Jacovich presents a mixed view since he both resembles Stoner's and Walker's connections to the early detectives and in his family life displays the more whole-life, connected view of the moderns. Divorced, Jacovich keeps in touch with his ex-wife through their two sons. The latter frequently stay at his apartment, and he clearly shows that they matter to him. Stephen Greenleaf's John Marshall Tanner is an example of the naturally isolated male more often found in the animal world than the human. He does not quite have the hard, bitter edge of the early hard-boiled detectives, but in the early novels he survives apart as if that were his destiny. Jeremiah Healy's John Francis Cuddy not only mourns his dead wife but also reaches out to her for love and companionship. The dynamics of a Cuddy sacrifice the hard-boiled edge for a more complex portrait that disturbs the genre's sense of direction without lessening its ability to thrive. Earl Emerson's Seattle private eye Thomas Black is a good balance between self-sufficiency and the need for others. His developing friendship and then love for his former basement tenant Kathy Birchfield does not clash with his hard-boiled image. These detectives' actions might resemble a glacial move to a new hard-boiled dimension, but they resemble a move nonetheless.

The clear examples of homophobia in the early hard-boiled detective novel contrast sharply with the introduction of homosexual detectives, male and female, in the two later Periods. Joseph Hansen's David Brandstetter in the 1970s and J.M. Redmann's Michelle "Micky" Knight and Sandra Scoppetone's Lauren Laurano in the 1990s introduce new attitudes toward sexual orientation in the genre. Raymond Chandler's Philip Marlowe and Mickey Spillane's Mike Hammer crudely dismiss homosexuals as warped exotics. However, the above three more recent writers not only have homosexual protagonists, they parallel heterosexual experiences. Brandstetter and Scoppetone are monogamous, and although the former goes through romantic upheavals, he looks for someone to love. Scoppetone's Laurano, as *Everything You Have Is Mine* starts, has an eleven-year relationship with Kip Adams. They own a home together in Greenwich Village and are committed to one another. While in the real world, genuine lasting love relationships are as possible among homosexuals as heterosexuals, they do not easily fit into the traditional hard-boiled environment. However, nearly every aspect of life, e.g., love, friendship, home, work, worry, joy, and sadness, appears in these works as part of the homosexual lifestyle, presenting them as "normal" there as in real life. Redmann expands this image with the promiscuous Micky Knight. Knight does have longer-term relationships than the proverbial one-night stands in *The Intersection of Law and Desire* (1995), but at times she revels in the excitement of meeting and having sex with strangers. Hard-boiled detectives, whether in the Early, Transitional, or Modern periods, male or female, and gay or straight, seldom indulge so whole-heartedly in sexual relationships. Mickey Spillane's Mike Hammer, John D. MacDonald's Travis McGee, and Robert B. Parker's Spenser, in *The Godwulf Manuscript* in which he makes love to a mother and daughter on the same day, are among the few exceptions and not consistent ones at that.

It is difficult to determine whether or not the elasticity of the genre is greater in terms of sexual orientation or race and ethnicity. Minorities do not figure as protagonists in either the Early or, for the most part, Transitional Period. But in the Modern Period, they *are* often the focus in their novels. Blacks generally do not start working with whites to learn the business and prepare for independence. Walter Mosley's Easy Rawlins and James Sallis's Lew Griffin, functioning in both minority and majority cultures, proceed to solve their cases without nods to progenitors. Rawlins is thrust more into dangerous situations than Griffin who harks back to the hard separateness and control of the Early Period. Rawlins' greatest aspiration is to keep his home and other property, and he becomes a private investigator to effect this. Griffin, alone, with bitter memories, exemplifies in *The Long-Legged Fly* the private investigator with little else. Bruce Cook's Antonio "Chico" Cervantes in *The Mexican Standoff* occupies a middle ground between the two. Born in the United States, Cervantes comes from a family that has to a certain extent, assimilated. He is a Chicano who speaks English with no accent but Spanish with one and thus remains suspect to the more alienated youth of South and East Los Angeles. Cervantes seems to represent a modern America still in the future, neither Chicano nor Anglo. Valerie Wilson Wesley's Tamara Hayle in *When Death Comes Stealing* operates in Newark and appears more remote from mainstream American culture than Cook. However, she lives a middle-class lifestyle as a black hard-boiled private eye. Divorced with a teenaged son, Hayle works hard at keeping a roof over their heads and maintains a relationship with her exhusband for the sake of her son. Her sometimes dangerous profession occasionally spills over into her life, but she works at keeping them separate. Like Hayle, Reginald Hill's Joe Sixsmith, a black man whose family came from the West Indies, endures a family relationship. His Aunt Mirabelle keeps close tabs on him and is forever attempting to match him up with Beryl Boddington, a nurse who attends their church and sings in the Boyling Corner Chapel Concert Choir with Sixsmith. This improbable environment is matched with Sixsmith's accidental venture into private investigation after he is laid off from his lathe operator's job. Gar Anthony Haywood's Aaron Gunner operates in *Fear of the Dark* (1988) primarily in South Central Los Angeles and holds his own, however precariously, with blacks, whites, and Chicanos.

Several other themes demonstrate the genre's ability to maintain a stable form through varied changes. Beginning in Chapters 4 and 6 in the Early Period, violence and work, respectively, are dominant elements, but the former is progressively less so in the Transitional and Modern Periods. Violence closely accompanies the early hard-boiled detectives as they do their jobs. Daly's Race Williams, Hammett's Continental Op, and Spillane's Mike Hammer have the most conspicuous connections to the use of force. Williams and Hammer not only use violence but boast about it. As mentioned in earlier chapters, Williams influences Hammer in this area. Although he uses violence, the Continental Op is more surrounded by it in *Red Harvest* and *The Dain Curse* than the initiator. As with Cooper's Leatherstocking, the Op more often responds to others' violence. Even though violence abates somewhat in the Transitional and Modern Periods, some protagonists, at least in part, are throwbacks to the early detectives. MacDonald's Travis McGee, Parker's Spenser, and Crumley's Milo Milodragovitch are examples in the former period of this split personality regarding violence. In *The Green Ripper*, McGee becomes almost insanely violent after the murder of his lover Gretel Howard, but in *The Lonely Silver Rain*, violence largely surrounds McGee who mellows even further when he learns he has a daughter. Spenser acts more like a kindly uncle to Kevin Bartlett in *God Save the Child*, but in *Mortal Stakes*, the next novel, commits a violent act, doubtful both morally and legally, when he ambushes the black-mailers Wally Hogg and Frank Doerr. Milo becomes so disgusted in Crum-ley's *Dancing Bear* from the violence that he has both seen and committed that he quits his profession as a private detective and works as a bartender. Estleman's Walker and Valin's Stoner in the Modern Period revert to the harder and more violent image of the private investigator, but Timlin's Nick Sharman is probably involved in the most violence in the Modern Period, whether reactively or proactively. *Romeo's Tune* involves shootouts using heavy weaponry and even a helicopter. Timlin's Sharman thus verges on a caricature of the hard-boiled private detective. The female detectives in this period use violence but almost always defensively. They act to protect themselves and others. Good examples of this occur in Grafton's *"A" Is for Alibi*, Scoppetone's *Everything You Have Is Mine*, and Garcia-Aguilera's *Bloody Waters*.

Work absorbs most of the hard-boiled detective's time. Obviously true for many people, this needs stressing since the detectives have so many other dramatic experiences than just trying to earn their fees. Checking facts, interviewing people, and writing reports along with waiting for new cases connect them to the real world and give them a certain believability against the sometimes incredible events they undergo. Danger is part of their work, but other things clarify what they do to a greater extent. For example, the quality of experience, demonstrated in a variety of ways, marks these men and women. Daly's Race Williams and Hammett's Continental Op establish an early image of someone who will not quit once hired. Nat-urally, the detective's character affects the way that one perceives and appre-ciates their persistence. What impresses in the Continental Op may not be easily observed in Prather's Shell Scott, and yet the latter pursues his cases to the end. His flamboyance contrasts with the Op's stolid, more reassur-ing qualities. MacDonald's Travis McGee has the image of a beach bum, a cultivated image, but when he takes a salvage, as he calls his cases, he does not stop until he finishes it to the best of his ability and frequently after suffering serious injuries. Block's Matthew Scudder, alcoholic and sunk in gloom, functions similarly to McGee. Both have that Holmesian commit-ment to the client that modern detectives demonstrate as well. As demon-strably dangerous as involving himself with Los Angeles gangbangers is, Gar Anthony Haywood's Aaron Gunner goes to their areas in South Cen-tral Los Angeles in *Not Long For This World* (1990) to interview members of "the Imperial Blues, a local Cuz set" (12) when he takes a case against his better judgment to help prove the innocence of a "hard-nosed little man-child" (15) named Toby Mills. Denver P.I. Jacob Lomax does not con-front as extensive a collection of criminals in Michael Allegretto's *Death on the Rocks* (1987) as does Haywood's Gunner, but perennial criminals and misfits Leonard Reese and Herman "Tiny" Blatt make Lomax's efforts to show that local oil man Phillip Townsend did not commit suicide but rather was murdered just as difficult and dangerous. Once he learns that the above two men did indeed kill Townsend, he pushes the police to reopen the case and keeps after them until they agree. While other qualities appear in the genre, one detective more analytical and another more physical, one working well with the police and another constantly experiencing friction, throughout the genre detectives exhibit the idea of persistence. Neither age, class, gender, race, nor ethnic differences affect its appearance in their various cases.

Character and change are also important themes in this work. The character of the detective dominates the genre. The many plots are, as it were, drawn into the character of the detective. Daly's Williams is less effective in achieving this than Hammett's Continental Op and Sam Spade. As soon as they appear in *Red Harvest* and *The Maltese Falcon* respectively, one knows that as significant as the other themes are in understanding what defines the genre, character is central. Chandler's Philip Marlowe strongly confirms character's role followed by Spillane's Mike Hammer and Ross Macdonald's Lew Archer. After the Early Period, the change that character undergoes and the possibilities that accrue to later writers in developing their detectives begin in the Transitional Period with John D. MacDonald's Travis McGee. McGee heralds a resurgence in the genre that still has not run its course in the Modern Period. MacDonald, whose publications before 1964 include more than five hundred short stories and forty-two novels, learned his craft well. He writes about his careful planning for the series, and once launched, he introduces a character whose creative possibilities are not used up after twenty-one novels. Only MacDonald's death ended the series, and by then, 1986, the changes in the genre were accelerating. However, like signposts, certain writers not only clearly link their detectives to the Early Period but also to the Transitional Period. In Timlin's *Romeo's Tune*, Nick Sharman sits in his office reading MacDonald's *The Lonely Silver Rain*, the last novel in the series, although he is unaware of it at the time. More similar to Spillane's Mike Hammer than McGee, Sharman nonetheless knows his roots. In general, these allusions, from Poe's Dupin and Conan Doyle's Sherlock Holmes on, acknowledge sources as well as differences. While allusion establishes a sense of tradition, the genre shows no tendency toward inhibiting change. In Stuart Kaminsky's *Vengeance*, Lew Fonesca travels to Sarasota, Florida, from Chicago after his wife's death in a car accident. He sets up as a private detective, even without a license, though he is careful not openly to break the law. In addition to being a lovely Gulf Coast city, Sarasota was MacDonald's hometown. Fonesca does not physically resemble McGee, but he more than handles himself against the predators he encounters. In William J. Reynolds' *Moving Targets* (1986), Nebraska, a writer of a detective novel and a private investigator, makes eight allusions in the first few chapters to private detectives and/or their authors. Additionally, Omaha Police Detective Kim Banner refers to Nebraska's arrival on a "white stallion" (5), a possible allusion both to Marlowe, the knight in the stained glass window in *The Big Sleep*, and to medieval knights in general. Nebraska also alludes indirectly to Don Quixote (33), something that MacDonald's Travis McGee often does. These and other examples establish the connection between the various detectives whose images rise up in the novels to remind one from where they have come but not necessarily where the character as character is going. The only certainty is that one will know him or her as a hard-boiled private detective.

Klein says, "Between 1987 [...] and 1994, women private eyes have flourished in detective fiction; some might say they have taken over" (*Woman Detective* 232). For the hard-boiled detectives considered, this is not exactly true; they represent a little less than fifty percent in the Modern Period. However, this is a significant number for a genre that has had to change and still maintain its own boundaries. Opinions differ as to whether this change has successfully occurred or even whether it can. The apparent dynamism of the form will decide if, as argued, it has the ability to absorb the world around it, politically, socially, or culturally, and transform it into literature while holding on to its past literary conventions and traditions.

Bibliography

Allegretto, Michael. *Death on the Rocks*. 1987. Toronto: Paperjacks, 1988.

Baker, John. *Death Minus Zero*. London: Vista, 1996.

_____. *Poet in the Gutter*. London: Vista, 1995.

Baker, Robert A. and Michael T. Nietzel. *Private Eyes: One Hundred and One Knights: A Survey of American Detective Fiction 1922–1984*. Bowling Green, OH: Bowling Green State University Popular Press, 1985.

Bakhtin, M.M. *The Dialogic Imagination: Four Essays*. Ed. Michael Holquist. Trans. Caryl Emerson and Michael Holquist. Austin: University of Texas Press, 1981.

Barnes, Linda. *A Trouble of Fools*. 1987. New York: Fawcett Crest–Ballantine, 1988.

Barzun, Jacques. *A Stroll with William James*. Chicago: University of Chicago Press, 1984.

Bergman, Andrew. *The Big Kiss-Off of 1944: A Jack LeVine Mystery*. 1974. New York: Ballantine, 1975.

_____. *Hollywood and LeVine*. 1975. New York: Perennial-Harper, 1983.

Block, Lawrence. *The Devil Knows You're Dead*. 1993. New York: Avon, 1994.

_____. *In the Midst of Death: A Matthew Scudder Novel*. New York: Avon, 1992.

_____. *The Sins of the Fathers: A Matthew Scudder Novel*. 1976. New York: Avon, 1991.

Burns, Landon. "*Fadeout*: Dave Brandstetter's First Case." *In the Beginning: First Novels in Mystery Series*. Ed. Mary Jean DeMarr. Bowling Green, OH: Bowling Green State University Popular Press, 1995. 171–84.

Campbell, Robert. *In La-La Land We Trust*. 1986. New York: Mysterious, 1987.

Casella, Donna R. "The Matt Scudder Series: The Saga of an Alcoholic Hardboiled Detective." *Clues: A Journal of Detection* 14.2 (1993): 31–49.

Cawelti, John G. *Adventure, Mystery, and Romance: Formula Stories as Art and Popular Culture*. Chicago: University of Chicago Press, 1976.

_____. *The Six-Gun Mystique*. 2nd ed. Bowling Green, OH: Bowling Green State University Popular Press, 1984.

Chandler, Raymond. *The Big Sleep*. 1939. New York: Vintage-Random, 1992.

_____. *Farewell, My Lovely*. 1940. New York: Black Lizard–Vintage Crime, 1992.

_____. *The High Window*. 1942. New York: Black Lizard–Vintage Crime, 1992.

_____. *The Lady in the Lake*. 1943. New York: Black Lizard–Vintage Crime, 1992.

_____. *The Long Goodbye*. 1953. New York: Black Lizard–Vintage Crime, 1992.

_____. *Playback*. 1958. New York: Vintage, 1988.

_____. "The Simple Art of Murder: An Essay." 1950. *The Simple Art of Murder*. New York: Vintage, 1988. 1–18.

Christianson, Scott R. "A Heap of Broken Images: Hardboiled Detective Fiction and the Discourse(s) of Modernity." *The Cunning Craft: Original Essays on Detective Fiction and Contemporary Literary Theory*. Ed. Ronald G. Walker and June M. Frazer. Afterword David R. Anderson. Macomb: Western Illinois University Press, 1990. 135–48.

Cody, Liza. *Dupe*. 1980. London: Arrow, 1993.

Collins, Max Allan and James L. Traylor. *One Lonely Knight: Mickey Spillane's Mike Hammer*. Bowling Green, OH: Bowling Green State University Popular Press, 1984.

Collins, Michael. *Act of Fear*. 1967. New York: Bantam, 1969.

_____. *The Brass Rainbow*. 1969. New York: Bantam, 1970.

_____. *Walk a Black Wind*. 1971. New York: Carroll & Graf, 1989.

Collins, Wilkie. *Basil*. 1852, 1862. New York: Dover, 1980.

_____. *The Moonstone*. 1868. Intro. Frederick R. Karl. New York: Signet-Dutton, 1984.

Cook, Bruce. *Mexican Standoff*. 1988. New York: St. Martin's, 1990.

Crais, Robert. *Indigo Slam*. New York: Hyperion, 1997.

_____. *The Monkey's Raincoat*. New York: Bantam, 1987.

_____. *Voodoo River*. New York: Hyperion, 1995.

Crider, Allen B. "Race Williams— Private Investigator." *Dimensions of Detective Fiction*. Ed. Larry N. Landrum, Pat Browne, and Ray B. Browne. Bowling Green, OH: Popular Press, 1976. 110–13.

Crumley, James. *Dancing Bear*. 1983. New York: Vintage-Random, 1984.

_____. *The Wrong Case: A Novel*. 1975. Vintage-Random, 1986.

Daly, Carroll John. *The Hidden Hand*. 1928, 1929. New York: HarperPerennial, 1992.

_____. *Murder from the East: A Race Williams Story*. 1935. Intro. Tony Sparafucile. New York: International Polygonics, 1978.

_____. *The Snarl of the Beast*. 1927. New York: HarperPerennial-HarperCollins, 1992.

_____. "Three Gun Terry." *Black Mask Boys: Masters in the Hard-Boiled School of Detective Fiction*. Ed. William F. Nolan. New York: William Morrow, 1958. 43–72.

Dawson, Janet. *Kindred Crimes*.1990. New York: Fawcett Crest–Ballantine, 1992.

_____. *Till the Old Men Die*. New York: Fawcett Crest, 1993.

Dewey, Thomas B. *Draw the Curtain Close*. 1947. New York: Pocket, 1968.

_____. *Every Bet's a Sure Thing*. New York: Simon and Schuster, 1953.

Dickens, Charles. *Bleak House*. Afterword Geoffrey Tillotson. 1853. New York: Signet–New American, 1964.

Dobyns, Stephen. *Saratoga Trifecta: Saratoga Longshot, Saratoga Swimmer, Saratoga Headhunter*. 1976, 1981, 1985. New York: Penguin, 1995.

Doyle, Sir Arthur Conan. *The Complete Sherlock Holmes*. Pref. Christopher Morley. New York and London: Doubleday, 1930.

Dunant, Sarah. *Birth Marks*. 1991. London: Penguin, 1992.

_____. *Fatlands*. 1993. London: Penguin, 1994.

Durham, Philip. *Down These Mean Streets a Man Must Go: Raymond Chandler's Knight*. Chapel Hill: University of North Carolina Press, 1963.

Eliot, T.S. *The Complete Poems and Plays: 1909–1950*. New York: Harcourt, Brace, 1971.

Emerson, Earl. *Nervous Laughter*. New York: Avon, 1986.

_____. *Poverty Bay*. 1985. New York: Ballantine, 1997.

_____. *The Rainy City*. 1985. New York: Ballantine, 1997.

_____. *The Vanishing Smile*. 1995. New York: Ballantine, 1996.

_____. *Yellow Dog Party*. New York: Morrow, 1991.

Estleman, Loren D. *Angel Eyes*. 1981. New York: Fawcett Crest–Ballantine, 1987.

_____. *Motor City Blue*. Boston: Houghton, 1980.

Fiedler, Leslie A. *Love and Death in the American Novel*. 1960, 1966. New rev. ed. New York: Laurel-Dell, 1969.

Fontana, Ernest. "Joseph Hansen's Anti-Pastoral Crime Fiction." *Clues: A Journal of Detection* 7.1 (1986): 89–97.

Ford, G.M. *Who in Hell Is Wanda Fuca?: A Leo Waterman Mystery*. 1995. New York: Avon, 1996.

Francis, Dick. *Dead Cert*. 1962. New York: Fawcett Crest–Ballantine, 1987.

Garcia-Aguilera, Carolina. *Bloody Waters: A Lupe Solano Mystery*. 1996. New York: Berkley, 1997.

Gash, Jonathan. *The Judas Pair*. 1977. London and New York: Penguin, 1989.

Gault, William Campbell. *Day of the Ram*. 1956. New York: Bantam, 1957.

_____. *Ring Around Rosa*. New York: Dutton, 1955.

Geherin, David. *The American Private Eye: The Image in Fiction*. New York: Ungar, 1985.

_____. *Sons of Sam Spade: The Private-Eye Novel in the 70s: Robert B. Parker, Roger L. Simon, Andrew Bergman*. New York: Ungar, 1980.

Grafton, Sue. *"A" Is for Alibi: A Kinsey Millhone Mystery*. 1982. New York: Bantam, 1987.

_____. *"B" Is for Burglar*. 1985. New York: Bantam, 1986.

_____. *"D" Is for Deadbeat: A Kinsey Millhone Mystery*. 1987. New York: Bantam, 1988

_____. *"E" Is for Evidence*. New York: Holt, 1988.

_____. *"J" Is for Judgment*. 1993. New York: Fawcett Crest–Ballantine, 1994.

Greenleaf, Stephen. *Grave Error*. New York: Dial, 1979.

Grella, George. "The Hard-Boiled Detective Novel." *Detective Fiction: A Collection of Critical Essays*. Ed. Robin W. Winks. Rev.ed. Woodstock, VT: Foul Play–Countryman, 1988. 103–20.

_____. "Murder and Manners: The Formal Detective Novel." *Dimensions of Detective Fiction*. Ed. Larry N. Landrum, Pat Browne, and Ray B. Browne. Bowling Green, OH: Bowling Green State University Popular Press, 1976.

Hall, James W. *Under Cover of Daylight: A Novel*. 1987. New York: Warner, 1988.

Hall, Parnell. *Detective: A Novel*. 1987. New York: Onyx–New American, 1988.

Halliday, Brett. *Dividend on Death*. 1939. Toronto: Raven-Worldwide, 1982.

_____. *The Private Practice of Michael Shayne: A Michael Shayne Murder Mystery*. New York: Dell, 1940.

_____. *A Taste for Violence*. New York: Dodd, Mead, 1949.

_____. *The Uncomplaining Corpses*. 1940. New York: Dell, 1963.

Hammett, Dashiell. *The Dain Curse*. 1929, 1957. New York: Vintage-Random, 1972.

_____. "From the Memoirs of a Private Detective." *The Art of the Mystery Story: A Collection of Critical Essays*. 1946. Ed. Howard Haycraft. Intro. Robin W. Winks. 2nd ed. New York: Carroll & Graf, 1992.

_____. *The Maltese Falcon*. 1930. New York:Vintage-Random, 1972.

_____. *Red Harvest*. 1929. New York: Vintage-Random, 1992.

Hansen, Joseph. *Death Claims*. 1973. Harpenden, Herts.: No Exit, 1996.

_____. *Fadeout*. 1970. Harpenden, England: No Exit, 1996.

_____. *Troublemaker: A Dave Brandstetter Mystery*. 1975. Harpenden, Herts.: No Exit, 1997.

Harris, Timothy. *Kyd for Hire*. 1977. New York: Dell, 1978.

Haycraft, Howard. *Murder for Pleasure: The Life and Times of the Detective Story*. 1941. New York: Carroll & Graf, 1984.

Haywood, Gar Anthony. *Fear of the Dark*. London: Macmillan, 1988.

_____. *Not Long for This World: An Aaron Gunner Mystery*. New York: St. Martin's, 1990.

Healy, Jeremiah. *Blunt Darts*. 1984. New York: Pocket, 1991.

Hill, Reginald. *Blood Sympathy*. London: HarperCollins, 1993.

_____. *Born Guilty*. 1994. London: HarperCollins, 1995.

_____. *Singing the Sadness*. 1999. London: HarperCollins, 2000.

Hirshberg, Edgar W. *John D. MacDonald*. Twayne's United States Authors Series. Ed. Warren French. 1985. Boston: Twayne, 1986.

Isaac, Frederick. "Situation, Motivation, Resolution: An Afternoon with Marcia Muller." *Clues: A Journal of Detection* 5.2 (1984): 20–34.

Jones, Louise Conley. "Feminism and the P.I. Code: or 'Is a Hard-boiled Warshawski Unsuitable to be Called a Feminist?'" *Clues: A Journal of Detection* 16.1 (1995): 77–87.

Kaminsky, Stuart M. *Vengeance: A Lew Fonesca Mystery*. 1999. New York: Forge–Tom Doherty, 2000.

Kelly, R. Gordon. *Mystery Fiction and Modern Life*. Jackson: University of Mississippi Press, 1998.

Kijewski, Karen. *Katapult*. 1990. New York: Avon, 1992.

_____. *Katwalk*. 1989. New York: Avon, 1990.

Klein, Kathleen Gregory. *The Woman Detective: Gender & Genre*. 2nd ed. Urbana, IL: University of Illinois Press, 1995.

_____. *Women Times Three: Writers, Detectives, Readers*. Bowling Green, OH: Bowling Green State University Popular Press, 1995.

Lehane, Dennis. *Darkness, Take My Hand*. 1996. London and New York: Bantam, 1997.

_____. *A Drink Before the War*. 1994. New York: Avon, 1996.

_____. *Sacred*. 1997. London and New York: Bantam, 1998.

Lehman, David. *The Perfect Murder: A Study in Detection*. Ann Arbor: University of Michigan Press, 1989, 2000.

Lewin, Michael Z. *Ask the Right Question*. 1971. New York: Mysterious-Warner, 1991.

_____. *The Enemies Within*. 1974. New York: Perennial-Harper, 1984.

_____. *The Way We Die Now*. 1973. New York: Perennial-Harper, 1984.

Lippman, Laura. *Baltimore Blues*. New York: Avon-HarperCollins, 1997.

Lutz, John. *Bloodfire: A Fred Carver Mystery*. 1991. New York: Avon, 1992.

_____. *Buyer Beware*. 1976. New York: Carroll & Graf, 1992.

_____. *Kiss*. 1988. New York: Avon, 1990.

_____. *Nightlines*. New York: St. Martin's, 1984.

_____. *Scorcher: A Fred Carver Mystery*. 1987. New York: Owl-Holt, 1995.

_____. *Tropical Heat*. 1986. New York: Avon, 1987.

Lyons, Arthur. *All God's Children: A Jacob Asch Mystery*. 1975. New York: Owl-Holt, 1982.

_____. *The Dead Are Discreet*. 1974. Harpenden, Herts.: No Exit, 1990.

_____. *The Killing Floor*. 1976. Harpenden, Herts.: No Exit, 1988.

MacDonald, John D. *Bright Orange for the Shroud*. Greenwich, CT: Fawcett Gold Medal, 1965.

_____. *Cinnamon Skin: The Twentieth Adventure of Travis McGee*. 1982. New York: Fawcett Gold Medal–Ballantine, 1983.

_____. *Darker than Amber*. 1966. New York: Fawcett Gold Medal–Ballantine, 1982.

_____. *A Deadly Shade of Gold*. 1965. New York: Fawcett Gold Medal–Ballantine, 1982.

_____. *The Deep Blue Good-by*. 1964. New York: Fawcett Gold Medal–Ballantine, 1982.

_____. *The Dreadful Lemon Sky*. 1975. New York: Fawcett Gold Medal–Ballantine, 1982.

_____. *Dress Her in Indigo*. 1969. New York: Fawcett Gold Medal–Ballantine, 1982.

_____. *The Empty Copper Sea*. New York: Fawcett Gold Medal, 1978.

_____. *Free Fall in Crimson*. 1981. New York: Fawcett Gold Medal–Ballantine, 1982.

_____. *The Girl in the Plain Brown Wrapper*. Greenwich, CT: Fawcett Gold Medal, 1968.

_____. *The Green Ripper*. 1979. New York: Fawcett Gold Medal, 1980.

_____. "Introduction and Comment." *Clues: A Journal of Detection* 1.1 (1980): 63–74.

_____. *The Lonely Silver Rain*. 1985. New York: Fawcett Gold Medal–Ballantine, 1986.

_____. *The Long Lavender Look*. 1970. New York: Fawcett Gold Medal–Ballantine, 1982.

_____. *Nightmare in Pink*. 1964. New York: Fawcett Gold Medal–Ballantine, 1983.

_____. *One Fearful Yellow Eye*. 1966. New York: Fawcett Gold Medal–Ballantine, 1982.

_____. *Pale Gray for Guilt*. Greenwich, CT: Fawcett Gold Medal, 1968.

_____. *A Purple Place for Dying*. Greenwich, CT: Fawcett Gold Medal, 1964.

_____. *The Quick Red Fox*. Greenwich, CT: Fawcett Gold Medal, 1964.

_____. *Reading for Survival*. Washington: Library of Congress, 1987.

_____. *The Scarlet Ruse*. 1973. New York: Fawcett Gold Medal–Ballantine, 1983.

_____. *A Tan and Sandy Silence*. New York: Fawcett Gold Medal, 1971.

_____. *The Turquoise Lament*. 1973. Greenwhich, CT: Fawcett Gold Medal, 1974.

Macdonald, Ross. *The Moving Target: A Lew Archer Novel*. 1949. New York: Warner, 1990.

_____. *The Drowning Pool*. 1950. New York: Bantam, 1970.

_____. *The Way Some People Die*. 1951. New York: Bantam, 1971.

MacShane, Frank. *The Life of Raymond Chandler*. London: Hamish Hamilton, 1976.

Maxwell, A.E. *Just Another Day in Paradise: A Fiddler and Fiora Mystery*. New York: HarperPaperbacks, 1985.

McDermid, Val. *Dead Beat*. 1992. London: Gollancz Crime, 1993.

Moore, Lewis D. *Meditations on America: John D. MacDonald's Travis McGee Series and Other Fiction*. Bowling Green, OH: Bowling Green State University Popular Press, 1994.

Mosley, Walter. *Devil in a Blue Dress*. 1990. New York: Pocket, 1991.

Muller, Marcia. *Ask the Cards a Question*. 1982. New York: Mysterious-Warner, 1990.

_____. *Edwin of the Iron Shoes: The First Sharon McCone Mystery*. 1977. New York: Mysterious, 1990.

Nolan, William F. *Hammett: A Life at the Edge*. New York: Congdon & Weed, 1983.

Nugent, Harold, and Susan Nugent. "Noir: Keys' Style." *Crime Fiction and Film in the Sunshine State: Florida Noir*. Ed. Steve Glassman and Maurice O'Sullivan. Bowling Green, OH: Bowling Green State University Popular Press, 1997.

Nyman, Jopi. "Images of Social Change in Dashiell Hammett's *Red Harvest*." *Clues: A Journal of Detection* 21.2 (2000): 77–93.

O'Brien, Geoffrey. *Hardboiled America: Lurid Paperbacks and The Masters of Noir*. 1981. Expanded ed. New York: Capo, 1997.

O'Sullivan, Maurice. "Ecological Noir." *Crime Fiction and Film in the Sunshine State: Florida Noir*. Ed. Steve Glassman and Maurice O'Sullivan. Bowling Green, OH: Bowling Green State University Popular Press, 1997. 119–26.

Panek, LeRoy Lad. *An Introduction to the Detective Story*. Bowling Green, OH: Bowling Green State University Popular Press, 1987.

_____. *New Hard-Boiled Writers 1970s — 1990s*. Bowling Green, OH: Bowling Green State University Popular Press, 2000.

Paretsky, Sara. *Indemnity Only: A Novel*. 1982. New York: Dell, 1991.

_____. *Killing Orders*. 1985. New York: Ballantine, 1986.

Parker, Robert B. *Early Autumn*. 1981. New York: Dell, 1983.

_____. *God Save the Child*. 1974. New York: Dell, 1983.

_____. *The Godwulf Manuscript*. 1973. New York: Dell, 1983.

_____. *The Judas Goat*. New York: Seymour Lawrence–Dell, 1978.

_____. *Mortal Stakes*. 1975. New York: Dell, 1983.

_____. *Promised Land*. 1976. New York: Seymour Lawrence–Dell, 1983.

_____. *Valediction*. 1984. New York: Seymour Lawrence–Dell, 1985.

Pasachoff, Jay M. "Cosmology." *Microsoft Encarta Encyclopedia*. 1999.

Pinker, Steven. *The Blank Slate: The Modern Denial of Human Nature*. 2002. New York: Penguin, 2003.

Poe, Edgar Allan. *Complete Stories and Poems*. Garden City, NY: Doubleday, 1966.

Porter, Dennis. *The Pursuit of Crime: Art and Ideology in Detective Fiction*. New Haven: Yale University Press, 1981.

Prather, Richard S. *Bodies in Bedlam*. Greenwich, Conn.: Fawcett Gold Medal, 1951.

_____. *Case of the Vanishing Beauty*. Greenwich, Conn.: Fawcett Gold Medal, 1950.

_____. *Dance with the Dead*. Greenwich, Conn.: Fawcett Gold Medal, 1960.

Priestman, Martin. *Detective Fiction and Literature: The Figure in the Carpet*. New York: St. Martin's, 1991.

Pronzini, Bill. *Blowback*. New York: Random, 1977.

_____. *Hoodwink*. 1981. New York: Knightsbridge, 1990.

_____. *Scattershot*. 1982. New York: Knightsbridge, 1990.

_____. *The Snatch*. 1971. London: Sphere, 1975.

_____. *Undercurrent*. New York: Random, 1973.

_____. *The Vanished*. New York: Random, 1973.

Pronzini, Bill and Collin Wilcox. *Twospot*. 1978. New York: Carroll & Graf, 1993.

Reddy, Maureen T. *Sisters in Crime: Feminism and the Crime Novel*. New York: Ungar-Continuum, 1988.

Redmann, J.M. *Death by the Riverside*. Norwich, VT: New Victoria, 1990.

_____. *The Intersection of Law and Desire*. New York: Norton, 1995.

_____. *Lost Daughters*. New York: Norton, 1999.

Reynolds, William J. *Moving Targets*. 1986. New York: Ballantine, 1987.

_____. *The Nebraska Quotient*. 1984. New York: Ballantine, 1986.

Roberts, Les. *Full Cleveland*. 1989. New York: St. Martin's, 1990.

_____. *Pepper Pike*. 1988. New York: St. Martin's, 1990.

Ruehlmann, William. *Saint with a Gun: The Unlawful American Private Eye*. New York: New York University Press, 1984.

Sallis, James. *The Long-Legged Fly*. 1992. New York: Avon, 1994.

Sangster, Jimmy. *Snowball*. New York: Holt, 1986.

Schutz, Benjamin M. *Embrace the Wolf*. 1985. New York: Bantam, 1986.

Scoppetone, Sandra. *Everything You Have Is Mine*. 1991. New York: Ballantine, 1992.

Simon, Roger L. *The Big Fix*. 1973. New York: Warner, 1986.

Slotkin, Richard. "The Hard-Boiled Detective Story: From the Open Range to the Mean Streets." *The Sleuth and the Scholar: Origins, Evolution, and Current Trends in Detective Fiction*. Ed. Barbara A. Rader and Howard G. Zettler. Contributions to the Study of Popular Culture, Number 19. New York: Greenwood, 1988. 91–100.

Slovo, Gillian. *Death Comes Staccato*. London: Women's Press, 1987.

_____. *Morbid Symptoms: A Murder Mystery*. New York: Dembner, 1984.

Spenser, Edmund. *The Faerie Queene*. 1590, 1596, 1609. Ed. Thomas P. Roche, Jr. and C. Patrick O'Donnell, Jr. London: Penguin, 1978.

Spillane, Mickey. *The Big Kill*. New York: Signet–New American, 1951.

_____. *I, the Jury*. New York: Signet–New American, 1947.

_____. *My Gun Is Quick*. New York: Signet–New American, 1950.

_____. *One Lonely Night*. New York: Signet–New American, 1951.

_____. *The Snake*.New York: Signet–New American, 1964.

_____. *Vengeance Is Mine*. 1950. *Mickey Spillane: The Mike Hammer Collection: I, the Jury, My Gun Is Quick, Vengeance Is Mine!* Intro. Max Allan Collins. New York: New American, 2001.

Spring, Michelle. *Every Breath You Take*. 1994. New York: Ballantine, 1999.

Symons, Julian. *Bloody Murder: From the Detective Story to the Crime Novel: A History*. Rev. ed. London: Pan, 1994.

Timlin, Mark. *A Good Year for the Roses*. 1988. London: Headline, 1990.

_____. *Romeo's Tune*. London: Headline, 1990.

_____. *A Street That Rhymed at 3 AM*. 1997. London: Vista, 1998.

Valin, Jonathan. *The Lime Pit*. New York: Dell, 1980.

VanderVen, Karen. "Psyhological Genesis of the Prototype Hero in Mystery/Detective Fiction as Embodied by Travis McGee: A Retrospective Analysis of his Development as a Child and Youth." *Clues: A Journal Detection* 11.1 (1990): 31–56.

Van Dover, J.K. *You Know My Method: The Science of the Detective*. Bowling Green, OH: Bowling Green State University Popular Press, 1994.

Wesley, Valerie Wilson. *When Death Comes Stealing: A Tamara Hayle Mystery*. 1994. New York: Avon, 1995.

Wolfe, Peter. *Beams Falling: The Art of Dashiell Hammett*. Bowling Green, OH: Bowling Green State University Popular Press, 1980.

_____. *Dreamers Who Live Their Dreams: The World of Ross Macdonald's Novels*. Bowling Green, OH: Bowling Green State University Popular Press, 1976.

_____. *Something More than Night: The Case of Raymond Chandler*. Bowling Green, OH: Bowling Green State University Popular Press, 1985.

Young, Mary. "Walter Mosley, Detective Fiction and Black Culture." *Journal of Popular Culture* 32.1 (1998): 141–50.

Zimmerman, J.E. *Dictionary of Classical Mythology*. 1964. New York: Bantam, 1971.

Index